LESBIAN PHILOSOPHIES AND CULTURES

SUNY Series in Feminist Philosophy
Jeffner Allen, Editor

LESBIAN
PHILOSOPHIES AND CULTURES

EDITED BY
JEFFNER ALLEN

STATE UNIVERSITY OF NEW YORK PRESS

Published by State University of New York Press
© 1990 to each author. "Coincidences" and "Certain Words"
by Nicole Brossard, © The Woman's Press, 1988. "The Trojan
Horse," by Monique Wittig, © Beacon Press, 1990.
All rights reserved
Printed in the United States of America
Cover and Text design by Lou Robinson

For information, address State University of New York Press,
State University Plaza, Albany, NY 12246

Library of Congress Cataloging-in-Publication Data
Lesbian philosophies and cultures/edited by Jeffner Allen.
p.   cm — (SUNY series in feminist philosophy)
ISBN 0-7914-0383-1. — ISBN 0-7914-0384-X (pbk.)
1. Lesbianism.   I. Allen, Jeffner, 1947-   II. Series
HQ75.5.L443 1990   90-9554
306.76'63 — dc 20   CIP

10 9 8 7 6 5 4 3 2 1

Contents

Contents

Introduction

The lesbians who have contributed to this book are theorists and activists who write as members of diverse lesbian cultures. Each lesbian has her ways of knowing, her voices, approaches, methodologies, languages. Each lesbian reflects, directly and indirectly, her relations to her own and to other ethnicities, races, social classes, physical abilities, ages, and nationalities. Each lesbian has distinctive perspectives on lesbian existence, friendships and sexualities, separatism and coalition building, theories of knowledge and ethics, language and writing. *Lesbian Philosophies and Cultures* is a hybrid site for discussion of, work on, and delight in this sometimes uneasy, sometimes painful, sometimes surprising and wonderful, lesbian pluralism.

For this collection, some of the authors have chosen to write in essay style, and some have chosen to write in fiction, autobiography, poetic prose, and experimental forms. Many of the authors have chosen to mix, innovatively, feminist writing from experience, remembering and research into history, textual analysis, new age meditation, deconstruction and postmodernism, and theoretical explorations as yet unnamed. All of the authors live currently in the u.s.a. or quebec. Shared by the contributors is a sense of urgency that each, in her writing, might make a difference.

The primary emphasis of this book is *lesbian* philosophies and cultures, rather than lesbianism considered in relation to or in contrast to, patriarchy, or heterosexuality. Yet the authors arrive at no single point of convergence; and in that plurality is inseparable from lesbian philosophies and cultures, this is necessarily so. The authors' writings, not variations on one theme, not a collection of many that have risen out of the same, form irreducible pluralities of shifting continuities and discontinuities. While some chapters may overlap, often in ways that defy anticipation, none coincide.

The authors talk to and among each other, and sometimes, at the same time, they talk at and talk past each other. Each attempt to find what this talking means is itself an interpretation that reflects diverse political, methodological, aesthetic, personal, and other criteria. An author may simply be moving in a specific direction, or she may not have noticed the existence of other directions, and her not noticing may or may not matter; what counts as 'real' for some perspectives may not count as 'real' from other standpoints, and that difference may or may not be considered important. Agreement among lesbians is not necessary for, and if assumed superficially may impede, conversations, reflections, and the creation of multiple realities. However, attention in daily life, and as authors and readers, to how each lesbian, including oneself, inhabits the cultures where she lives is crucial if theorizing by lesbians is to be useful. And attention to how each lesbian, especially oneself, may and may not connect to those cultures she does not inhabit is vital, if theorizing by lesbians is, as I believe it must, to challenge and to dismantle positions of privilege. This book is dedicated to the creation of spaces in which such attention can thrive.

How to articulate this living in the plural, where each author, each reader, each lesbian herself inhabits multiple cultures, at least some of which may be in constant transformation at any given time, has been for me an energizing question. When the writings for this book arrived one by one in the mail and I began to arrange them, there came a time, slowly but surely, when the writings began gradually to form connections among themselves, until none was the same as it had been before, at least, none was the same to me. Each writing discussed matters that the others considered, or did not consider, or more often, considered but in different ways. Each author referred to some authors in the anthology, and also to other authors. There were voices from off these pages, as well, voices that had been referred to but that had not spoken themselves, and voices that had not been referred to at all. Slowly, ever so slowly, I began to hear chorusing

> tones   different tones   and then rhythms
> several rhythms at once   rhythms changing
> songs   several songs at once   voices
> some voices taking up when others were fading out
>   some insistent   some more tenuous
> others not distinguishable   as yet   by me

Although I felt closer to some writings than to others, and to parts of some writings more than to parts of others, there came moments when, as I talked with each writing, asked her questions, imagined and dreamed her, and tried to listen to what she said, that I, too, began to change. I did not appropriate the writings. Indeed, they were not mine to 'have,' but only to edit. And some of the writings said that I must change still more, if I were to edit with honesty to myself or to them. Yet in time, sometimes easily, sometimes by hard work, contexts for a friendship with each of these writings developed. I now reread them not so much to make them clearer, or to get clearer myself, but to hear their, and my

> dissonances harmonies   rational
> arguments   abstract   emotional
>   momentum
> screams   anger   incantations   joy   rituals
>   chants   dances

While rereading these writings I recently happened to find that, *if such songs are sung and heard and danced night and day, for three nights and days unending, and if she who sings also listens and she who listens dances, and she who hears her sing or sees her dance herself sings three nights and days unending and questions imagines dreams, then by incalcuable magic, any lingering belief in an instant total unanimity among lesbians may let go, displaced, slowly so slowly, by a trust in a discerning, critical and loving, attention to the irreducible pluralities that sustain lesbians' lives.*

"Living in the Plural," the opening section of *Lesbian Philosophies and Cultures*, focuses on daily dilemmas of creating lesbian spaces, and of lesbian visibility. In "Dyke Methods," Joyce Trebilcot proposes principles, clusters of values, which she finds help her to not impose her 'truths', or a 'we', on others. Joyce shows that a female may have shifting identities, as a 'woman' and as a 'womon,' relative to how she positions herself in regard to issues of control, and she illustrates how her own awareness of these identities informs her actions. "I speak only for myself," her first principle, may well be her most suggestive and most controversial. "The Invisible Woman," a lesbian political fantasy by Vivienne Louise, presents some of the breath-taking events experienced by Fay, whether gardening, doing her errands, playing poker with friends, making herself a cup of tea. Vivienne tells how Fay realizes that others are not aware that she is there, and the sometimes liberating potential of that invisibility; how Fay recognizes an energy or feeling about some women that makes it possible for them to see her.

"Locations," the next section of this book, discusses geographies of lesbian cultures: How might lesbian cultures by conceptualized? Where are lesbian cultures? What can lesbians do to make these locations not simply visions, but actualities? In "Breaking Silences, Making Waves and Loving Ourselves: The Politics of Coming Out and Coming Home," Kitty Tsui, speaking at the Second Annual Third World/Lesbians of Color Conference, invokes an energy that connects memories, the joy of living, and love: a sense of oneness. While recalling the importance of talking story and writing it down, Kitty herself tells stories within stories of fire and power: the lives of Kwan Ying Lin and Hsu Hung Lum, her work on the book *Third World Women*, the first Asian Pacific

Lesbians conference, body building, building character, and staying close to her heart. "What is lesbianism?" Ann Ferguson asks in, "Is There a Lesbian Culture?" Ann formulates a dialectical theory of lesbian cultures as cultures of resistance, and a critique of the historical inadequacies and political implications of current theories of lesbianism. Against the cultural imperialism that attempts to imprint a model of Western lesbian liberation movements onto other societies, she argues for the development of international lesbian, feminist, and gay liberation movements which promote a plurality of lesbian cultures, and for a coalitionist and non-separatist politics. Julia Penelope, in "The Lesbian Perspective," proposes not that there is a single lesbian perspective, but that there is the possibility of a lesbian consensus reality. She shows how this lesbian perspective has as its basis the ambiguity of lesbians' lives, both as oppressed, and as creating, in an uncharted world, our own grounds and values. Julia urges not that lesbians avoid making any generalizations about lesbians, which, she states, would entail that we stop identifying ourselves as lesbians and dykes, but that lesbians realize our visions of a lesbian community by working on honesty, language, and self-definition.

In "Jewish Lesbians in France: The Issue of Multiple Cultures," Marthe Rosenfeld finds french radical feminist and lesbian theories of gender and race liberating insofar as they challenge biological determinism, but limiting insofar as they often exhibit universalizing tendencies that marginalize race and ethnicity. She studies personal, historical and contemporary situations that complicate the development of a functional vocabulary to express multiple allegiances, a vocabulary that is vital for a lesbian movement that depends on the empowerment of all its members to express ourselves in our own ways. Many feminist lesbians have a vision of pluralist separatism embodying ethnic and cultural diversity, states Claudia Card in "Pluralist Lesbian Separatism," but can separatist politics nourish the understanding requisite to realizing such pluralism? Claudia finds the greatest flexibility in separatism that is based on opposition and that emphasizes analysis of kinds of connections, rather than in separatism that relies primarily on shared beliefs about being lesbian. Lesbian community is no more than how we relate with each other, Anna Lee maintains in "For the Love of Separatism." Anna emphasizes the importance of valuing differences, not merely from afar, but in intimate relations. Black lesbians, she writes, need to take black lesbian interactions and self-definition seriously. Anna calls upon white lesbians who have not examined their bond with white men to begin to consider that bond, itself a block to the creation of meaning-ful diversity, to stop using black women to strengthen con-nections between white women and men, and to examine the meaning of privilege.

How to live and how to theorize differences of race, eth-nicity, abilities, class, age, appearance, nationalities, one's own and those of others, is at the heart of *Lesbian Philoso-phies and Cultures*. How these questions are, and are not, addressed marks not simply dis/connections *between* exist-ing cultures, or lifeworlds, but dis/connections which shape cultures, which make them what they are. "Dis/Con-nections," the third section of this book, traces move-ments—intersecting, overlapping, intruding, conflicting, absent—among lesbians, among one's selves, and among theories by lesbians.

María Lugones, in "Playfulness, 'World'-Travelling, and Loving Perception," proposes a pluralistic feminism that affirms the plurality in each woman and among women as valuable and as central to feminist epistemology and ontolo-gy. María interweaves her coming to consciousness as a daughter and her coming to consciousness as a woman of color in her analysis of a complex failure of love: the failure of one woman to identify with another woman. She recom-mends travelling across 'worlds' as partly formative of cross-cultural and cross-racial loving. Edwina Franchild, in "'You do so well.': A Blind Lesbian Responds to her Sighted Sis-ters," reflects on her struggles to help create a cultural and

political community of choice. By discussion of world-travelling as a blind lesbian, not as identical to the world-travelling
described by María Lugones, but with its distinctive moments,
Edwina shows how living with differences of physical abilities
and disabilities may not be parallel to living with race and ethnic differences. She maintains that blind lesbians cannot exist
entirely apart from sighted lesbians, and that sighted lesbians
must come to terms with disability and its consequences in an
ableist society. "Lesbian Revolution and the 50 Minute Hour:
A Working-Class Look at Therapy and the Movement," by
Caryatis Cardea, traces classism within the lesbian feminist
movement to the power of therapy in lesbians' lives. Caryatis's analysis of intellect and emotion demonstrates how feminist process, in therapy and elsewhere, benefits middle-class
lesbians and denies working-class ways of life. Among Caryatis's proposals for change are that middle-class lesbians listen
to their working-class sisters, and that lesbians, instead of
seeking therapy, cultivate solid friendships and politics. "The
View from Over the Hill, Notes on Ageism between Lesbians," by Baba Copper, articulates the complexity of ageism
among women, a problem which she renames 'daughterism.'
Baba analyzes how oppression by age steals upon lesbians
gradually. Although lesbianism offers women the opportunity
to explore a fundamentally new social identity, Baba writes,
lesbian communities have tended to maintain patriarchal
practices of rendering old women absent, rather than listening
to old lesbians and exploring ageing and ageism.

The "Dis/Connections" described by Bette S. Tallen,
Michèle Causse, and Sarah Lucia Hoagland, focus, respectively, on questions of political theory, ways of knowing or
epistemology, and ethics. The authors radically reconfigure
these fields so that they address, and are of value to, lesbians'
experiences and concerns. In "How Inclusive is Feminist
Political Theory?: Questions for Lesbians," Bette S. Tallen
shows that much feminism and feminist political theory
excludes her life as a Jewish lesbian, both by its subtly anti-
Semitic feminist process, critical of Jewish conversational

styles and cultural values, and by the tendency of non-lesbians not to include lesbians when they use the terms 'woman' or 'feminist'. Bette argues that if the basis of feminism and feminist theory is that it applies to all women, 'woman' should be an inclusive term, and non-lesbians must begin to understand how a lesbian context and meaning can apply to their lives. Michèle Causse, in "The World as Will and Representation," writes innovatively of an epistemological revolution in which, for women as subjects, the world becomes our will and our representation, to create new relations between self and world. Michèle details moments of increasingly reciprocal self-recognition where women rebel against all hierarchy. She suggests a gynaesthesia in which women, by overcoming past breaks between heart and will, take on cuttings and grafts that will become our flesh and give birth to ourselves. Moral revolution is the theme of Sarah Lucia Hoagland's "A Lesbian Ethics and Female Agency." Just as the previous authors criticize English liberal theory and contemporary male European philosophy, Sarah criticizes traditional anglo-european ethics, whose foundation, she claims, is dominance and subordination, and which serves to interrupt rather than promote lesbian connection. Rejecting moral reform that appeals to the feminine, to self-sacrifice, and to mothering as unconditional loving, Sarah describes an ability to act that is not defined in terms of an other. Interactions between lesbians become, then, a perceiving ourselves as both separated and related, which Sarah terms 'amazoning,' and choice becomes a process of engagement and creation, a source of power.

"Writing Desire," the final section of *Lesbian Philosophies and Cultures*, explores desire, spirituality, sexuality and sensuality with particular emphasis on how languages and writing chart these experiences. Nett Hart, in "Lesbian Desire as Social Action," writes that to be lesbian, to act and name oneself a lover of women, presents an unmitigated challenge to the belief system that structures reality. Rejecting duty, as fervently loyal to the status quo and to the expectations others have of her, Nett calls upon desire: she who flows in the most erratic of manners toward the least likely of goals, and who, when she succeeds, creates new worlds. A lesbian separatist perspective, an approach not reactive, but self-authorized, informs Nett's painting of a landscape/seascape where lesbians name our desire. In "Lesbian 'Sex,'" Marilyn Frye, after examining a questionnaire on sex practices, reflects on a dilemma: if the term 'sex' is an inappropriate term for what some lesbians experience, how to approach whatever it is that lesbians do that has been designated 'sexual,' especially if there is no language, no linguistic community, for such experience? Marilyn purposes to address this question by beginning with her own experiences, a start which, she notes, has at least the virtue of firm connection with someone's actual life. She suggests that a vocabulary will arise among lesbians when we talk with each other about our passions and bodily pleasures.

In "Learning to Touch Honestly: A White Lesbian's Struggle with Racism," Kim Hall moves between her memories of 'you,' brown skinned, filipina, and 'I,' white, anglo, and her current life. While trying to come to terms with her whiteness, and to love womyn better, Kim shows how white lesbians frequently abstract racism from white lesbians' personal experiences, thereby analyzing whiteness from a distance, or not at all. This abstractness can dissolve, she suggests, if white lesbians explore relationships with womyn of color and with each other in ways that take risks and that are committed to change. "Lesbian Body Journeys: Desire Making Difference," by Jacquelyn N. Zita, has as its theme a politic of body journeys in which a body is marked by many differences and partial homes. Jacquelyn writes of narratives that return to the body as a point of desire, pleasure, and connection. These narratives are constantly recontextualized across differences of class, race, gender, sexualities and history. Jacquelyn shows that the lesbians in the narratives she describes have in common not a presumed essence, but a primacy of sexual desire for other lesbians. Language, Monique

Wittig maintains in "The Trojan Horse," is a direct exercise of power. Any work with a new form operates as a war machine, for its goal is to pulverize old forms and formal conventions. Monique claims that language is comprised of disparate elements and is, therefore, heterogenous. This heterogeneity appears in writing, where the form of words is not dictated by facts, actions, ideas, but arises through a detour in which words, the material of writing, are worked, and the shock of words is produced.

Nicole Brossard, in "Coincidence" and "Certain Words," writes with an enthusiasm for figures that change the image of reality. A lesbian does not catch sight of herself in another woman, Nicole writes, rather, she crosses into a new dimension. Nicole's text begins where there is no center, no axis, and this is in no way chaos. The magnitude of the expression, 'To do without a man,' becomes apparent when she writes the pleasant effects of slowly touching, as well as in her theory of reading, where lesbians become what we desire. Gloria E. Anzaldúa, in "She Ate Horses," tells of a relationship between Prieta and Llosí, a love that had started so well, but that had come to stand still. She writes with stunning images of a love where the instinct to unite has forgotten its counter-movement, the loosening, the letting-go, the acceptance of contradictions. How to begin when the ligament holding the two together breaks, and the halves fall apart; when *la orilla*, an edge of some sort, finally has split them; when each deals in different ways with the wild horse making thunder? "On the Seashore, A Writing of Abundance," by Jeffner Allen, recounts a time before abundance was rendered scarce and the many were dominated by the same. Amid tales of wimmin's alphabets, nebular selves, and clitoral currents, Jeffner develops a theory of writing. She writes in poetic prose of a shore that is effervescent, shifting sands, rubble washed by the sea, layers under layers upon layers; and of a transformation of energies in these multiple shifting grounds.

The contributors to this anthology are lesbians who are engaged in philosophical writing, including lesbians teaching philosophy in academic institutions who responded to a call for papers. In this sense, *Lesbian Philosophies and Cultures* is an outcome of an ongoing process made possible by conferences and publications frequently outside mainstream u.s.a., and by discussions among lesbians. Some of the contributors have come to know each other's work while attending gatherings such as the National Radical Thought Conference for Women, of which Lee Evans was a primary organizer, the biannual meetings of the Midwest Society for Women in Philosophy, the annual Third World/Lesbians of Color Conference, the National Women's Studies Association, readings in women's bookstores, and elsewhere. Some of the contributors have met through, or have had our writings cross in, books and anthologies, especially those published by women's presses, and in journals that have supported theoretical writing by lesbians, including *Sinister Wisdom, TRIVIA: A Journal of Ideas, Lesbian Ethics, Maize, Conditions, Amazones d'hier, lesbiennes d'aujourd'hui, VLASTA, and Hypatia: A Journal of Feminist Philosophy.*

I would like to thank Peggy Gifford and Lois Patton, at SUNY Press, for their support. I also thank Lauren Crux, Rosemary Curb, Kathryn Edwards, Kim Hall, Melyssa Jo Kelly, Anne Mamary, Connie Pacillo, Nathalie de la Rozière, and Joyce Trebilcot, each of whom, in special ways, has helped to make this book a reality. I am grateful to all of the contributors, many of whom gave invaluable suggestions for *Lesbian Philosophies and Cultures*, for reminding me of the gentle surprise of the unexpected.

J.A.

LIVING IN THE PLURAL

Dyke Methods

JOYCE TREBILCOT

First principle:	I speak only for myself
Second principle:	I do not try to get other wimmin to accept my beliefs in place of their own.
Third principle:	There is no given.[1]

The methods I discuss in this essay are, most narrowly conceived, methods for using language. They are, therefore, methods for a great deal else as well—experiencing, thinking, acting. But my focus is on language, on verbal language, on English; my focus is on how, as a dyke—a conscious, committed, political lesbian—I can use words to contribute to the discovery/creation of consciously lesbian realities.

The center of the essay is the statement of three principles. The principles are not rules to be followed. They are, rather, summaries of values that I frequently have and currently like having. I do not intend them to be adhered to by others and I can "violate" them myself if I want, with no negative consequences, no guilt.

Sources of the principles in my experience. The principles come mainly from anger, from anger about being controlled.

This control is exercised by men and male-identified women over women/wimmin and girls in a variety of ways, of which — as I have learned through feminism — two of the most effective are erasure and false naming. In erasure, men make us invisible either by claiming that we are included when we are not (as in terms such as "mankind") or by simply ignoring us; in false naming, they define us and then enforce their definitions upon us (as in their concept of woman).

Another manifestation of control by men is that women/wimmin adopt the very means of oppression that the dominators use and apply those techniques against ourselves and one another. For example, I have been in the audience of sessions of the Society for Women in Philosophy and of the National Women's Studies Association when lesbian feminist speakers have made claims about wimmin, about dykes, about "we," that erase or misdescribe me. In such cases, if I maintain my sense of who I am, I am excluded; if I feel myself a part of the "we" being discussed, I distort who I am. This difficulty is not only mine; I have heard other wimmin say that the misuse of "we" in lesbian and feminist settings is hurtful for them as well.

But long before feminism, I was angry because of attempts—often successful—to control me. My earliest experience of being controlled was as the only child of a mother who, with single-minded dedication, attempted to make me carry on her husband's values. I was also controlled and, in certain respects, continue to be controlled by institutions designed by powerful men to keep other people in line: the catholic church, heterosexuality, academe, capitalism, and so on.

In connection with the work of this essay, it is important to understand that these and similar institutions participate in the truth industry—heteropatriarchal science, religion, scholarship, education, media—that is used by men as a means of exercising power. In dominant culture "truths" are presented as claims that people are required to accept as bases for their thinking and action and hence identities, regardless of how *they* feel about the "truths" and regardless of their relevant experiences. By means of the apparatuses of "truth," "knowledge," "science," "revelation," "faith," etc. (it matters little whether the methodology is scientific or religious), men are able not only to project their personalities as reality, but also to require that other people participate in those realities and accept them as their own. Recipients of the "truth" (ie., all those not certified to create it) are expected to long for truth, to respect it, to bow down to it, and especially, to honor—and obey—those who are authorities on it. The system is thoroughly corrupt; it hurts me, angers me, and, when I have my wits about me, strikes me as silly. How ridiculous, for example, for men to go on an archaeological dig and report that what they have found is what is there, when I would come back with quite a different story were I to dig, and other wimmin would come back with yet other stories. Just as I am committed to writing philosophy without excluding or distorting any wimmin, so I am also committed to finding ways of working without imposing my "truths"—the descriptions, definitions, explanations, ideals, that are meaningful to me—on other wimmin. The three principles I explicate here help me in this process.

Where the principles apply. My life is like a muddy lake with some clear pools and rivulets—wimmin's spaces—but many areas thick, in one degree or another, with the silt and poisons of patriarchy. The principles I articulate here belong to the clear (relatively clear) waters.

The principles are not intended to be used in situations that are predominantly patriarchal, that is, when getting something from men is at stake, as when one is working in the patriarchy for money, doing business with men and male-identified women, etc. In these contexts, I find that it is often most effective—that is, helpful rather than harmful to wimmin/women—to operate according to patriarchal ideas of knowledge and truth.

When both patriarchal and feminist elements have a significant part in a situation, the principles do apply, although in ways limited by patriarchal power. Women's studies classes sometimes have this character; sometimes, for example, for a class to work, both in relation to the institution and in relation to the students in it, the teacher must operate partly with patriarchal principles and partly as a co-discoverer/creator of wimmin's spaces.

In situations that are predominantly wimmin-identified, in contrast, I attempt to throw off mainstream habits and values in favor of the more direct and diverse patterns of wimmin. I should add that, for me, patriarchy is always present: there is no "pure" wimmin's space. (As if in compensation, when wimmin are present there is no pure patriarchy—we are always violating and sabotaging it.)

The Principles

First Principle: I speak only for myself. I speak "only for myself" not in the sense that only I am my intended audience but, rather, in the sense that I intend my words to express only my understanding of the world. I expect that some wimmin will find that what I say is more or less true for them and that some will find that it is false, distorted, or irrelevant. The latter sort of case may hurt because I often want what I say to be accepted by wimmin I respect and love. But it is more important to me to acknowledge plenty of spaces for differences.

Let me give an example of how the idea that I speak only for myself works. Suppose I am inclined to write "We all need love." Because I wish to speak only for myself and thereby to acknowledge the likelihood that there are wimmin who do not believe that *they* need love, I refrain from the plural "we." There are several alternatives. First, instead of "We all need love," I may write "I need love and some other wimmin report that they also need love." This social science sort of approach presupposes data—written or verbal avowals from other wimmin. In what I would take to be the best scholarship, the wimmin who are reported on have themselves authorized the use of their words in the context in question; they themselves participate, as it were as co-authors, in the work. With this approach to fulfilling the principle that I write only for myself, feminist scholarship moves in the direction of becoming collective scholarship, a not surprising outcome.

A second way of reacting to the inclination to write "We

all need love" in a way consistent with speaking only for oneself is to write instead something like "I need love and it seems to me that some other wimmin also need love"; or, perhaps better, "My image of wimmin is that we all need love." In formulations like these I remind myself and my audience that I am talking about only my own beliefs, concepts, definitions, imagings—and that I respectfully leave space for the accounts of the wimmin I am describing, whether or not those accounts are significantly different from mine. With this approach I remind the reader that when I am writing about other wimmin, the distinction between my opinion and their own is (even when the opinions themselves are identical) methodologically significant.

The third and perhaps best alternative is that, in place of "We all need love," I write simply, "I need love." If I choose this approach, I clearly speak only for myself, and so attach my theorizings—that is, whatever explications, explanations, predictions, or exhortations I may connect to the claim that I need love—clearly and closely to my self, in accordance with the feminist belief that the personal is essentially involved in both knowledge (and hence theorizing) and liberation.

I have said that I intend my words to express only my own understanding. But my understanding is formed partly by men. Hence, in speaking for my self, often—to my horror, when I realize it—I am speaking also for men, for patriarchy. For example, when I, a white woman, speak in racist ways, I express white men's racism as well as my own. In order to speak only for my chosen dyke self and not for men as well, I work to recognize and eliminate oppressive ways of thinking and speaking and the forces that create them.

Second principle: I do not try to get other wimmin to accept my beliefs in place of their own. The first principle, that I speak only for myself, suggests the second, that in talking about my beliefs I reject the purpose of trying to bring it about that other wimmin substitute my beliefs for their own. I sometimes call this the principle of nonpersuasion. In this context, the term "persuasion" must be construed broadly so as to include not only argument and discussion but also other forms of deliberately influencing people's beliefs, such as emotional manipulation of various kinds.

Of course the principle of nonpersuasion does not preclude my telling other wimmin what my beliefs and values are, and I may certainly give them information, whether of a particular and perhaps trivial sort (e.g., "I'll be there at ten-thirty") or, for example, information I might relate to a class about herstory or feminist theory. The principle of nonpersuasion holds that I should not try to mold wimmin's minds, not that I should not give them information and ideas that they can use, if they choose, in making up their own minds, in making up their own realities.

Not trying to get other wimmin to accept my ideas in place of their own is a principle primarily about intention rather than about behavior. Whether a particular kind of behavior counts as persuasion varies from situation to situation and among cultures, so there is no kind of behavior that is always precluded by the principle. Indeed, I find that applying the principle does not require much change in how I act—I can still set out my convictions and my reasons for them (as I do, for example, here). But my attitude changes—it no longer includes the intention to persuade, an intention to which I became habituated in patriarchy.

Despite my renunciation of persuasion, wimmin may, of course, be influenced by me to adopt as their own certain of my beliefs, even though those beliefs are not authentic for them; this is especially likely in situations in which I am perceived as having higher rank or status. The principle of nonpersuasion can not and does not require that I in fact do not cause other wimmin to believe in certain ways, but only that I refrain from trying to do so.

This principle, then, takes seriously the cliche that everyone should think for herself. In patriarchal scholarship, this notion is likely to be presented against a background image of "a marketplace of ideas" where many producers present their wares, hawking them with arguments, competing with one another for attention and allegiance, and consumers buy some ideas but not others. The principle that in making a statement I do not try to get others to accept it suggests not an image of such a marketplace but one of a potluck: we each contribute something and thereby create a whole meal. It is understood that our contributions may be diverse and may seem, on some standards, not to go well together, but we are not bothered by that, for those standards are not ours. We each eat from our own and other dishes. The dish I bring is something I like myself, but also I want to share it—I hope that at least some others will like it too.

In writing dyke philosophy it is essential to me that someone else thinks that at least some of my work is worthwhile. But I want my work to be used by other wimmin because they find it helpful in terms of their own experiences, not because I have persuaded them, however gently, that what I say is true. I wish to learn to present my work not as ideas for sale in a competitive marketplace but as fruit to be shared with those who are so inclined.

Third principle: There is no "given." This principle, like the second, is suggested by the first. Not only do I speak only for myself but, ultimately and in principle, *only* I speak for myself. That is, the task of discovering/creating reality requires in the long run the exploration of every facet of existence through my feminist lesbian consciousness. In principle, I need to rewrite for myself the entire world as patriarchy has presented it to me. In practice, a finite lifetime and the call of other amusements make doing so impossible. Further, other wimmin with dyke consciousnesses are doing some of the work, and in many cases I can integrate their analyses into my own. Still, the principle that there is no given reminds me that at every step I need to consider how patriarchal assumptions my be distorting who I am and what I think, leading me back into the service of men.

The claim that there is no given does *not* mean that there is no oppression, that the baby is not actually crying in the next room, and so on. I understand that daily life may be experienced as replete with givens, with phenomena imposed from the outside; I do not mean to deny this experience, which I share. In saying that there is no given, I mean, rather, that every patriarchal assumption, every axiom of received reality, is ultimately to be questioned for the purpose of deciding whether to accept it as it is, change it, or reject it entirely: all the alleged immutables of nature, of the human condition, of ultimate reality, must be identified and evaluated.

Consider how controlling and pervasive patriarchal givens are. For example, in writing about wimmin's lives, part of the background of my discussion is the many assumptions shared by me and my readers about the necessary conditions of human life—that, for example, humans and hence wimmin must have food and water and air to survive; that our lives generally last less than a hundred years; that we are subject to pain; and so on. When these topics are not themselves the subjects of my discourse, I am likely, as a matter of habit and convenience, to accept such assumptions not merely as true but as givens in the sense that I take them to be immutable, to be written into the nature of things. And, indeed, they are written into the nature of things—but not by me, nor, yet, by any womon. So they are "givens" only on sufferance: temporarily and, even then, suspect.

The idea that there is no given means not just that every "given" needs to be reexamined in dyke consciousnesses, but also that dyke consciousnesses may define reality in such a way that there are no givens at all, that is, no "nature" (or deity) no immutable facts of nature (or metaphysics) that wimmin are forced to accept and build upon. In developing ideas in one area it may be helpful or even necessary to assume a fixed background of as-it-were immutable conditions, but these may be understood as assumptions for the sake of discussion and further creation/discovery rather than as facts of nature. The principle that there is no given not only calls attention to the need to question the assumptions and presuppositions of a particular focus, it also is a reminder that many familiar conceptual schemes that require givens are designed by privileged men in their own interests.

Queries and Replies

In this section I address what seem to me to be the most important objections and puzzles inspired by the three principles. These are organized as three queries: the query about persuasion, the query about community, and the query about pie-in-the-sky.

Query about persuasion. Joyce (I say to myself), probably the most serious worry I have about what I have written so far has to do with the second principle, which is that I do not try to get other wimmin to accept my beliefs as their own. I have two concerns about this claim. First, it is not true: I sometimes do try to persuade others. Second, and more important, I wonder whether it ought to be true: surely there are situations in which I *should* try to get others to agree with me.

Reply to the first part. Yes, I often do try to persuade others to accept what I say as their own. Sometimes I do this for the fun of arguing and sometimes I do it out of moral and political conviction. In some of the situations when I try to persuade others to adopt my views, resisting the temptation to attempt to persuade would be appropriate but, rather than resist, I act out of old habits. All three of the principles are ideals, and I do not always live up to them. On other occasions, however, the principle of nonpersuasion does not apply because the situation is patriarchal; these principles, as I have already said, are designed for wimmin's spaces.

But part of what constitutes wimmin's space is the exercise of these principles. That is, wimmin's space is defined partly by ways wimmin treat one another; the absence of conceptual/intellectual hegemony or, more broadly, serious respect for differences among wimmin, which is the point of the principle of nonpersuasion, is one of the characteristics of wimmin's space. Thus, there is an intimate relationship between acting in accordance with the second principle (and, indeed, with all three of the principles I have articulated here, as well as others) and the nature of the space one is in. I define whether a space or situation is wimmin's partly in terms of whether the principles I am discussing here apply; conversely, whether the principles apply depends on whether the space is wimmin's.

Consider a case in which I am a teacher in a women's studies classroom in a mainstream university. If the classroom situation is very patriarchal—a large beginning class of 50 or 60 students, say, with few feminist students—I am likely to define my task as largely one of recruitment and so to find persuasion—for example, persuading students that women are oppressed—an essential tool. I do not follow the principle against persuasion, which does not apply here. In contrast, in a smaller and more advanced class, I may enter into the exploration of the views of a student where these views are inconsistent with my own, not with the prospect of her beliefs changing but, rather, with the intention of participating in the articulation of those beliefs. By acting in accordance with the principle of nonpersuasion, I contribute to the creation of wimmin's space in this classroom.

Reply to the second part. The second part of the query about persuasion urges that in wimmin's spaces there sometimes are situations in which I *should* try to persuade others to accept my beliefs as their own. This idea is based on the conviction that some beliefs are so harmful that changing them, or trying to change them, is more important than avoiding the imposition of one's own beliefs on others.

My understanding of such situations is that they are defined by patriarchal values and so are not wimmin's spaces. Imagine, for example, a group of women/wimmin in which a white woman says something racist. I want her to be quiet, to take it back, not to talk like that, and I tell her so, and why. So far, I have acted consistently with the second principle. I have told her how I feel and what I think about her words, but I have not asked her to cease her racist talk nor argued that she should do so.

In fact, of course, my telling her my reaction to her words may function as a sanction, so that she may change her behavior and even her beliefs in order to please me—but this response is a patriarchal one, part of the traditional female role of acting according to the wishes of others. On the other hand, the womon may consider what I say on its own merits, without regard to her relationship to me, and decide, in the light of what she has heard, that she wants to change. In the former case, I persuade despite my intention not to; in the latter, I do not persuade, but the womon nevertheless changes.

But suppose that the woman who makes the racist remarks continues in a racist way despite being told that her words are heard as racist. Now it is clear that the space we share is not wimmin's, for in wimmin's spaces, patriarchy, including racism, is rejected whenever it is recognized. At this point, I may decide to attempt to persuade this woman to disavow racism, but this decision does not abrogate the second principle, for that principle applies only in wimmin's spaces. Thus, there are situations in which persuasion is appropriate, but the very existence of such a situation means, to me, that the space in question is not wimmin's.

Query about community. In a voice of challenge I say to myself that feminism, especially lesbian feminism, is essentially based on"we," on communities of wimmin conscious of ourselves as wimmin. But in my emphasis on difference, I obliterate community; in my emphasis on the many (to use terms from patriarchal philosophy as a reminder of the source of the objection), I lose sight of the one.

Another way of formulating this idea is to ask whether there must not be something or other that all feminists, or all dykes, agree on, whereby we are all entitled to be called "feminist" or "dyke." Surely being a dyke, while partly a matter of action and style, is also partly a matter of having certain beliefs. And, indeed, it might be argued, it is essential for wimmin to have shared beliefs as a basis for solidarity, so that we may stand together in strength against patriarchy. The query that emerges from these considerations, then, is whether the principles articulated here protect differences among wimmin but sacrifice our being together as wimmin.

Reply. Communities of wimmin are wimmin acting, singing, speaking, thinking, playing, feeling, not necessarily the same but in concert, together. The three principles imply that I will not try to bring this about by persuading wimmin to accept some set of beliefs, but they do not prevent my participating in and encouraging community. The principles preclude my imposing a "we" on others, but they do not mean that wimmin cannot share values and beliefs and self-definitions; they do not mean that wimmin cannot move together, thus creating a "we."

More explicitly, while being a dyke is in part to have certain beliefs—for example, belief in the creative power of wimmin—it is dykiest, I think, to come to these beliefs oneself, not to internalize them in reaction to someone else's intention that one do so. Of course, wimmin generally learn dyke beliefs partly from one another—indeed, community consists partly in this interaction. But learning from one another does not require the intention to persuade. Nor does sharing beliefs presuppose persuasion. Dyke communities, where wimmin share some central beliefs and values, may come into being without persuasion, through wimmin defining and redefining ourselves in interaction with one another.

I want to add that although I try to refrain from acting so as to get other wimmin to adopt the principles I articulate here, I would *like* other wimmin to adopt them. I like to be with wimmin where no one is imposing her views and there is no competition about who has the truth. When wimmin who share my anti-hierarchical, anti-competitive values get together, we tend not to argue or to try to persuade, but to tell our stories—past, present, and future, actual and fantastical—and to make plans. In these situations it seems that the stories are understood and enjoyed and the plans carried out just as well or better than when some womon is trying to convince us to accept her ideas. Sometimes an idea for an action or project for us all to participate in together elicits disagreement and is therefore allowed to drop. But in other cases, we agree, and we act jointly. Because of these experiences, I do not think that abandoning the purpose of getting others to adopt one's own beliefs lessens community; on the contrary, it seems to me that such restraint can strengthen wimmin's sense of shared convictions and commitments.

Finally, I should note that as I use these principles of dyke method, they do not imply that other wimmin should not act as leaders and persuade wimmin to accept *their* beliefs and values. I do not universalize the principles. My purpose is to announce my own (perhaps temporary) adoption of them, not to try to persuade others to accept them.

Query about pie-in-the-sky. Assuming a somewhat scolding and definitely pragmatic voice, I say to myself: Joyce, there you go off again, all by yourself, to some imaginary dyke heaven where each woman speaks only for herself, we love one another's differences, and not even nature limits us. I understand that this tendency comes from your separatist heart, but you are wasting your energies. Pure wimmin's spaces can't exist—we are interfused everywhere with patriarchy—and, anyway, we need to be dealing with patriarchal reality now, for they are truly out to get us.

Reply. First, a semantic point: pure wimmin's spaces can't exist in that when they do, the word "wimmin" itself will not be part of them, for despite the spelling, that word refers back to patriarchy; in pure wimmin's spaces, patriarchy is inconceivable. (It does not follow, however, that "pure wimmin's spaces" [with the quotation marks] cannot exist.)

As to the central concern of the query, the need to confront patriarchy: the anger from which the theorizing in this essay comes is like a two-headed snake, one head attacking patriarchy directly (and often in its own terms), the other slithering its way *through* patriarchy, making its own spaces, pushing aside men and their products, eliminating patriarchy from its path. Thus, the principles for discovering/creating wimmin's spaces do not preclude attacking patriarchy in its own arena. Indeed, commitment to wimmin's spaces is in fact often conjoined with a commitment to defend and support wimmin/women who are being harmed by patriarchy. In particular, some separatists are regular organizers of and participants in actions that involve dealing with men both in confrontation and in coalition. Moreover, the development of wimmin's spaces may itself lead wimmin to decide on direct political action, as, for instance, in the case of an academic, fired because her research is about separatism, who then chooses to confront the university directly in a campaign to get her job back. The central response I want to make to this query here, however, is that it is a mistake to suppose that devotion to wimmin's spaces means that a woman can not or does not engage in political actions involving confrontations with men.

The methods discussed here are *dyke* methods because dykism, as I understand it, is a rejection of/separation from patriarchy, a movement to which these principles contribute. One who consciously and on political grounds adopts them thereby participates in dyke process. (It is men, of course, who make sex the center of lesbianism, as they make sex the center of every female identity.)

As what I have already said indicates, my main motive (as far as I know) for developing these dyke methods is one that has always been at the center of my life: that others not control me. My logic here is in part like that of the pacifist who responds to violent treatment with a refusal to be violent in return. I respond to domination with a commitment to discover/create spaces in which domination cannot exist. But unlike the pacifist, who renounces all violence, I do not renounce all attempts to persuade: rather, I sometimes use the master's methods within the master's house for the sake of wimmin/women; in wimmin's spaces, however, I abjure those methods. The principles discussed here may seem an unacceptable renunciation of power to some wimmin. For me, however, they feel empowering; they embody my deepest values.[2]

Notes

[1] In this essay I use two sets of spellings for words referring to human females: the conventional "women" (plural) and "woman"(singular) and the less familiar "wimmin" (plural) and "womon" (singular). The difference between the two spellings is that a woman is defined by men, whereas a womon, usually in interaction with other wimmin, defines herself. But most wimmin some times, in some respects, conform to definitions imposed by men and so are (at those times and in those respects) women; similarly, most women at some times, in some respects, act independently of men and so are (at those times and in those respects) wimmin. Hence, the two sets of spelling do not distinguish two kinds of females. It is usually a mistake to try to figure out whether a particular female is a womon or a woman, although it is sometimes useful to think about whether particular ideas and behaviors are more harmonious with the values of wimmin or with those of women.

[2] I appreciate contributions to the content of this essay by Anne Waters, Claudia Card, Jacquelyn N. Zita, Janneke van der Ros, Jeanette Silveira, Jeffner Allen, Julia Penelope, Kim Hall, María Lugones, Marilyn Frye, Ryn Edwards, and Sarah Lucia Hoagland. Also, the writing of Liz Stanley and Sue Wise in their book *Breaking Out: Feminist Consciousness and Feminist Research* (London: Routledge and Kegan Paul, 1983) has given me both content and courage.

For additional discussion of these ideas, see the longer version of "Dyke Methods" in *Hypatia* vol. 3, no. 2 (Summer 1988) and the commentary on it, "Lesbian Angels and Other Matters," by Jacquelyn N. Zita along with my response in *Hypatia* vol. 4, No. 3. "Dyke Methods" also appears in the Wisconsin lesbian-feminist periodical, *Hag Rag*, in two parts in Vol. 3, Nos. 4 and 5.

After I presented some of this material at a session of the Midwest Society for Women in Philosophy in the fall of 1986, Sarah Lucia Hoagland sent me a copy of an earlier essay by Sally Miller Gearhart in which Gearhart develops an idea closely related to part of what I say here. Gearhart's thesis is that "any intent to persuade is an act of violence." Her essay is "The Womanization of Rhetoric," *Women's Studies International Quarterly*, 1979, Vol. 2, pp. 195-201.

The Invisible Woman

VIVIENNE LOUISE

Fay picks the most intruding weeds from the garden. It is time to plan her winter crops, mustard greens, kale and tulip bulbs for the spring. The autumn chill is damp, but with the exception of her hands, she is comfortably warm. Her hands grind through the brown earth, almost becoming the earth as the colors in her hand and the earth match. She digs determinedly and comes across a small piece of metal. It's a bullet. Probably dropped by someone, maybe even Ruby. Fay fingers the cold object turning it over and over trying to beat back the memories that it brings.

Ruby had bought the gun years ago. She insisted that they needed it to protect themselves from the trifling no-accounts in the world. There had been a rash of burglaries and physical attacks on neighbors and Ruby's brashness was really a cover-up for her own fear. Fay objected, of course.

"A gun is dangerous. Someone could get hurt. We might even have an accident and shoot each other."

But in the end the gun came into the house.

Ruby convinced Edith, Germaine and Tiehl to purchase guns also. Many Sunday afternoons were spent with the five of them at the firing range shooting until their ears hurt from the noise. In spite of herself, Fay learned how to shoot quite well and enjoyed practicing such a precise skill. Detailed work came easy to her so the simple concentration necessary to shoot a gun accurately calmed her. Target practice soon became her favorite past-time, relishing in the controlled release of aggression.

However, no one ever burglarized their home nor threatened them in any way. Their friends and co-workers were not so lucky, though, and Ruby's and Fay's anger mounted at these unprovoked attacks.

Fay chuckles to herself as she remembers that they used to keep the gun in the top drawer of the china cabinet, underneath her grandmother's mauve table linen. How impractical. How were they ever going to get it from there if someone did come in and threaten them?

Fay finishes weeding and goes into the house. The hot air from the furnace envelopes her in a sheet of warmth as she moves to turn down the thermostat. Reaching for a sheet of note paper on the table, she begins to write a shopping list for plants from the nursery. Tunisia will be by later on and Fay will ask her to pick up the plants.

Fay then starts up the stairs to get dressed for her poker game this afternoon. As she runs her hand along the banister for support she catches a splinter in her finger. She leans over and is reminded of the jagged area of exposed wood on the banister. It stands out naked against the neighboring wood all sanded, polished and shining. Fay grimaces at the pained finger and picks at the splinter with her fingernails. It remains stubbornly embedded and she sits down on the step, determined to be spared the burden of finding a pair of tweezers.

Fay's granddaughter, Tunisia, had begged Fay to have that section of the banister repaired. But Fay held out wanting, or maybe needing, a reminder of that fateful night.

Ruby had been gone for maybe two years by that time. Fay's heart still ached from longing but she had learned to let go of the anger that death so deftly instills. However, often she felt lonely, finding friendships just not enough after so many years with a close lover. It was while she was in a particularly gruesome funk that she realized something was wrong. She had an eery feeling of dread and for the first time since living in her house she felt fearful of some sort of attack. She interpreted this intuitive message as a warning that maybe some trifling no-accounts were going to break in that night. She had no rational reason for this assumption but decided that preparation was the best medicine. So she cleaned the gun, and just after sunset positioned herself in a rocking chair by the stairway, facing the front door. Her plan was to shoot them as they entered the house, picking them off one by one.

As she sat there rocking back and forth, fear mounting with every second, she realized that she hadn't acted quite as wisely as she thought. Why didn't she call someone and tell them of her feelings? Why hadn't she at least called Tunisia to let her in on the situation: Why was she so sure she was going to be invaded anyway? It had never happened before. Why should it happen now?

Just as she was about to reach for the light and use the telephone, she heard someone jimmying her lock. In no time at all, four strident males had entered the house. The lights from the street lamps streamed into the room causing shadows to dance across the wall and on the floor. The whole front area of the house appeared as a dark landscape with deep black holes juxtaposed against varying shades of grey figures. Before Fay could catch her breath one of the men had turned on the hall light. They were evidently not afraid of being discovered by her or anyone else. Their boldness surprised her, even with her knowledge of many other similar situations.

As the hallway filled with light the greys and blacks gave way to stark outlines and clear, complete objects. The four no-accounts were standing in the hallway, talking among themselves. Fay sat for a moment looking at them, pointing the gun with an inwardly shaking hand. But they paid no attention to her. She was plainly visible, with the angular dark object resting neatly in her hand, and yet they acted as though she wasn't there.

Fay then spoke, something between a normal speaking tone and a shout. They didn't flinch a muscle, nor cast a nod in her direction. She then got up and walked toward them with the gun ready for firing. Again no response. Fay stood still, not three steps from them. Her mind tumbled as pieces of a plaguing puzzle fell together. They didn't see her. And even more astounding, they also didn't hear her. They were not aware that she was there. This realization shocked her. If she was really invisible then that explained why she was constantly overlooked at the meat counter, or passed over in lines at the post office, or unable to get decent service at certain dress shops. These people simply didn't see her. She was invisible so they weren't being rude, they just weren't seeing.

This clarity came to Fay in a few moments, flashing through her mind with lightening speed as the pieces fell into place. In the next few moments Fay adopted her survival mode. She remembered the assaults against her friends and neighbors, pulling the rage from her visceral depths. Visible or not this was her house and they had invaded it. She went to the front door and locked it. She then turned off the light and shot the nearest no-account in the back of the head. The sound of the gun shocked the other three and they turned too late to see their companion fall. Before another breath was drawn Fay moved to the next one and shot him through the heart.

By this time the other two were terrified and the necessity for escape had become apparent. One ran towards the living room aiming for a window. Fay shot him in the leg and when he had slowed down, finished the job with a bullet in his brain.

The fourth, not thinking clearly, ran upstairs. Fay, not caring to chase an agile young man, turned off the hallway light, sat down in the rocker and waited. She made no sounds as she waited for him to descend. Eventually he did and she sent him to his maker with no hesitation. The bullet grazed the banister on the way to its host and left the splintered chips. Fay considered this a baptism of sorts and thus continued to refuse Tunisia's pleas to repair it.

Not sure what to do after such a grizzly task, Fay reverted back to the posture of the obedient citizen and called the police. She had to call five times before she got someone on the phone who could hear her. Everyone else merely repeated their initial salutation, "Police department may I help you, police department may I help you, police department may I help you." A couple of times they cursed at her, but she persevered. The woman who finally could hear her was polite, concise and took the time to ask her if she was alright. She said that she would send a squad car as soon as possible.

Fay then called Tunisia, needing a comforting, take-charge person with her at that time.

Tunisia arrived a few minutes after the police. Fay had opened the door for the police but they didn't see her so they informed Tunisia that the door had been left open. They asked Tunisia if she lived in the house and Tunisia told them that her grandmother lived in the house. When asked where her grandmother was, Tunisia nimbly replied that she was sitting on the sofa. The police detective looked in the direction of the sofa, saw no one sitting there, and stiffly told Tunisia that this was no laughing matter and she needed to stop playing games.

Tunisia, not understanding their reluctance to acknowledge her grandmother, who was in plain view, became annoyed.

"Detective Thurman, my grandmother is sitting on that sofa in plain view. If you want to talk to her then go right ahead. I'm sure she has an explanation. However, don't continue to be insulting, insinuating that I don't want to cooperate."

Tunisia's very black eyes rolled in anger as she pursed her full lips into a thin line of irritation. She folded her arms across her ample bosom and paced back and forth. Tunisia was a striking woman, having much of Ruby's personality. She was actually Ruby's granddaughter. But Ruby and Fay had been together all of Tunisia's life and so she grew up regarding both of them as her grandmothers. However, her impatient balderdash marked her as a sure descendant of Ruby.

Detective Thurman snorted, shrugged, asked Tunisia a few questions, vowed to check out her alibi and left. The other police fiddled and searched and finally removed the bodies. It was several hours before the house was cleared and Fay and Tunisia were able to sit down and talk privately.

Fay told Tunisia what happened, including her realization of invisibility. Tunisia looked at her grandmother thoughtfully and calmly replied,

"Gran Fay you aren't invisible. I can see you very well. No probably someone else killed these men and you just don't remember what happened. Yes, that's it," replied Tunisia confidently, gathering speed with each new assertion.

"Maybe these men were being chased, randomly picked your house as a refuge only to be caught anyway. You must have left the door unlocked." Then with condescending compassion, "You must be in shock and don't remember or realize what happened. Gran Fay are you alright? Do you want me to spend the night? Or would you rather spend the night with me? I'm worried about you."

Tunisia's furrowed brow was set above dark brown eyes that probed her grandmother's face for an entrance to intimate thoughts. No entrance was found but Tunisia continued to study intently.

"No dear I'll be alright. Go home and call me in the morning," sighed Fay, accepting the position of aged incompetence. She knew she had been invisible to those men but convincing Tunisia would be no less miraculous than stopping the flow of the ocean.

"I'll drink something hot and go to bed," promised Fay, acquiescing to the familiar role of harmless old lady who tires early in the evening and needs to rest when there is too much excitement.

However, after everyone left Fay found sleep entirely out of the question. She put down sheets on the carpet where blood was stained. She washed down the walls and door as much as possible. And she sprayed air freshener and opened the windows to rid the room of the aroma of death. Pleased with herself she then baked a chocolate cake with mocha frosting, her favorite.

Fay got no sleep that night as she thought on the turn of events. The whole evening had been a series of surprises; the intuitive dread, the now-deceased intruders and the invisibility. She was an embryo wrapped in a cocoon gradually unfolding into a butterfly. She felt exhilarated, happy, and for once in her life, powerful.

How the police finally resolved the case was unknown to Fay. Although they searched her house they didn't find the gun as it was on her, and of course they couldn't see her. They did watch her house and follow Tunisia, but eventually gave up on finding any leads. Tunisia received a few hate letters from members of the deceased's family, but that never came to anything. In the meantime, Fay went about adjusting and changing her life to accommodate her new found freedom.

That was four years ago.

Fay is finally able to remove the splinter with a few good tugs. She then gets up and goes upstairs to change for her poker game. Fay calls a cab, hoping that one of the regulars will answer the phone. The phone rings and luck is not with her. A young woman chants, "Confidence Cab." Fay swallows, states her name and her desire for a taxicab. The new voice just continued to chant, "Confidence Cab may I help you? Is anyone there? Confidence Cab." Just as the speaker is becoming exasperated another female voice comes on the line. It is familiar and her first words are,

"Ms. Wilson is that you?"

"Yes, it's me. Thanks for picking the phone up. I would like a cab here in about 20 minutes please."

"Well we only have two new drivers available but I'll send both of them. If it doesn't work out then call me again?"

"Thank you. I really appreciate your consideration."

"We really appreciate your business. Now they are both new and we don't know them very well, but maybe it will be okay."

"Okay, I'll let you know."

"Thanks, do that."

Fay hangs up the phone with a sigh. Confidence Cab is a woman-owned company that runs on a shoe string. She has been dealing with them for four years and counts on them for a great deal of her transportation needs. They hire only women and most of the drivers have no trouble seeing her. Fay notes that the ones that do have trouble usually don't last very long.

When she first started dealing with Confidence Cab all of the drivers were able to see her. It wasn't until about a year and a half into their relationship that a problem arose. A driver came to her house, didn't see her standing on the front steps, honked the horn and didn't see her approach the cab. When Fay opened the back door the driver became alarmed and reached to pull the door shut. A minor tug of war ensued with Fay being thrown off balance and falling in the street.

She called the company, complained and was immediately sent another driver. The owner later stated that some of her drivers were just not very polite and didn't want to deal with senior citizens. Fay knew better, but kept her own counsel.

Fay had not learned to drive; at first stating that her reflexes weren't sharp enough and then later crying poor eye sight. The real reason was that she secretly liked being driven around. She didn't want to be bothered with concentrating on traffic when it was so much more amusing to look out the window and daydream. Ruby liked driving so this was not an issue between them. And now most of Fay's friends drove so she could usually get a ride. When it was an inconvenience for her friends to pick her up she called a cab.

After that fateful night when she realized she was invisible, she had begun to understand who can see her and who can't. Absolutely no men can see her. But some women, especially those in her types of circles, can see her. However, some women can't see her either. It is tricky figuring out who can see what. But Fay had started to be able to recognize a certain posture, gleam in the eye, energy or feeling about some women that makes it possible for them to see her.

Fay is drawn back to the present by the sound of a horn honk. She hurries down the stairs and out the door. She makes a mental note to tell the company to train these new drivers in taxicab etiquette, such as ringing doorbells. Fay locks the front door and eyes the drivers as she walks briskly down the walkway. The one in cab no. 9 will see her, she is sure of it. As it turns out, she is right. The driver looks her dead in the eye, speaks and simply asks her destination. Fay notes the name of the cabbie as one she will request in the future.

Tiehl answers the door, wearing a red sweat suit and her poker cap. Germaine and Edith are already sitting at the table nervously shuffling the cards, prematurely counting their winnings no doubt. They greet Fay, giving her smiles, hugs and sweet kisses. Judy and Carmen come in from the kitchen laden with trays full of sandwiches, freshly baked cookies, potato chips and fruit. The coffee maker is already on the buffet and the smell of fresh brew permeates the air. Lenore is the last to arrive, breezing in with brisk excitement, wearing cool autumn colors matching her latest hair tint.

"You'll never guess who I saw today," breathes Lenore. And before anyone can reply she states,

"Kitty. She was with her husband and she all but tried to ignore me. But I wasn't having any of that. No one ignores me. So I went right up to her and said hello. She backed off like I had something but that didn't stop me. I introduced myself to her husband and told her that we hadn't seen her in a long time. Asked why she had been away so long. As I moved on I could hear him asking her who I was and why hadn't he met me before. I could also just imagine what she said."

Everyone laughed at this, but an undertone of sadness is unmistakable. Kitty had been a friend for many years. Then she started to change. Fay had been oblivious of the changes in Kitty until one evening at Kitty's house. The poker game was over and everyone had left, except for Fay. Fay was putting on her sweater when she caught Kitty looking at her through squinting eyes. Fay had seen this expression often enough to know what it meant. The woman was having trouble seeing her.

"Fay, you know maybe my eyesight is going but sometimes I could swear that you are a ghost, or transparent or something like that." Then shocked at the illogic of what she had said Kitty hurriedly added, "Oh, but that must be nonsense. I mean you are flesh and blood just like me. Maybe I just need my eyes checked." But she continued to look at Fay through squinting eyes and sometimes didn't see her at all. Fay knew by the expressions on women's faces whether they saw her or not. And Kitty sometimes didn't see her at all.

Undaunted by this situation Kitty caught herself asking the other players, "Where's Fay? She was just here a minute ago." Then someone would look up from her cards, and absent-mindedly reply that Fay was sitting right next to her or across the table from her. Kitty would mask her shock by an over-jocular laugh but still apparently be unable to see Fay.

Eventually Kitty stopped coming to the poker game. She made excuses; no time, illness, other commitments. But when Kitty married a neighboring widower six months later, Fay knew why she had become unable to see her.

The game is fun. Germaine and Edith do go away with the pot but Judy's cookies sweeten the plight of the losers.

Fay gets a ride home with Carmen and Tunisia drives up just as they arrive. Upon entering the house Fay gives Tunisia the nursery shopping list and asks if she wants to stay for dinner. Tunisia accepts and together they prepare a simple meal.

Tunisia is currently involved with another project to bring down the system. She is a grad student at the university and is responsible for establishing Adamu, a Black lesbian feminist organization on campus. Adamu is a name for the female principle of matter. It means red and represents the blood of the womb and menstruation. This organization has been active in promoting positive change around a myriad of discrimination issues on campus.

Adamu has: protested the dismissal of a woman professor launching a campaign to gain her tenure; contributed to the Pan-African celebrations by bringing in Black lesbian poets and musicians; and worked hard with other lesbian groups on campus to institute a few lesbian culture classes. Presently Adamu is involved in pushing the administration to recruit more older women students. The university evidently has money set aside for these special students but is lax in disseminating information about the availability of this money. Adamu is attempting to correct that. They are also writing a guideline sheet for changing the language, moving away from words that insult those who have been incarcerated in mental institutions.

To Fay, Tunisia and her organization seem indefatigable in their relentless pursuit of justice from the system. Tunisia's enthusiasm is inspiring and Fay enjoys her stories involving tactics to use on the offending entity and the soap opera dynamics of sabotage and power plays among the members. She is grateful that she isn't involved, but is happy to know that the legacy of political action continues.

Fay and Ruby were quite active in the civil rights movement through their participation in various Negro women's clubs. She did her share of marching, petitioning and door knocking when she was younger. Now she reminisces the vibrancy of those times through Tunisia's renditions.

Tunisia often invites Fay and her friends to Adamu's events, such as speeches, readings, concerts and the like. Although Tunisia introduces Fay to a wide variety of people, only a select few actually see her. Tunisia is oblivious to this, however, and when by chance she does notice her grandmother being ignored she chalks it up to the appropriate ism—ageism, racism, sexism—never discussing the situation with Fay.

At 7:30 p.m. Tunisia leaves, stating that she is late for a meeting. Fay settles in her favorite overstuffed chair with a mystery while listening to jazz on the radio. It is a thrilling who-dunit and she wants to finish it tonight.

At 11:00 p.m. she finds herself on the last page of the book. Finishing with satisfied relish she gets up, goes to the closet and reaches for her plaid cape. This is her favorite part of the day, the midnight stroll.

Being invisible to all but a chosen few has its drawbacks. However, it does make it possible to walk in the moonlight, carefree and unfettered. This one luxury is worth all the inconvenience that sometimes surrounds her daily life. She wraps a scarf around her neck, grabs her purse and leaves one lamp on before walking into the chilled night air.

It is colder now than earlier but the sky is clear and the waning moon smiles benevolently on her as she promenades down the street. She usually does her grocery shopping at this time. As it so happens not only is she invisible, but anything she touches or holds is also invisible. So she is able to get groceries without paying for them. Spending the money is not the problem. Ruby and Fay owned a small business for years, invested wisely, and Fay is now quite comfortable on the financial end. But just the notion that she *can* get groceries for free is the thrill. Taking them, or as Tunisia, would say, liberating them, is the fun; especially taking them out from under the noses of clerks and managers.

Her neighborhood store is one of a chain that stays open all night. However, after 11:00 p.m. the employees are usually all men and she can shop quite freely, knowing there is no danger of discovery. She moves through the aisles, picking up this and that, always opting for the most expensive items. Fay then gathers her packages at the front, puts them in a bag and sprightly walks back home.

This evening pleasure has sometimes been interrupted by the inclusion on the night shifts of women. More often than not they can't see her. But she has to take a risk to ascertain this.

A couple of months ago a young woman began working on the night shift. This woman sees her quite clearly. Fay noticed that the clerk didn't blink or squint but looked directly at her. Tempting fate just for a little added amusement, Fay gathered up her groceries as always. She bagged them and walked out without paying. She knew the woman saw her, but ignored this, glancing back only once to catch her incredulous expression. Fay shopped two more times before the woman approached her in the aisles of the store.

"Mam, you will have to pay for these things if you want to take them out of the store. I know that you didn't pay the last couple of times you came in here. But you will have to pay tonight," she said pointedly.

Fay looked at her wearily and asked,

"Why?"

The clerk becomes slightly flustered at what she perceives as impudence and answers,

"Because that is the way it is done. The store can't make any money if everyone comes in here and just takes what they want."

"But everyone doesn't come in here taking whatever they want. Only I do that. So your logic doesn't hold up. Leave me alone, so that I can finish what I came in here for."

"I'll call the manager if you try to take these things without paying for them. I'll have to."

"Why will you have to?"

"Because it is my job."

"But no one else is concerned. You are not the only one present here. They leave me alone, why won't you?"

At this the woman was visibly uncomfortable. She had, indeed, wondered why no one ever stopped the shoplifting old woman. Fay had located a sensitive nerve. She then retorted curtly,

"Just don't try it again tonight or I will have to call the manager."

Fay didn't deign to reply, just kept putting groceries into her basket. When it came time for her to bag her groceries the woman came and stood watching her. When Fay started to walk out the door the woman called the manager. "This woman is attempting to leave the store without paying for her groceries." The manager looked around and then at her and asked, "What woman?"

"That woman, the old lady walking towards the front door," pointed the clerk.

The manager sucked his teeth and said with annoyance and a sneer,

"I don't see anyone going towards the front door. In fact I don't see any customers in the store at all. What are you talking about?"

Then dubiously,

"You're not on drugs are you?"

Fay lingered a moment to watch the manager leave the clerk and disappear down one of the aisles. She then said,

"They don't care about you. Why do you care so much about them?" The woman didn't respond. She stared at Fay with tears welling up in her eyes.

Since that evening Fay shops when she feels like it. When she needs no groceries she merely waves at the bewildered clerk through the store front window. Despite her confusion, the store employee continues to look at Fay directly, not feigning a dismissal or attempting to make her invisible. Fay thinks there is hope for the young woman.

Tonight, however, the woman isn't there. It is an all male night shift again, and Fay hums a favorite tune while she shops.

As she walks back home the silken rays of the moon soften her heart and she thinks of other walks that were taken with Ruby. She remembers when they were much younger and lived downtown. They would walk at night, arm in arm, two maiden ladies out for a stroll or going to one of the colored clubs. She could almost hear the delicate strains of Ella, Sarah or Dinah as she noted the heavy dampness of the air against her skin. Those were magical times; feeling loved, building a business, constructing a life together and feeling secure.

Of course, these are magical times too, she reminds herself, reluctant to slip too deeply into the nostalgic repartee.

'What would Ruby say now? Would she be invisible too? Would I be invisible if Ruby was still alive? If I was invisible would Ruby acknowledge it or would she simply dismiss it, like Tunisia?'

As Fay doesn't know why she is invisible or how she came to be invisible, she quizzes herself daily with questions on this line; but with no answers, the questions just float into the atmosphere.

Welcoming the warmth of her home Fay puts the groceries away and makes a cup of tea. Tea helps her sleep after a busy day and insures a sound rest for the next.

LOCATIONS

Breaking Silence, Making Waves and Loving Ourselves

The Politics of Coming Out and Coming Home

Kitty Tsui

My family name is Tsui. My first name is Kit Fan, Fragrant Purity. I was born in the Year of the Dragon in the City of Nine Dragons, Kowloon, Hong Kong. I am the first daughter in a family of three girls and a son. My father was the first—and youngest—captain of Chinese descent for the British Blue Funnel Lines based in Liverpool, England.

My grandmother brought me up in Hong Kong until I was five years old. At that time, my parents sent for me. I remember looking out of the airplane and seeing my grandmother, a tall, slender woman, standing on the runway waving a handkerchief. She was crying. I was busy chewing on a piece of beef jerky from a large tin she had filled with some of my favorite goodies to distract me, no doubt, from the pain of parting. She was crying. I was busy eating.

Another vivid memory from childhood is one of silence. My grandma, parents, siblings and members of our extended family sitting down to dinner. And silence. No conversation or laughter. Just the sound of soup spoons and chopsticks against the rice bowls.

My fondest memory from childhood is one where my grandmother is holding me in her arms. We are backstage. All around us are actors resplendent in their robes, their faces awash in color, made up as courtesans, women warriors, immortals, scholars or clowns. I remember seeing them drinking tea from the spouts of miniature teapots so they wouldn't smear their makeup. This memory is one that is filled with many sounds: the sound of children playing in the aisles, people cracking open melon seeds and spitting them out mingling with the strident chords of the *erh-hu* and the clashing of the cymbals.

In the summer of 1968 my family came to Gold Mountain following the footsteps of 175,000 Chinese immigrants who entered from 1910 to 1940. That first wave entered the country at Angel Island, a detention center for Chinese awaiting jurisdiction on the outcome of medical examinations and immigration papers. It was also the holding ground for detainees awaiting deportation.

Mrs. Fong, who was imprisoned on Angel Island in 1922 says: "One woman failed the interrogation and tried to drown herself, so the husband returned to China with her."

Looked upon as undesirables who were taking jobs away from the white citizenry, the Chinese were targets of many racist laws that began in 1870 with the Cubic Air Ordinance, culminated with the Chinese Exclusion Act of 1882, and that lasted until 1943.

Over the years more than 50,000 Chinese were held at Angel Island for weeks, months, even years while the government decided whether to admit or deport them. Many carved poems of pain, anger and frustration on the walls of their wooden prison. Some of them committed suicide rather than face the humiliation of being sent home.

One detainee wrote:

> Originally I had intended to come to America
>   last year.
> Lack of money delayed me until early autumn.
> It was on the day that the Weaver Maiden
>   met the Cow Herd
> That I took passage on the President Lincoln.
> I ate wind and tasted waves for more than
>   twenty days.
> Fortunately I arrived safely on the
>   American continent.
> I thought I could land in a few days.

How was I to know I would become a prisoner
    suffering in the wooden building.
The barbarians' abuse is really difficult to take.
When my family's circumstance stir my emotions
    a double stream of tears flow.
I only wish I can land in San Francisco soon,
Thus sparing me this additional sorrow here.[1]

My family arrived in the summer of '68 on a cool, foggy day at San Francisco International. I remember seeing my grandmother again after almost a decade of separation and thinking: I'm taller than she is. In the ten years since our separation I had grown into a tall, gawky adolescent and she had shrunk into old age.

We rode in my uncle's big American car to a small, unfurnished apartment on Washington and Powell where the cable cars clanged through Chinatown every few minutes. Grandma taught me to eat steak rare and the technique of fine dicing onions without slicing off my fingertips. She took me to Ping Yuen Restaurant on Du Pont Gai for Coke, apple pie, custard tarts and bought me whatever I wanted from the Five and Dime. She cooked my favorite foods: short ribs with fermented black beans, bittermelon and chicken, steamed pork with salted duck eggs, chicken feet and peanut soup. We had white rice and black tea. She fed me chicken and mushrooms, beef and greens. She didn't tell me of the years of eating meals of plain rice and hot tea. She wouldn't talk of her life. She never chattered, she rarely spoke. I had to beg for stories of her life, her husband, my grandfather. "What for, you wanna know?" she'd ask. "Why you asking? Too many questions you young kid asking."

So I went to the library to find stories to fill the gaps. There were books about America and books about China. There were books about Hong Kong, the Pearl of the Orient. But there was nothing about a place and a language and a culture called Asian Pacific America. And certainly nothing about a renowned Chinese opera singer named Kwan Ying Lin, my grandmother.

It was about this time that I realized the importance of talking story and writing it down, the importance of documentation and the power of words. If nobody writes anything down our history will be lost. Who will know of our work, our struggles, our victories, our joys, our loves, our lives? Who will remember? Who will care?

My foreparents began emigrating to Gold Mountain during the Gold Rush, necessitated by political chaos and economic hardship at home. From the beginning they were met with prejudice, discrimination and bigotry. But their contribution to this country was invaluable. China Men built the transcontinental railroad, reclaimed swamplands in California's Sacramento-San Joaquin River delta, developed the shrimp and abalone fisheries, the Napa-Sonoma vineyards, new strains of fruit, and provided the needed labor for this State's agriculture and other light industries.

While the China Men built the iron horse and worked the land, the China Women were, for the most part, denied entry by the laws of the new country and relegated to no-class citizenship by the unwritten laws of their homeland. In my grandmother's day, girls born into poverty were killed or sold into prostitution, girl children born into prosperity had their feet bound, their marriages arranged. My grandmother herself escaped this fate by being sold, instead, into the theater, where she spent her early years as a slave and then an apprentice to the reigning stars of the Chinese opera. By the time she was in her teens, she was already famous for her acting, her beauty, the power of her voice and the seduction in her eyes.

In 1922 when she was barely twenty-two years old, she was invited to travel across the great ocean and perform at the Liberty Theater in San Francisco Chinatown. It was there on the West Coast that she met actor Au Yun Choy and married him at the home of her godmother on Walker Street behind the Grand Lake Theater in Oakland.

The China Men said the eyes of Kwan Ying Lin had the power to strike you dead. The China Men said Kwan Ying Lin was as graceful as a peach blossom in the wind. The

China Men said when Kwan Ying Lin went on stage even the electric fans stopped.

The two actors returned to China after the expiration of their contract. It was then that Kwan Ying Lin discovered that her husband already had two wives. Though as a Chinese woman of that time she was able to accept the fact of their existence, it was painful for her to accept the fact that she had been deceived by the man she called husband.

My grandmother had three daughters: Siew Han born in Seattle, Chee Han born in China and Suk Han, my mother, also born in China on the same year the stock market crashed on Wall Street. Kwan Ying Lin was often away from home touring in Hong Kong, Macao, and to other places in southern China, Guangxi and parts of south east Asia. Her husband, who was more popular in the Chinatowns in America than in China, did not work for long periods and was in failing health. The responsibility of supporting the family rested solely on the shoulders of Kwan Ying Lin.

It was a large household comprised of Kwan Ying Lin and her three daughters, her husband, his son, his wives and servants. Shortly after the birth of the second daughter, her husband brought into the household a young woman barely out of her teens to share his bed.

Kwan Ying Lin had met and worked with an actress by the name of Hsu Hung Lum when they were both part of an all-girl troupe performing at the Lai Yuen Amusement Park in Guangzhou. After the birth of her third child, my grandmother, finding the crowded house more than she could cope with, took her daughters and left her husband. She established another household with Hsu Hung Lum, the woman with whom she was to spend the next decade of her life. Hsu Hung Lum was a tall, handsome woman with a commanding presence, well-suited to taking the male roles on stage. They lived together in China and Hong Kong, and then travelled to New York and California when the theater producers called. The China Men said they were always together, like two peach blossoms growing on the same branch. They were together for ten years; two independent, strong-willed, creative women. They were together for ten years, companions and friends.

As a Chinese woman I have a great heritage of rejection to overcome. In Hong Kong when I was growing up I heard all around me mothers shouting in exasperation at their children: *"Say nui, mow yung, ngai say."* Dead girl, no use, you dead. And *"ngai ge sai yun tow!"* Your dead head.

We were not just called bad girls or naughty brats. We were called dead girls. What a way to begin life! Hearing myself called dead girl so many times I was sure I *was* a dead girl, meaningless, useless, worthless. In addition to this, I was always told what I couldn't do, what I couldn't say, what I couldn't be. I could dream but I could never be.

In the China of my grandmother's time, girl children born into poor families were drowned or sold. Girl children born into prosperity had their feet bound, their marriages arranged. My grandmother escaped the horror of having her feet bound because she was born poor. I and all my contemporaries escaped because we were born to a new generation. But we were not born free. We cannot walk on the streets without being accosted by a whistle, a catcall or a car horn. Taunts ranging from "Ching chong Chinaman" to "Suzy Wong" to "china doll" are never far away. Social stereotyping is still running rampant in this modern age. Every moment, every day a woman is victimized, beaten, raped and murdered. It is no wonder we feel numb, oppressed, depressed, powerless.

But when we speak out, communicate, reach out, we challenge the stereotypes. We breathe, we shout, we live. We must be acknowledged as who we are: women with a history, women with voices, women who live, breathe and sing. Women to whom words like weak, passive, ugly, fat, poor, meek and stupid mean nothing. Women who can turn the heritage of silence and oppression into strength, solidarity and sunshine.

As a Chinese woman I have a great heritage of rejection

to reject. I have come a long way since my childhood. I ran away from my traditional Chinese upbringing when I was fifteen. I lied about my age, got a job in a hospital kitchen making salads and put myself through college. I became a community activist, a poet and a cultural worker. When I was twenty-one I came out as a lesbian.

It was one of the hardest periods of my life. I was rejected by my family, rejected by my peers, rejected by my community, rejected by my friends. It was a rough period but I had my tools for survival: a typewriter, a voice that was screaming to be heard, and my best friend, alcohol.

I wrote, I paced around my small apartment. I went to Chinatown and ate with my grandmother. I asked her questions about her life. I coaxed her to break silence.

I broke my silence and came out to her. I love women, I said. They are my closest friends, my companions, my sister spirits, my lovers. What will you do when you get old, she asked, you will be alone and without children? No. *Poa Poa*, I said, you will be my role model. I will be strong, independent and creative. I will live a long and full life and I will have a woman as my companion and my friend, just like you.

I persisted in my questions, I wrote down her stories. I persevered, I grew. I cooked her favorite foods: spaghetti with mushrooms and meat balls, garlic bread, white cut chicken, pan fried steak. I wrote poems and plays and stories. I paced around my apartment, I ate with my grandmother. I coaxed her to tell of her life and her pain and her struggles. I wrote down her stories. I wrote down her stories so her history will never be lost; she will be remembered, she will never die.

In 1971 I was introduced to a group of women of color who were part of Third World Communications, a media collective comprised of media people, artists, writers, and poets, cultural workers and community activists. One of their goals was to set up a publishing house run by the collective. The Third World womens' group set out to compile an anthology of writings by and about the lives, histories and cultures of women of color. The book, *Third World Women*, grew out of our need to express ourselves as Third World women.

Our core group started with Janice Mirikitani, Diana Lin, Nina Serrano, Thulani Nkabinde, Geraldine Kutaka and myself. Over the months it grew to include other writers: Avotcja, Penny Williams, Jessica Hagedorn and Ntozake Shange among them. We met in each other's homes, talked and ate meals together. We shared our own work and began the monumental task of reading through piles of material that began to arrive non-stop! We saw our reflection in each other's lives and struggles and began to find strength in the knowledge that we are not alone. Through learning, working together, and sharing experiences and by uniting in a real way we became a stronger force. We gave birth to the book in a long and hard eighteen months.

Part of the introduction reads:

> We, the Third World people of Asia, Africa and the original Americas, are the victims of the United States and the western European world. We are the workers who have not reaped the profits of the land. We are the descendants of captives from Africa, of coolied workers from Asia, and of the natives of this land. We are "those people," the "minority." Victims of racism and ghetto colonies within the United States, we have been divided. We have been subjected to "white is right," to Max Factor, to "blonds have more fun," to bleaching creams. No heat in winter, welfare lines, rat-infested homes, unemployment are all symptoms of our colonial status.
>
> No, we are not conquered. We, the people of color, make up nine-tenths of the world. We have a heritage of civilization extending back thousands of years. We are the most oppressed class in the United States and in the world. As Third World women, we are oppressed because of our color, sex and class. We compose the lowest paid workers. We have raised families alone, we have been forced to prostitution. Because of our daily battle for survival, we are strong.
>
> As Third World people we come from different cultures and histories, but are involved with a common struggle against capitalism, racism and sexism. We decided that art for art's sake was not where we were at. We cannot isolate ourselves from our communities, we had to redefine the criterion of art, literature, poetry

and political analysis. We agreed that work should reflect Third World consciousness, that it should relate to the realities of what is happening in our respective communities. . . We had untruths to uncover about each other and within ourselves. We cannot be hampered by the divisions that are imposed on us—race, class and sex. Instead of hiding our differences we discussed our cultural biases, creating a stronger comraderie.[2]

I grew up in England, Hong Kong and the United States surrounded by advertising images of white privilege, power and attractiveness. I wanted to be white. I grew up hating myself. I wanted to be white, to have blonde hair and blue eyes. But I was a short, skinny Chinese girl who wore glasses, had bad skin, bow legs and bit her nails. I was painfully shy, always sat in the back of the class and buried myself in books. But I wanted friends and I wanted a beau.

All my life I've felt different. When I was in England I was the only Chinese kid in the school, in the whole town, it seemed. Class bullies chased me through the school yard calling me names and pushed me into rain puddles. When I went back to Hong Kong I was put in a very exclusive private school for whites, foreigners and rich Chinese. Coming to America I was an immigrant. Coming out I was the only Chinese lesbian I knew, the only one I saw at bars.

Alcohol was a friend. Alcohol made me feel good. It made me feel okay about myself and my surroundings. When I was high I didn't feel lonely or different or scared or angry. Alcohol numbed me; I didn't care about anything or anybody, including myself. I continued reinforcing my internalized oppression and self-hatred by abusing alcohol and drugs. I lived years as a "dead girl", meaningless, useless, worthless.

I started drinking in my senior year at Lowell High. Many years were lost in a drunken fog. I had known for a long time that I was an alcoholic and I've stopped for months, even years, and fallen back into the old pattern of self-hatred and self-destruction.

The last dry episode ended when my best friend of thirteen years, Anita Onang, was dying of cancer in the spring of

1986. Anita was one of the few people I had let into my heart. She was a warm and wonderful sister and friend and someone who always called me on my shit! Anita died in the spring. After her death I knew I had two choices: continue drinking myself into the gutter and self-fulfill the prophecy of becoming a "dead girl," or get sober.

I knew that neither Anita nor my grandmother wanted me to kill myself with alcohol and drugs. So I made the decision to quit drinking and to start living with and loving myself. I got my weight belt, knee wraps and gloves out of the closet, sought out my former coach and returned to the gym. I started bodybuilding and chose as my goal the Physique Competition at Gay Games II that was three months away!

Bodybuilding is the ultimate sport. Not only must a dedicated bodybuilder train with weights four to six days a week, often double split (training different body parts twice a day), she also has to follow a strict diet, practise her posing routine, do rigorous aerobic activity to burn off body fat and get as dark a tan as possible. It is not only a full-time activity, but a very demanding lifestyle.

Bodybuilding is an art, a science and a sport. It is the art of sculpting your body to perfection taking into consideration body symmetry, proportion, and muscle size, shape and definition. Pumping iron has changed my life. It is a constant challenge and an activity I enjoy more and more with each session at the gym. I follow my progress, I see the changes in my body, I get in touch with my power.

For me, bodybuilding is more than just pumping iron to look good. It is a way of rejecting all the putdowns and stereotypes I grew up with. The familiar girls can't, won't, don't, shouldn't. It is a positive statement about my body and myself. To push myself physically to my full potential helps me find the courage and the strength to challenge myself mentally and spiritually. When I drank I was hating myself. When I bodybuild I am loving my body and loving myself.

The sport is more than just developing muscle; it is building character, developing discipline and making discoveries about your innermost being. Bodybuilding is also a way in which I as a woman can challenge and change the traditional male standard of beauty that is measured in terms of face, tits and ass. To show the physicality of a muscular body is to declare to the world: I can, I will, I do, I dare. I am strong. I am powerful. All of this physique is beauty. All of this is me loving myself.

Last month I had the privilege and the pleasure of attending a historic three-day event. It was a retreat organized for Asian Pacific lesbians to come together to explore, share, validate and celebrate ourselves. Eight Asian Pacific lesbians of all ages and backgrounds came from New York, Chicago, Los Angeles, Santa Cruz and the San Francisco Bay Area. It was an incredible experience to look around and see all of those beautiful Asian Pacific lesbians together in one place! And to think when I first came out thirteen years ago, I thought I was the only one!

The weekend was jampacked with events and activity and filled with emotions. I cried throughout much of the slideshow that Trinity Ordona created for the retreat. It was a profoundly beautiful, powerful and deeply moving account of our histories, our heritage and a celebration of who we are. We saw the homelands of our ancestors, we saw our parents building a life, assimilating, working, struggling and surviving. We saw ourselves here in America together, our faces, our bodies, yellow and brown, strong and proud.

At the retreat we experienced the joy of seeing ourselves reflected in each other, felt comfort in our commonalities and talked through past hurts and differences. We reconnected with old friends and renewed acquaintances. We met new friends, exchanged phone numbers, hugged and laughed and danced through the night.

I came out to myself and to the world thirteen years ago. At the retreat was the first time in my life that I felt I had come home.

Anita's mom, Nina Mayeda, said: "Always listen to your heart first and to others second." My heart tells me to stay open, to continue talking story and writing it down, to not be afraid of my emotions, to keep on making waves and speaking out, to stay clear of alcohol and drugs, to live life to the fullest and not be afraid of my own power and potential. My heart tells me: dare to be different, dare to dream.

I want to ask all of you out there who sit side by side, who stand shoulder to shoulder to take a minute and turn to the woman on your left and on your right. Look into her eyes, smile, speak without words. Those of you who have a free hand, reach out and join hands with the ones next to you, link arms, stand close to one another and let your shoulders touch. Let us be one. Feel the energy connecting all of us. Let us take a moment to remember our grandmothers, our mothers, our lovers past and present, our friends. Those who are here and those who have gone on before us. Let us remember the women warriors all over the world who battle apartheid, oppression and poverty. Let us remember the women who have suffered, the ones who survived, the ones who did not. Let our footsteps shake the sidewalk, let our voices proclaim that we fear no man. Let each breath declare that we are strong, that we are survivors. Snap out of our numbness, shake the despair, rise out of depression. Say no to all those things that hold us back.

Listen to your heart. Feel the power in your body, the energy in your hands, the fire in your eyes. Say, I love you. I love myself. Look around you and know, without a doubt, that we are not invisible. We are here in the community. We work, we smile, we sing, we live, we breathe, we love. We are here and the joy of living and the power of love flows through us.

We have all survived being dead girls. We are strong. We are powerful. We will grow and prosper. We are Lesbians of Color. We are women who are breaking silence, making waves and loving ourselves. We have come out and we have come home.

Notes

"Breaking Silence, Making Waves and Loving Ourselves: The Politics of Coming Out and Coming Home" was a keynote speech at the Second Annual Third World/Lesbians of Color Conference, San Francisco, 1987.

[1] From *Island: Poetry and History of Chinese Immigrants on Angel Island 1910-1940*, eds. Genny Lim, Him Mark-Lai, Judy Yung, [San Francisco: Hoc-Doi Project [History of Chinese Detained on Island], 1980).

[2] From *Third World Women*, eds. Kitty Tsui, Janice Mirikitani, Diana Lin, Nina Serrano, Thulani Nkabinde, Geraldine Kutaka, (San Francisco: Third World Communications, 1972).

Is There a Lesbian Culture?
ANN FERGUSON

What is lesbianism?[1] Is it a universal, crosscultural concept and identity or is it historically specific to that period of world history in which industrial societies develop? Do lesbians have a culture that cuts across the cultures of race, class and society? If so, is it co-extensive with women's culture? If not, how does it differ? Is being a lesbian like being Jewish or Afro-American? That is, is it like an ethnic identity: a social aspect of self that is deeper than a mere "preference" which can be changed by individual whim? Or, are homosexual desires a part of every human Unconscious even though repressed by the majority? Finally, is it plausible to argue that being a lesbian is a political act: an act of resistance to patriarchy? If so, how is it related to feminism?

Feminist theoretical answers to these questions have presupposed either a continuous, a discontinuous or a deconstructivist approach to understanding lesbianism. I shall critique all of these approaches, as much for their political implications as for their historical inadequacies, and offer a dialectical theory of lesbian cultures as cultures of resistance. Due to different systems of social domination in different countries, including forms of patriarchy (Ferguson, 1984, 1989, in press), class-divided production, racism and ethni-

---

[1] The original paper from which this version is drawn is longer and more fully argued. It is to be found in Ann Ferguson, *Sexual Democracy: Women, Oppression and Revolution* (Boulder, CO: Westview Press, forthcoming).

cism, there is at present no international lesbian culture, though there are women who primarily love and/or have sex with women in every society. Lesbian-feminist theory and politics must acknowledge this discontinuity in our sisterhood before we can change it.

An international lesbian culture cannot be just defined or wished into existence, in the manner implied by some radical feminist theorists (cf. Cook, 1977; Daly, 1979, 1982; Rich, 1980). Indeed, as I shall argue, the very *concept* of an international lesbian culture is politically problematic, for the most likely model under which it could come into existence is a cultural imperialist one, of Western lesbian liberation movements importing our notions of the proper values for a lesbian culture of resistance onto other societies. Rather than taking as our political project the creation of an international lesbian culture, we would do better to work for the construction of international lesbian, feminist and gay liberation *movements* which develop a radical democratic form for promoting the development of indigenous national and local lesbian, feminist and gay oppositional cultures in their particular locales, social classes and racial and ethnic groups.[2] Only after such a political movement is created would the pre-conditions for a universal lesbian culture be present.

In order to develop the view that there is no international lesbian culture and the political implications of this for lesbian and feminist theory, let us consider different ways of conceptualizing culture and of framing lesbian history.

Lesbian Culture

What is a culture? Before we can answer the question of whether a lesbian culture exists, we need to define our terms. Lesbian-feminist theorists have claimed that there is a universal women's culture hidden under patriarchal cultures (Barry, 1969). Some say women's communities preceded patriarchal

---

[2] I owe this distinction between an international *movement* and an international *culture* to Cindy Patton.

societies 2(cf. Reed, 1973, Grahn, 1974, Cavin, 1985). Within women's cultural networks, some argue, women-loving women from an even more invisible lesbian culture (Cook, 1977, Rich, 1980). A more recent approach is to look at women's separate institutions and communities — convents, Chinese marriage resisters, contemporary lesbian communities—as examples of "gyn/affectionate" women's oppositional cultures without labelling them as "lesbian" (Raymond, 1986). This is at odds with Judy Grahn's view, since for her a distinctive social group of women, say spinsters, can be defined as lesbian, and as part of a gay culture, independently of whether they identify as such, just in case they perform what she calls a "gay office". But other lesbian-feminist theorists (MacKinnon, 1986) suggest that neither an authentic nor a women's culture exist in male dominant societies, for gender identity and sexual desires are patriarchally constructed. To assess these opposing claims we need to understand what constitutes a culture.

Anthropologists have studied different societies using a very broad concept of culture, as a cluster of activities by which a social group is distinguished from and distinguishes itself from other social groups; common language, values, habits, rituals, arts, religion, philosophy and so forth. Clifford Geertz (1973) argues that culture involves a public sharing of symbols, which Fern Johnson (1987) divides into three interrelated systems of meaning: (1) language and communication; (2) artifacts; and (3) abstractions.

In Geertz's sense of culture, the gender division of labor between domestic household activity and public market or organized state activity can ground differences in values, artifacts, and personalities and thus produce different "gender cultures" in every human society.[3] Certainly the work by

---

[3] This theses is problematic in complex societies in which those in the same gender may have more in common culturally with those of their same class, race or ethnicity than those of the same gender in different classes, races or ethnic groups. To be plausible, it would have to be modified to the claim that there are different gender subcultures within class, race and ethnic parameters which may or may not overlap across these lines.

Chodorow (1974, 1978), Gilligan (1982), Lakoff (1975) and Johnson and Aries (1983) suggests that women's personalities, ethical thinking and language, all important elements of culture, may differ from men's.

However, there is a problem with the characterization of culture as a shared symbol system. Languages, values, and production of artifacts may overlap so that people can be members of different cultural systems at the same time. For example, people can be said to be in subcultures connected to gender, race, ethnicity, religion—even occupation—as well as in a dominant culture defined by nationality, e.g. citizen of the United States. How do we decide when people's shared activities are sufficiently similar to constitute a common culture?

For example, Afro-American female slaves cared for planters' children as well as their own. And until recently, a large number of Afro-American women were employed as domestics in other people's homes. Does such activity constitute a common women's culture uniting Black women and white women slaveowners who also cared for their children, or white women who do domestic chores in their own homes?

What these examples point up is that there are two ways of defining membership in a culture or subculture. First, there is an "objective" sense of culture, defined by the theorist as sufficient social attributes in common for members to constitute a distinctive social group. Second, there is the "subjective" sense of culture; i.e. culture in the sense of a consciously held identification of others as members, along with self, as part of a particular group. This second sense of culture, which we can call the "identity sense", requires that one be recognized, both by oneself and by others in one's society, as being a part of a social category. Without such a recognition, as, for example, with societies who lack one of the several Western conceptions of race that developed with the institutions of imperialism and slavery (Harris, 1964), any so-called "natural" similarities between people, even when they involve shared tasks and values, will lack social implications for one's sense of self.

A problem with the objectivist approach pursued by Barry, Grahn, Gilligan, Ruddick (1984), Ortner (1974), Johnson and Rich are the political conclusions that some theorists draw from assuming a group has a common culture. This is, that such a group has a common interest, if a social domination system such as male dominance, capitalism or racism oppresses them, to "unite and fight" their oppressors. Such an analysis often ignores other social activities and structural positions of individuals which may keep them from feeling any common identification, hence common political cause, with each other (cf. women as a sex/class analyses, as in my earlier work, Ferguson, 1979; Delphy, 1984; Wittig, 1982).

The identity sense of culture insists that members of the same culture must identify as such. That is, every individual assumed to be a part of a culture or subculture must consciously accept, at least on reflection, this characterization of themselves. On this view it is problematic to assume that nonwhite and white women share a common women's culture in racist societies. Rather, such a sense of common culture must be struggled for and created by feminist and anti-racist movements in which women acknowledge their other social differences, privileges and oppressions vis a vis each other.[4]

The identity approach has another important consequence: it allows us to point out the asymmetry of gender cultures in patriarchal society and thus note the negative consequences of domination on women. Some of the objectivist theorists of culture tend to ignore the effects of domination in limiting the possibilities of women's culture. For example, Gilligan's theory of a women's ethical point of view assumes that men's and women's ethical voices are complementary not antagonistic. But patriarchal culture does not allow such a conclusion. For since dominant public cul-

---

[4] It was the failure of white middle class women in the first wave U.S. Women's Movement to do this, argue Angela Davis (1981) and Bettina Aptheker (1983), that was ultimately responsible for the end of militant feminism during this period. Similarly Black and Third World feminists have taken the second wave U.S. Women's Movement to task for its white middle class bias (Anzaldua and Moraga, 1981; Lorde, 1984; Combahee River Collective, 1979; Hull, Scott and Smith, eds., 1982).

ture is controlled by men, men both identify themselves with such a culture and exclude women as contributing members. They thus do not acknowledge the value of women's cultural activities. Women on the other hand, since our cultural activities tend to be devalued and less visible, are less able to identity ourselves proudly as members of a cultural group which produces valued artifacts, has its own distinctive language and values (Miller, 1976). In this sense McKinnon (1986) is correct to question the extent to which patriarchal cultures have allowed any independent women's culture to exist. And Daly (1982) and Rich (1979) argue that an important part of our task is not to uncover a hidden women's culture but to create it, which they (Daly, 1987, Rich, 1978) and Wittig (1971, 1986) have set out to do.

A problem with the identity sense of culture when applied to those who share in lesbian culture is that it defines out of existence "false consciousness", i.e. women whose sexual and affectional preferences are for other women but because of internalized homophobia refuse to acknowledge themselves as lesbians. Is it not an arbitrary solution to the political issue of who should "come out" to eliminate the issue by a mere definition of the term "lesbian" which implies that women can never be mistaken about whether or not they are members of this culture? (cf. Zita's critique of my earlier work: Zita, 1981, Ferguson, 1981).

The shortcomings of both the objectivist and identity senses of culture seem to create a dilemma for lesbian theory. For the objectivist theorist can pick out any set of social activities shared by individuals and label that a "culture", regardless of whether the participants accept that designation. On the other hand, the identity sense of culture suggests that most human societies have been lacking a lesbian culture: since it was not until the late nineteenth and early twentieth century that a distinctive self-identified lesbian subculture arose. Is lesbian theory forced to choose between a notion of lesbian culture that is so broad as to include any woman who challenges gender roles or so narrow as to exclude us from any authentic lesbian history before the nineteenth century?

A way to avoid these problems is to change the nature of our search: instead of looking in general for common subcultures involving women, we should be looking instead at cultures of whole societies in a more historical and dialectical way. If we do we may be able to identify lesbian and feminist oppositional and proto-oppositional subcultures, that is those which, in their historical context, generated or have the possibility to generate a political resistance to patriarchy and compulsory heterosexuality. A culture of resistance is one which challenges the social roles and valuation given to it by the dominant culture. It is when such an oppositional culture has arisen, or is in the process of arising, that individuals can make, and be asked to make, identity decisions as to whether they are members of the culture or not.

Contemporary lesbian-feminist theorizing has arisen in just such a historical situation, as a tool of lesbian, gay and feminist social movements seeking to re-evaluate and reconstruct existing lesbian, gay and feminist subcultures so as to forge them into a unified culture of resistance to a dominant culture seen as patriarchal and heterosexist. A dialectical historical approach can explain our historical uniqueness without sacrificing a broader sense of continuity to other actual and potential lesbian and gay cultures of resistance in other historical settings.

Feminist theories of lesbianism revisited: continuity, discontinuity and deconstructionist approaches. Before I discuss further my alternative approach to lesbian herstory, let us review other approaches to the subject. In doing so, it is important to keep in mind that the argument about how to define lesbianism, like most theoretical debates, is not simply a factual dispute about what is included in the concept. Rather, it also has political implications about the best way to conceive lesbianism in order to advance the cause of lesbian/gay liberation and feminism. Thus, it is important to look for the sometimes hidden political agendas and disagreements of those who enter the fray. Let us now revisit the debate about the definition of "lesbian" engaged in by a number of lesbian scholars since 1977 to examine the political implications of theoretical differences

In my 1981 dispute with Rich I put forth three criteria for evaluating a successful definition which Rich and others in the debate seemed to assume: 1) that a definition should valorize the concept *lesbian* by freeing it from clinical and pejorative associations with deviancy, sinfulness and psychological sickness and neurosis; 2) that a definition should help us with a new approach to the project of lesbian history, which could help us uncover evidences of past lesbians so that present lesbian culture could have a sense of belonging to a valuable if hidden tradition that 3) could help us to grasp the magnitude of the underground resistance to the institution of compulsory heterosexuality.[5]

Looking back on this debate today, I think that it is not possible to characterize lesbians in a way so as to fulfill these three criteria—indeed I think this is a misguided task. What strikes me is that there are two conflicting emphases in these definitions which connect to two opposing needs of contemporary self-identified lesbian communities.

On the one hand, there is the need for historical *continuity*: we seek to identify with foresisters who also deviated from the strictures of compulsory heterosexuality in their age and society. On the other hand, there are also good reasons to stress historical *discontinuity*: there have never been gay liberation movements of the contemporary sort before, nor have there been lesbian-feminist movements like those in advanced capitalist societies today. What does this tell us about our historical uniqueness, both

---

[5] What is missing in this list of tasks for lesbian history is the political dimension. That is, knowingly or not, lesbian-feminist theories of lesbianism are used as tools in ideological and political debates in the contemporary lesbian community as to who counts as a "real lesbian" and a "real feminist". A clear example of this is Rich's view that lesbian existence should be dissociated from male homosexual values and allegiances (Rich, 1980: 65). This strongly implies that lesbians who identify with a mixed gay community rather than a separate lesbian one are lower down on the "lesbian continuum", thus not in the political vanguard of "woman-identified women" she wants to valorize.

as political subjects and as warriors against heterosexism and patriarchy? We need to pay attention to our historical context in order to develop an effective political strategy for our place and time.

CONTINUITY APPROACHES TO LESBIANISM There are three major overlapping continuity approaches employed by lesbian-feminist theorists. The first identifies lesbians crossculturally and transhistorically with"women-loving women" i.e. those who prioritize relations with women (cf. Radicalesbians, 1970; Cook, 1977; Sahli, 1979; Faderman, 1981).

A second approach, articulated by Adrienne Rich, places all women on a lesbian continuum, with respect to those of their practices which resist compulsory heterosexuality and dependence on men. A third approach developed by Judy Grahn (1984), assumes that gayness is connected to a universal gay social role, or office, to convey cross gender information to human societies, which since they are otherwise gender segregated, lack access to this integrative function. This view maintains that women who reverse gender roles—"mannish" women and those who cross-dress—are examples of lesbians and that societies which institutionalize such possibilities for men and women, such as many native American cultures, are more "permissive" to homosexuality.

Though these continuity approaches overlap, they also involve implausible and incompatible conclusions. For example, Rich, Cook and Grahn assume that all women-loving women are patriarchal resisters. But though this may be plausible as a psychological description of such women, it may be questionable as a political judgement, depending on the historical context. So, in the nineteenth century in Western Europe, England and the U.S. when the prevalent ideology of true womanhood held that women were more spiritual and less sexual than men, women's romantic friendships were not seen as a challenge to patriarchal ideology, but rather a confirmation of it. And what of the "mannish" women that Judy Grahn describes in many native American cultures who cross-dressed and reversed gender roles? Are they challenging patriarchal assumptions of bi-polar gender roles or just further supporting them?

Another disagreement concerns the status of men who reversed or challenged gender roles, e.g. the berdaches or holy men of some native American cultures, and those who cross-dressed, did women's work and married other men (cf. Grah, 1984, Roscoe, 1988). Were they patriarchal resisters, members of an oppositional gay culture and precursors of a unified feminist and gay liberation movement? Or were they simply breaking *one* general rule of patriarchal societies—the gender division of social roles based on biological sex—in order to validate a more important rule: that of male bonding by all possible means (Frye, 1983)?

Lesbian herstorian Judy Grahn tends to equate any gay activity, whether by men or women, with a challenge to patriarchy. Interestingly, she and others who identify as part of a subculture with gay men are either older lesbians who banded together in mixed gay bars and gay organizations in the 1940s and 1950s (cf. Nestle, 1987) or younger lesbians whose political work, e.g. organizing around AIDS or opposing radical feminist views of pornography, connect them more primarily with the mixed gay community than with lesbian separatist or feminist subcultures. On the other hand, those who identity with lesbian separatist and feminist subcultures seek a lesbian herstory that dissociates lesbian from gay male culture past and present (Rich, Frye).[6]

---

[6] The first model of gay liberation tends to conceive gayness as similar to ethnicity: it is something one is born into and does not choose (cf. Epstein, 1987). Gays like Jews are seen to be in minority subcultures oppressed in most human societies. Thus, unless we defend the value of gay ethnicity to challenge cultural homophobia, we will never be accepted as individuals. On the contrary the radical lesbian-feminist model may be either *essentialist* in the biological sense: women by nature have superior values to men (cf. Barry, 1979; Cavin, 1985), or else they are extreme *voluntarists*: any woman can choose to be a lesbian. These latter hold a social constructionism which maintains that women's developed personalities are superior to men's (Bunch, 1975). In either case, the political and theoretical strategy ends up being what has been called "cultural feminism"; women should separate ourselves from men in order to create a superior, and liberated, women's culture.

What these disagreements among continuity theorists demonstrate is that there is no one common characterization of *lesbian* that applies transhistorically and crossculturally. Instead, each of these approaches involves an implicit appeal to an objectivist sense of lesbian culture which picks out one cluster of commonalities between gender rebellious women or women and men and *re-articulates* (cf. Omi and Wynant, 1986) for contemporary lesbians one possible historical set of past women to identify as part of one's self-conscious lesbian community. But the competing clusters are not co-extensive and there is no objective way to resolve the issue.

LESBIAN AS A DECONSTRUCTIVE CATEGORY One way to avoid the problem of assigning a specific denotation to "lesbian" in order to do lesbian history is to argue that there is no specific denotation because of the logic of the term "lesbian" itself. On this view, "lesbian" is a sliding signifier with no fixed positive content: rather it is a *deconstructive* concept which can be applied to any woman who violates assumptions of gender dualism which are themselves historically specific.

Monique Wittig develops this idea of lesbianism in her essay "One Is Not Born A Woman" (Wittig, 1981). On her view, *lesbian* challenges the gender binary categories of compulsory heterosexuality. A lesbian is an anomaly in terms of these categories: someone who is No/Woman, Not/Man. No wonder then that lesbian existence is invisible in dominant culture (Frye, 1983). The possibility of lesbianism challenges the naturalness of the category "woman" as it is defined socially by systems of compulsory heterosexuality. Lesbian as a category challenges the essentialism of the idea of the eternal masculine vs. the eternal feminine, defined as natural complements, but does not itself have a fixed content or essence. It is merely a negative category, and as such empty of specific positive expectations. Nonetheless it creates the possibility of a radical third gender—presumably "gay male" would be a fourth gender (cf. Butler, 1987)—to challenge the dual gender systems of compulsory heterosexuality and male dominance.

There are two problems with this deconstructive analysis of the concept "lesbian". The idea that "lesbian" is used in a normatively negative way implies that it does have a denotation in our society, and thus that it is false that lesbians are invisible in our society. The concept "lesbian" denotes quite visible lesbians, e.g. working class butches, those who appear to act like men as well as to have sex with women. In so far as this role is viewed as a type of deviant womanhood, it is on the same level as prostitution: both lesbians and whores *are* women, but they are bad or "failed" women. In neither case does the existence of bad women threaten the hegemonic characterization of good, "true", "natural" women as nonpromiscuous, heterosexual and, eventually, married and mothers.

Second, even if Wittig is correct that compulsory heterosexuality in our society reinforces patriarchy by promoting a gender dualism that makes the concept of "lesbian" a challenge to the concept "woman," her point does not necessarily apply to other historical types of patriarchy, compulsory heterosexuality and gender dualism. For example, it might be argued that those cultures such as the native American ones cited by Grahn which institutionalize forms of homosexuality do not have concepts exactly equivalent to our concept "lesbian" or "gay." If so, any deconstructive and hence patriarchy-challenging use of that concept in our society does not necessarily carry over to those and other non-Western societies.

THE DISCONTINUITY APPROACH: LESBIAN AS A HISTORICALLY DEVELOPED IDENTITY Whether or not one is willing to grant sufficient commonality to structures of male domination across race, ethnic group, class and culture to allow the univocal use of "feminist" to women who resist patriarchal structures, the concept "lesbian" seems more historically discontinuous. Perhaps this is because capitalist development has led to the historical separation of kinship and economic organization in a way which creates a much more open sexual economy for women. Wage earning allows the possibility that unmarried women can live independently of kin, thus that for some women, living with and engaging in sex with women could take the place of heterosexual marriage. "Lesbian" acquires a unique meaning as networks of female homosex practitioners are enabled to create their own unique networks and subcultures facilitated by available wage labor and the development of urban centers. Key features in such urban centers are the possibility of living separate from kin in boarding houses and apartments, and the development of gay bars, which allows for a sexual economy permitting a cultural area and set of rituals for women to engage in lesbian sexual exchanges.

Another important factor is the success of late nineteenth and early twentieth century sexology (Krafft-Ebing, Freud, Ellis) in promoting a theory of essential self identity based on sexual identity. In the process, the new concept of a distinctive homosexual *identity* which is not simply reducible to homosexual sexual *practices* allowed the development of a sense of group identity and the possibility of a self conscious subculture (Foucault, 1978). A somewhat later development for lesbians was the "woman-identified woman"—a way of seeing lesbian love that resists the merely negative pathological implications of the sexologists (Ferguson, 1981).

The idea of *gay* and *lesbian* as distinctive historically developed identities connects to the identity sense of culture discussed earlier. It has the obvious advantages of allowing us to explain how and why the new social movements of the sixties and seventies in the United States and Europe led to more radical gay liberation movements. For though there were gay political organizations in these countries before the sixties, the idea that institutional racism infringes on the civil rights of radical minorities enabled the conception to develop of an analogous structure of compulsory heterosexuality, or heterosexism, which infringes on gays and lesbians as a sexual minority. Thinking of gays as an oppressed social minority rather than a set of individual deviants was made historically possible by the existence of a gay and lesbian bar culture, social clubs and friendship networks that constituted a segregated subculture in some ways similar to the U.S. Afro-American subculture produced by slavery and social segregation.

Though the discontinuity approach to lesbian identity is helpful in understanding the unique aspects of contemporary women's history, some of the political appropriations of this approach are problematic. For one thing, many assume that the new homosexual identity is analogous to an ethnic identity; i.e., one that though socially constructed, is nonetheless fixed for those defined by it. Such an assumption is used to base an Identity politics: viz., of acknowledging one's inner "essence" as a lesbian or gay man, of "coming out" and of defining one's interests as centrally involved with promoting those of the lesbian and/or gay community. This is the deterministic pole of Identity politics: that individuals should not try to escape what they "really" are, in order to avoid social repression. As such, it is characteristic of much of "old" lesbian and gay politics of the 1950s in the U.S. and Europe as well of much of contemporary gay politics in these countries which centers itself around gaining civil rights for gays (cf. Plummer, Ed., 1981: Epstein, 1987).

The other pole of Identity politics is implicitly anti-deterministic. This was, ironically, both a feature of early lesbian-feminist separatism (cf. Myron and Bunch, eds., 1973) and radical humanist lesbian and gay liberation (Dworkin, 1974, 1978, Altman, 1973). Early lesbian-feminist separatism stresses that since heterosexuality is itself socially constructed, all women have a choice as to whether to be lesbian or heterosexual. Thus, women should choose lesbianism as the vanguard of feminism. Radical humanist gay liberation, on the other hand, stressed that all humans have unconscious homosexual tendencies, so coming out will ultimately allow the development of a bisexual or pansexual orientation for everyone. On this view that we are all homosexuals as well as all dual gendered, the best strategy is a non-separatist sexual liberation movement which attacks homophobia and sexism within and without its ranks (Altman, 1973, Escoffler, 1985). This view, like the corresponding ideal of androgyny in the women's movement (Ferguson, 1977) has now been discounted as utopian by most feminist and gay liberation activists (Raymond, 1979, Altman, 1983).

The discontinuity approach, though it suggests an Identity politics, gives us no way to adjudicate between the politicization of conflicting identities (Weeks, 1985). For example, though some lesbians identify as a vanguard against patriarchy, others make common cause with gay men in a struggle against heterosexism, for example by working against the homophobia engendered by the AIDS crisis. Since lesbians and gays do have a common interest in fighting heterosexism, why not then identify ourselves as part of a mixed lesbian/gay community?

A Dialectical Approach to Lesbian Cultures

In the review of continuous, deconstructive and discontinuous approaches to lesbian history, I have argued that none gives us a totally satisfactory approach to understanding lesbianism and what constitutes a lesbian culture.

The alternative approach that I recommend, a dialectical and historical approach to the question of lesbian culture, assumes that there is a historical discontinuity between societies in which women have a high status and homosexuality is legitimated and those whose forms of patriarchy involve some type of compulsory heterosexuality[7] for most women, though types of male homosexuality may still be permitted, for example, in Hellenic Greece and various mid-Eastern cultures (cf. Allen, 1986; Hatem, 1986). Lesbian practices which are legitimated because they are connected to the religious

---

[7] Even the analytic concept of "compulsory heterosexuality" needs to be used with care, for it may lead us to ignore historical differences between our own contemporary social formation and others. For example, a case can be made that the concept of "heterosexual identity" is itself a contemporary one. Previous types of patriarchy—father patriarchy, husband patriarchy—based on kin organization of the economy did not require the self-identification of individuals as having a heterosexual sexuality, since men's sexual control of women was guaranteed by patriarchal marriage and property laws. Thus, both men and women could engage in homosexual practices which did not challenge their gender identity as long as they were, or planned to be, married.

rituals of priestesses or corss-dressing women who are given an accepted social status in a society, for example, Mohave and other native American societies, do not constitute a lesbian culture in the dialectical sense in which I am interested.

Rather, I want to focus on lesbian cultures which are, or have the potential to be, oppositional subcultures, that rise or continue as a feminist practice of resistance in a primarily patriarchal society. Some interesting cases involve those peoples that have developed a mixed culture with both patriarchal and women-empowering elements because a conquering more patriarchal group has failed to completely eradicate women-centered practices from the culture as a whole. More empirical work needs to be done on Judy Grahn's theory that there was a real human culture of Fairies in the British Isles, which was a women-centered and homosexually permissive society. Grahn's view is that this people were conquered by the Celts and incorporated into their culture, making the product a mix of patriarchal and women-empowering elements. This would explain the features of Celtic society which allowed for warrior queens like Boadicca to exist alongside of male warriors, the fact that women had many more rights to property than in more patriarchal societies, and for the presence of religious rites involving lesbian practices.

After the Roman conquest of the Celts and the opposition of the patriarchal and heterosexist Roman Catholic religion on the populace, we can hypothesize that an oppositional lesbian culture formed from the remnants of Celtic culture. This was connected to witchcraft and pagan nonpatriarchal religious practices that also involved some men engaged in gay religious rites (cf. Dworkin, 1974). This would explain why the Inquisition regularly charged witches with lesbian sexual practices, and why Joan of Arc was targeted as part of such a heretical woman-centered culture since she insisted on wearing men's clothes, thus challenging patriarchal privilege as well as the Catholic male clergy's right to interpret the will of God. It would also explain the elevation of the Virgin Mary to high status in an otherwise patriarchal religion, as an attempt to co-opt some of those who would otherwise have rejected Roman Catholicism for more women-empowering pagan religions.

The thesis that lesbian subcultures tend to form when a mixed culture composed of dominant patriarchal and subordinate matrilocal and more women-centered peoples has developed also makes sense of the lesbian culture in Mombasa, researched by Gill Shepherd (1987). In this society the Swahili, who long ago merged with invading Islamic Arabs, have a religion and familial-gender ideology which is patriarchal but a social reality which is more bilateral and matrifocal. Thus, women are veiled, have limited legal autonomy, are expected to marry and be obedient to their husbands and ought to inherit only half as much property as their brothers. Nonetheless, the high divorce rate, the practice of leaving children of divorces with the mother and of divorced women leaving property to their daughters has created a situation where 50% of Swahili women live independently of provision by a husband. There is a lesbian subculture consisting both of lesbian couples living together—usually a high status, wealthy woman with a low status dependent woman — and a social life of salons of lesbian women which meet regularly in one another's houses. A sexual economy permitting such lesbian relationships is based on the higher status a poor woman achieves by being paired with a wealthy lesbian than by being a dependent first or second wife of a poor man.

A sign of the matrifocal nature of the whole society in spite of the patriarchal Islamic culture imposed on married women is that lesbian women do not need to cross-dress to have high status: rather, this is achieved by wealth which allows them to outdo married women in feminine finery at all women activities surrounding marriages and funerals. Also poor homosexual men achieve status by cross-dressing and being accepted into the salons of wealthy lesbian women.

The United States is another example of a society which has developed lesbian oppositional cultures, though these

have been importantly divided by race and economic class.[8]
Nonetheless, our society has unifying common social
spaces for lesbians. Bars, women's bookstores, lesbian magazines and newsletters exist which allow any woman
regardless of class, racial or ethnic background to find a
common identification as lesbian. Thus, with a coalitionist
politics that is sensitive to race, class and ethnic differences
there is the potential of a minimally unified lesbian oppositional culture in the U.S.[9] But this is not necessarily so in
many third world subcultures.

This is not surprising if we acknowledge that there are
different forms of patriarchy and compulsory heterosexuality
in different societies. Though most existing societies could be
said to have some degree of compulsory hetrosexuality, this
condition is enforced by a number of mechanisms. Since any
of these can vary in strength depending on the context, resistance to patriarchy can take any one of a number of different
forms which may have no common "core" of cultural practices or self-identifications. Post-industrial capitalist patriarchal societies create the material conditions for a contemporary lesbian-feminist culture that challenges gender roles.
But such conditions are not present in every society. Thus, in
some societies and some historical periods, resistance to
patriarchy may involve women "passing" as men or women
banding together with gay men to identify a common gay
culture (cf. Myron and Bunch, 2973, Katz, 1978). This seems
to be true today where marriage is such a dominant institution that even those engaging in lesbian and gay practices

---

[8] Work by Davis and Kennedy (1986) has explored the butch/femme relationships of
a typical American working class lesbian bar culture of the 1940s and 1950s. The
Daughters of Bilitis, a middle class lesbian organization of the 1950s, attempted
to make lesbianism respectable by rejecting butch/femme roles and bar culture
(Van Staveren, 1987). The lesbian-feminist movement of the 1970s also showed a
class intolerance to working class lesbian culture by challenging butch-femme
roles and implying that those who engaged in them were not real feminists
(Nestle, 1987).

[9] But a tightly unified American lesbian culture is probably not possible due to serious value disagreements. For example American lesbian-feminists disagree about
the propriety of butch/femme roles, S/M sex, cruising sex, bisexuality, penetra-
tive sex, motherhood, pornography and separatist politics, to name a few!

must first marry, unless they find a religious role as monks, nuns or priests, or drop to the bottom of the social ranking altogether by becoming prostitutes. For example, in most Latin American countries, what constitutes a lesbian or gay identity has been very different from first world countries. That is, the key distinction is between "activos", or those who play the macho role, and "passivos", or those who play the feminine role (Adam, 1987). The activo men and the passivo women are not considered "real" gays or lesbians, respectively, since they act according to correct gender roles with the exception of their sexual preference. Thus there is a lack of a sense of common gay or lesbian culture: passivo gays and lesbians identify primarily with straight women and feminists, not a unified gay male or a unified lesbian community in our sense. This makes it difficult for independent gay liberation movements to develop in these countries or for organized feminism to develop a strong demand for lesbian liberation.

These cross cultural and historical examples make it plausible to argue that there are historically different gender and sexual formations in place in different societies—different family structures, economies, forms of the state, which embed different forms of patriarchy and sexual hierarchy. In other writings I have called such systems "modes of patriarchal sex/affective production." (Ferguson, 1984, 1989 in press). In different sexual formations there will be somewhat different ways available to resist patriarchy and sexual hierarchy. Many of these can be associated with lesbian sexual practices that will involve different senses of self identification, not only between one country or region of the world and another, but within cultures, between different economic classes, racial and ethnic groups. Our lesbian history thus should conceive of a number of lesbian subcultures rather than one universal lesbian culture.

The politics of a lesbian-feminist dialectical approach to lesbian cultures as potential cultures of resistance against dominant patriarchal cultures are coalitionist and non-separatist. We must reject the comforting image that there is one correct way to construct a model lesbian identity with a specific cultural content which will allow us to build a vanguard lesbian culture of resistance. A more democratic approach would conceive of an international lesbian culture to be possible, if at all, only after a long process of networking among those disparate subcultures of women, all of which engage in same sex sexual practices but whose conception of lesbianism may be very different. We need, as I shall explain below, to conceive of our goal as international political *movement* building (of interconnected lesbian, gay and feminist movements) rather than *culture* building.

Building an International Lesbian Movement

What is the difference between the goal of building international lesbian, gay and feminist *movements* and building *cultures*? My view is that those who see themselves as building a political movement are more able to tolerate value disagreement than those who see themselves as building a culture. Those who define their task as movement building will tend to recognize the need for strategic and tactical thinking which inevitably involves disagreements, experimentation and changes in political positions as a result of perceived failures in the results of political actions. On the other hand, those concerned with culture building will tend to fall into the pitfalls of Identity politics. That is, they will emphasize the importance of symbolic unity in oppositional lifestyles, rituals, social practices, that is, of agreement on all values of the relevant oppositional community, on order to validate an alternative way of living to the dominant culture.

To avoid the weakening of potential sisterhood that lesbian vanguardism involves, we should conceive of ourselves not as building one unified lesbian culture, but as building a plurality of lesbian cultures, each with its own set of self-definitions, and each of which can, out of its reconstructed sense of its own self-interest, choose to involve itself with the lesbian and feminist liberation movements, but none of which gets to define itself as "the" vanguard of that movement. Hopefully then we will feel more free to disagree yet to support each other on general campaigns challenging sexism and heterosexism.

This point is even more important for international lesbian-feminist politics. Since the aim of international sisterhood requires that any feminist culture-building be democratic, we must adopt a model that permits the self-determination of local and national lesbian cultures. But such a process, to involve self-determination, would have to suppose a cultural pluralism and not a cultural imperialism.[10] This presents the paradox for American lesbian-feminists: to avoid cultural imperialism we can only aid in the constructing of such a culture by not defining international culture-building as our goal! Another way to express this result is that aiming for an international lesbian-feminist culture is subject to the same problem involved in the paradox of hedonism: that the desired result cannot be achieved if directly aimed at.[11]

---

[10] The partial success of women's, gay and lesbian liberation movements in some Western democracies, particularly in the U.S., have given us access to institutional resources—academic jobs, women's and gender studies programs, and support from parts of the political liberal establishment for gay liberation issues. We have won the political space for lesbian/gay pride marches on the national level and in many local spaces. The space for gay and lesbian research and some financial resources means that international lesbian and gay academic conferences and political networks are dominated by Western gay and lesbian sensibilities, and even more by American gay and lesbian consciousness. Not only does this tend to lead us to ignore differences in the histories of lesbian/gay politics but to assume that Second and Third World countries should develop lesbian and gay countercultures and politics after the American model.

An example of American gay cultural imperialism occurred in the early seventies when gay American volunteers to cut cane in Cuba staged a gay pride march and were met with incomprehension and embarrassment by Cuban gays and repression by the Cuban authorities. Since Cuban lesbians are invisible and only the "femme" gay men even define themselves as gay, the gay subculture in Cuba requires a different model for liberation than gay pride marches. This does not imply that Latin American lesbian and gay cultures will never use such tactics—indeed some small lesbian and gay public demonstrations have occurred. Rather, it implies that North Americans must be respectful of local lesbian and gay judgments about the value of such tactics in their particular contexts.

Conclusion

In this paper I have distinguished two senses of culture: an objectivist and an identity sense. Both of these senses, employed by continuity and discontinuity approaches to lesbian history, involve theoretical and political problems. Instead I have defended a historical and dialectical approach to thinking of lesbian cultures as potential cultures of resistance within historically specific patriarchal cultures. I have maintained not only that no international lesbian culture exists, but that the goal of lesbian-feminists who seek to promote an international sisterhood opposing compulsory heterosexuality and patriarchy should be, not to construct such a culture, but to work instead for the creation of an international lesbian movement which is culturally pluralist in its approach to defending lesbian subcultures.

---

[11] The paradox of hedonism is this: she who seeks pleasure directly or as her sole end will find it difficult to achieve, while she who seeks activities for their own sakes will tend to realize pleasure as a byproduct of these activities! Similarly, lesbians who seek not to impose our values by defining a common culture for women-loving women from different cultural contexts, may succeed better in creating such a culture than those who do. This may be true if we pursue friendships and minimum agreed on political goals to defend our perceived common interests as women and as lesbians.

References

1. Adam, Barry (1987a) *The Rise of a Gay and Lesbian Movement*, Boston: Twayne/G.K. Hall.
2. Adam, Barry (1987b) "Homosexuality without a Gay World: the case of Nicaragua", Proceedings, "Homosexuality, Which Homosexuality?" Conference, Amsterdam: Free University.
3. Allen, Jeffner (1986) *Lesbian Philosophy: Explorations*, Palo Alto, Ca.: Institute of Lesbian Studies.
4. Altman, Dennis (1974) *Homosexual, Oppression and Liberation*, London: Allan Lane.
5. Altman, Dennis (9183) *The Homosexualization of America*, Boston: Beacon.
6. Anzaldúa, Gloria and Moraga, Cherri, eds. (1981) *This Bridge Called My Back: Writings by Women of Color*, Watertown, Ma.: Persephone Press.
7. Aptheker, Bettina (1983) *Woman's Legacy: Essays on Race, Class and Gender*, Amherst, Ma.: University of Mass.
8. Barry, Kathleen et al (1969) "The Fourth World Manifesto", Anne Koedt et al, eds., 1973.
9. Bunch, Charlotte (1975) "Lesbians in Revolt", Myron and Bunch, eds. (1975): 29-38.
10. Butler, Judy (1987) "Variations on Sex and Gender: Beauvoir, Wittig and Foucault:, Seyla Benhabib and Drucilla Cornell, eds. (1987) *Feminism as Critique*, Minneapolis: University of Minn.: 128-142.
11. Cavin, Susan (1985) *Lesbian Origins*, San Francisco: Ism Press.
12. Chodorow, Nancy (1974) "Family Structure and Feminine Personality" Rosaldo and Lamphere, eds. (1974).
13. Chodorow, Nancy (1978) *The Reproduction of Mothering*, Berkeley: University of Cal.
14. Combahee River Collective (1979) "A Black Feminist Statement", Anzaldúa and Moraga, eds. (1981).
15. Cook, Blanche Weisen (1977) "Female Support Networks and Political Activism", *Chrysalis* no. 3: 43-61.
16. Daly, Mary (1978) *Gyn/Ecology: The Meta-Ethics of Radical Feminism*, Boston: Beacon.
17. Daly, Mary (1982) *Pure Lust: Elemental Feminist Philosophy*, Boston: Beacon.
18. Daly, Mary and Caputi, Jane (1987) *Webster's First Intergalactic Wickedary of the English Language*, Boston: Beacon.
19. Davis, Angela (1981) *Women, Race and Class*, New York: Random House.
20. Davis, Madeline and Kennedy, Elizabeth Lapovsky (1986), "Oral History and the Study of Sexuality in the Lesbian Community: Buffalo, New York 1940-1960", *Feminist Studies*, v. 12, #1, Spring, 1986: 7-26.

21. de Castro, Ines Orobio (1987) "How Lesbian is a Female Trans-sexual?", Proceedings, "Homosexuality, Which Homosexuality?" Conference, Social Sciences, vol. 2 (Amsterdam: Free University): 110-115.

22. Delphy, Christine (1984) *Close to Home: A Materialist Analysis of Women's Oppression*, Amherst: University of Mass.

23. Donovan, Josephine (1985) *Feminist Theory: The Intellectual Traditions of American Feminism* (New York: Frederick Ungar).

24. Dworkin, Andrea (1974) *Womanhating*, New York: Dutton.

25. Dworkin, Andrea (1978) "Biological Superiority: The World's Most Dangerous Idea", *Heresies*, issue on Women and Violence, no. 6 (Summer 1978).

26. Dworkin, Andrea (1987) *Intercourse*, New York: Free Press.

27. Ehrenreich, Barbara, Elizabeth Hess and Gloria Jacobs (1986) *Re-Making Love: The Feminization of Sex*, New York: Doubleday.

28. Epstein, Steven (1987) "Gay Politics, Ethnic Identity: The Limits of Social Constructionism" *Socialist Review* 93/94 (v. 17, #3 & 4), May/August 1987: 9-56.

29. Escoffler, Jeffry (1985) "Sexual Revolution and the Politics of Gay Identity", *Socialist Review* 82/83 (v. 15, #4 & 5), July-Oct. 1985: 119-154.

30. Faderman, Lilian (1981) *Surpassing the Love of Men*, London: Junction.

31. Ferguson, Ann (1977) "Androgyny as an Ideal for Human Development", Mary Vetterling-Braggin, Frederick Elliston and Jane English, eds. (1977) *Feminism and Philosophy*, Totowa, N.J.: Littlefield/Adams.

32. Ferguson, Ann (1979) "Women as a New Revolutionary Class in the U.S.", Pat Walker, ed. (1979) *Between Labor and Capital*, Boston: South End.

33. Ferguson, Ann (1981) "Patriarchy, Sexual Identity and Sexual Revolution", *Signs*, v. 10, no. 1 (Autumn 1981): 158-172.

34. Ferguson, Ann (1984) "On Conceiving Motherhood and Sexuality: A Feminist Materialist Approach", Joyce Treblicot, ed. (1984): 153-184.

35. Ferguson, Ann (1989, in press) *Blood at the Root: Motherhood, Sexuality and Male Dominance*, New York: Pandora/Unwin & Hyman.

36. Foucault, Michel (1978) *The History of Sexuality*, v. 1, New York: Pantheon.

37. Frye, Marilyn (1983) *The Politics of Reality*, Trumansburg, N.Y.: Crossing Press.

38. Geerz, Clifford (1973) *The Interpretation of Cultures*, New York: Basic Books.

39. Gilligan, Carol (1982) *In a Different Voice: Psychological Theory and Women's Development* (Cambridge, Ma.: Harvard University).

40. Grahn, Judy (1984) *Another Mother Tongue: Gay Words, Gay Worlds* (Boston: Beacon).

41. Harris, Marvin (1964) *Patterns of Race in the Americas*, New York: Norton.

42. Hatem, Mervat (1986) "The Politics of Sexuality and Gender in Segregated Patriarchal Systems: The Case of Eighteenth and Nineteenth Century Egypt", *Feminist Studies*, v. 121, #2 (Summer 1986): 251-274.

43. Hull, Gloria, Scott, Patricia and Smith, Barbara, eds. (1982) *But Some of Us Are Brave*, Old Westbury, N.Y.: Feminist Press.

44. Johnson, Fern (1987) "Women's Culture and Communication: An Analytical Perspective", Cynthia M. Lout and Sheryl Friedley, eds. *Beyond Boundaries: Sex and Gender Diversity in Education*, forthcoming.

46. Katz, Jonathan (1978) *Gay American History: Lesbian and Gay Men in the U.S.A.*, New York: Avon.

47. Kitzinger, Celia (1987) *The Social Construction of Lesbianism*, London: Sage.

48. Koedt, Anne (1970) "The Myth of the Vaginal Orgasm", Anne Koedt et al, eds. (1973).

49. Koedt, Anne, Levine, Ellen and Rapone, Anita, eds. (1973) *Radical Feminism*, New York: Quadrangle/New York Times Book Co.

50. Kristeva, Julia (1977) *About Chinese Women*, London: Marion Boyers.

51. Lakoff, Robin (1975) *Language and Women's Place*, London: Harper & Row.

52. MacKinnon, Catharine (1987) *Feminism Unmodified: Discourses on Life and the Law*, Cambridge, Ma.: Harvard University.

53. Marx, Karl (1972) *The Eighteenth Brumaire of Louis Bonaparte*, New York: International Publishers.

54. Miller, Jean Baker (1976) *Toward a New Psychology of Women*, Boston: Beacon.

55. Myron, Nancy and Bunch, Charlotte, eds. (1975) *Lesbianism and the Women's Movement* (Baltimore: Diana Press).

56. Nestle, Joan (1987) *A Restricted Country*, Ithaca, N.Y.: Firebrand Books.

57. Omi, Michael and Winant, Howard (1986) *Racial Formation in the United States*, New York: Routledge/Methuen.

58. Ortner, Sherry (1974) "Is Female to Male as Nature is to Culture?", Rosaldo and Lamphere, eds. (1974).

59. Ortner, Sherry (1982) "Gender and Sexuality in Hierarchical Societies: The Case of Polynesia and Some Comparative Implications", Sherry Ortner and Harriet Whitehead, eds. (1982): 359-409.

60. Ortner, Sherry and Whitehead, Harriet (1982) *Sexual meanings: The Cultural Construction of Gender and Sexuality*, New York: Cambridge University.

61. Patton, Cindy (1985) *Sex and Germs: The Politics of AIDS*, Boston: South End Press.

62. Plummer, Kenneth, ed. (1981) *The Making of the Modern Homosexual*, London: Hutchinson.

63. Ponse, Barbara (1978) *Identities in the Western World: The Social Construction of Self*, Westport, Ct.: Greenwood Press.

64. Radicalesbians (1970) "The Woman-Identified Woman", Anne Koedt, et al, eds. (1973): 240-245.

65. Raymond, Janice (1979) *The Trans-sexual Empire: The Making of the She-Male*, Boston: Beacon.

66. Raymond, Janice (1986) *A Passion for Friends*, Boston: Beacon.

67. Reed, Evelyn (1973) *Women's Evolution from matriarchal clan to patriarchal family*, New York: Pathfinder.

68. Rich, Adrienne (1978) *The Dream of a Common Language*, New York: W.W. Norton.

69. Rich, Adrienne (1979) *On Lies, Secrets and Silence*, New York: W.W. Norton.
70. Rich, Adrienne (1980) "Compulsory Heterosexuality and Lesbian Existence", *Signs*, v. 5, no. 4 (Summer 1980): 631-60.
71. Rosaldo, Michelle and Lamphere, Louise eds. (1974) *Women, Culture and Society*, Stanford, Ca.: Stanford University.
72. Roscoe, Will (1988) "The Zuni Man-Woman", *Outlook*, v. 1, #2 (Summer 1988): 56-67.
73. Rubin, Gayle (1975) "The Traffic in Women", Rayna Reiter, ed. (1975) *Toward an Anthropology of Women*, New York: Monthly Review: 157-210.
74. Rubin, Gayle (1984) "Thinking Sex: Notes for a Radical Theory of the Politics of Sexuality", Carole Vance, ed. (1984) *Pleasure and Danger: Exploring Female Sexuality*, London: Routledge Kegan Paul: 267-319.
75. Ruddick, Sara (1984) "Maternal Thinking", Joyce Trebilcot, ed. (1984): 213-230.
76. Runte, Annette (1987) "Male Identity as a Phantasm: the Difficult Borderline between Lesbianism and Female Trans-sexualism in Autobiographical Literature", *Proceedings, "Homosexuality Which Homosexuality?" Conference*, Social Sciences, v. 2, Amsterdam: Free University: 216-229.
77. Sahli, Nancy (1979) "Smashing: Women's Relationships Before the Fall", *Chrysalis*, no. 8: 17-28.
78. Shepherd, Gill (1987) "Rank, Gender and Homosexuality: Mombasa as a key to Understanding Sexual Options", Pat Caplan, ed. (1987) *The Cultural Construction of Sexuality*, London: Tavistock: 240-270.
79. Treblicot, Joyce, ed. (1984) *Mothering: Essays in Feminist Theory*, Totowa, N.J.: Rowman and Allenheld.
80. Van Staveren, Mariette (1987) "Bars and Butches: The Respectability Pursued by Daughters of Bilitis", *Proceedings, "Homosexuality, Which Homosexuality?" Conference*, Social Science Supplement, Amsterdam: Free University: 46-58.
81. Weeks, Jeffrey (1979) *Coming Out: A History of Homosexuality from the nineteenth century to the present*, London: Quartet Books.
82. Weeks, Jeffrey (1981) *Sex, Politics and Society*, New York: Longman.
83. Weeks, Jeffrey (1985) *Sexuality and Its Discontents: Meanings, Myths and Modern Sexualities*, London: Routledge Kegan Paul.
84. Whitehead, Harriet (1982) "The Bow and the Burden Strap: A New Look at Institutionalized Homosexuality in Native North America", Ortner and Whitehead, eds. (1982): 80-115.
85. Willis, Ellen (1984) "Radical Feminism and Feminist Radicalism, Kate Soper, ed. *The Sixties Without Apology*, Minneapolis: University of Minnesota.
86. Wittig, Monique (1971) *Les Guérrillères*, New York: Viking.
87. Wittig, Monique (1981) "One is Not Born a Woman", *Feminist Issues*, (Winter 1981), v. 1, no. 3: 47-54.
88. Wittig, Monique (1986) *The Lesbian Body*, Boston: Beacon.
89. Zita, Jacquelyn, "Historical Amnesia and the Lesbian Continuum", *Signs*, v. 10, no. 1 (Autumn 1981): 172-187.

The Lesbian Perspective
Julia Penelope

I call this "The Lesbian Perspective," not because I imagine
there is **one** Lesbian perspective, but to suggest the possibility of a Lesbian consensus reality, a Lesbian-centered view of
the world, and the aspects of Lesbian experience on which
we can ground a self-defined consensus reality. When Lesbians work and create together, we live the vision of a Lesbian community. "That is the whole meaning of lesbian
works, magazines, videos, movies, research, all of which
shape our collectivity into reality. A collectivity becomes
flesh and bone each time one of us thinks of herself as par-
taking in an actual lesbian community" (Grimard-Leduc, p.
494). Given the depth of the differences in the ways we
understand ourselves, can there be such a being as "the Lesbian"? I think yes. Our perspective inheres in all our works.
If we are not trying to articulate a Lesbian view of the world,
why do we create the artifacts of a self-realizing culture?
Although I am unable to flesh out the anatomy of the Lesbian Body, I want to emphasize the unique potential inherent
in the Lesbian experience, a potential so dangerous to the
heterosexual body politic that it's exhilarating.

Obviously, easy generalizations about **all** Lesbians are
impossible because each of us participates in male culture to
some degree. But I cannot use that fact to avoid generalizing.
If we think that any generalizing about Lesbians is wrong,

then we should also stop identifying ourselves as *Lesbian* and *Dyke*, and adopt the point of view that there is nothing significant about being Lesbians. By placing the Lesbian experience clearly in relation to male culture, however, I will show how our apparent differences arise from specific contexts and our responses to those contexts. I want to outline the common ground on which I think we can create a Lesbian community that will support even those who may not want it or know that it exists.

What I call the "Lesbian Perspective" is a "turn of mind," a stance in the world, that asks unpopular questions, that can be comfortable only when it confronts the sources of its discomfort, a frame of mind that refuses to accept what most people believe to be "true." This turn of mind I identify as "Lesbian." It is what enabled us to reject heterosexual bribery. (This different way of perceiving and responding to the world is frequently called having a "bad attitude.") It is a mind that must have its own integrity on its own terms. Just as being a living, breathing Lesbian exposes the lie of heterosexuality as "normal" and "natural," the Lesbian Perspective challenges every lie on which male society is founded. And there are lots of those. We don't submit willingly to the dogmas of authority. Even when we try to hide our bad attitude from those who have power over us by retreating into silence, we stand out like dandelions in neatly-manicured lawns. Lesbians are the weeds that blossom proudly, stubbornly, in heterosexual families; no matter what lethal methods they use to eradicate us, we keep springing back. We are resilient, and our roots go deep.

What's Wrong with This Picture?

Where do we begin to define our Selves? How are Lesbians unique? In spite of our occasional craving to be "like everybody else," we know that we **aren't**. If we were, we wouldn't be Lesbians. Some deep-seated consciousness knows that the world presented to us as "real" is false. There's something wrong with the picture. The Lesbian Perspective originates in our sense of "difference," however vague the feeling may be, however much we resist that knowledge, and in our certainty that what others seem happy to accept as "real" is seriously flawed. In order to conceive and define ourselves as Lesbians, we have to defy the "wisdom of the ages." Nobody held up a picture of a wonderful dyke for us and said, "You could grow up to be strong and defiant like her." From the day a girl child is born, everyone who exercises control and authority in her life assumes that she will grow up to "fall in love" with a male, as though that were an "accidental" misstep, and that she will inevitably marry one. All the messages she hears about WHO she is and WHO she's expected to become assume that there's only one kind of love and one kind of sexuality, and that's HETEROSEXUAL. One of those messages informs us that we possess a biologically-determined "maternal instinct"; another croons at us, "Every woman needs a man." Imagine how many Lesbians there would be in the world if we got the kind of air-time and publicity that heterosexuality gets. In spite of liberal feminist proclamations to the contrary, we're a long, long way from Marlo Thomas's world of "Free to be You and Me." What we're "free to be" is heterosexual. That, and that only.

If we must speak of choice, it is the Lesbian who **chooses** to accept the terms of the heterosexual imperative, not the heterosexual. Heterosexuals don't choose their sexuality, because they believe it's "natural," the only way there is to be. Only Lesbians can choose to define ourselves. Being a Lesbian or a heterosexual isn't a matter of "choosing" a lifestyle or a "sexual preference" from the table spread before us by parents, teachers, and other authority figures. There's only one dish on the social menu—heterosexuality—and we are given to understand that we swallow it or go without. The only options we have are those we create for ourselves because we must do so. Who we decide we are isn't a matter of "taste," although some Lesbians do try to acquire a "taste" for heterosexuality.

There's a large difference between "being heterosexual" and "being" a Lesbian. "Being" heterosexual means conforming, living safely, if uncomfortably, within the limits established by men. "Being" a Lesbian means living marginally, often in secrecy, often shamefully, but always as different, as the "deviant." Some Lesbians have sex with men, often marry one, two, three, or four men, have numerous children, and may even live as heterosexuals for some portion of their lives. Lesbians are coming out at every age, and, regardless of how old we are when we decide to act on our self-knowledge, we say, "I've always been a Lesbian." Some Lesbians die without once acting on their deep feelings for other wimmin. Some Lesbians live someone else's life. Deciding to act on our emotional and sexual attractions to other wimmin is usually a long-drawn-out process of introspection and self-examination that can take years, because the social and emotional pressure surrounding us is so powerful and inescapable. There's no visible, easily accessible support in our society for being Lesbians, which explains why we have so much trouble imagining what "being Lesbian" means. In many ways, we remain opaque even to our Selves because we haven't yet developed a language that describes our experiences.

The differences among us have to do with our level of tolerance for discomfort, how thoroughly we have learned to mistrust and deny our Lesbian selves. Lesbians can deny ourselves endlessly because we are told that we "should." Being heterosexual is the only identity offered, coerced, supported and validated by male society. Male society makes it easy to deny our inner selves, to disbelieve the integrity of our feelings, to discount the necessity of our love for each other, at the same time making it difficult for us to act on our own behalf. Ask a Lesbian who has lived as a heterosexual if she knew she was a Lesbian early in her life, and most will say "yes." Maybe some didn't know the world *Lesbian*, but they'll talk about their childhood love for teachers and girlfriends. Most will say, after they've named themselves Lesbians, "I've always been a Lesbian." Most will say, "I didn't believe there were others like me. I thought I was the only one." This is reinterpretation of experience from a new perspective, *not* revision. Once a Lesbian identifies herself as *lesbian*, she brings all of her earlier experiences with and feelings for other women into focus; she crosses the conceptual line that separates the known (the "safe") of the social validation awarded to heterosexuals and the tabooed unknown of deviance. Crossing into this territory, she begins to remember experiences she had "forgotten," recalling women and her feelings for them that she had analyzed or named differently; she examines memories of her past from a new perspective. Events and experiences that once "made no sense" to her are now full of meanings she had ignored, denied, or discarded. Reconceiving herself as Lesbian, she doesn't change or revise women, events, and experiences in her past, she reinterprets them, understanding them anew from her Lesbian Perspective in the present.

When we fail to be visible to each other, we invalidate the Lesbian Perspective and the meanings it attaches to our experiences. Each of us pays a price for Lesbian invisibility, in our self-esteem, in years of our lives, in energy spent trying to deny our Selves. But it is a fact that millions of us name ourselves "Lesbian" even when we have no sense of a community, when we know no one else who is like us, when we believe we will live as outcasts and alone for the remainder of our lives. How do we become that which is nameless, or, named shameful, sinful, despised? The Lesbian stands against the world created by the male imagination. What **willfulness** we possess when we claim our lives!

The Lesbian Perspective develops directly out of our experiences in the world: How other people treat us as Lesbians, the negative and positive reactions we get in specific situations, what we're told (and believe) we "ought" to feel about ourselves as Lesbians, and the degree of honesty we come to feel we can exercise in our various relationships. What appear to be important differences among Lesbians are survival skills that enable us to survive in hostile territory. Some of us, for example, have had mostly positive or less damaging reactions to our Lesbianism from others who "count" in our estimation. Some Lesbians have experienced varying degrees of acceptance, tolerance, and open-heartedness from their heterosexual families and friends. Some Lesbians say they've had "no problems" in their lives connected with their Lesbianism. Not every Lesbian has had portions of her mind destroyed by drugs and repeated shock treatments, or been disowned by her genetic family, or had to survive on her own in the streets, but lots of Lesbians have suffered greatly, have been abused, rejected, ridiculed, committed to psychiatric hospitals, jailed, and tortured. For some, the pain of loving as a Lesbian made death a reasonable choice, and many Lesbians have killed themselves rather than endure an existence that seemed to have no hope. Suicide is a valid choice. Whatever our personal experience is, we are always at risk in this society.

Choosing Our Selves

Being a Lesbian isn't a "choice." We **choose** whether or not we'll live as **who we are**. Naming ourselves *Lesbian* is a decision to ACT on our truest feelings. The Lesbian who decides to live as a heterosexual does so at great cost to her self-esteem. Heterosexuals don't have to question the assumptions on which they construct their lives and then defend them to a hostile society. I can't estimate the damage done to our emotional lives by the dishonesty forced on us by male dogma, but I know how much of my own life has been lies, lies, and more lies.

We live in a society where dishonesty is prized far above honesty, and Lesbians learn the necessity of lying early on. Parents may tell us to "be ourselves," but we find out quickly, after only one or two "experiments," that honesty is punished, that "being ourselves" really means "Be who we want you to be." I know how much of myself I've tried to cover up, deny, and lie about in order to escape the most violent, lethal methods of suppression. The people who represent "society" for us when we're growing up teach us all we need to know about what being an "adult" means. "Growing up" for females in male societies means *choosing men*, and then lying about how "happy" they are. Naming ourselves Lesbian is one of the most significant steps we take to affirm our integrity, to choose honesty over deception, and to become real to ourselves.

This is why the consensus reality of heteropatriarchy describes Lesbianism as "a phase," as something we're supposed to "grow out of." Adopting the protective coloration of heterosexuality is thus equated with "maturity." "Growing up" is a code phrase signalling one's willingness to perform in specific ways: compromise principles, deny feelings, provide **and** accept descriptions one knows to be false, and read along from the heteropatriarchal script. Some are more adept and credible at acting "mature," but adults lie, and they lie all the time—to their children, loved ones, friends, bosses—but mostly to themselves.

Even after we've begun to explore and expand the meanings of our Lesbian Perspective, we bring that learned dishonesty, and our painful experiences about the cost of being honest, into our Lesbian lives. Unlearning years of heterosexual training isn't something we can expect to accomplish quickly or easily. Staying honest about ourselves takes lots of practice. We bring our lessons about the necessity of disguising ourselves, of lying about our innermost feelings, and a sincere reluctance to self-disclose with us when we become members of Lesbian society. The results can be far more damaging to our attempts to communicate and create a community than they are in male society.

On the one hand, lying, not being honest about who we are or how we feel, is a **survival skill** we have developed. We have to lie to get by in most heterosexual contexts. I realize there are some exceptions to this—there are always exceptions to any generalization. But a majority of Lesbians—today, in 1990—are **afraid** to be honest about their

Lesbian identity, and with good reason. As an outfront Lesbian, one of the exceptions, I want to validate their fear. It's real, it's based on real or likely experiences, and no Lesbian should feel she's expected to apologize for protecting herself in the only way she knows.

On the other hand, we've internalized the ethic of fear and secrecy so thoroughly that we discover we can't simply shed it when we're in Lesbian contexts. Again, though, previous experiences suggest that self-disclosure and honesty aren't entirely wise even among Lesbians. Too many Lesbians simply don't feel "safe" among other Lesbians on an emotional level, because of previous experiences, and so we're constantly on guard, prepared to protect ourselves. If we're committed to creating Lesbian communities in which we can work together, we have to deal up front with the fact that Lesbians hurt other Lesbians, not just sometimes, but frequently. We can only stop it when we recognize it, name it for what it is, resolve not to do it, and eliminate it as a behavior.

Choosing Each Other

Those of us who call ourselves Dyke or Lesbian talk often about a Lesbian community, whether we're "in" or "out" of it, whether or not such a thing can be said to exist, whether we approve or disapprove of some events or behaviors. Some of our talk may be negative, bitter, wishful, even fanciful, but it has a basis in our experience as well as our desire. However we may feel about Lesbian community, negative, positive, or indifferent, we call it into existence because we **do** talk about it.

One Lesbian or another can be heard denying that there's any such thing as a Lesbian "community" because she hasn't gotten support for one thing or another. It's easy to deny ourselves, to remove ourselves from a Lesbian context, to refuse to argue with each other. I have to point out what I fear may be obvious: Denying the existence of something acknowledges its potential existence. Those who say the Lesbian community doesn't exist are simultaneously asserting that it **should** exist, thereby calling it into being. I think we deny the existence of Lesbian community when someone or some group fails to meet our expectations of what we believe a Lesbian community should be. Rather than risk exposing our expectations of ourselves and other Lesbians, we erase the community we're working hard to create. Something that doesn't exist cannot be blamed for betraying or failing us.

However we conceive our Selves, when each of us decided to name ourselves Lesbians, we were simultaneously estranged form our first "community," the male society into which we were born and in which we were raised. Our decision to be Lesbians cut us off from the forms of validation available to nonLesbians. Even if a Lesbian gladly embraces male values in every other aspect of her life, if her only act of rebellion is her decision to relate sexually and emotionally with other Lesbians, she will never be rewarded as heterosexuals are. Whether we like it or not, our Lesbianism isn't valued by male society; it's devalued—discouraged, derided, punished—no matter how we choose, individually, to accommodate estrangement in our lives. We may find occasional support and validation here and there among heterosexuals, but it's not something we can rely on or count as permanent. Our greatest hope for steady, reliable support lies with each other, within the Lesbian community.

I'm going to suggest that a lot, not all, but a lot of our internal dis-eases, are essentially language problems. They originate in how we talk or don't talk to each other and how we listen or don't listen to each other. Talking, which implies the desire to share ideas, opinions, and feelings, is the essential feature of two pairs of words: *communicate* and *community* and *relate* and *relationship*. The word *community*, after all, has the same Latin root as the verb to *communicate, communicare*, 'to share', and its adjective, *communis*, meaning 'common'. In addition to their more specialized meanings in English, these words also mean 'to share with' and 'to be connected'. If we break the words *community* and *communicate* down further, the prefix *com-*, as in *complete* and *commute*, means 'with', and -*mun*- is the root of the Latin verb *munire*, meaning 'to fortify'. If we think about all these meanings, being connected, sharing, having something in common, and being fortified, we can better understand why a word like *community* resonates in us. We communicate most comfortably with those with whom we have something in common, and we're most likely to find them within a shared community. By sharing with other Lesbians, we fortify ourselves and grow stronger.

Relationship, that poor, tired, overused word, sounds empty these days, having been heterosexually reified as though it were an autonomous entity or therapized into a banal abstraction. Whether we can save it or not, we need to remember what it once meant: the willing telling of our Selves to those we connect with. Our relationships aren't limited to those that are sexual; sexual intimacy isn't the defining characteristic of a "relationship." Our friendships are "relationships," and our disagreements are relationships, too. Both our individual relationships as Lesbians and our community are premised on the same sharing, our willingness to **tell** our Selves, our stories, our fears, and our imaginings. The more we talk and listen to each other, the stronger each of us becomes. The stronger we are, the stronger our community. Too often, though, we talk **around** or **at** each other rather than **to** or **with**. Arguing is one kind of communication, but it's something we seem reluctant to do publicly, as if by suppressing our disagreements we can coerce unity from silence.

When we disagree, when we criticize other Lesbians, we're sharing ourselves and our own ideas and opinions. Disagreement isn't only a way of affirming ourselves; we also affirm the significance of the individuals we criticize. Arguing and disagreeing are ways of paying attention to the ideas and beliefs of others. When we argue, we're implying that the ideas we disagree with are important and merit attention. Silence often signals indifference. What we don't find worth responding to, we ignore. When we argue with other Lesbians, we also grow. Total agreement is total stagnation and boredom.

Consider this: In this society, we learn to think of argument as war (Lakoff and Johnson, pp. 4-6). ARGUMENT IS WAR is a cultural metaphor that turns up in the ways we describe the process of arguing. We talk about feeling "defensive," "defending our position," "shooting holes in someone else's argument," "holding opposing views," "demolishing an argument," "winning" and "losing arguments," having "weak points" in an argument, making claims that are "indefensible," "going on the offensive," and "being right on target." If we argue with each other as though ARGUMENT IS WAR, it's no wonder that criticisms are felt as "attacks" and disagreements are felt as "hostility." But arguing doesn't have to be experienced as a war. It's only the male description that makes the equation seem to be "inevitable" and "accurate."

If we believe that criticism is an "attack," and arguing is inherently "hostile," we're also likely to confuse unquestioning support with nurturance. If someone questions our opinions, behaviors, or attitudes, we may dismiss them as "unsupportive." Much is possible once we stop expecting to agree with each other on every single aspect of our lives. Like the members of any other society, we're not going to agree completely, ever. Yet, as a community, we don't handle our disagreements as well as we could.

I believe that inside each lesbian is the headstrong, willful core of Self that enabled her to choose to act on her Lesbianism, and we need to reclaim that initial certainty, to fulfill the promises we made to our Selves. A first step toward a real Lesbian community must be relearning honesty, a difficult project when all we know is lies. If we are to talk to each other, we must be able to believe that what we are hearing is honesty, even if we don't like it. Let's drop the fine rhetoric and the pretense to perfect understanding. If we're going to make a commitment to a viable, strong, Lesbian community, we have to begin by talking honestly to each other and listening carefully, too. We must take responsibility for articulating and acting on Lesbian values, values that empower our Lesbian Selves.

The BIG Picture

It's been a scary ten or eleven years for Lesbians, and many of us have slipped into an uneasy silence or slammed shut the doors of the closets behind us for a second or third time. We need to keep reminding each other that, *as far as we know,* **nothing like us has ever happened before.** *As far as we know,* there has never been a Lesbian Move-ment, and we are *global* in our connectedness. Too many Lesbians have learned, again, to think of themselves as "small," "tiny," insignificant. We've heard so much about "broader issues" and "the big picture" that some may think that the Lesbian Perspective is a "narrow" one, restricted to an "insignificant" minority.

"Narrow," when applied to concrete, physical dimen-sions, is used positively, because it means 'slender' in width, and being 'slender' in our society has become a moral imper-ative for those born female. But "narrow," used abstractly to describe ideas, implies a primarily negative evaluation of whatever concepts it's used of. We speak, for example, of "narrow opinions," "narrow perspectives," "narrow con-cerns," and we're much taken by points of view that adver-tise themselves as part of "the broader picture," as affording us "a broader perspective," a "wider scope," or an opportu-nity to join the "larger revolution." The word "narrow" is used to trivialize, diminish, and discredit a point of view that some people, usually those with socially-validated power, find threatening, repugnant, and downright outrageous. It is my intention to be outrageous. The "Lesbian Perspective" is certainly no less "real" or compelling than the dominant per-spective of the white, heterosexual majority, and it is by no means as "narrow" in the negative sense of that word. We rightly avoid the "straight and narrow path."

Our unacknowledged allegiance to male thought pat-terns can hypnotize us into passivity, and men frequently succeed in paralyzing us with that word (and others). There is nothing "narrow" about being and thinking **Lesbian**. What I'm warming up to here is a discussion of "category width" in English and where we think we might "fit" into the categories of the man-made framework. The language most Lesbians in the U.S. speak, by choice or coercion, is English (Native American, Black, and Hispanic Lesbians know first-hand about the cultural imperialism of imposed language), and it's the semantic structure of English that binds our minds, squishing our ideas into tidy, binary codes: this/not-this, female/male, big/small, Black/white, poor/rich, fat/thin, seeing/unseeing, powerless/powerful, wide/narrow, guilty/innocent. These are narrow concepts in the most negative sense of the word, but they are the semantic basis of the pale male perspective, and we need to understand the conceptual territory those semantic categories map before we can set about the task of creating a new map that charts the territory of the Lesbian Perspective.

Learning a first language socializes us, and we're dependent creatures when our minds are guided into the conceptual grooves created by the map of the territory men want us to follow. The language forces us to perceive the world as men present it to us. If we describe some behaviors as "feminine" and others as "masculine," we're perceiving ourselves in male terms. Or, we fail to perceive what is not described for us and fall back on male constructs, such as "butch" and "femme," as inherently explanatory labels for our self-conceptions.

Those of us raised speaking English weren't offered any choice in the matter. While we were passive in the indoctrination process for the first few years, however, there comes a time when we have to put aside the fact that we began as innocent victims and undertake the active process of self-reclamation that starts with understanding what happened to us and questioning the conceptual premises on which male societies are based. Learning to think around categorial givens is hard, but it's something we have to do in order to think well of ourselves. If we refuse to do this, we abandon ourSelves.

What is called "consensus reality" is the male-defined,

male-described version of "what is," and we are obliged to live around, under, and sometimes within what men say is "reality," even as we strive to conceive and define a Lesbian "consensus reality." The duality of our position as Lesbians, simultaneously oppressed by a society in which we are unwanted and marginal and envisioning for ourselves a culture defined by our values, with Lesbian identity at its core, is, I maintain, a position of strength if we take advantage of it.

First, we must undertake the tedious process of examining and re-examining **every** aspect of how we've been taught to "think," including the process of thinking itself. Every one of us raised in an English-speaking household was programmed to perceive the world, and ourselves in the world, according to the special map of the pale male perspective. Any map is always, and only, a **partial description** of the territory it claims to chart. Each map draws attention only to those topographical features that the map creator thinks are "relevant' or "significant"; each map creator perceives only some of the aspects of the territory while other, perhaps equally important features, remain invisible, unperceived. Some things are left out on purpose, others are distorted. Black and dark, for example, are given negative values in the pale male conceptual structure, while white and light are assigned positive values; being able to see is a "good thing"; not being able to see is a "bad thing." These descriptions, and the values attached to them, are not "the nature of the world," and that is not a coincidence. Whatever conceptual changes are eventually condoned by male culture can occur only by enlarging existing category widths, in particular the referential scope of words like *people* and *gay*. The semantic categories themselves don't change; they aren't allowed to change. They expand and contract, but the essential thought structures remain the same.

One of our difficulties with describing a Lesbian consensus reality is a language problem, the contradictory labels we use to name ourselves, a terminology that's sometimes useful, and often divisive. The way we name ourselves reflects how we understand what we mean in the world. We call our-selves, for example, "people," "human beings," "women," "gays," "Lesbians," "Dykes." Because we're biologically cate-gorized as female, it seems meaningful to say that, by inclu-sion with heterosexual women, we're oppressed as "women," and our experience of socialization confirms this category overlap. Likewise, because we aren't hetero, we're also oppressed as "homosexuals," so some Lesbians identify with gay men, in which case they call themselves "gay women," as I did for many years. Our invisibility, even to ourselves, is at least partially due to the fact that our identity is subsumed by two groups: women and gays. As a result, Lesbian issues seem to find their way, by neglect or elimination, to the bot-tom of both liberation agendas. The liberation of Lesbians is supposed to wait for the liberation of all women, or be absorbed and evaporate into the agenda compiled by gay men. Instead of creating free space for ourselves, we allow men to oppress us invisibly in both categories, as "women" or as "gays," without even the token dignity of being named "Lesbians." How we name ourselves determines how visible we are, even to each other.

If we allow ourselves to imagine ourselves as something other than "woman" or "gay," if we try to conceive of our Selves beyond those labels, what comes into our minds? Is it no-thing, or is it some-thing? Even if it is hazy, vague, with-out clear definition, isn't it some-thing we know but haven't yet been able to articulate? The issue here is making explicit the basis of our prioritizing, which is the idea that we are "sub-" somebody else. I think we are much, much more if we choose our Selves. The problem, as I identify it, is calling ourselves *women*. Monique Wittig (1988), and others, have argued that the category *woman* is a man-made category that serves men's purposes. In this case, the label *woman* diffuses Lesbian movement toward our Selves, to divert our attention from Lesbian issues and Lesbian needs. The label shifts our focus, directing our attention away form Lesbian community. As soon as we name ourselves Lesbians, we step outside of the category 'woman'. What we experience as Lesbians and identify as "women's oppression" is the socialization process that tried to coerce us into 'womanhood'. As a result of this tailoring of our identities, when we change categories from 'woman' to 'lesbian', we're still oppressed as 'female' and oppressed for daring to be 'non-woman'. While both Lesbians and hetero women experience misogyny as biological females, our experience of that oppression is very different.

The L-word continually disappears into the labels "gay" and "woman," along with our energy, our money, and our hope. So much Lesbian creativity and activity is called "women's this" or "gay that," making Lesbians invisible and giving heterosexual women or gay men credit for what they can't imagine and haven't accomplished. We need to think LESBIAN. We need to think DYKE. We need to stop being complacent about our self-erasure.

The male map cannot be trusted because the territory it describes isn't a healthy place for us to live in. Accepting male descriptions of the world endangers Lesbians. We can fight for inclusion within already sanctioned categories, such as *people, human being,* or *woman,* thereby forcing other speakers to enlarge them, or we can remain outside of patriarchally-given categories and endeavor to construct a different, more accurate map of the Lesbian conceptual territory. We have internalized a description of the world that erodes our self-esteem, damages our self-image, and poisons our capacity for self-love. If the children we were lacked options for the process of self-creation, the Lesbians we've become have the potential, as well as the responsibility, for redefining ourselves, learning to perceive the world in new and different ways from what we were taught, and setting about making maps that accurately describe the territory of our envisioning.

We can choose whether or not we will conform to heterosexual values, and even the degree to which we'll conform to the map men have imposed on reality. How we choose to deal with the defining categories of male culture places us within its boundaries or at its periphery. (See my essay, "Heteropatriarchal Semantics: 'Just Two Kinds of People in the World'," for an analysis of these defining categories.) We are never "outside" the reach of society, because even the negative evaluation of who we are can limit and control our lives. How we describe for ourselves that first wary step into an uncharted world determines how we think of ourselves as Lesbians. The Lesbian situation is essentially **ambiguous**, and that ambiguity provides the foundation of the Lesbian perspective. We must start from where we are.

Terra Incognita

Deciding to act on our Lesbian perceptions requires each of us to conceive ourselves as someone other than what male society has said we are. The Lesbian process of self-definition, however long it takes, begins with the recognition and certainty that our perceptions are fundamentally accurate, regardless of what male societies say. This is a STRONG place in us. In order to trust ourselves, we have to be able to push through the lies and contradictions presented to us as "truths," cast them aside, and stand, for that moment, in our own clarity. Every Lesbian takes that step into *terra incognita*, the undescribed or falsely described, the "unknown," beyond the limits posted by the pale male map of reality. Picture for yourself the map of the "known" world presented to us every moment, every day of our lives. Label that map HETEROPATRIARCHY out to the very neatly trimmed edges. Now read the warning signs along the edge: "Dangerous," "monstrous," "sick," "sinful," "illegal," "unsafe," "Keep Out! Trespassers will be violated!" Remember how long you deliberated with yourself before stepping across that boundary, before you decided you had to ignore the warning signs and take your chances in an ill-defined geography.

It's the clarity of that moment, the confidence of self-creation, that creates the "euphoria" so many Lesbians experience when we first come out. We do not forget that moment of clarity, ever. Lesbians think and behave differently because we've had to fight constantly to establish and maintain our identity in spite of covert and overt attempts, some of them violent, all of them degrading, to coerce us into heterosexuality. The Lesbian Self must stand alone, sometimes for years, against the force of the heterosexual imperative, until she can find other Lesbians who will support and affirm her. The out Lesbian has denied the validity of what men call "reality" in order to be Her Self. We do think differently. We perceive the world as aliens, as outcasts. No matter how hard some Lesbians try to "fit in," pale male societies define us as outside the boundary of the categories that maintain its coherence. We are made outcasts, but we can empower our Selves on that ground.

Although we may look back at times with yearning toward the heterosexual land of make-believe, we know that delusion for what it is: a man-made smog that pollutes and poisons all life. We must choose our own clarity, our willfulness, and reject the orthodoxy, "right-thinking," of men. Being Lesbian **is** nonconforming. The Lesbian perspective demands heterodoxy, deviant and unpopular thinking, requires us to love ourselves for being outcasts, not in spite of it, to create for ourselves the grounds of our being. The Lesbian Perspective isn't something we acquire as soon as we step out of our closets. It's as much a process of unlearning as it is learning. It's something we have to work at, nurture, encourage, and develop. The Lesbian Perspective is furious self-creation.

If we can imagine ourselves into being, if we can refuse to accept the labels and descriptions of men, the "possibilities **are** endless." We **are** outcasts from male society. We have no choice in that. What we can choose is how we define ourselves with respect to our outcast status. The Lesbian Perspective always asks "unpopular" questions. They're not popular because they threatened the interior structure of societies erected by men. What, exactly, does the Lesbian Perspective look like? Because we're already living in a way that men say is impossible, we gradually shed the dichotomies and distinctions we learned as children. The labels, names, and compartmentalizations that accompany those ways come to have less and less relevance in our thought processes, and we find new ways of interpreting our experience in the world because we perceive it differently. What we once memorized and accepted as "facts" no longer accurately describes our perceptions of reality. We realize that what we were taught to think was "real" or "natural" are only man-made constructs imposed on acts and events, ready-made representations of thoughts and feelings that we can, and must, reject. This is a difficult, gradual, uncertain process only because male societies don't want us to enjoy being outcasts. It's definitely **not** in the interests of men for us to like ourselves. Although it's men who established the boundaries that made us outcasts, what counts is how we organize that information in our minds and act on it in our lives.

The Lesbian Perspective challenges what heterosexuals choose to believe is "fact." As our joy in being outcasts expands, so does our ability to ask dangerous questions and dis-cover magical answers. We have no "givens" beyond that which is "other than": "deviant," "abnormal," "unnatural," "queer," false descriptions we begin with and cannot afford to forget. Indeed, we should wear them proudly. But our major endeavor must be self-definition. We have much to learn yet about ourselves, *our* culture, and we have new maps to draw that show the significant features of our worlds. The Lesbian Perspective makes it possible to challenge the accuracy of male consensus reality, and to create a reality that is Lesbian-defined and Lesbian-sustaining. Once we learn to perceive the world from our own perspective, outside the edges of the pale male map, we'll find it not only recognizable, but familiar.

Note

Different versions of this paper have been read at the University of Illinois-Champaign/Urbana, Southern Illinois University-Edwardsville, Washington University, the Building Community Conference held in Portland, Oregon

(November, 1986), and in Cleveland, Ohio. I want to thank the Lesbians in those audiences for their valuable suggestions and comments, and Joyce Trebilcot for urging me to talk about Lesbian consensus reality. The insights of my Dyke friends and their willingness to share their ideas have helped me to clarify my own thinking.

References

Grimard-Leduc, Micheline. "The Mind-Drifting Islands," in *For Lesbians Only*, eds. Sarah Lucia Hoagland and Julia Penelope. London: Onlywomen Press, 1988, 489-500.

Lakoff, G. and M. Johnson. *The Metaphors We Live By*. Chicago: University of Chicago Press, 1980.

Penelope, Julia. "Heteropatriarchal Semantics: 'Just Two Kinds of People in the World;," *Lesbian Ethics* 2, 2 (Fall, 1986) 58-80.

Wittig, Monique. "One is Not Born a Woman," in *For Lesbians Only*, eds. Sarah Lucia Hoagland and Julia Penelope. London: Onlywomen Press, 1988, 439-48.

Jewish Lesbians in France

The Issue of Multiple Cultures

MARTHE ROSENFELD

While the myth of the American melting pot gave way in the late sixties and the seventies to the reemergence of ethnic consciousness in the United States, there is little evidence to support the idea that French society is moving toward some form of cultural pluralism.[1] In fact, in France relations between the dominant culture and ethnic minorities seem to have worsened since the rise of an extreme right-wing political party, the National Front.[2] Other factors in contemporary France which account for the marginalization of immigrants and ethnic groups have to do with the reinforcement of the State at the expense of local power, the growing inequality between the working classes and the bourgeoisie, and the tendency of many French people to consider things French part of an old and prestigious civilization that is universally valid for everyone.[3]

In the lesbian movement in France, as well, one wonders whether, at an entirely different level, the reproduction of norms, values and theories that marginalize ethnicity may

---

[1] Jeffry [Shaye] Mallow, "Politics of Language," in *Chutzpah: A Jewish Liberation Anthology* (San Francisco: New Glide Publications, 1977), p. 146; Paula Hyman, *From Dreyfus to Vichy: The Remaking of French Jewry, 1906-1939* (New York: Columbia University Press, 1979), p. 234.

[2] Richard Bernstein, "Chirac Bill on Citizenship Raises Debate on How to Become French," *The New York Times*, 13 November, 1986.

[3] Stanley Hoffmann, "Transformations et contradictions de la Ve République," in *Société de la France contemporaine*, ed. Georges Santoni (Albany: State University of New York Press, 1981), pp. 280, 284, 371.

not prevail. In any case, an uncomfortable feeling looms on the horizon whenever one raises the question of lesbians who identify with another group, or with other groups.[4] Won't these multiple bonds divide a movement already threatened by factionalism from within, and threatened from without by the repressive measures of traditional politics? Are not those who claim dual identities keeping the lesbian movement from achieving its principal goal: to analyze all of society from a lesbian point of view?[5]

A brief account of radical feminist and lesbian theories in France might clarify these universalizing tendencies. Forty years ago Simone de Beauvoir, in *The Second Sex*, brought to light the oppressive situation of 'woman'. By asserting that it is civilization as a whole which has shaped her image in society as an inessential being, Beauvoir rejected all biological explanations of the inequalities between the sexes.[6] Similarly, Monique Wittig has shown that the idea underlying 'woman' is a politically constructed myth.[7] In "One is not Born A Woman," and in other essays, Wittig shows how females, appropriated by men to fulfill the requirements of the dominant class, have been portrayed primarily and above all else as sexual beings, and how this artificial image has become the sign of their intrinsic difference.[8] That is why Wittig insists on the necessary relationship between lesbianism and female autonomy.[9] Indeed Sapphic love appears in the work of Wittig

---

[4] At a women-only discussion meeting organized by two lesbian groups and which took place in Paris February 27, 1985, I heard remarks that poked fun at the idea of inviting lesbians from different cultures to widen the debate. But other people who were present at that meeting felt that such a project would be desirable.

[5] "Espaces: entrevue avec Irène et Martine," interview carried out by Louise Turcotte in *Amazones d'hier Lesbiennes d'aujourd'hui*, 2, No. 4 [Montréal] (March 1984), pp. 83-101.

[6] Simone de Beauvoir, *Le Deuxième sexe*, I (Paris: Editions Gallimard, 1949), pp. 11-32.

[7] Monique Wittig, "On ne naît pas femme," Questions féministes, 8 [Paris] (May 1980), pp. 75-84. Originally written in English, this article appeared under the title "One is not Born a Woman," in *Feminist Issues 1*, No. 2 (Winter 1981), pp. 47-54.

[8] Monique Wittig, "The Category of Sex," Feminist Issues 2, No. 2 (Fall 1982), pp. 63-68.

[9] Monique Wittig, "La pensé Straight," *Questions féministes* 7 (February 1980), pp. 52-53. Wittig's article was translated under the title "The Straight Mind," *Feminist Issues*, 1, No. 1 (Summer 1980), pp. 108-111.

as a very ancient social practice, a practice which stands for the female spirit of resistance against the arbitrary division of humanity into two distinct groups: those who constitute the norm and those who are perceived as the Others.[10]

In many respects, Colette Guillaumin's study of the concept of race in "Race and Nature: The System of Marks, The Idea of a Natural Group and Social Relationships" parallels Wittig's analysis of the structuring of gender. Both of these writers note that the subordinate conditions of women as a class, and of people of color, are often attributed to physical and innate characteristics. The relationships of power which maintain these oppressive hierarchies thus tend to remain hidden from consciousness.[11] By showing how biological interpretations of race and sex have been used throughout modern history to legitimize the persecution of entire groups of people, French radical feminism and lesbianism have emphasized the dangers of naturalistic ideologies. However this justifiable critique of an essentialist mode of thinking should not prevent feminists or lesbians from exploring our cultural diversities. Nor should the radical feminist and lesbian rejection of the hierarchic differences between the sexes anesthetize women to the nondominant differences in our oppressions.[12] Thus Arab and Jewish women in France, while differing among themselves, experience a triple oppression: as females they are strongly conditioned to fill the part of the dutiful wife and mother, as Jews or Moslems they are kept at a distance, the religion being mostly in the hands of men, as immigrants they share some of the characteristics of the people of the country where they were born and some of the characteristics of the culture of their adoptive country.

---

[10]Wittig, "One is not Born a Woman," pp. 52-53; Wittig, "The Category of Sex," pp. 66-68. See also Marthe Rosenfeld, "The Linguistic Aspect of Sexual Conflict: Monique Wittig's *Le corps lesbien*," Mosaic, XVII/2 [Winnipeg, Canada] Spring 1984, pp. 235-241.

[11]Colette Guillaumin, "Race and Nature: The System of Marks. The Idea of a Natural Group and Social Relationships," *Feminist Issues*, 8, No. 2 (Fall 1988), pp. 34-42.

[12]I owe a great deal to Audre Lorde for the concept of "nondominant differences." See her essay: "The Master's Tools Will Never Dismantle the Master's House," in *Sister Outsider* (Trumansburg, New York: The Crossing Press, 1984), pp. 110-113.

Given the conflicts of values and the anxieties which invariably touch the lives of multi-cultural peoples, it is not surprising that a small group of Jewish women should have decided to meet in Paris twice a month during the year 1976-77, not only for the pleasure of being together, but also to discuss issues of mutual interest.[13] The members of this group, consisting of Sephardic and Ashkenazi feminists between the ages of twenty and forty, embarked on a voyage to discover their identities. All of them agreed that their mothers had played a major role in their lives as persons who transmitted to them the values of their cultures.[14] With regard to their sexual attitudes, however, the two groups differed from one another. While the Ashkenazi women expressed many ideas about theory, they readily admitted that a certain puritanism affected their daily lives. The Sephardic women, on the other hand, revealed a greater familiarity with their bodies and a much greater freedom of gesture among themselves.[15]

My purpose is to inquire whether Jewish lesbians in France have experienced a similar need to exchange ideas with one another concerning how multi-cultural experiences affect their lesbianism and in turn how their lesbianism affects their Jewishness. But before tackling this important question, I should like to describe the early manifestations of my own lesbianism as well as my growing sense of solidarity with other Jewish women.

I was born in Antwerp in 1928 and grew up in that city until the outbreak of World War II. Though raised in a secular

---

[13] Judith Stora-Sandor, "Bilan d'une expérience," *La Presse Nouvelle Hebdomadaire* [Paris], (December 1, 1978), pp. 6-7.

[14] While the word Ashkenazi originally denoted German Jewry, it also refers to the Jews from Poland and Lithuania, many of whom immigrated to Western Europe and the United States. The Sephardim are descendants of Jews who lived in Spain or Portugal. After their expulsion from Spain in 1492, the Sephardim fled to North Africa, Western Europe, the New East. Important Sephardic communities were established also in the Balkans, particularly in Constantinople, Izmir and Salonika.

[15] One of the reasons mentioned for the easiness with which Sephardic women related to each other was the *hammam* or Turkish baths which they had gone to as young girls while they were living in North Africa.

environment, I was aware of belonging to a group on the edge of society, for the remarks made by people around me insinuated that Jews were foreigners. The holidays moreover, especially the Passover seder, had taught me the Exodus from Egypt and its symbolic meaning of liberation from servitude. The stories of I.L. Peretz, such as "Between Two Peaks," "If Not Higher," and "Three Gifts," which I read in French, put me in touch with the life of East European Jews. In Peretz's sympathetic portrayal of working class people and their search for community, I found role models which were extremely appealing.[16] Those stories that brought out the oppression of ordinary folk gave evidence also of the unbreakable qualities of Jewish strength. My feeling of alienation towards the dominant culture intensified when I learned around the age of eleven that Jews were being tortured in the concentration camps in Germany and that my Orthodox Jewish classmates would now be compelled to go to school on Saturday. When it was our turn to flee southward in the face of the German onslaught, I began to experience the dread of those who have lost all their rights. As the leader of an authoritarian regime in the southern, so called "Free Zone" with Vichy as its capital, Henri Philippe Pétain showed his contempt for democracy by abolishing all the principles on which the Third Republic had rested. Moreover, he tried to ingratiate himself with the conqueror by passing anti-Semitic legislation. The law of October 4, 1940, for example, permitted the internment of Jewish aliens living in France. During the same year, Jewish members of the teaching profession were excluded from public educational institutions.[17] A year and a half before the great roundup of July 16-17, 1942, I had the exceptional good fortune to be able to leave Europe with

---

[16] A writer of the Yiddish renaissance in the closing decades of the nineteenth century, I.L. Peretz shared the heterosexist prejudices of his time. What I appreciated in his short stories was the humorous and sympathetic portrayal of East European Jewish life.

[17] Rabi, *Anatomie du judaisme français* (Paris: Les Editions de Minuit, 1962), p. 120.

my close relatives on one of the last boats sailing from Marseilles to the Americas.

New York City in the forties had become a center for refugees from all over the world. In high school I was close to other Jewish young women, immigrants from Europe like myself, and soon fell in love with one of their girlfriends, a student at the university. Though barely sixteen at the time, I still remember how much joy I experienced in the company of this young person. Indeed, whenever I evoke that period of my life, a sense of well-being rises from the past for, without being conscious of any reasons, I felt good about loving someone of my own sex. It was only toward the end of the war, when I discovered the unspeakable fate which my cousins, my aunts and uncles had endured in the inferno of the extermination camps, that I became obsessed with a feeling of culpability. Eventually the pressures to become assimilated into the new culture would lead to the erasure of my Jewish experience and of my nascent lesbianism. Not until the late 60's did I, upon becoming aware of women's oppression, and of the subversive character of lesbianism as revealed in the powerful and innovative writings of Monique Wittig, rediscover the person I had been twenty years earlier. After coming out as a lesbian in 1977, I understood that I needed to make contact with the other person who had dozed within me all this time and who now yearned to express herself.[18]

During the summer of 1979, as a member of an NEH seminar for college teachers at the University of Wisconsin, I was introduced to the Madison Jewish Lesbian Group. Meeting at each others' homes, we discussed topics such as the bonding of women in Jewish culture and the strength which our Jewish upbringing had given us to come out as lesbians. Two summers later, during the meeting of the NWSA in Storrs, Connecticut and during a trip to Montreal, where I had a chance to become acquainted with the daughter of a

---

[18]And yet I had not forgotten the example of Anne Frank, who in an almost desperate situation never renounced her Jewishness.

Holocaust survivor, the connections between my being a lesbian and being Jewish became growing questions in my mind. Here I was influenced by *Nice Jewish Girls*, the lesbian anthology edited by Evelyn Torton Beck, a book which has struck a receptive note in the consciousness of certain francophone lesbians in France as well as in Quebec, and also by *Periods of Stress*, by Irena Klepfisz.[19]

As a teacher I had the opportunity of staying in Paris during the school year '84-'85, and in the course of that time, of meeting a few Jewish lesbians. What impressed me as I chatted with them was the fact that although they identified as lesbians, they did not seem interested in discussing the question of ethnicity. I wondered, therefore, what historical factors accounted for the difference of situation between myself, a Jewish lesbian with a francophone background who had become assimilated into American modes of thinking, and the French Jewish lesbians with whom I had the opportunity to speak. Among the issues that I tried to address were: the effects of nationalism, of anti-Semitic beliefs, of the impact of events in French history during the first and second world wars, of the less known but tremendously important history of Jewish women in France in the Resistance.

Unlike the Jews in the *shtetls*, small-town communities of Eastern Europe, who had maintained a rich and varied Yiddish culture until the beginning of World War II, the Jews in France as descendants of the Revolution gained civic and political rights provided that they limit themselves to becoming French citizens of the Jewish faith.[20] In a similar manner the Sephardic women of Algeria adopted French around 1910, instead of Judeo-Arabic, the local language of their

---

[19] *Nice Jewish Girls: A Lesbian Anthology*, ed. Evelyn Torton Beck (Watertown, MA: Persephone Press, 1982; reprinted and distributed by The Crossing Press, 1984). I am indebted to my friend Laura Yaros for the information which she sent me about cross-cultural lesbian influences in the francophone world.

[20] Hyman, pp. 4-5.

community.[21] Modern nationalism, by linking the concepts of State and unified culture, thus tended to stifle the expression of ethnic diversity.

Anti-Semitism, with its long history of discrimination and hostility, has also influenced assimilation, including assimilation by French lesbians, into the dominant French culture. One of the most persistent themes of modern anti-Semitism is the myth of the Jewish conspiracy, namely, that guided by a group of elders, the Jews would destroy Christian values, impose their own laws on every people of the earth and ultimately rule the world.[22] Closely related to this theme is the idea of Jewish profiteering, another widely circulated myth which enabled victims of bankruptcy or business failings to blame the Jews for their economic woes.[23] But it was Edouard Drumont's *La France Juive*, published in the spring of 1886, that disseminated these ideas. In his voluminous study of French society, Drumont maintained that the Semite when compared to the Aryan is inferior in every way. If this book proved to be so successful it is not only because the author appealed to a nostalgia for the "good old days," the period of the old regime, but because he based his argument on the "science" of his own time.[24] Other books and articles inspired by *La France Juive* continued to fuel the anti-Semitic frenzy which prevailed during the Dreyfus Case.[25]

---

[21]Joëlle Allouche-Benayoun, "Mémoires juives et acculturation à la France à propos des femmes juives d'Algérie," *Traces*, 9/10 [Paris] (1984), p. 59.

[22] Described at the beginning of the twentieth century in a forgery prepared for the Tsar under the title: "Protocols of the Elders of Zion," the notion of Jewish world domination was used by the extreme right wing, particularly in Western Europe, to stir up hatred of the Jews and of their alleged "socialist plot."

[23]Léon Poliakov, *Suicidal Europe: 1870-1933*, Vol. IV of *The History of Anti-Semitism*, trans. George Klim (New York: The Vanguard Press, 1985), pp. 38-39.

[24]Among other proponents of racist ideologies in nineteenth century France there were: Joseph Arthur de Govineau with *L'Essai sur l'inégalité des races humaines*, 1855; Georges Vacher de Lapouge with *L'Aryen*, 1886; and Gustave Le Bon, who wrote pseudo-scientific essays on the negative role of the Jews in European civilization.

[25]The following is a summary of the events: In 1894 Alfred Dreyfus, a captain in the French army and a Jew, was accused on the basis of an unsigned letter or bordereau of having passed army information to the Germans and was sentenced to

Although that trial was viewed as a great misfortune by the majority of French Jews, they did not protest against Dreyfus's sentence. Their political neutrality, as Paula Hyman has shown, resulted from the ideology of emancipation, a concept of human rights which had granted equality to the Jews as individuals but which had denied their existence as a people.[26]

That it took a great upheaval such as World War I to limit the hate campaign against the Jews is a sad commentary on the modern world. But there were signs before the end of the hostilities which indicated that the leaders of the Right had put their anti-Semitism aside only for a few years. Thus in 1917, fearing the loss of an important ally, a number of French intellectuals began to blame the Jews for having incited the Bolshevik Revolution. Similarly, the issue of a Jewish homeland gave rise at that time to a virulent anti-Semitism within the higher ranks of the Catholic clergy, a number of whose members denounced the Zionist movement as yet another plot to control and subjugate the world.[27] Although the stereotype of the Bolshevik Jew subverting the established order began to fade after the resumption of diplomatic relations with Moscow, the Socialist figure of the Jew became the target of the bourgeoisie's class consciousness and xenophobia. Thus Léon Blum's Popular Front, which sought to effect a more equi-

---

life imprisonment on Devil's Island. Two years later another document was discovered proving that information was still being passed. Major Esterhazy, an officer riddled with debts, became a suspect. But Commandant Hubert Joseph Henry, a staff member in the French Intelligence, forged documents to strengthen the army's case against Dreyfus. When Esterhazy was tried and found innocent, Emile Zola published an open letter to the President of the Republic accusing the chiefs of staff and the military tribunals of having falsified evidence to save face. In 1898 the forgery was discovered; Commandant Henry was accused and committed suicide. The next year Dreyfus was returned to France for a retrial and pronounced guilty once again. Only in 1906, twelve years after the initial condemnation, was he finally exonerated. See Jean-Denis Bredin, *The Affair: The Case of Alfred Dreyfus,* trans. Jeffrey Mehlman (New York: George Braziller, 1986) for a full account.

[26] Hyman, pp. 4-11.
[27] Poliakov, pp. 278-285.

table distribution of wealth among the working classes and which took that figure's place in the unstable France of the mid-thirties was, nevertheless, doomed to fall.[28]

An unmistakable sign of France's political instability at the time of World War II was the sudden and drastic shift in political allegiances. So hopelessly was France divided that one could no longer recognize either the Right or the Left. Thus, while the Socialists had participated massively in the anti-Fascist demonstration of 1936, the majority of those Socialists voted four years later to transfer the powers of government to Pétain.[29] Indeed the changing attitudes of the Left under the impact of events brought out the precariousness of coalitions and solidarities. When 7,000 Jews, of which 4,051 were children, found themselves excluded from French society, having been imprisoned by the police July 16, 1942, in a stadium without water or toilets and almost without nourishment, there was no longer any doubt about it, the Jews were alone.[30]

One of the most remarkable chapters of this ominous period of history is the participation, which is little known, of Jewish women in the Resistance. Macha Ravin and Eva Goldgevid, two of those resisters who immigrated to Paris from Poland in the 1930's, became involved after the occupation in saving the lives of Jewish children. They left no stone unturned to find a place for them among peasant families who would agree to hide Jewish children.[31] Moreover, while working for the relief organization *Solidarité*, they helped Jewish women with dependents who found themselves stranded and without any means of support. At a time when

[28] Poliakov, p. 302; See also Marc Bloch, *L'Etrange défaite* (Paris: Société des Editions Franc-Tireur, 1946), pp. 179-184.

[29] Milton Dank, *The French against the French: Collaboration and Resistance* (Philadelphia and New York: J.B. Lippincott Company, 1974), pp. 31-32.

[30] Claude Lévy and Paul Tillard, *Betrayal at the Vel d'Hiv*, trans. Inea Bushnaq (New York: Hill and Wang, 1969), pp. 25-59.

[31] Ania Francos, herself a daughter of Jewish immigrants, praises those French people who, often at the risk of their own lives, gave sanctuary to Jewish children. See *Il était des femmes dans la Résistance. . .* (Paris: Editions Stock, 1978), p. 111.

Fascist repression struck terror in the hearts of the immigrants, Macha, Eva and their female comrades crisscrossed the sections of Paris with the largest Jewish populations and brought leaflets to them in Yiddish urging the Jewish women to fight on.[32]

Marie-Elisa Nordmann and France Bloch-Serazin were close friends who helped each other keep the enemy on the alert. Chemists by training, they produced explosives. In 1937, France Bloch joined the Communist party out of concern for the working classes. During the war, her commitment to freedom became so strong that she did not hesitate to fight beside the partisans who attacked a factory that was working for the Nazis and who blew up railroad tracks. Since she was not allowed to hold a job, she gave private lessons to keep herself and her two children alive.[33] She was arrested May 16, 1942 and she was beheaded in a German prison at the age of twenty-nine. Having struggled with courage to uphold her ideals, however, she died serene and without flinching.[34] The other three resisters: Macha, Eva and Marie-Elisa were departed to Auschwitz in July of 1943. If these women managed to survive the hell of the concentration camp universe, it was thanks to the mutual friendship, thanks to the words and the affection that passed between them.[35]

In a fascinating article on Jewish women in the Resistance in France, Penelope Hamm has shown that a number of immigrant women undertook the dangerous task of working as "liaison agents" between the clandestine world of the Resistance and the mercilessly bureaucratic world of the German occupation. By using wiles and charm, they succeeded in passing from one sphere to the other without arousing the suspicion of the authorities. Among the women whom Penelope mentions as having been involved in direct action were: Golda Bancic, Andrée Barral, Cecile Weidzman, Betty Knout.

---

[32] *Ibid.*, pp. 111-113.
[33] *Ibid.*, pp. 130-131.
[34] *Ibid,* pp. 125-126.
[35] *Ibid.*, pp. 397-403.

Other immigrants from Poland, such as Riga Levin and Hella Igla, acquired weapons and fought the enemy as members of the guerrilla group F.T.P. (*Francs Tireurs et Partisans*).[36] Although numerous documents show that Jewish women participated at every level of the Resistance in France, the fact that this information has begun to appear in feminist and lesbian publications only within the last decade and that these materials are not widely publicized helps to explain the lack of knowledge concerning this activism and bravery. Hence the indifference of many lesbians toward a heritage with which they may not be familiar. For in spite of the long history of Jewish rebellion against tyranny, in spite of the distinguished record of the Jewish Maquis in France and of the courageous Jewish uprising in the Warsaw Ghetto, the stereotype of the fearful and submissive Jew continues to falsify the truth and to impede the development of an authentic Jewish identity.

Undoubtedly these historical reflections relate to the situation of French Jewish lesbians and the reluctance which many of them feel to discuss issues of ethnicity. Indeed the difficulty of multi-cultural peoples to reconcile the various components of their personalities was well illustrated toward the end of 1984 when *Lesbia*, a French magazine, published the interviews which it had carried out with six Jewish lesbians. Like the feminist group that we met earlier, the lesbians represented various generations, classes and communities. Equally divided between the Sephardic and Ashkenazi groups, the interviewees were between the ages of nineteen and fifty-six, two of them coming from working-class and four of them from middle-class backgrounds. The differences of attitudes toward the question of Jewishness should come as no surprise, given the variety of their experiences. However all of them stated that they were confused at times by the problem of keeping their multiple identities from canceling each other out.

---

[36] Pénélope Hamm, "Les Femmes juives dans la Résistance en France," *Archives recherches et cultures lesbiennes*, 3 (November '85), pp. 48-49.

For example, when two of the interviewees compare the vitality of modern Israel with the weakness and fatalism of the Jews before 1939, they reveal a tragic misunderstanding of the historical facts. But their candid appraisal of their own situation brings out the precariousness of multiple identities. One of them feels both Jewish and different from her people, a people who deliberately ignores her chosen way of life; another gives priority to her lesbianism, has difficulty connecting to a religious and cultural reality which basically she denies. Moreover, they dwell on the tensions which they experienced at home because of the perennial advice of parents, siblings, even casual acquaintances, on behalf of marriage and the survival of the ethnic group.[37] The other lesbians interviewed by the magazine, myself included, claim more than one identity not only because we draw inspiration from the strength and courage of our foremothers, but because we believe that our Jewish experience gives us a deeper understanding of other oppressions, as well as the incentive to fight racism in all its forms.[38]

In the summer of 1986, several conversations in Paris with Jewish lesbians who identify strongly with the culture convinced me that the progress of our lesbian movement depends on the empowerment of all its members to express themselves in their own ways. Interestingly enough, the meaning of remembering our past, of bearing witness, of preserving our individual and collective memories, was a common preoccupation. In addition, these interviews enabled me to understand more fully the difficulties which Jewish lesbians often encounter. Evoking a particularly stressful relationship, one of the interviewees observed that the hostility of her ex-lover toward Israel brought to light the gulf which separates Jewish lesbians from militant leftists.[39]

---

[37] Muriel Goldrajch and Christiane Jouve, "Lesbiennes et Juives," *Lesbia*, 22 (November '84), pp. 12-15.

[38] Muriel Goldrajch, "Lesbianisme et Minorités: Lesbiennes Juives," *Lesbia*, 23 (December '84), pp. 13-15.

[39] Many Jewish lesbians support Israeli and Palestinian women in their efforts to achieve a peaceful resolution of the conflict in the Middle East and we condemn the human rights violations by the Israeli government especially in the occupied

Another Jewish lesbian, answering a question on the relative importance of each of these identities, reveals her dilemma: In Jewish circles which by and large ignore homosexuality, she feels misunderstood as a lesbian; in lesbian gatherings where people often keep silent about other oppressed groups, she longs to come out as a Jew. In one community as well as in the other, she feels divided and estranged.

Nevertheless, except for the Beit-Haverim, a mixed Jewish gay organization which maintains the culture, and a group of four Jewish lesbians who meet in Paris at regular intervals, there has not been much activity in France until now in favor of ethnic minorities.[40] This lack of support does not stem solely from the fear of divisiveness whose influence on the movement we observed at the beginning of this essay. Indeed a current of radical lesbians accuse those lesbians who claim another identity of practicing racism in reverse. Thus Irène of the now defunct magazine *Espaces*, though she is Jewish herself, excoriates the movement abroad for having transformed itself into a supermarket of narrowly sectarian interests. Because she has completely absorbed the ideology of emancipation, she cannot imagine that Jewish lesbians might wish to discuss other subjects besides religion. She does not hesitate, therefore, to label workshops on anti-Semitism in the movement, on Jewish-lesbian culture and on older Jewish lesbians as "the great naturalistic mystic," but her reasoning is flawed and her irony out of place.[41]

French radical lesbianism, as we saw, challenges the naturalist discourse.[42] It questions the language that describes as "natural" a prefabricated and mandatory heterosexuality; it

---

territories. But it is the hatred of Israel, the unwillingness to distinguish between its various political parties or to recognize the existence of its progressive organizations, which is regarded as a new mask of anti-Semitism.

[40] A Jewish lesbian in Paris kindly gave me this information in a recent letter.

[41] Irène, "Racisme: conférence nationale des lesbiennes juives à Londres," *Espaces*, 13 (April 1983), pp. 3-4.

[42] I use the terms "radical lesbianism" and "radical lesbians" to refer to my interpretation of the theories of such writers as Monique Wittig, Colette Guillaumin and Nicole-Claude Mathieu; I am not alluding to the way these writers choose to live or to define themselves.

refutes all arguments which base themselves on biology to explain the behavior of distinct groups.[43] This critique of biological determinism is a major contribution to lesbian and feminist theories. Not only does it keep one from falling into the trap of essentialist thinking, it puts us on guard against making assumptions about people on the basis of sex, color, names or other characteristics. Above all it encourages women, trapped in the hierarchic system of gender, to escape from their class or to seek liberation in the world of lesbianism.

Radical French lesbianism, however, has not fostered the development of ethnic awareness. Given the long history of racist ideology in France, in which the dominant culture attempted to marginalize and thereby to obliterate non-dominant cultures, and its catastrophic consequences, French radical lesbians tend to question those ideas which conjure up notions of "exclusion," "specificity," or "race." They view with misgiving the frequent usage of words such as "identity," "roots," "culture," "difference," and prefer, instead, to bring out the resemblances between peoples as well as their commonalities.[44] But even with a functional vocabulary, the task of expressing multiple allegiances among lesbians of different backgrounds is painstaking, and without a functional vocabulary, that task becomes virtually impossible. Moreover, the notion that minority identities are exclusively historical products of oppression and resistance undermines the exploration of individual and collective consciousnesses. For even if the struggle against anti-Semitism forms an integral part of Jewish identity, this identity is also related to culture, a rich and diverse culture which cannot be reduced to the terms of dominance and submission. A distinction should be made here between identity, a form of extreme nationalism

---

[43] By comparing several non-Western societies, Nicole-Claude Mathieu shows that it is education, not genetics which influences the behavior of children and adults. See "Masculinité/féminité," *Questions féministes*, 1 (November 1977), pp. 51-67; trans. "Masculinity/Feminity," *Feminist Issues*, 1, NO. 1 (Summer 1980), pp. 51-69.

[44] Colette Guillaumin feels that any appeal to the race even under the pretext of going back to one's roots or of nurturing a specific culture reveals a political tendency which is not harmless, given the omnipresence of racism in modern societies. See "'Je sais bien mais quand même' ou les avatars de la notion 'race'," *Le Genre humain*, 1 (1981), issue on *La science face au racisme*, pp. 55-65.

that can easily turn into racist propaganda, and the desire which many of us share to retrieve a profoundly valuable language, theater, history, music or dance.[45]

But there are a few indicators within the radical French lesbian movement which show a greater concern for the ethnic diversity of its lesbian population. Not only have articles appeared recently on this subject in the journal of the Lesbian Archives of Paris; this organization also formed an anti-racist group in 1985, a group whose purpose is to study the issues and to celebrate acts of resistance by lesbians against fascism and anti-Semitism.[46] Should this trend continue, as I fervently hope it will, lesbians, including Jewish and other minority lesbians in France, would be encouraged to discover the meaning of lesbianism for themselves. Likewise, by studying the diversity of experiences and social conditions of these lesbians, by confronting the inequalities, by looking at the interrelationship of all the oppressions, French radical lesbians could broaden the conceptual framework of their analyses.[47] In that way they would also show some of the multiple connections among paths of lesbians from various classes, backgrounds and ethnic affiliations.

Note

I would like to thank Claudie Lesselier, founding member of the Lesbian Archives of Paris, for her helpful criticism of an earlier version of this essay. I also thank Sara Halperyn, librarian of the *Centre de Documentation Juive Contemporaine* for sending me valuable materials. Jeffner Allen's continuous support and her critical readings are deeply appreciated.

---

[45] Melanie Kaye/Kantrowitz, "To Be a Radical Jew in the Late 20th Century," in *The Tribe of Dina: A Jewish Women's Anthology*, eds. Melanie Kaye/Kantrowitz and Irena Klepfisz, Sinister Wisdom 29/30 (Montpelier, Vermont, 1986), p. 276.

[46] *Archives recherches et cultures lesbiennes* 3 (November '85), p. 40. This publication reprinted the leaflet which was distributed at a lesbian demonstration against racism, anti-Semitism and Fascism held in Paris on the 8th of May 1985 to celebrate the resistance of Algerian and French women against colonialism.

[47] The importance of the "conceptual framework" in developing feminist or lesbian theory became clear to me after reading Evelyn Beck's article "The Politics of Jewish Invisibility," *NWSA Journal, A Publication of the National Women's Studies Association*, 1, No. 1 (Autumn 1988), pp. 93-102.

Pluralist Lesbian Separatism[1]

CLAUDIA CARD

Many feminist lesbians have a vision of pluralist separatism embodying ethnic and cultural diversity as well as appreciation of differences in political history.[2] It is not obvious, however, that separatism coheres well with muticultural pluralism. Can separatist politics nourish the understanding requisite to realizing combined resistance to white supremacism, anti-Semitism, homophobia, capitalist imperialism, and misogyny?[3] A widely joked-about yet persistently troubling "tyranny of political correctness" has the potential to undermine such understanding, to discourage an inherent-

---

[1] On feminist and lesbian separatism I found the following useful: Jeffner Allen, *Lesbian Philosophy: Explorations* (Palo Alto, CA: Institute of Lesbian Studies, 1986); Marilyn Frye, "Some Reflections on Separatism and Power," *The Politics of Reality* (Trumansburg, N.Y.: Crossing Press, 1983), pp. 95-109; Sarah Lucia Hoagland, "Lesbian Separatism: An Empowering Reality," *Sinister Wisdom* 34 (Spring 1988), 23-33; Christine Pierce and Sara Ann Ketchum, "Separatism and Sexual Relationships," in Sharon Bishop & Marjorie Weinzweig, eds., *Philosophy and Women* (Belmont, CA: Wadsworth, 1979), 163-171; Billie Luisi Potts, "Owning Jewish Separatism and Lesbian Separatism 9982," *The Lesbian Insider/Insighter/Inciter* #9 (Dec. 1982), pp. 3, 29, 30; Adrienne Rich, "Notes for a Magazine: What Does separatism Mean?" *Sinister Wisdom* 18 (Fall 1981), 83-91; Joyce Trebilcot, "In Partial Response to Those Who Worry That Separatism May Be a Political Cop-Out: An Expanded Definition of Activism," *off our backs*, May 1986; Ariane Brunet and Louise Turcotte, "Separatism and Radicalism: An Analysis of the Differences and Similarities," *Lesbian Ethics* 2: 1 (Spring 1986), 41-49; María Lugones, "On the Logic of Pluralist Feminism" (presented to the Spring conference of Midwest SWIP, E. Lansing, MI, March 1988, unpublished) and "Playfulness, 'World'-Travelling, and Loving Perception," *Hypatia* 2: 2 (Summer 1987), 3-19, and María C. Lugones and Elizabeth V. Spelman, "Have We Got a Theory for You! Feminist theory, cultural imperialism and the demand for 'the woman's voice'," *Women's Studies International Forum* 6: 6 (1983), 573-581.

ly valuable intercultural bonding which can also be useful in understanding and resisting complex sources of oppression.

Sexual liberationists have mocked value judgments as "politically correct," hoping thereby to gain acceptability for gay porn and sadomasochism—an endeavor undermined from the start, for "acceptable" *is* a value judgment. My purpose is not to defend sexual liberation. My purpose is to take seriously fear of peer rejection for dissent among separatists and to consider what can be done about that within a separatist framework. Without space for internal dissent, the internal critique needed to assess resistance strategies is not readily forthcoming, especially given the valuing of caring relationships described among us so well by Carol Gilligan.[4] Fear of rejection, pervasive among women in patriarchy, can be exacerbated among separatists. In this essay I examine this issue. I conclude that pluralism in separatist alliances leads to pluralism in the bases of separatism, both as a logical extension of separatist commitments and as a framework for constructive internal evaluation and growth.

What follows has four parts. Part I analyzes separatism, setting out variables that conceptually define it. Part II sup-

---

I benefited also from: Howard McGary, "Racial Integration and Racial Separatism: Conceptual Clarifications," in Leonard Harris, ed., *Philosophy Born of Struggle: Anthology of Afro-American Philosophy* from 1917 (Dubuque, IA: Kendall/Hunt, 1983), pp. 199-211; Raymond L. Hall, ed., *Black Separatism and Social Reality: Rhetoric and Reason* (New York: Pergamon, 1977); Arthur Hertberg, *The Zionist Idea* (New York: Atheneum, 1973); Ralph Barton Perry, *Puritanism and Democracy* (New York: Vangard, 1944).

I have been helped by comments from Terry Winant, Sharon Keller, Victoria Davion, Bat Ami Bar-On, Jeffner Allen, dykes attending the Burning Bush Midwest Lesbian Separatist Conference in Wisconsin, June 1988, and by encouragement from conferences of the Midwest Society of Women in Philosophy.

[2] See e.g., Hoagland, *ibid.*

[3] For skepticism on this issue, see The Combahee River collective, "A Black Feminist Statement," in Gloria T. Hull et al, eds., *All the Women Are White, All the Men Are Black; But Some of Us Are Brave: Black Women's Studies* (Feminist Press, 1982), *This Bridge Called My Back: Writings by Radical Women of Color*, ed. Cherrie Moraga and Gloria Anzaldua (Watertown, MA: Persephone, 1981), and "Racism and Classism in the Lesbian Community," *Top Ranking*, ed. Sara Bennett and Joan Gibbs (Brooklyn, N.Y.: Feb. 3rd Press, 1980).

[4] *In a Different Voice: Psychological Theory and Women's Development* (Cambridge, MA: Harvard, 1982).

ports separatism based on *oppression* rather than on *dissent*—two forms taken historically by oppositional separatisms, which suggest differing interpretations of lesbian separatism. Part III examines flexibility in withdrawal and connection as necessary for sensitivity to multiple sources and forms of oppression. Part IV considers difficulties for views in Parts II and III.

What is Separatism?

Current literature reveals no consensus about the meanings of and relationships between feminist and lesbian separatisms. Part of my object is to clarify that issue. I do not begin by defining either lesbian or feminist separatism. Rather, I look at structural possibilities and analogies.

From 17th C. Puritans to 20th C. Black Nationalists, separatists have united to resist oppressors.[5] Separating as an alternative to assimilating or integrating has been important to replacing hostile with friendly self-concepts. As Marilyn Frye has noted, separatism differs from segregation according to who initiates it and whose interests it serves: segregation is at the initiative of and in the service of oppressing or dominant groups; separation, a stance of political resistance, is at the initiative of and in the service of those oppressed or dominated.[6]

"Ism" words, like "separatism," carry a risk of carelessness of thought. Separatism is about many separations. Logically, separation is a relation. Relations are definable by variables. Separation has at least four important variables: (1) who is to separate, (2) from whom (suggesting, by implication, remaining affiliates), (3) kind(s) of connection to be severed, and (4) reasons for severing them. As these variables can be filled in differently, very different politics can equally be "separatist."

---

[5] Some—perhaps the Transcendentalists of Brook Farm—may simply have wanted a new beginning, free of distracting but not necessarily oppressive environments. Others, perhaps social sororities and fraternities, are not meant to be oppositional.

[6] Frye, *ibid.*

In controversy, we sometimes overlook the third vari-able—the severed connection—as though separating were "all or nothing." Since we are connected in many ways, how-ever, we can withdraw from some without withdrawing from all connections. We can (even must) also create new, different connections while withdrawing from old ones. Sep-aratists have always done this, established new connections on their own terms to maintain needed communications, defense, even economic exchanges.

The fourth variable—bases, grounds, or reasons—is most basic. It gives rationales in terms of which separations can be evaluated. Separatist movements tend to be named after the first variable—who is separating (as in black sepa-ratism or female separatism)—or the fourth, grounds of sep-aration (as in feminist separatism, Zionism, or Black Nation-alism). Menstrual huts may be female separatist, but it is questionable whether they are feminist. "Lesbian" in "les-bian separatism" sounds as though it names separators and, by implication, rejected connections. Racial separatisms have been distinguished by the third variable as "cultural," "economic," or "Political."[7] Contemporary feminist and les-bian separatist have found these categories misleading when they are treated as alternatives. For separations can have significant political implications which labels like "cul-tural" may disguise.[8] Still, there is a significant variable here—kinds of ties to be broken—whether or not "cultural" and "economic" are useful categories.

Feminist separatism has similarities to the labor union movement. Both are resistance movements. Neither is a nationalism. Each aims to empower an oppressed majority. The labor union movement is not ordinarily described as

---

[7] See, e.g., McGary, *ibid.* and Hall, *ibid.* for discussion of such distinctions among black separatists in the U.S.

[8] Some recent critics of lesbian and feminist separatism do apply those labels to sug-gest that the separations in question are not really or adequately political. Lori Saxe (U. WI-Madison, Dept. Philosophy) has responded to some of these critics in "The New Radical Feminist Attack on Lesbian Feminism," presented to the Mid-west Society of Women in Philosophy Fall Conference, 1985, Carbondale, Illinois.

"separatist." Its separations are not geographical but they are integral to healing the laborer's alienation from self. Such separations are central for feminists also: realignment of loyalties, redefining of identity apart from oppressive roles, acquisition of integrity and generation of energy for projects supportive of oneself and of good personal relationships.

Fundamental to feminism have been separations of women from men, not of feminists from non-feminists, nor even of separatists from non-separatists. In practice this is not obvious; separatism *has* divided feminists from non-feminists and separatists from non-separatists. Yet, not all women whose separations from men are supported on feminist grounds are themselves feminist; many are antifeminist domestic and sex industry workers. Feminist separatism, Black Nationalism, and Zionism have in common that they refer to *grounds* of separation, not to believers in those grounds.

The objections of some critics are really to separatisms identified simply by naming separators. When it is objected, for example, that women of color have more in common with *men* suffering racial oppression than with middle class white *women*, "feminist separatism" may be (mis)interpreted simply as "female separatism." So understood, it can be antifeminist. Critics have labeled it female supremacist, elitist, exacerbating the alienation of people of color in the U.S. from their histories and cultures, and, more recently, essentialist about the concept "woman."

However, feminist and lesbian separatist philosophers— such as Jeffner Allen, Marilyn Frye, Sarah Hoagland, Joyce Trebilcot—have understood separatism not in terms of separators and separatees but in terms of *grounds or bases*, leaving room for argument and interpretation regarding its forms.[9] Different grounds give different interpretations of lesbian separatism.

The next section examines two such interpretations. They are not clearly distinguished in the literature or in common parlance. Yet they seem implied by positions lesbians have

---

[9] See Note #1.

taken regarding affiliations to be welcomed and affirmed. On one interpretation, "lesbian" refers to those whose separations are supported and to possible affiliates, suggesting that *being lesbian*—defined by one's commitments, beliefs, and values—is the basis of separation and affiliation. On the other interpretation, "lesbian" describes *grounds* of separation, without identifying whose separations are supported or who are possible affiliates. It leaves open the possibility that the latter need not be believers who identify themselves as "lesbian." The first interpretation exemplifies *separatism based on dissent*. The second allows for a *separatism based on oppression* but not on dissent.

Separatism Based on Dissent vs. Separatism Based on Oppression

When separatism is based on dissent, the dissenting beliefs and practices define an identity which separatists aim to cultivate. Worthiness to affiliate is proved by dissent from the establishment in practice and belief. Dissent need not be the *only* basis of separation; indeed, if I am right, it cannot be. But being a dissenter is crucial to justifying separation or affiliation.

By contrast, separatism based on oppression supports separation of the oppressed, regardless of their beliefs or practices, although it also aims to raise consciousness among the oppressed. Many of those oppressed are politically oblivious of their history. Many, perhaps most, are not political dissenters, for oppression hinders dissent. Separatists may believe *all* the oppressed should separate from others, for a variety of reasons including that separate space facilitates political consciousness. This belief has consequences for loyalty alignments.

In advocating separation on the basis of oppression we identify neither those whose separation we advocate nor those from whom we advocate separation by their individual beliefs or practices but, rather, identify both by their relationships to a history of oppression. Since these relationships are not altogether within individual control, such separations may seem to the liberal mind unfair. But they are defended as necessary or effective for empowering the oppressed and for ending complicity in oppressive practices.

Let me try to forestall a misunderstanding. Unless we are dissenters, we will (probably) not be *attracted to* political separatism, though we may be curious about it. Separating usually *expresses* dissent; dissent is a *motive* to separate. This does not imply that *being a dissenter* is a *ground*, i.e., a justifying reason, for the separation. Grounds are contained in dissenting beliefs, if they are sound. But *holding* such beliefs is not thereby itself a ground. Grounds are the facts of oppression (which separatists believe) and certain values (which the separatist holds), but not the fact of holding either beliefs or values. Separatists may be ready to affiliate with the oppressed, whether they are believers or not.

In Western history, not only Puritanism but Christianity, generally, is a paradigm of separatism based on dissent. Lesbian separatism based on dissent may exhibit unwittingly a christian cultural bias. The purpose of dissent-based separation has been to create an environment for expressing and exploring dissenting beliefs and practices, free of interference from traditionalists. "Interference" ranges from the blatant—outright prohibition and penalization—to the subtle, such as putting a damper on activities. Sheer lack of support "interferes" when it acts as a damper. Thus whoever is not "for" may be perceived as "against."

Many feminist and lesbian separatists, however, have supported separations not on the basis of individually espoused beliefs but on the basis of socially inherited relationships to institutions with histories of oppression and domination. Superficially, we may appear to support separations on the basis of things utterly beyond anyone's control, such as gender, skin color, or ethnic heritage. Our separations can thus appear superficially to be based on femaleness rather than on a feminist analysis of history. We have been considered bigots, unable to appreciate or relate to diversity in humanity, in being wrongly assumed to be female supremacists. Because *oppressive* practices have used gender, race, and ethnic heritage as criteria marking the subordinate, those characteristics have become important to resisters for identifying the oppressed. Such traits, however, do not answer the question why separation is desirable. Femaleness is not the *basis* of feminist separatism; the bases are feminist understandings of the histories of sexual politics.

Nonseparatist critics commonly fear that separatism would be just another oppressive supremacism, if the power were there. My concern about separatist "correctness" is not about supremacism; it has different origins. Female supremacy no more follows from our capacity for endurance than male supremacy follows from men's capacity for domination. Supremacism is, in any case, implausible as an *origin* of oppression. Belief in male supremacy is a likely *consequence* of male domination, which *then* enters into its maintenance.[10] Belief in male intellectual and military supremacy follows easily upon a long history of intellectual and military training for men only. Denying women physical and intellectual educations, rewarding us for ingratiating, servile behavior while treating our anger as insane, produces visibly inferior female physiques and intellects. The truth in the suspicion that separatists are supremacists is that separatists are often visibly competent at maintenance, repairs, construction, and other tasks that patriarchy routinely forbids women and assigns to men. Refusing to depend on men, we have had to develop that competence. This is a far cry from "natural superiority." There are different reasons for *separatists* to worry about separatistism, reasons centering on attitudes toward dissent.

Commonly, all women are welcomed to *feminist* separatist events, which are billed "for women only," not "for feminists

---

[10] Some men grant the "natural superiority" of women to justify imposing extra burdens. Ashley Montagu's *The Natural Superiority of Women* glorifies endurance. Cf. Michele Wallace's "The Myth of the Superwoman," *Black Macho and The Myth of the Superwoman* (New York: Dial, 1978).

only." The same is less generally true of *lesbian* separatism. Lesbian separatist events are often billed "for lesbians only," not "for women only." This practice treats being lesbian as a ground of separation. Yet in practice, all women may be welcomed to lesbian separatist events if only they self-identify as "lesbian." This suggests that "being lesbian" is understood as an individual choice of affiliation and loyalty. Such a lesbian feminist separatism, like Puritanism (and *un*like the labor union movement, Zionism, or Black Nationalism), is of *dissenters* rather than of an oppressed group as such.

If openness in practice to any woman willing to identify herself as lesbian is *not* simply an expedient for finding women with certain loyalties, what is fundamental may be not having certain beliefs but, more promisingly, certain potentialities and relationships to histories of oppression. So understood, lesbian separatism would have as a purpose nurturing and supporting the lesbian(s)—the women-lovers—in *all* women. This implies a readiness to entertain and explore divergent ideas about what it means to be lesbian, about who the woman-lovers in us are and how we do it, a readiness to affiliate with women who do not (yet) identify as lesbian, a readiness to respect and value other paradigms than the lesbian paradigm for woman-loving. "Lesbian" derives from Sappho of Lesbos (ca 600 B.C.E.), an influential paradigm of woman-loving in European cultures.[11] There are no doubt equally valuable paradigms yet to be discovered by many of us. A lesbian separatism with such flexibility would not be *based* on dissent, although it would dissent from what Jan Raymond has recently called "heteropatriarchy."[12] Such lesbian separatism would interpret feminist separatism by finding the devaluing of women's woman-loving a key factor in women's oppression.

---

[11] On the Sappho and other paradigms, see Elaine Marks, "Lesbian Intertextuality" in Elaine Marks and George Stambolian, eds., *Homosexualities and French Literature: Cultural Contexts/Critical Texts* (Ithaca, N.Y.: Cornell; 1979), pp. 353-377.

[12] Janice G. Raymond, *A Passion for Friends: Toward a Philosophy of Female Affection* (Boston: Beacon, 1986).

On the other hand, when lesbian feminists concerned to separate from nonlesbian women, as well as from men, base their separations and affiliations on the lesbian commitment to loving women, there is a circle. If lesbianism so understood were the *only* basis of the separation, the question would arise whether that separation ultimately had a basis. For, on what basis is *any* lesbian committed to loving women?

In determining loyalties by belief and practice, dissent-based separatism interferes with the growth of belief and practice by inhibiting constructive critique and correction from within. Critics risk exclusion from separatist communities for dissenting from the dissenters, for not being a "true dissenter"—a "true feminist," a "real lesbian." Loyalty is better grounded in character, interests, histories, and mutual benefits than in something as fluid and, hopefully, growing, as political beliefs and practices. Loyalty based on shared belief and practice is more useful for temporary battles than satisfying in a deep way. As an ethical response, loyalty is based on gratitude and love. While beliefs and practices are not irrelevant to one's ability to love another, they are not sufficient nor even the most important things. More important is who others are, which is only partly captured by their beliefs—at least, by what they would sincerely report as their beliefs—at given times in their lives.

Separation based on dissent is not without ethical attractions, however. Feminist separation on the basis of oppression presents certain moral and political problems which separation on the basis of dissent may seem to solve. Women are oppressed not only as women and not only by men but also as people of color, as Jewish, as lesbian, as poor, fat, disabled, and by women. Women's roles in oppressive practices are not always reducible to that of the token torturer serving men.[13] Therefore, it can seem irrational to ally ourselves with only and all women. But it also seems self-defeating to try to

---

[13]Some have thought Mary Daly's point in discussing "token torturers" in Gyn/Ecology: *The Metaethics of Radical Feminism* (Boston: Beacon, 1979)—though she does not say so—was that women hurt women only in serving men.

avoid aligning ourselves with anyone who has participated in or stands to benefit from oppression. Carrying the latter to its logical conclusion would require turning against ourselves. And turning against ourselves is, after all, part of the problem, not the solution. Separation based on dissent may appear the logical solution. Since none of us can be confident of being altogether free of oppressive beliefs or practices or of not having benefited from such things, owing to histories pre-existing us that helped make us who we are, it may seem that the logical basis for alignment *is* shared belief and practice with respect to the stances that we can take now regarding such matters. That, at any rate, is something over which we have some control. It seems in this respect "fair."

However, this reasoning leaves untouched an inconsistency in the hybrid of a dissent-based lesbian separatism which is also feminist. The *feminist* part of the separation is *not* based on dissent; it is a separation of *women* from men, regardless of individual beliefs and practices of either. Only by such separations does the lesbian in us have much chance of surfacing with robustness. But if it were then justifiable to move *to* dissent as a basis for separation *among* women—to separate actual from potential lesbians—the question should arise why it would not be justifiable to *begin* with dissent as the basis for separation, with the result that some men would undoubtedly be included among "feminist separatists" on the basis of their beliefs and practice. If it is not justifiable to *begin* with separation based on dissent, on what basis is it justifiable to *move to* dissent in the case of lesbian separatism? If we maintain that it is a history of oppression, not one's lesbianism as such, that is the *basis* of separatism, such a move seems irrational. For women's refusals or inabilities to cherish the women-lovers in themselves can be construed as evidence of their oppression.

Zionism, Black Nationalism, the labor union movement, and most feminist separations based on oppression rather than on dissent have survived internal diversity of goals. Still, however pluralistic, no political theme is likely to be adequate to all our political concerns. Environmental and nuclear crises may require us to depart form separatism, compromise it or supplement it with other strategies.[14] Further, political separatism based on oppression seems logically committed, other things equal, to taking seriously separatist resistance to any kind of oppression for which such resistance is potentially important. Appreciating multiple forms of oppression indicates that separatists should be flexible enough to compromise for the sake of other equally justified separations.

As with anything valuable, there is a price for such flexibility. The price is some of the sense of security that comes with homogeneity in expectations. Sources of discomfort worth accepting, however, are at the same time resources for political resistance. Separatist space must offer support, but it may frequently not be cozy or reassuring

Separatism and Pluralism

It may be possible to separate with respect to many kinds of oppression if, instead of focussing on "from whom?" we think more about "from what kinds of connections?" and "why?," "with what aims in view?" To put it in terms of Part I above, instead of focussing on the first and second variables—separators, allies, and separatees—we do better to focus on the third and fourth variables, which are more basic: kinds of ties to sever and reasons to do so. We need to clarify the ties that have defined our oppressions and take seriously the task of inventing non-oppressive connections to people who would otherwise stand to benefit, by way of more traditional ties, from our oppression. Marilyn Frye argued a decade ago that a major point of separating from men is to gain control of our own accessibility.[15] If so, connections with men where we have such control may be consistent with, even necessary to, separatist goals.

---

[14] See Trebilcot, *ibid,* and Hoagland, *ibid.*
[15] Frye, *ibid.*

Just as unionizing redefines and formalizes a once relatively intimate, informal relationship serving employers at
the expense of employees, feminist sisterhood has the potential to redefine and formalize what have been highly intimate
and relatively informal connections of women to men that
have served men at women's expense. The procreative connection changes dramatically, for example, when severed
from erotic intimacy.

There is also potential to invent new informal connections. Nonsexual, nonintimate friendships and work-defined
connections between women and gay men may be nonop-
pressive and potentially resistant to both homophobia and
misogyny. Interracial friendships and work-defined connections regardless of gender may hold a similar potential for
resisting racism and misogyny.

I do not refer here to coalitions. Coalitions are formal
relationships among groups. Coalitions among parties very
unequal in power are not promising. I refer to connections
between individuals, not groups. If friendship is not basically a power relationship (not grounded, that is, on a distribution of what Sarah Hoagland has called "power over"), as I
believe it is not, inequality in political power between friends
may not be disastrous, depending on the social context nour-
ishing the friendship.[16]

The most difficult question of loyalty presents itself as
the question who can form *intimate* alliances that do not
undermine their participants. Where the question is intimate
relationships, "who" is at least as basic as "why." Whom can
we love without doing ourselves in? If we can love ourselves, we should be able to love others whose beliefs and
practices have been politically disappointing, provided they
have a certain depth of character, and provided their political
connections do not nullify our own resistance. Character is
indicated not only by beliefs and practices but, more importantly, by habits of attitude and response *to* beliefs and prac-

---

[16] See Sarah Hoagland, *Lesbian Ethics* (Palo Alto: Institute of Lesbian Studies, 1988).

tices. The requisite depth of character consists in having developed certain "higher order character traits," traits responding to other aspects of oneself.[17] An example is the humility that consists in appreciating that we have formerly rejected as mistaken or biased beliefs to which we were once committed and that in the future we may feel that way about some of our present beliefs. This is not a false humility that consists in assuming ourselves unworthy of anything important or valuable. It is a humility that appreciates workroom for diversity and dissent, an important virtue for separatists, for it may prevent degeneration into separatism based on dissent. Many who possess it may be worthy intimate allies, despite disagreement in belief and practice.

Some Difficulties

I have argued that separations are justifiable not by the holding of certain beliefs but by histories of oppressive relationships. Worthy allies are better identified by individual character, not reducible to a set of beliefs and somewhat up to the person, and by the person's relationship to oppressive institutions and practices, not entirely within individual control. How these factors are to be balanced is something I have not taken up. One's character is related to one's history in complex and interesting ways.

Basing separatism on oppression, rather than on dissent, also raises questions regarding problematic relationships to a history of oppression. Passing is one such widely discussed case. There is also, however, something like its converse. Some become targets of oppression through problematic or inaccurate identification. Children of non-Jewish mothers and children of fathers with Jewish surnames may become targets of anti-Semitism, regardless how they are recognized

---

[17] I use the term "higher order character traits" by analogy with and generalization from Harry Frankfurt's "second-order desires" in "Freedom of the Will and the Concept of a Person," *The Journal of Philosophy* LXVIII: 1 (Jan. 4, 1971). Similarly, Gabriele Taylor refers to integrity as a "higher order virtue" in *Proceedings of the Aristotelian Society*, Supp. Vol. 55 (1980-81), 143-157.

by those whose Jewish identity is unproblematic. Women overtly rejecting femininity may find themselves targets of homophobia. For separatist purposes, what is the status of such individuals?

A more serious problem, however, presents itself for the idea that separatism is not well-grounded on dissent. Not basing separatism on dissent seems to require not relying heavily on consensus as decision procedure in separatist communities. Yet consensus has become a central part of contemporary separatist attempts to abandon hierarchies. The difficulty is that consensus seems to have only two ways of dealing with dissenters: convert them or exclude them. I have argued that it is important to do neither, that room for dissent is necessary to the process of constructive self evaluation and correction. How, then, can we keep from opening the door to a "separatism" which is no longer distinguished from assimilationism? Ready to unite with all women, regardless of their beliefs and practices, since they too are victims of oppression, how can we develop and maintain identities resistant to those men have created for women? For many women support the latter, even claiming authorship of them for themselves.

Perhaps the distinction between separatism based on oppression and separatism based on dissent is not sharp. The other side of feminist separatism is sisterhood. But how can we unite without common commitments, at least, the commitment to resisting oppression? If a point of separating is to achieve greater strength through union for political resistance, do we not need to agree which institutions are oppressive and are to be resisted?

The objection is more clearly put in terms of values. A major reason for establishing separatist space is to encourage values supportive of those who inherit a history of oppression. Beliefs significantly ground values. Values are exhibited in practice. How, then, can separatism based on oppression not also be based on dissent—dissent regarding the values of the oppressive culture? Separatists work to establish alternative social environments, practices, and relationships, based on values alternative to those embodied in oppressive institutions. Is this possible without consensus on basic values to be implemented in the alternatives?

Must we all, then, be vegetarian, pacifist, drug-free, opposed to competition, anti-hierarchical, in favor of circles, committed to promiscuity with women, and free of the parochialism of erotic arousal? Is this too specific? These values are not peripheral to analyses of women's oppression.

Can we be sure our analyses of misogyny and oppression are undistorted by cultural biases? Perhaps what we need as separatists is some (indefinite) members of a *family* of attitudes, beliefs, and values, whose members are related by what Wittgenstein called a "family resemblance," rather than by possession of some common denominator.[18] Such looseness might allow enough "workroom" for the dissension involved in self evaluation and correction.

At an abstract level, some consensus may be needed. Perhaps, for example, we need consensus on the value of questioning received ideas, including the idea of consensus itself. Separatist space is also important to repairing and rebuilding self-esteem, and for undoing the damage of gas-lighting.[19] We need to be valued not only for what we can do for others. These goals may require consensus on the importance of valuing each other for ourselves.

However, the very naming of lesbian separatism suggests consensus on matters more specific. I favor understanding lesbian separatism as based on a feminist identification of the

---

[18] Ludwig Wittgenstein, *Philosophical Investigations I,* trans. G.E.M. Anscombe (Oxford: Blackwell, 1958), pars. 65-70 (pp. 31-33).

[19] See Florence Rush, "The Freudian Cover-Up: The Sexual Abuse of Children," *Chrysalis* #1, 31-45, esp. 31, reprinted as ch. 7 of Florence Rush, *The Best Kept Secret: The Sexual Abuse of Children* (Englewood Cliffs, N.J.: Prentice Hall, 1980), for the verb "gaslighting" after the movie *Gaslight* (1944), in which a husband attempts to drive his wife mad (to gain control of her money) by making the gaslights flicker and letting her think she is hallucinating. Rush used "gaslighting" to describe Freud's decision that women reporting memories of childhood sexual abuse were exhibiting wish-fulfillment fantasies, since he admitted in his correspondence with Fliess that he lacked empirical evidence that their reports were literally false.

devaluing of women's woman-loving as a key factor in women's oppression. But what are the implications of the idea that lesbian separatism can be *committed to a certain view* regarding the oppression of women?

Lesbian separatists so identifying themselves are so committed. Yet this does not imply that everyone with whom it is good to affiliate shares the belief. Certain beliefs inspire separatist alternatives. Lesbian separatism may name the inspiration without being committed to alliances with only those so inspired or to welcoming only them into separatist space. Lesbianism is about cherishing women and the women-lover in women. It is important to love women who have not learned to cherish the women-lover in themselves. Being so loved is probably the best catalyst of such learning.

The dissent issue is related to other issues for a pluralist lesbian separatism. Separation is not sufficient for woman-loving, even if separate space is needed for its cultivation. Even if we each first loved a woman, woman-loving does not now spring up wherever men are absent. It was not just "a woman" we each first loved, but a woman with a culture, ethnicity, and value-orientation. How much of our mothers' particularities, not to mention peculiarities, do we import into our own woman-loving? We need to learn each other's histories, languages, perspectives, values, and habits, before we know how to love each other well. This requires readiness to respect much that appears to be dissent, readiness to listen, experiment, re-evaluate, to live with what is unfamiliar and therefore not always comfortable. Getting to know each other is also getting to know ourselves, discovering, in the mirrors we can be for each other, selves we did not know we had.[20] Consensus on the value of such learning supports alertness to premature expectations of consensus elsewhere.

---

[20] Lugones, "The Logic of Pluralist Feminism."

For The Love Of Separatism

ANNA LEE

Separatism is focusing on each other as lesbians and minimizing the energy given to males. In focusing on lesbians I am including all lesbians who choose to focus on lesbians. The previous two statements are the intent of separatism. Obviously, the diversity among us is not a given, but it is also a fact that the lesbian community is more diverse than any other existing community. While it is important not to romanticize the lesbian community, we too often denigrate our accomplishments and intentions. The lesbian community continues to seek to enhance our interactions so that lesbian diversity occurs. I will return to what blocks that diversity later in my discussion.

In terms of my definition of separatism, I embraced the theory very slowly. Over a number of years, I gradually began to understand and accept separatism, while other separatists accepted separatism almost simultaneously with coming out. I also have heard that the separatist lifestyle was adopted by some prefeminist lesbians. While this community adopted the lifestyle, from my observations, ideological justification or theory was not important to prefeminist lesbians. All of this is to say that my journey is not necessarily true for other post-feminist lesbian separatists or the same kind of separatism practiced by prefeminist lesbians.My journey is mine with my perceptions of others' journeys.

I came out in 1969 believing that my loving a woman was happenstance and our love for each other was no different than heterosexual loving. At the same time, to say I loved a woman because she was a woman was too "queer".[1] The queerness of loving women in part explained my wish to believe that homosexuality was no different than heterosexuality. In 1969, no one was talking about women loving women, information was hard to find and the analysis was pretty unsophisticated. While the sixties are perceived as a free, loving and liberating period, it is often forgotten, if the observer had even once noticed, that free-love and liberation was male focused and directed. Women were the objects. Even though loving a woman was a radical departure from the predominant "predator"[2] heterosexual relations existing in the sixties, lesbian identification was outside of the constraints imposed by hip males. As I said, loving a woman because she was a woman was too queer. In addition to the silence around women loving women in the sixties, interracial relationships were becoming tolerable but not quite acceptable. As a black woman I loved a white woman. It would be four more years before *Rubyfruit Jungle*, which celebrated coming out gay and depicted an interracial relationship as acceptable although not as lovers, was published by Daughters in 1973.

I stepped into that void in a small midwestern town with four other queers. And we believed we were the only ones in the land. In fact, we felt we had attained nirvana and others were not as enlightened as we were, which explained why heterosexuals exhibited so much self hatred by choosing partners unlike themselves. Nineteen years later Katherine Forrest would write a short story describing homosexuals as possessing intelligence, sensitivity and creativity. The heterosexuals no longer had those characteristics so they were

---

[1] Julia Penelope, "The Mystery of Lesbians", *Lesbian Ethics* (Vol 1 No. 2). While Julia discusses how her overt lesbianism made her the target for anti-lesbian violence, it was not fear of violence which made me reluctant to use the word queer. It was, however, the fear of moving beyond the pale of male-defined acceptable beliefs.

[2] Sarah Lucia Hoagland, *Lesbian Ethics: Toward New Value* (Palo Alto: Institute of Lesbian Studies 1988). Sarah expands her concept of predator-protector in the above mentioned book.

becoming extinct. The homosexuals explained to each other that the knowledge that heterosexuals were becoming extinct was the reason that heterosexuals had persecuted homosexuals throughout our history.[3]

Believing we were superior to heterosexuals led me to my next step. That step was the realization that I loved my lover (a different woman from the first) because she was a woman. The idea of separating from males was totally foreign to me. While I believed that it was significant that I loved a woman because she was a woman, I believed that my love for a woman was no different than a woman's love for a man. The early D.O.B. (Daughters of Bilitis) sought toleration for female homosexuals, even encouraging lesbians to dress in drag. In this case, drag meant dressing as if lesbians were heterosexual feminine women. D.O.B. argued that female homosexuals needed to make ourselves acceptable to heterosexuals through dress and behavior. In the early seventies, D.O.B., and particularly its publication, *The Ladder*, had begun to question the female role and to use the word lesbian. Coincidentally, as *The Ladder* became independent from D.O. B. the use of the word lesbian became more acceptable and in fact the norm. Even though *The Ladder* had exhibited radical change, the context in my small midwestern town in which I came out was more similar to the civil rights approach advocated by D.O.B. in the early fifties.

The feeling of homosexual superiority was just beginning in the early seventies, but the predominant trend was the pleas for toleration and acceptance from heterosexuals. It is important to note that ability to resist is in part dependent on the context within which one finds herself. For example, if a feminist or visible lesbian community had existed, I would have perceived myself as a follower of those who had preceded me instead of a pathfinder who had to make it (whatever it was at that moment) up as I went along. The context is only a part of the ability to resist heterosexual domination.

---

[3] Katherine V. Forrest, "The Test", *Dreams and Swords* (The Naiad Press Inc. 1987), pp. 167-177.

The other part is the individual wherewithal to resist "normalcy".[4] I believe this is the reason so many lesbians call it a miracle that any of us were able to come out.

So not having a social context or political analysis which challenged my search for toleration from heterosexuals or my acceptance that heterosexuality was the norm by which all relationships were judged, I continued to fall in and out of love for a number of years. I certainly had a fledgling feminist consciousness, but the way I participated in relationships as lover and friend was not examined. When I moved to the east coast, a whole new world opened for me.

I met white socialists versus the black nationalists and socialists with whom I had interacted. It was the late seventies and I was amazed that a whole group of people could write pages and pages of, and speak in, marxist rhetoric. I thought that that rhetorical ability was limited to the college radicals I had known. With concentrated effort, I could only do a few sentences and then would forget what the point was. I had a larger group to observe as I attended Worker's World party meetings. I noticed some characteristics similar to the black nationalists and socialists. One obviously was the speaking in tongues or jargon. Two, the leadership was primarily male and the women concerned themselves with women's issues and the recruiting of women. I had many lively arguments with my lover at the time and my friend from the midwest who had also moved to the east coast. I didn't have any political analysis for this, but I knew something was wrong. I mentioned to my lover that Worker's World Party discussed rape only in terms of black males being unfairly accused. We both agreed that black males were disproportionately accused, prosecuted and convicted. We disagreed about the significance of women always being disbelieved about our experiences. She believed that when the class revolution occurred then women would not be

---

[4] Ruston, Bev Jo, and Linga Strega, "Heterosexism Causes Lesbophobia Causes Butch-phobia Part II of the Big Sell-Out: Lesbian femininity", *Lesbian Ethics* (Vol 2 No 2), pp. 22-43.

raped or forced to accept a subservient role at any time. She held this belief even though all the significant roles were performed by males within the Party. I had seen this same refusal to define relationships between males and females as harmful within the black nationalist movement. I would later learn that mixed groups encourage the women to believe that our issues are less important than the issues with which males are concerned.

My lover did introduce me to a feminist business and that allowed me to perceive the world from an entirely different perspective and gave me a context for the concerns I had about the various movements in which I had been involved. The feminist business was a context in which I could observe a world which was truly women identified. That women identification encouraged my examination of relationships with women and engendered me to refocus away from male actions.

The group who ran the feminist business valued women. Each woman in the group believed that women's work and ideas were important. They wanted a woman owned, operated and identified collective. There were mistakes made, but their intent was to create a world of women who challenged, inspired and nourished themselves and other women. So in 1979, I embarked on my greatest adventure in which all of the things I had taken for granted were questioned. I had to rethink almost every assumption I had made about how the world operated and my part in it. I also had the opportunity to interact with other women, particularly lesbians, in a context which assumed that we could change the world, and our movement was growing. I had choices that I had never had.

The choices concerned both resistance to males and connection to women. At that time we defined women as lesbians. We never considered women who would want to involve males to be in our community. The lesbians, and the few straight women who were part of that community, considered women only space as a given. Women energy and relationships were primary for both groups. Separatism was valued by both groups. For the first time my political activities occurred in a women only context.

The issues that were seen as secondary by male dominated groups were examined as if our lives depended on it. In fact, our lives did depend on understanding the ways males sought to control us through violence against us. Male violence against women ranged, and ranges, from defining who we can be to killing us. Because males defined the acceptable way racism could be discussed, lesbian ability to develop anti racist postures was undermined. Our ability even to perceive racism between women was minimal. Racism was concerned with black males as if black women did not exist.

Big Mama Rag, a now defunct newspaper, argued that women should support national liberation struggles. Women should support national liberation struggles even though the males who participate in them defined women's issues as secondary to the liberation of the country or community.[5] For a number of years and even today, the male-defined scope of racism has meant that if males, including black males, are excluded, then an act of racism has occurred. In 1987, a black male hit a white lesbian after she excluded him from viewing her sculpture at Sisterfire, an event described by the organizers as a celebration of women's culture. The organizers argued that the white lesbian had provoked the incident. As a result the organizers suggested that mutual violence had occurred. Their argument defines exclusion as violence and hitting as violence. Is there anything wrong with this equation? What is wrong with this equation is that racism is defined as the exclusion of black males. The white lesbian did exclude white males, but not black women, from viewing her sculpture. The organizers of Sisterfire ignored black women in their definition of racism and what counts as a

---

[5] Elaine Henrichs, "A Call To Resist", *Big Mama Rag* (May 1982). In her discussion of forming coalition with national liberation struggles, note the absence of women in the policy making bodies of those struggles. In addition, the traditional role of women in African countries is undermined or eliminated. When u.s. agriculture policy and national liberation struggles foster subservient roles for women, whose interest is being served?

racist act. *Big Mama Rag*, in a similar vein, had discounted the interest of noneuropean women in their advocacy of national liberation struggles. Whether it was the intent of *Big Mama Rag* or Sisterfire, the result is that women bonded with males under the guise of protecting nonwhite males. In fact, the following discussion will demonstrate that that bond was with white males.

The original radical analysis of rape by organizers of rape crisis centers was replaced with their acceptance, even desire, for police participation in preventing the crime of rape. Organizers of rape crisis centers eagerly sought police involvement even though police had never demonstrated a concern with or success in finding the male rapist of black women. The police, however, have shown a willingness to rape black women.[6] The police also had shown a very successful record of protecting white men from facing the penalties for their rapist acts. As I commented earlier, black males are disproportionately targeted to pay the penalty for the crime of rape. Who benefitted from police involvement with rape crisis centers? Not black women. Not black men. But white males did benefit. While white feminists' agenda may not have been articulated, their desire to bond with white males was not unnoticed. In the example of Sisterfire, the organizers' claim is that coalition building is important and essential. The coalition building is the bonding with males who numerically are white males.

Another example of the bond between white lesbians and white males is the almost wholehearted endorsement of the need to support males dying of AIDS. As Jeannette Silveira pointed out to me in a conversation, she considers the support for AIDS as the litmus test for separatism. Although a number of white lesbians, both separatist and nonseparatist, believe that aids is important and women should be involved in that struggle, I would agree with Silveira that AIDS is not a separatist issue. It is true that black males and females die from AIDS. It is not true that AIDS is transmitted through the

---

[6] A conversation with Lee Evans.

air we breathe or the water we drink. It is transmitted through sexual contact with someone who has AIDS and through blood exchange with someone who has AIDS. Because of the ways AIDS is transmitted, lesbians are a low risk group. The problem is that the definition of lesbianism is diluted to include women who have sexual contact with men. If that definition is true, then what is a heterosexual woman?

Again it does not matter to me if the lumping together of heterosexual women and lesbians is intentional. What does concern me is the masking of white female-male bonding by claiming the reason AIDS is significant to women is that black women are dying from AIDS. Because black women are dying, then some lesbians say AIDS is a lesbian issue. This is not the first time that white women have used black women to advocate an agenda which results in a stronger bond between white women and men.

This bond between white women and white men is motivated by white women's desire for power for white women and white males' desire to recapture women's attentions, as I discuss in more depth in my paper on new age spirituality.[7] I have had to reexamine my relationship to black males. I'm not sure white women have examined their relationship to white men. I'm not sure because the bond between them goes unspoken, but exists and manifests itself in lots of ways, some of which I have already mentioned. I am very clear that my brothers hold the power of the penis. Any male, regardless of class, income or race, holds power in the world. Truly, some males have more control in the world than others, but each has, if nothing else, a woman or woman-substitute as his slave, i.e., wife, mother, girlfriend and so forth. A male, regardless of this status in the world, can exercise his power over at least one woman virtually without interference. A cursory examination of the statistics concerning males battering women or raping their daugh-

---

[7]Anna Lee, "New Age Spirituality Is the Invention of Heteropatriarchy." Unpublished paper given as a talk at the 1988 National Women's Studies Association as part of a panel on Lesbian Theory organized by Sarah Hoagland.

ters demonstrates these actions are seldom punished. At the same time, women and daughters who object to these male activities are severely penalized.[8]

What all of us, and especially white lesbians, must be clear about is the difference between power and privilege. Power-over is the necessary resources to decide what the outcome of a situation will be. Privilege, which is revokable, is the ability to carry out someone else's decisions and agenda. As long as someone else's decisions and agenda are followed, privilege can be wielded. White women have revokable privilege. When they serve white male interests, resources are made available to them. When they do not, the availability of resources decreases. When battered women's shelters hire openly out lesbians or make services available to lesbians who have been battered, funding from city, county, state or national government is cancelled. It is important to males that women be patched up and returned to them. It is not important to males that lesbians be patched up and returned to a lesbian battering situation.

White lesbians or feminists may know that the availability of resources is dependent upon making the male givers of the resources comfortable, or they may not want to examine the gift horse's mouth too closely. When certain actions result in predictable, consistent outcomes, then the actions must be examined and not the rhetoric. I'm still waiting for white women who have not examined their bond with white men and what that bond means to creating a diverse lesbian community to begin to consider that unacknowledged bond. The bond between white women and men currently is a stumbling clock to the creation of meaningful diversity.

The accepted definition of black culture is also a stumbling block. We as black lesbians are allowing black men to define the meaning of our blackness. While I will specifically discuss the need for black lesbians to promote our own defi-

---

[8] Note the discussion of the Karen Newson case in *Off Our Backs* (October 1988), pg. 3. Karen Newson went to jail for six weeks to attempt to protect her child from being sexually assaulted by her father. The father was awarded custody of the child.

nitions of blackness, I believe all of our communities of origin need to be examined for the female centeredness of each community in order to determine what qualities we can bring to the lesbian community that enhance lesbian value.

Within the black community, I grew up with strong women role models. These models were not lesbian, but the women understood that their survival was dependent on their ability to move through the world without a male intermediary. They knew that they could not depend on males. Black women in my community created networks in which we could call on each other. It did not surprise me that the women around me encouraged me to rely upon myself or believed in me. What those strong black women nourished in me was a strong egoism, an egoism sufficient to survive in a world which would not necessarily look kindly upon me, a world which too often hated me. That black female community taught me loyalty to myself and to others. It also taught me to face the truth. For not only would the truth set me free, it would also insure my survival. Of course if I didn't like the truth I found, then I should change that truth and not pretend it didn't exist. Middle class pretensions were reserved for those who could afford them. Middle class pretensions would not save my hide.

Even though most of us grew up with strong black female models, even though we learned that we could never be white and therefore acceptable, we have refused to take black lesbian interactions seriously. We deny our female centeredness and get caught up with accepting black male definitions of blackness. Instead of defining us for ourselves, we use the male norm to evaluate our blackness. The closer an activity or performance is to black males, the more the activity or performance is seen as black. In a conversation, a sister supported the black muslims even though she could not be one herself and even though the black muslims insist that women be subordinate to men. In another conversation, a sister pereived a black woman who performed from a heterosexual position as more professional than an openly black lesbian who performed in a woman identified context. In each case black lesbians were not valued. It is a common world view among oppressed groups that what we create among ourselves is not really worth having and lacks the professionalism and validity that is exhibited by the oppressor and his lackeys.

Black lesbians reject whites defining who we can be, but accept black males defining who we can be. Until we can value what we create, we will not exist except in the distorted house of mirrors at the carnival. Since we have not seriously considered our position in the world as black lesbians, we too often become more concerned with our appearances than with our minds or developing a political analysis that begins with us, a political analysis which places black lesbians central to understanding the world or our relationship to the world. I am certainly not suggesting that black lesbians are mindless or do not think. What I am suggesting is that the definitions of who we are have not been created by us. We have some hard work ahead of us. It is necessary we do that work.

Separating from black males is scary. It is scary because we are stepping into a void. it is a void through which even the strong black women role models we have known cannot help us. The strong black women can help provide an impetus to seek our answers, but not the answer itself. The creation of ourselves can be exciting. Excitement, by its very nature, is leaving the familiar and comfortable. Bernice Reagon has suggested that coalition work is difficult because we must go beyond the safety of being comfortable. In fact, coalition work resembles our community of origins inasmuch as males are valued members of the coalitions she wants to create. It is creating lesbian community which is unfamiliar to us, or at least to most of us, since very few of us grew up in a lesbian context. Coalition work is a return to what is known.

We face this void named lesbian centrality with only the barest hint of how to create it. We have made some serious mistakes and we will probably make many more. Yet it is within the context of lesbian separatism that we have achieved our greatest accomplishments. We have created spaces to know each other. We have developed an analysis which utilizes lesbians as the basis. We have acknowledged our differences and sought to validate our various ablisms. We have created economic lesbian networks. We have developed lesbian skills in carpentry, music, production, printing, selling, and so forth. These abilities, skills, analyses have flourished in a lesbian context. We have surpassed our wildest dreams.

Our dreams are not ashes, but we must continue to develop new dreams and vistas. The next step must address how we interact with intimates. By intimates I am suggesting that we examine all of our relationships, for lesbian community is no more than how we relate with each other. I hope our lesbian community never becomes so institutionalized that we as individuals do not have to contribute anything for it to continue. Once community becomes institutionalized it becomes fossilized. Something fossilized is unable to nourish the joy of creation. It just is. It is unchangeable and unchanging. It is dead.

Lesbian community is a community of intimates, a diverse collection of intimates. That is our greatest challenge. It is our challenge to establish intimacy with those who grew up different from us. Even within groups whose members could be classified as similar to ourselves, there will be differences among us. So each of us must stretch herself to value differences in intimate relationships. It is fairly easy to value differences from afar. It is much harder to include differences in our intimate circles. It is even harder to seek out those who are different because we need those differences in our own lives in order to grow, to be challenged, and to create values we have not dreamed.

Note

While this paper is loosely based on "A Black Separatist," which is published in the separatist anthology, *For Lesbians Only* (Onlywomen Press), I have retitled this paper to minimize confusion with the revised version appearing in the anthology. I want to thank Jeannette Silveira for giving me a chance to substantially change that earlier paper. I had wanted to do so for the anthology, but time and money constraints prevented this from occurring. I want to thank the many lesbians who have encouraged me over the years to rethink some of my analysis. I want to thank Tara Ayres who loves me enough to continue to argue with me even when I am my most stubborn. I want to thank Julia Penelope and Sarah Hoagland for continually inspiring me by their writing and their willingness to critique my writing. I want to thank Lee Evans who listened to my ranting and raving and offered helpful suggestions that pulled me from my dilemmas. Finally I want to thank Noel Furie, Selma Miriam, Betsey Beaven, and Denslow Brown, who have always challenged me to explore further what separatism means to me. Of course, I take responsibility for the arguments found in this essay.

DIS / CONNECTIONS

Playfulness, "World"-Travelling, and Loving Perception

MARÍA LUGONES

This paper weaves two aspects of life together. My coming to consciousness as a daughter and my coming to consciousness as a woman of color have made this weaving possible. This weaving reveals the possibility and complexity of a pluralistic feminism, a feminism that affirms the plurality in each of us and among us as richness and as central to feminist ontology and epistemology.

The paper describes the experience of 'outsiders' to the mainstream of, for example, White/Anglo organization of life in the U.S. and stresses a particular feature of the outsider's existence: the outsider has necessarily acquired flexibility in shifting from the mainstream construction of life where she is constructed as an outsider to other constructions of life where she is more or less 'at home.' This flexibility is necessary for the outsider but it can also be willfully exercised by the outsider or by those who are at ease in the mainstream. I recommend this willful exercise which I call "world"-travelling and I also recommend that the willful exercise be animated by an attitude that I describe as playful.

As outsiders to the mainstream, women of color in the U.S. practice "world"-travelling, mostly out of necessity. I affirm this practice as a skillful, creative, rich, enriching and, given certain circumstances, as a loving way of being and living. I recognize that much of our travelling is done unwillfully to hostile White/Anglo "worlds." The hostility of these "worlds" and the compulsory nature of the "travelling" have obscured for us the enormous value of this aspect of our living and its connection to loving. Racism has a vested interest in obscuring and devaluing the complex skills involved in it. I recommend that we affirm this travelling across "worlds" as partly constitutive of cross-cultural and cross-racial loving. Thus I recommend to women of color in the U.S. that we learn to love each other by learning to travel to each other's "worlds."

On the other hand, the paper makes a connection between what Marilyn Frye has named "arrogant perception" and the failure to identify with persons that one views arrogantly or has come to see as the products of arrogant perception. A further connection is made between this failure of identification and a failure of love, and thus between loving and identifying with another person. The sense of love is not the one Frye has identified as both consistent with arrogant perception and as promoting unconditional servitude. "We can be taken in by this equation of servitude with love," Frye (1983, 73) says, "because we make two mistakes at once: we think, of both servitude and love that they are selfless or unselfish." Rather, the identification of which I speak is constituted by what I come to characterize as playful "world"-travelling. To the extent that we learn to perceive others arrogantly or come to see them only as products of arrogant perception and continue to perceive them that way, we fail to identify with them—fail to love them—in this particular way.

Identification and Love

As a child, I was taught to perceive arrogantly. I have also been the object of arrogant perception. Though I am not a White/Anglo woman, it is clear to me that I can understand both my childhood training as an arrogant perceiver and my having been the object of arrogant perception without any reference to White/Anglo men, which is some indication that the concept of arrogant perception can be used cross-culturally and that White/Anglo men are not the only arrogant perceivers. I was brought up in Argentina watching men and women of moderate and of considerable means graft the substance[1] of their servants to themselves. I also learned to graft my mother's substance to my own. It was clear to me that both men and women were the victims of arrogant perception and that arrogant perception was systematically organized to break the spirit of all women and of most men. I valued my rural 'gaucho' ancestry because its ethos has always been one of independence in poverty through enormous loneliness, courage and self-reliance. I found inspiration in this ethos and committed myself never to be broken by arrogant perception. I can say all of this in this way only because I have learned from Frye's "In and Out of Harm's Way: Arrogance and Love." She has given me a way of understanding and articulating something important in my own life.

Frye is not particularly concerned with women as arrogant perceivers but as the objects of arrogant perception. Her concern is, in part, to enhance our understanding of women "untouched by phallocratic machinations" (Frye 1983, 53), by understanding the harm done to women through such machinations. In this case she proposes that we could understand women untouched by arrogant perception through an understanding of what arrogant perception does to women. She also proposes an understanding of what it is to love women that is inspired by a vision of women unharmed by arrogant perception. To love women is, at least in part, to perceive them with loving eyes. "The loving eye is a contrary of the arrogant eye" (Frye 1983, 75).

I am concerned with women as arrogant perceivers because I want to explore further what it is to love women. I want to explore two failures of love: my failure to love my mother and White/Anglo women's failure to love women across racial and cultural boundaries in the U.S. As a consequence of exploring these failures I will offer a loving solu-

---

[1] Grafting the substance of another to oneself is partly constitutive of arrogant perception. See M. Frye (1983, 66)

tion to them. My solution modifies Frye's account of loving perception by adding what I call playful "world"-travel.

It is clear to me that at least in the U.S. and Argentina women are taught to perceive many other women arrogantly. Being taught to perceive arrogantly is part of being taught to be a woman of a certain class in both the U.S. and Argentina, it is part of being taught to be a White/Anglo woman in the U.S. and it is part of being taught to be a women in both places: to be both the agent and the object of arrogant perception. My love for my mother seemed to me thoroughly imperfect as I was growing up because I was unwilling to become what I had been taught to see my mother as being. I thought that to love her was consistent with my abusing her (using, taking for granted, and demanding her services in a far reaching way that, since four other people engaged in the same grafting of her substance onto themselves, left her little of herself to herself) and was to be in part constituted by my identifying with her, my seeing myself in her: to love her was supposed to be of a piece with both my abusing her and with my being open to being abused. It is clear to me that I was not supposed to love servants: I could abuse them without identifying with them, without seeing myself in them. When I came to the U.S. I learned that part of racism is the internalization of the propriety of abuse without identification: I learned that I could be seen as a being to be used by White/Anglo men and women without the possibility of identification, i.e. without their act of attempting to graft my substance onto theirs, rubbing off on them at all. They could remain untouched, without any sense of loss.

So, women who are perceived arrogantly can perceive other women arrogantly in their turn. To what extent those women are responsible for their arrogant perceptions of other women is certainly open to question, but I do not have any doubt that many women have been taught to abuse women in this particular way. I am not interested in assigning responsibility. I am interested in understanding the phenomenon so as to understand a loving way out of it.

There is something obviously wrong with the love that I was taught and something right with my failure to love my mother in this way. But I do not think that what is wrong is my profound desire to identify with her, to see myself in her; what is wrong is that I was taught to identify with a victim of enslavement. What is wrong is that I was taught to practice enslavement of my mother and to learn to become a slave through this practice. There is something obviously wrong with my having been taught that love is consistent with abuse, consistent with arrogant perception. Notice that the love I was taught is the love that Frye (1983, 73) speaks of when she says "We can be taken in by this equation of servitude with love." Even though I could both abuse and love my mother, I was not supposed to love servants. This is because in the case of servants one is and is supposed to be clear about their servitude and the "equation of servitude with love" is never to be thought clearly in those terms. So, I was not supposed to love and could not love servants. But I could love my mother because deception (in particular, self-deception) is part of this "loving." Servitude is called abnegation and abnegation is not analyzed any further. Abnegation is not instilled in us through an analysis of its nature but rather through a heralding of it as beautiful and noble. We are coaxed, seduced into abnegation not through analysis but through emotive persuasion. Frye makes the connection between deception and this sense of "loving" clear. When I say that there is something obviously wrong with the loving that I was taught, I do not mean to say that the connection between this loving and abuse is obvious. Rather I mean that once the connection between this loving and abuse has been unveiled, there is something obviously wrong with the loving given that it is obvious that it is wrong to abuse others.

I am glad that I did not learn my lessons well, but it is clear that part of the mechanism that permitted my not learning well involved a separation from my mother: I saw us as beings of quite a different sort. It involved an abandoning of my mother while I longed not to abandon her. I wanted to love my mother, though, given what I was taught, "love" could not be the right word for what I longed for.

I was disturbed by my not wanting to be what she was. I had a sense of not being quite integrated, my self was missing because I could not identify with her, I could not see myself in her, I could not welcome her world. I saw myself as separate from her, a different sort of being, not quite of the same species. This separation, this lack of love, I saw, and I think that I saw correctly as a lack in myself (not a fault, but a lack). I also see that if this was a lack of love, love cannot be what I was taught. Love has to be rethought, made anew.

There is something in common between the relation between myself and my mother as someone I did not use to be able to love and the relation between myself or other women of color in the U.S. and White/Anglo women: there is a failure of love. I want to suggest here that Frye has helped me understand one of the aspects of this failure, the directly abusive aspect. But I also think that there is a complex failure of love in the failure to identify with another woman, the failure to see oneself in other women who are quite different from oneself. I want to begin to analyze this complex failure.

Notice that Frye's emphasis on independence in her analysis of loving perception is not particularly helpful in explaining this failure. She says that in loving perception, "the object of the seeing is another being whose existence and character are logically independent of the seer and who may be practically or empirically independent in any particular respect at any particular time" (Frye 1983, 77). But this is not helpful in allowing me to understand how my failure of love toward my mother (when I ceased to be her parasite) left me not quite whole. It is not helpful since I saw her as logically independent from me. It also does not help me to understand why the racist or ethnocentric failure of love of White/anglo women—in particular of those White/Anglo women who are not pained by their failure—should leave me not quite substantive among them. Here I am not particularly interested in cases of White women's parasitism onto women of color but more pointedly in cases where the failure of identification is the manifestation of the "relation." I am particularly interested here in those many cases in which White/Anglo women do one or more of the following to women of color: they ignore us, ostracize us, render us invisible, stereotype us, leave us completely alone, interpret us as crazy. All of this *while we are in their midst*. The more independent I am, the more independent I am left to be. Their world and their integrity do not require me at all. There is no sense of self-loss in them for my own lack of solidity. But they rob me of my solidity through indifference, an indifference they can afford and which seems sometimes studied. (All of this points of course toward separatism in communities where our substance is seen and celebrated, where we become substantive through this celebration. But many of us have to work among White/Anglo folk and our best shot at recognition has seemed to be among White/Anglo women because many of them have expressed a *general* sense of being pained at their failure of love.)

Many times White/Anglo women want us out of their field of vision. Their lack of concern is a harmful failure of love that leaves me independent from them in a way similar to the way in which, once I ceased to be my mother's parasite, she became, though not independent from all others, certainly independent from me. But of course, because my mother and I wanted to love each other well, we were not whole in this independence. White/Anglo women are independent from me, I am independent from them, I am independent from my mother, she is independent from me, and none of us loves each other in this independence.

I am incomplete and unreal without other women. I am profoundly dependent on others without having to be their subordinate, their slave, their servant.

Frye (1983, 75) also says that the loving eye is "the eye of one who knows that to know the seen, one must consult something other than one's own will and interests and fears and imagination." This is much more helpful to me so long as I do not understand Frye to mean that I should not consult my own interests nor that I should exclude the possibility that my self and the self of the one I love may be importantly tied to each other in many complicated ways. Since I am emphasizing here that the failure of love lies in part in the failure to identify and since I agree with Frye that one "must consult something other than one's own will and interests and fears and imagination," I will proceed to try to explain what I think needs to be consulted. To love my mother was not possible for me while I retained a sense that it was fine for me and others to see her arrogantly. Loving my mother also required that I see with her eyes, that I go into my mother's world, that I see both of us as we are constructed in her world, that I witness her own sense of herself from within her world. Only through this travelling to her "world" could I identify with her because only then could I cease to ignore her and to be excluded and separate from her. Only then could I see her as a subject even if one subjected and only then could I see at all how meaning could arise fully between us. We are fully dependent on each other for the possibility of being understood and without this understanding we are not intelligible, we do not make sense, we are not solid, visible, integrated; we are lacking. So travelling to each other's "worlds" would enable us to *be* through loving each other.

Hopefully the sense of identification I have in mind is becoming clear. But if it is to become clearer, I need to explain what I mean by a "world" and by "travelling" to another "world."

In explaining what I mean by a "world" I will not appeal to travelling to other women's worlds. Rather I will lead you to see what I mean by a "world" the way I came to propose the concept to myself: through the kind of ontological confusion about myself that we, women of color, refer to half-jokingly as "schizophrenia" (we feel schizophrenic in our goings back and forth between different "communities") and through my effort to make some sense of this ontological confusion.

"Worlds" and "World" Travelling

Some time ago I came to be in a state of profound confusion as I experienced myself as both having and not having a particular attribute. I was sure I had the attribute in question and, on the other hand, I was sure that I did not have it. I remain convinced that I both have and do not have this attribute. The attribute is playfulness. I am sure that I am a playful person. On the other hand, I can say, painfully, that I am not a playful person. I am not a playful person in certain worlds. One of the things I did as I became confused was to call my friends, far away people who knew me well, to see whether or not I was playful. Maybe they could help me out of my confusion. They said to me, "Of course you are playful" and they said it with the same conviction that I had about it. Of course I am playful. Those people who were around me said to me, "No, you are not playful. You are a serious woman. You just take everything seriously." They were just as sure about what they said to me and could offer me every bit of evidence that one could need to conclude that they were right. So I said to myself: "Okay, maybe what's happening here is that there is an attribute that I do have but there are certain worlds in which I am not at ease and it is because I'm not at ease in those worlds that I don't have that attribute in those worlds. But what does that mean?" I was worried both about what I meant by "worlds" when I said "in some worlds I do not have the attribute" and what I meant by saying that lack of ease was what led me not to be playful in those worlds. Because you see, if it was just a matter of lack of ease, I could work on it.

I can explain some of what I mean by a "world." I do not want the fixity of a definition at this point, because I think the term is suggestive and I do not want to close the suggestiveness of it too soon. I can offer some characteristics that serve to distinguish between a "world," a utopia, a possible world in the philosophical sense, and a world view. By a "world" I do not mean a utopia at all. A utopia does not count as a world in my sense. The "worlds" that I am talking about are possible. But a possible world is not what I mean by a "world" and I do not mean a world-view, though something like a world-view is involved here.

For something to be a "world" in my sense it has to be inhabited at present by some flesh and blood people. That is why it cannot be a utopia. It may also be inhabited by some imaginary people. It may be inhabited by people who are dead or people that the inhabitants of this "world" met in some other "world" and now have in this "world" in imagination.

A "world" in my sense may be an actual society given its dominant culture's description and construction of life, including a construction of the relationships of production, of gender, race, etc. But a "world" can also be such a society given a non-dominant construction, or it can be such a society or *a* society given an idiosyncratic construction. As we will see it is problematic to say that these are all constructions of the same society. But they are different "worlds."

A "world" need not be a construction of a whole society. It may be a construction of a tiny portion of a particular society. It may be inhabited by just a few people. Some "worlds" are bigger than others.

A "world" may be incomplete in that things in it may not be altogether constructed or some things may be constructed negatively (they are not what 'they' are in some other "world.") Or the "world" may be incomplete because it may have references to things that do not quite exist in it, references to things like Brazil, where Brazil is not quite part of that "world." Given lesbian feminism, the construction of 'lesbian' is purposefully and healthily still up in the air, in the process of becoming. What it is to be a Hispanic in this country is, in a dominant Anglo construction purposefully incomplete. Thus one cannot really answer questions of the sort "What is a Hispanic?", "Who counts as a Hispanic?", "Are Latinos, Chicanos, Hispanos, black dominicans, white cubans, korean-columbians, italian-argentinians hispanic?" What it is to be a 'hispanic' in the varied so-called hispanic communities in the U.S. is also yet up in the air. We have not yet decided whether there is something like a 'hispanic' in our varied "worlds." So, a "world" may be an incomplete visionary non-utopian construction of life or it may be a traditional construction of life. A traditional Hispano construction of Northern New Mexican life is a "world." Such a traditional construction, in the face of a racist, ethnocentrist, money-centered anglo construction of Northern New Mexican life is highly unstable because Anglos have the means for imperialist destruction of traditional Hispano "worlds."

In a "world" some of the inhabitants may not understand or hold the particular construction of them that constructs them in that "world." So, there may be "worlds" that construct me in ways that I do not even understand. Or it may be that I understand the construction, but do not hold it of myself. I may not accept it as an account of myself, a construction of myself. And yet, I may be *animating* such a construction.

One can "travel" between these "worlds" and one can inhabit more than one of these "worlds" at the very same time. I think that most of us who are outside the mainstream of, for example, the U.S. dominant construction or organization of life are "world travellers" as a matter of necessity and of survival. It seems to me that inhabiting more than one "world" at the same time and "travelling" between "worlds" is part and parcel of our experience and our situation. One can be at the same time in a "world" that constructs one as stereotypically latin, for example, and in a "world" that constructs one as latin. Being stereotypically latin and being simply latin are different simultaneous constructions of persons that are part of different "worlds." One animates one or the other or both at the same time without necessarily confusing them, though simultaneous enactment can be confusing if one is not on one's guard.

In describing my sense of a "world," I mean to be offering a description of experience, something that is true to experience even if it is ontologically problematic. Though I would think that any account of identity that could not be true to this experience of outsiders to the mainstream would be faulty even if ontologically unproblematic. Its ease would constrain, erase, or deem aberrant experience that has within it significant insights into non-imperialistic understanding between people.

Those of us who are "world"-travellers have the distinct experience of being different in different "worlds" and of having the capacity to remember other "worlds" and ourselves in them. We can say "That is me there, and I am happy in that "world." So, the experience is of being a different person in different "worlds" and yet of having memory of oneself as different without quite having the sense of there being any underlying "I." So I can say "that is me there and I am so playful in that "world." I say "That is *me* in that "world" not because I recognize myself in that person, rather the first person statement is non-inferential. I may well recognize that that person has abilities that I do not have and yet the having or not having of the abilities is always an "I have…" and "I do not have…", i.e. it is always experienced in the first person.

The shift from being one person to being a different person is what I call "travel." This shift may not be willful or even conscious, and one may be completely unaware of being different than one is in a different "world," and may not recognize that one is in a different "world." Even though the shift can be done willfully, it is not a matter of acting. One does not pose as someone else, one does not pretend to be, for example, someone of a different personality or character or someone who uses space or language differently than the other person. Rather one is someone who has that personality or character or uses space and language in that particular way. The "one" here does not refer to some underlying "I." One does not *experience* any underlying "I."

Being at Ease in a "World"

In investigating what I mean by "being at ease in a 'world'," I will describe different ways of being at ease. One may be at ease in one or in all of these ways. There is a maximal way of being at ease, viz. being at ease in all of these ways. I take this maximal way of being at ease to be somewhat dangerous because it tends to produce people who have no inclination to travel across "worlds" or have no experience of "world" travelling.

The first way of being at ease in a particular "world" is by being a fluent speaker in that "world." I know all the norms that there are to be followed. I know all the words that there are to be spoken. I know all the moves. I am confident.

Another way of being at ease is by being normatively happy. I agree with all the norms, I could not love any norms better. I am asked to do just what I want to do or what I think I should do. At ease.

Another way of being at ease in a "world" is by being humanly bonded. I am with those I love and they love me too. It should be noticed that I may be with those I love and be at ease because of them in a "world" that is otherwise as hostile to me as "worlds" get.

Finally one may be at ease because one has a history with others that is shared, especially daily history, the kind of shared history that one sees exemplified by the response to the "Do you remember poodle skirts?" question. There you are, with people you do not know at all. The question is posed and then they all begin talking about their poodle skirt stores. I have been in such situations without knowing what poodle skirts, for example, were and I felt so ill at ease because it was not *my* history. The other people did not particularly know each other. It is not that they were humanly bonded. Probably they did not have much politically in common either. But poodle skirts were in their shared history.

One may be at ease in one of these ways or in all of them. Notice that when one says meaningfully "This is *my* world," one may not be at ease in it. Or one may be at ease in it only in some of these respects and not in others. To say of some "world" that it is "*my* world" is to make an evaluation. One may privilege one or more "worlds" in this way for a variety of reasons: for example because one experiences oneself as an agent in a fuller sense than one experiences "oneself" in other "worlds." One may disown a "world" because one has first person memories of a person who is so thoroughly dominated that she has no sense of exercising her own will or has a sense of having serious difficulties in performing actions that are willed by herself and no difficulty in performing actions willed by others. One may say of a "world" that it is "my world" because one is at ease in it, i.e. being at ease in a "world" may be the basis for the evaluation.

Given the clarification of what I mean by a "world," "world"-travel, and being at ease in a "world," we are in a position to return to my problematic attribute, playfulness. It may be that in this "world" in which I am so unplayful, I am a different person than in the "world" in which I am playful. Or it may be that the "world" in which I am unplayful is constructed in such a way that I could be playful in it. I could practice, even though that "world" is constructed in such a way that my being playful in it is kind of hard. In describing what I take a "world" to be, I emphasized the first possibility as both the one that is truest to the experience of "outsiders" to the mainstream and as ontologically problematic because the "I" is identified in some sense as one and in some sense as a plurality. I identify myself as myself through memory and I retain myself as different in memory. When I travel from one "world" to another, I have this image, this memory of myself as playful in this other "world." I can then be in a particular "world" and have a double image of myself as, for example, playful and as not playful. But this is a very familiar and recognizable phenomenon to the outsider to the mainstream in some central cases: when in one "world" I animate, for example, that "world's" caricature of the person I am in the other "world." I can have both images of myself and to the extent that I can materialize or animate both images at the same time I become an ambiguous being. This is very much a part of trickery and foolery. It is worth remembering that the trickster and the fool are significant characters in many non-dominant or outsider cultures. One then sees any particular "world" with these double edges and sees absurdity in them and so inhabits oneself differently. Given that latins are constructed in Anglo "worlds" as stereotypically intense—intensity being a central characteristic of at least one of the anglo stereotypes of latins—and given that many latins, myself included, are genuinely intense, I can say to myself "I am intense" and take a hold of the double meaning. And furthermore, I can be stereotypically intense or be the real thing and, if you are Anglo, you do not know when I am which *because* I am Latin-American. As Latin-American I am an ambiguous being, a two-imaged self: I can see that gringos see me as stereotypically intense because I am, as a Latin-American, constructed that way but I may or may not *intentionally* animate the stereotype or the real thing knowing that you may not see it in anything other than in the stereotypical construction. This ambiguity is funny and is not just funny, it is survival-rich. We can also make the picture of those who dominate us funny precisely because we can see the double edge, we can see them doubly constructed, we can see the plurality in them. So we know truths that only the fool can speak and only the trickster can play out without harm. We inhabit "worlds" and travel across them and keep all the memories.

Sometimes the "world"-traveller has a double image of herself and each self includes as important ingredients of itself one or more attributes that are *incompatible* with one or more of the attributes of the other self: for example being playful and being unplayful. To the extent that the attribute is an important ingredient of the self she is in that "world," i.e., to the extent that there is a particularly good fit between that "world" and her having that attribute in it and to the extent that the attribute is personality or character central, that "world" would have to be changed if she is to be playful in it. It is not the case that if she could come to be at ease in it, she would be her own playful self. Because the attribute is personality or character central and there is such a good fit between that "world" and her being constructed with that attribute as central, *she* cannot become playful, she is unplayful. To become playful would be for her to become a contradictory being. So I am suggesting that the lack of ease solution cannot be a solution to my problematic case. My problem is not one of lack of ease. I am suggesting that I can understand my confusion about whether I am or am not playful by saying that I am both and that I am different persons in different "world" and can remember myself in both as I am in the other. I am a plurality of selves. This is to understand my confusion because *it is to come to see it as a piece* with much of the rest of my experience as an outsider in some of the "worlds" that I inhabit and of a piece with significant aspects of the experience of non-dominant people in the "worlds" of their dominators.

So, though I may not be at ease in the "worlds" in which I am not constructed playful, it is not that I am not playful *because* I am not at ease. The two are compatible. But lack of playfulness is not caused by lack of ease. Lack of playfulness is not symptomatic of lack of ease but of lack of health. I am not a healthy being in the "worlds" that construct me unplayful.

Playfulness

I had a very personal stake in investigating this topic. Playfulness is not only the attribute that was the source of my confusion and the attitude that I recommend as the loving attitude in travelling across "worlds," I am also scared of ending up a serious human being, someone with no multidimensionality, with no fun in life, someone who is just someone who has had the fun constructed out of her. I am seriously scared of getting stuck in a "world" that constructs me that way. A world that I have no escape from and in which I cannot be playful.

I thought about what it is to be playful and what it is to play and I did this thinking in a "world" in which I only remember myself as playful and in which all of those who know me as playful are imaginary beings. A "world" in which I am scared of losing my memories of myself as playful or have them erased from me. Because I live in such a "world," after I formulated my own sense of what it is to be playful and to play I decided that I needed to "go to the literature." I read two classics on the subject: Johan Huizinga's *Homo Ludens* and Hans-Georg Gadamer's chapter on the concept of play in his *Truth and Method*. I discovered, to my amazement, that what I thought about play and playfulness, if they were right, was absolutely wrong. Though I will not provide the arguments for this interpretation of Gadamer and Huizinga here, I understood that both of them have an agonistic sense of 'play.' Play and playfulness have, ultimately, to do with contest, with winning, losing, battling. The sense of playfulness that I have in mind has nothing to do with those things. So, I tried to elucidate both senses of play and playfulness by contrasting them to each other. The contrast helped me see the attitude that I have in mind as the loving attitude in travelling across "worlds" more clearly.

An agonistic sense of playfulness is one in which *competence* is supreme. You better know the rules of the game. In agonistic play there is risk, there is *uncertainty*, but the uncertainty is about who is going to win and who is going to lose. There are rules that inspire hostility. The attitude of *playfulness is conceived as secondary to or derivative from play.* Since play is agon, then the only conceivable playful attitude is an agonistic one (the attitude does not turn an activity into play, but rather presupposes an activity that is play). One of the paradigmatic ways of playing for both Gadamer and Huizinga is role-playing. In role-playing, the person who is a participant in the game has a *fixed conception of him or herself.* I also think that the players are imbued with *self-importance* in agonistic play since they are so keen on winning given their own merits, their very own competence.

When considering the value of "world"-travelling and whether playfulness is the loving attitude to have while travelling, I recognized the agonistic attitude as inimical to travelling across "worlds." The agonistic traveller is a conqueror, an imperialist. Huizinga, in his classic book on play, interprets Western civilization as play. That is an interesting thing for Third World people to think about. Western civilization has been interpreted by a white western man as play in the agonistic sense of play. Huizinga reviews western law, art, and any other aspects of western culture and sees agon in all of them. Agonistic playfulness leads those who attempt to travel to another "world" with this attitude to failure. Agonistic travellers fail consistently in their attempt to travel because what they do is to try to conquer the other "world." The attempt is not an attempt to try to erase the other "world." That is what assimilation is all about. Assimilation is the destruction of other people's "worlds." So, the agonistic attitude, the playful attitude given western man's construction of playfulness, is not a healthy, loving attitude to have in travelling across "worlds." Notice that given the agonistic attitude one *cannot* travel across "worlds," though one can kill other "worlds" with it. So for people who are interested in crossing racial and ethnic boundaries, an arrogant western man's construction of playfulness is deadly. One cannot cross the boundaries with it. One needs to give up such an attitude if one wants to travel.

So then, what is the loving playfulness that I have in mind? Let me begin with one example: We are by the river bank. The river is very, very low. Almost dry. Bits of water here and there. Little pools with a few trout hiding under the rocks. But mostly is wet stones, grey on the outside. We walk on the stones for awhile. You pick up a stone and crash it onto the others. As it breaks, it is quite wet inside and it is very colorful, very pretty. I pick up a stone and break it and run toward the pieces to see the colors. They are beautiful. I laugh and bring the pieces back to you and you are doing the same with your pieces. We keep on crashing stones for hours, anxious to see the beautiful new colors. We are playing. The playfulness of our activity does not presuppose that there is something like "crashing stones" that is a particular form of play with its own rules. Rather *the attitude that carries us through the activity, a playful attitude, turns the activity into play.* Our activity has no rules, though it is certainly intentional activity and we both understand what we are doing. The playfulness that gives meaning to our activity includes uncertainty, but in this case the uncertainty is an *openness to surprise.* This is a particular metaphysical attitude that does not expect the world to be neatly packaged, ruly. Rules may fail to explain what we are doing. We are not self-important, we are not fixed in particular constructions of ourselves, which is part of saying that we are *open to self-construction.* We may not have rules, and when we do have rules, *there are no rules that are to us sacred.* We are not worried about competence. We are not wedded to a particular way of doing things. While playful we have not abandoned ourselves to, nor are we stuck in, any particular "world." We *are there creatively.* We are not passive.

Playfulness is, in part, an openness to being a fool, which is a combination of not worrying about competence, not being self-important, not taking norms as sacred and finding ambiguity and double edges a source of wisdom and delight.

So, positively, the playful attitude involves openness to surprise, openness to being a fool, openness to self-construction or reconstruction and to construction or reconstruction of the "worlds" we inhabit playfully. Negatively, playfulness is characterized by uncertainty, lack of self-importance, absence of rules or a not taking rules as sacred, a not worrying about competence and a lack of abandonment to a particular construction of oneself, others and one's relation to them. In attempting to take a hold of oneself and of one's relation to others in a particular "world," one may study, examine and come to understand oneself. One may then see what the possibilities for play are for the being one is in that "world." One may even decide to inhabit that self fully in order to understand it better and find its creative possibilities. All of this is just self-reflection and it is quite different from resigning or abandoning oneself to the particular construction of oneself that one is attempting to take a hold of.

Conclusion

There are "worlds" we enter at our own risk, "worlds" that have agon, conquest, and arrogance as the main ingredients in their ethos. These are "worlds" that we enter out of necessity and which would be foolish to enter playfully in either the agonistic sense or in my sense. In such "worlds" *we* are not playful.

But there are "worlds" that we can travel to lovingly and travelling to them is part of loving at least some of their inhabitants. The reason why I think that travelling to someone's "world" is a way of identifying with them is because by travelling to their "world" we can understand *what it is to be them and what it is to be ourselves in their eyes*. Only when we have travelled to each other's "worlds" are we fully subjects to each other (I agree with Hegel that self-recognition requires other subjects, but I disagree with his claim that it requires tension or hostility).

Knowing other women's "worlds" is part of knowing them and knowing them is part of loving them. Notice that the knowing can be done in greater or lesser depth, as can the loving. Also notice that travelling to another's "world" is not the same as becoming intimate with them. Intimacy is constituted in part by a very deep knowledge of the other self and "world" travelling is only part of having this knowledge. Also notice that some people, in particular those who are outsiders to the mainstream, can be known only to the extent that they are known in several "worlds" and as "world"-travellers.

Without knowing the other's "world," one does not know the other, and without knowing the other one is really alone in the other's presence because the other is only dimly present to one.

Through travelling to other people's "worlds" we discover that there are "worlds" in which those who are the victims of arrogant perception are really subjects, lively beings, resistors, constructors of visions even though in the mainstream construction they are animated only by the arrogant perceiver and are pliable, foldable, file-awayable, classifiable. I always imagine the Aristotelian slave as pliable and foldable at night or after he or she cannot work anymore (when he or she dies as a tool). Aristotle tells us nothing about the slave *apart from the master*. We know the slave only through the master. The slave is a tool of the master. After working hours he or she is folded and placed in a drawer till the next morning. My mother was apparent to me mostly as a victim of arrogant perception. I was loyal to the arrogant perceiver's construction of her and thus disloyal to her in assuming that she was exhausted by that construction. I was unwilling to be like her and thought that identifying with her, seeing myself in her necessitated that I become like her. I was wrong both in assuming that she was exhausted by the arrogant perceiver's construction of her and in my understanding of identification, though I was not wrong in thinking that identification was part of loving and that it involved in part my seeing myself in her. I came to realize through travelling to her "world" that she is not foldable and pliable, that she is not exhausted by the mainstream argentinian patriarchal construction of her. I came to realize that there are "worlds" in which she shines as a creative being. Seeing myself in her through travelling to her "world" has meant seeing how different from her I am in her "world."

So, in recommending "world"-travelling and identification through "world"-travelling as part of loving other women, I am suggesting disloyalty to arrogant perceivers, including the arrogant perceiver in ourselves, and to their constructions of women. In revealing agonistic playfulness as incompatible with "world"-travelling, I am revealing both its affinity with imperialism and arrogant perception and its incompatibility with loving and loving perception.

Note

This essay has appeared in *Hypatia: A Journal of Feminist Philosophy*, vol. 2, no. 2 (Summer 1987), and in *Women, Knowledge, and Reality*, edited by Ann Garry and Marilyn Pearsall (Unwin and Hyman, 1989).

References

Frye, Marilyn. 1983. *The politics of reality: Essays in feminist theory.* Trumansburg, N.Y.: Crossing Press.
Gadamer, Hans-George. 1975. *Truth and method.* New York: Seabury Press.
Huizinga, Johan. 1968. *Homo ludens.* Buenos Aires, Argentina: Emecé Edi-
   tores.

"You do so well."

A Blind Lesbian Responds To Her Sighted Sisters

Michigan Womyn's Music Festival, 1981 . . . *I have come here on a bus with a bunch of women from Minneapolis, none of whom I know well. It is my very first experience of camping, as well as being the first time that I have attended a huge lesbian cultural event. I have come out only a year before at the age of twenty-eight. All day I have had trouble keeping up with my friends with whom I have camped, confused and disoriented by the lack of streets and corners or sidewalks or hallways or any such landmarks that I have used as a blind person to get around. I am feeling ashamed and irritable, and my new friends are beginning to lose patience with me. Finally, one turns to me and says, "Look, we really aren't able to meet your needs. Why don't you move over to the DART camp area, so that you can be with other disabled women and network with them?" I am crushed, but do not argue. I have been relegated to the leper colony, fenced in and patrolled by guards. I have failed in my attempt to be one of the regular guys. The euphemistically named Differently Abled Resource Tent turns out to be a sad place to be indeed, and I realize that I don't really belong here, or at outdoor music festivals at all.*

As a blind lesbian who has been struggling for years to belong to and to help create a cultural and political community of choice, I have gone through a kind of evolving cycle of attitudes towards lesbian feminism and my position in or feelings towards it. A couple of years ago, I arrived at a point where the extreme marginality of my position as a blind lesbian led me to suspect that it was in fact impossible to really *be* both blind and a lesbian. Though I knew blind women who were very sure of their lesbian identity and who would certainly have strongly disagreed with this idea, I decided to stop fighting and fearing the feeling. I decided to quit calling myself a lesbian. Almost immediately, though, I was hit with the question: how does one be a non-lesbian? I was clearly not something else like heterosexual, so there was simply no positive way to define myself as a sexual being, an identity I refused to part with. I found myself stuck on a sharp and slippery definition: I *was* the Impossible blind Lesbian.

Before I ever dreamed of being a lesbian, I came out as a blind woman. Because I had always had a little sight, my family and others had managed to deny the fact that I was blind. In fact, I was two or three years old before they began to understand that I was different at all. The damage was to my retina, and so was invisible. I always knew that it was a disgraceful thing to be unable to see, and had learned to help others feel more comfortable with me by tending to give them the impression that I could see better than I really could. I did this quite without thinking, and it was very easy to do, since people wanted to believe that I was sighted. There were, of course, many negative side effects of this "passing": people would often think that I was only pretending to be blind, rather than the other way around. This would make them very angry, and put me in terrible danger. (I should add that this still happens, although I now am as clear as I can possibly be about the fact that I am blind.)

I was seventeen when I was finally able to name myself "blind". That was when I first met other blind teenagers, and I was overjoyed to discover that there were people like me. For the first time in my life, I felt I belonged with another group of human beings. My acceptance into the blind community was never complete, and this became more and more clear to me as the years went by. But in 1969, at seventeen, I didn't care. The feeling of having come home that I felt then was completely wonderful and quite unexpected. A very bleak world had suddenly opened up, just a little. I no longer was ashamed of being blind. Instead I was conscious of and resistant towards the irrational social and cultural attitudes towards us as blind people. The small part of me that had always believed that I did not deserve to be treated the way I was treated, as though I were evil and worthless, was at last justified . . . a little bit. Whatever doubts I still had about myself, I was convinced that my new friends did not deserve to be treated badly. Although my acceptance by these friends was marginal and limited, it was enough to show me that oppression was shared, and that I needed to work with these people to fight against discrimination based on blindness. And we needed to work on this *together*.

When I came out lesbian in my very late twenties, at first marginal acceptance was wonderful. I was delighted to have new friends, and was happier to think of myself as a lesbian than as an ugly old maid who got "left on the shelf". Although I understood that being a lesbian was more than just love and sex, being a lesbian without ever experiencing the joys and sorrows of being in a Relationship seemed, and does seem, somewhat lacking. After all, when we read a lesbian story or novel, or see a lesbian play, we expect that there will be at least some talk of sex and Relationships.

We would be very disappointed if our lesbian cartoons and comedians didn't mention love and sex. And if I couldn't find anyone willing or able to be involved with a blind lesbian for a lover, how could I really get away with saying I was gay? Wasn't I really still that ugly old maid, just denying my true identity?

And before anybody asks: Yes it's true that some blind dykes do find lovers. But my informal survey of all the blind lesbians I know tells me that for us, relationships are very much fewer and farther between, and there are a high proportion of us who spend many years, or indeed our whole lives, celibate.

Autumn, 1983...*I was among the first guests to arrive at this party. I am seated as the other guests arrive. They are mostly lesbians that I haven't met before. I am feeling strong and comfortable tonight, and I am really enjoying meeting and talking with these women. I like them. They are interesting and friendly; I feel very glad that I was invited to this party. After a long while, I decide to get up and go to the bathroom, picking up my white cane from the floor beside me as I get up. When I return, I find several women speaking softly to each other. One of them turns to me, and says brightly and tensely, but without any hint of embarrassment: "We were just talking about you!" She is speaking in a new voice that I have not heard her use before. She almost seems to be a completely different person than the one I was chatting with moments before. "We had no idea that you were...well, that you had a sight problem. We think you're amazing!" Another woman adds: "Yes, you don't look like you are different at all...I just never would have known!"*

I feel disappointed, sadly realizing what has happened. I thought I was meeting some terrific women, some women who were accepting me so well that I thought at last I was bridging the barriers to acceptability. These women liked me; I didn't feel strange or awkward or horrible with them. I was pleased and happy, I felt like a real lesbian at last! But I had in truth been unwittingly conning these women into thinking that I was more like them than I was. Despite their strong exclamations of admiration for my astounding accomplishments, their voices revealed their horror in discovering that I was not who they thought I was. I had fallen drastically in their estimation (they were amazed that I could find the bathroom by myself), and they in mine. It was not the first time I had had this experience, yet I had not seen it coming. I had just been given another lesson, and an unusually clear glimpse, at the difference in the way blind women are perceived by the sighted. Now that these women had discovered that I was not their equal, as they had thought, the most I could expect from them was a warmly proffered ride home, a ride where I heard many exclamations of amazement at my stunning abilities to think and speak and walk just as though I were an ordinary human being. There was no longer even the slightest chance that any of these women would become friends with me. They were deeply impressed by me, and they would perhaps tell their friends how "courageous" I was ("Do you know she rides the bus all by herself?"), but they would be unable to take me seriously. I had crossed no barrier, after all. I was still strange, different and unacceptable. I would continue to feel isolated and alone within, or at the margins of, my lesbian community.

We have internalized the general fear of disability that we have been indoctrinated in since we were babies. This goes for both the newly disabled adult lesbian and those of us who have always been disabled. Those of us who have grown up disabled don't always connect our negative self image with our disabilities. We may simply feel inferior without knowing why. Those who have become disabled more recently may feel cheated and angry that they can no longer be thought of by others as normal. They may tend to blame the disability itself for their change in social status, rather than the cultural precepts that have taught them and others that to be disabled is to be worthless. They find that they are unable to do important things that they once were able to take for granted, and so, not surprisingly, they see the culprit as the disability which has changed their lives for the worse.

Our feelings about each other have also been seriously distorted by our ancient and deep feelings about disability. Some blind lesbians want to make sure that they are seen as being "in the sighted world," and may even shun much contact at all with any blind people. Those whose physical limitations are less are often taught to think of themselves as luckier or superior to those who might be, for example, totally blind. They are encouraged to avoid the use of Braille, white canes, and dog guides. Even some totally blind women work desperately to avoid being identified as such, and think of themselves as exceptions: they are somehow smarter or better than ordinary blind folk. While their sighted friends will often encourage and reinforce this attitude, resentment is built up between them and other members of the blind community.

Coalition and network building between and among lesbians with different disabilities has been slow to start, and has not seemed to really progress very far. This is partly because of the practical considerations that divide the different disability groups, as well as the resentment members of any particular group might feel toward one another. Because there are so few of us in any given lesbian community, we often know each other, sometimes with a great degree of intimacy. I have sometimes felt a kind of sibling rivalry between the blind lesbians in my community, and this is in part based on social and economic factors. There is such a thing as tokenism, and when I hear that another blind woman has gotten a job, though I am always glad, there is a part of me that says, "there it is . . . one less place for you." Socially, too, I suspect that there is a limit to the number of blind lesbians that any particular community might be willing to accept. This may be a false presumption, since it seems to me that so far none of us have really been accepted; but it is a feeling that I have nonetheless. It is true that we are compared to each other quite frequently, not to mention mistaken for each other constantly, and this can add to the competitive tension we sometimes feel towards one another.

Yet we are perhaps unlike genuine cultural minorities who may indeed have enough commonality, if not the critical mass, to give each other enough strength and support to continue to struggle in our lives for acceptance by the larger community. While Black, Hispanic, Asian, or Indian lesbians may find it important to make contact with each other for reasons of a shared and different culture, I don't believe that disabled lesbians receive the same benefits from contact with each other. My friend María Lugones speaks of possessing "two worlds" as a U.S. Latina lesbian. For me, it seems that there is the mainstream world of lesbian feminism to which I do belong as a white Anglo American, but from which I am excluded as a blind woman; and there is the contact that I have with my blind lesbian friends who all have a similar cultural background to mine. If María possesses two worlds, then I possess a world and an unformed place that is not quite a void, but is rather empty. I am not entirely alone there, but I am sharply aware of my individual differences that separate me from the other blind lesbians that I know. This unformed place of contact or noncontact is nowhere near to being something that I can call a world. There is no "world of the blind", no place of tragic bitterness. As blind lesbians, we cannot exist entirely apart; we need each other but we need the others, too. When we are rejected by the sighted community, we are left floating. When we come together, our "networking" is inevitably full of attempts to understand that rejection as something that is not our fault, not our lack. There are moments of intense bonding and solidarity between us as we discuss and share the ways in which we are able or unable to interact with our sighted counterparts. Still, when one of us achieves something, she tends to feel that it was due to her special talent or moral worthiness. She tends to deny that it was based on luck, and that she is not superior to her blind sisters; and the shame, pain, and divisions continue.

While these problems are our own to work through, and sighted women have no direct role to play in helping us work through them, it is important for me to point out that it is inappropriate for lesbians to do what my friends at the music festival did: to dump us on each other to "network", thus avoiding dealing with us themselves.

The Cheese Stands Alone...*The lesbian poetry reading is delightful; I sit and listen to each writer who daringly shares her work. I am struck by the diversity of experience labelled lesbian that is presented here, I feel good about my community, I feel myself to be a part of its richness. A blind lesbian friend and her "date" for the evening have been sitting nearby, and have offered me a ride home. After the performance, I stand up in a roomful of milling, noisy lesbians. I ask my friend if she has enjoyed the reading, and she doesn't answer. Perhaps she did not hear, the room is quite noisy, but I decide not to risk embarrassing her by raising my voice to ask again. Her companion has left to greet someone she sees across the room. I stand silent and alone in the bustle; I have run out of things to say. I suppose that there are women that I know in the room, but no one approaches me. I wonder if I could think of something interesting to talk about if they did. I wish I had something to say, someone besides my silent friend to speak to. I wonder if she wishes the same thing. After a long while, a woman I know slightly approaches and greets my friend; they know each other well. They chat briefly, and arrange a time to get together. My friend's companion returns, and we leave, no one having spoken to me after the reading.*

Once again, it has been brought home to me how few friends I have in this community. Of course, this is not a new or unique feeling for me, and I have no way of knowing how much of my isolation is due to lesbian non-acceptance of my disability and how much is due to my own many failings as an individual. Everyone here is socializing, but few have thought of making contact with the two blind women among them. This is despite the fact that we have both been around for a long time, and my friend has been actively working in the community and has made undeniable contributions to this community. Are they glad that we are here? Do they wish that we would go away? Are they unconcerned, figuring that they will put up with us if we continue to silently accept what feels to us like continual rejection? This sort of thing used to make me angry, but now I am only sad.

Just what is it that sets blind lesbians apart? Why should I, a white midwesterner of the baby boom generation, feel separate from the life of my lesbian community?

The first part of the answer is fairly obvious: it of course is not possible for lesbians of any particular cultural background to find themselves automatically free of the preconceptions and stereotypes that we have been trained to carry with us everywhere, even after we have discovered that they are false and destructive. As far as blindness goes, there are still many lesbians who have not yet questioned their assumptions about who blind people are, let alone begun to try to change them. I continue to hear from feminist lips all the derogatory language involving blindness (such as the use of the term "blind" as a synonym for ignorant, or helpless, or foolish) that I have always heard from the mouths of those in more "mainstream" or patriarchal establishment points of view.

But a lesbian culture has its own special norms that are enforced and sometimes broken by the members of our communities. Some of these rules are based on ways of being personally and politically defiant; a few years ago, for example, a short haircut was highly preferred among many groups in my local lesbian community. Some of the standards required by the acceptability boundaries are ostensibly defiant of the patriarchy, yet are also, paradoxically perhaps, deeply rooted in and supportive of, the ideologies that we as lesbian feminists say that we reject. For example, the feminist ideal of the independent woman, while it quite rightly rejects the feminine ideal of the helpless female that at least the middle-class or the aspiring middle-class upholds, at the same time supports that good old American individualism and can even imply and/or support a social Darwinist, victim blaming attitude. The very healthy feminist rejection of "care-taking" and "co-dependency" can lead quite easily, for women who don't want to accept any shared responsibility, to a self-righteous and self-indulgent code of ethics. The importance given to "independence" and "strength," combined with an attitude that associates disability with dependence and weakness, has obvious destructive consequences for disabled members of a group that holds these views.

Very practically speaking, what are the things that any lesbian might want to do in order to participate in and support her community, to meet friends and potential lovers? Well, there are lesbian softball leagues . . . not much room for a blind lesbian there. There are concerts and lectures and readings—a blind lesbian can attend as many of these as her usually very low income will permit, but she isn't very likely to meet new people at these. Among my own friends, and my community in the Twin Cities is blessed with an unusually large number of blind lesbians (at least half a dozen), we find that the committee and other work that we do is often the only place where we manage to meet new friends, and practically the only place that we have any social contact with other lesbians. To the extent that in these task-oriented groups we meet women who like us and want to include us in other parts of their lives, we are able to build a non-work social life.

I haven't yet mentioned the lesbian bars. Where I live, the way to really have a good time, even for sober dykes, is to go to the bars and dance. Sometimes my friends will invite me along to go dancing with them. I can be anti-social and miss joining them by declining the invitation, or I can go along. Once at the bar, I often find myself with even more difficult choices. I can let someone find me a chair, and sit there in the deafening din quite isolated from my friends, or I can allow myself to be escorted to and from the dance floor, the bathroom, the bar. …With the way those places are laid out, with all the people moving about and the loud music that deprives me of my most useful hearing, I am rather helpless. To my friends, I am a burden, a piece of luggage who can't share in their visual communication. I cannot even be relied on to stay anywhere near them on the dance floor. To someone who doesn't know me, I appear to be clumsy and useless. Why would anyone want to be with such a liability? How could anyone possibly be *attracted* to her? How on earth could she be a real lesbian?

Although these thoughts are my own, I am convinced that they are in fact similar to what many lesbians consciously or unconsciously think when reacting to the presence of a disabled lesbian. It is the only explanation for the fear and disrespect with which we are so often treated. And I am not saying this in order to snipe at nondisabled lesbians, but rather to show that their feelings and responses to us are in fact completely natural and understandable.

Nonetheless, it is important to discuss what the role of the disabled lesbian herself is in all of this. I have no interest in the attitude that says it is all, or even mostly, in our own heads, that if we only believed in and respected ourselves, others would too. I mention this because a surprisingly large number of women who are aware of the way oppression works against other groups will totally deny its existence when it comes to the disabled, cheerfully pointing to those amazing exceptions who overcame all odds, and so forth.

I used to feel very angry about my own and other disabled women's banishment from true and complete participation in lesbian life. Nowadays, though, I am weary of anger, and I mostly feel sad. Instead of indignantly judging nondisabled dykes for their inability to love us, I understand (although reluctantly) their limitations. It is very hard, maybe impossible, to love those you have spent a lifetime learning to fear and despise. But I do not intend to let nondisabled lesbians off the hook. This understanding of mine does not justify your walking away from us; disabled lesbians don't want any more "thank you for sharing" nonresponse when we voice our sense of isolation, frustration, or sadness. If we can learn to have real, whole communities, then it will not be only the disabled women among us who must live with and come to terms with disability and its consequences in an ablist society. More and more abled lesbians could learn, as a few already have, that disabled lesbians are as worthwhile as they and their abled friends are, and they could work with us, both inside and outside the lesbian community. The support and participation of nondisabled lesbians in the disability rights movement validates and strengthens that movement.

It is not now or ever okay with disabled lesbians to be regarded as inferior. The truth is that we, the impossible disabled lesbians, are valuable; in fact, we are necessary for the strength, growth, and survival of *all* lesbian communities. We really must all work together so that I and my disabled sisters can become fully realized lesbians in every sense of the word.

Lesbian Revolution
And The 50 Minute Hour
A Working-Class Look At Therapy And The Movement
CARYATIS CARDEA

> . . . liberty loses its meaning when women are not in fact free to change their situation or when *they participate in limiting others' freedom* . . .
>
> Kathleen Barry[1]

In Spring of 1980, I began this effort to elucidate classism within the lesbian feminist movement. As I developed my ideas in the three main areas of feminist process, humanism, and lesbian relationships, I noted that the classist aspects of each could be traced to the powerful effect therapy had acquired in lesbian life.

Feminist process, with its emphasis on courtesy, and on a firm separation of thought and feeling, exists for the comfort, benefit and continued power of middle-class lesbians. And it is to therapy that they go to acquire and maintain this mind-spirit divorce.

Humanism, with its obsessive inclusion of everyone and everything under the formerly womyn's banner of feminism [See, there's really no one to be angry with!] is reinforced by, and had its origins in, therapy's insistence that we each move beyond our anger and create our own reality. And we were to create this reality in our own space, one of individual prosperity and individual happiness.

Lesbian relationships have been newly defined as the place to get one's needs met, and to enter on a never-ending struggle to process honest political and personal differences. Here, therapy has provided perhaps its must popular justification for the imposition of middle-class manners and values under which lesbians like myself, from working-class backgrounds, have been suffocating.

Everywhere I looked, during the latter years of the 1970s, lesbians were going to therapists, becoming therapists, changing therapists, discussing their therapists, being abused by their therapists. If any other topic of conversation was introduced, it was phrased in the language of therapy. The heart of fire which our movement once contained was gone, replaced by what Mary Daly has termed "plastic passions." Lesbians no longer had opinions, they had "energy around some issues"; they didn't even get mad any more, they only "experienced some anger." I have no doubt that I will receive several suggestions that I enter therapy to deal with my excessive hostility in mentioning all of this.

This article is essentially a plea that we try to reverse the tide of "valueless individualism"[2] which stems from therapy. Therapy is not politics; it is not feminism. It is dangerous.

The attitudes and actions which I will describe as middle-class are exhibited to greater or lesser degrees within all strata of the economically privileged in U.S. society. I *attack* the values, and *challenge* the lesbians who hold them.

The Drift From Radical Feminism

By early 1975, I had come out as a lesbian and a separatist. I thought it awesome and beautiful that our horizons, already incredibly broad from the boundaries we had pushed out, moved apace with us, at lightning speed. Radicalism was present in what would now be seen as the least likely places. Concepts of world feminism, separatism, visions of lesbian nation, and a firm grasp of sexual politics could be found everywhere.

Across the country, in the coffeehouses, buildings and centers we had braved everything to establish, the movement sat back to take a breath. Besides the needed rest, challenges were coming from within and without the movement: race, class and other issues were being raised to challenge what we had finally acknowledged to be the white, middle-class domination of the movement.

Our Movement had become a Community. Its goals and methods were soon perverted. Few real challenges, and fewer changes, occurred. Political self-examination of ourselves as a group was abandoned. Those dominant in the community had opted for a way palatable to them: self-examination on a private level. Therapy. Thus was one of the most dangerous elements of the patriarchy introduced into our midst.

Lesbians acknowledge that we live in a patriarchy, but we have failed to recognize that the patriarchy lives in each of us. Had we faced this, we might have taken each political challenge as an opportunity to stretch our horizons further yet. Instead, everything being done by lesbian/feminists was explained, denied, responded to in the terms of therapy, an element of white, middle-class life.

Those of us not involved in—or even familiar with—therapy felt as though the earth were shifting beneath our feet. The change was not overnight, though it seemed to be. Attending meetings became an ordeal, conducted according to alien rules. Lesbians who had been by our sides for years grew scornful at our lack of familiarity with the territory into which they were dragging us. Language and vocabulary skidded away from us; words skirted around the edges of clear meaning. Lesbian and womyn's centers (and book-stores and restaurants and buildings) were effectively closed to separatist and other radical lesbians by their switch from revolutionary forums to social reform, and later still to a focus on personal growth. Relationships between lesbians were similarly undermined as privileged lesbians, bolstered by their therapists, sought not love and mutual respect, but a place to have their needs met. The key word was "process"; its concepts, goals and vocabulary were drawn from therapy.

Feminist Process

It is claimed by those who employ it that feminist process was devised to correct inequities in our political meetings such as domination by a minority of the lesbians present (those most verbal and assertive, infighting, a lack of structure, certain lesbians not being heard). Each of us knew who we believed responsible for these problems; each of us thought all the others meant the same ones.

Throughout the decade of feminist process' hold on the lesbian movement, I have watched the growing perplexity of poor and working-class dykes as the proffered solution to our problems—feminist process—has proved not only to exclude us further, but to oppress us. [I have shared the ideas contained in this paper with many lesbians who feel excluded and oppressed by these same things, but on the basis of their race or ethnicity. As a white working-class lesbian, I will approach it from my personal perspective in this paper.] Feminist process is based on middle-class values and experience, and justified by the middle-class phenomenon of therapy.

I was among those who complained loud and long about some lesbians controlling all meetings. Like other outsiders (non-WASP, non-middle-class), I meant the middle-class WASPs. But, while I wished to stop their long, personal discourses, they wished to stop my loud complaints.

The elements of feminist process so differed from the lives of nonprivileged dykes that we could not understand their enormous attractiveness to other lesbians. First is the request (read: demand) at the opening of political gatherings (including one-time forums, support groups, work groups, etc.) that each lesbian relate her feelings, memories, fears and so forth on the topic of discussion. [The voice of the therapist is saying, So, how have you been this week?] This sort of vulnerability and emotional exposure is strange to working-class and poor lesbians: encounter groups, after all, are not a lower-class phenomenon.

How the classes differ in this respect is really rather simple. Working-class people tend to **express our *ideas with feeling*, but we do not necessarily express our *feelings*.** Middle-class people maintain a level of coolness about ideas which baffles us (and is designed to make us feel vulgar), while displaying a willingness to reveal personal feelings which seems positively uncouth to many of us. It would be considered poor taste in our cultures. But since the middle class rules, working-class lesbians are continually reprimanded for our "excitability" in meetings, while also being reproached for our failure to "open up" personally.

Second, in my world, trust (which is what is being asked in these check-ins) was to be earned, not granted at first contact. Even within the confines of our community, all we have in common is our existence as lesbians. Trust on a personal, emotional level, that which implies a shared understanding of these experiences as lesbians in the patriarchy, is something I do not accept as a given. The dykes comfortable with these circumstances therefore do most of the talking. Anyone who thinks this is all a voluntary procedure should try passing her turn some time and observe the ensuing suspicious glances. If our meetings are such safe, supportive environments, why is it so threatening for anyone to decline to "share feelings?"

Lesbians have countless unshared experiences. As a minor example I once attempted to relate an amusing family anecdote to a middle-class acquaintance. It was relevant to my story that there had been insufficient food the night of the story, but this was *not* the story and *not* important to me by itself. Middle-class pity, however, made the listener so distraught the tale was never completed. We just don't always communicate.

The third practice instituted at political meetings was that of always having a facilitator. From the initial custom of designating one member to prevent irretrievable drift from the agenda, facilitation became a rigid control of all aspects of meetings. Facilitators keep time, limit how long each may speak; they take names of those who have raised their hands and call them in the order in which they saw them, or perhaps in clockwise order around the inevitable circle in which we sit, with no weight given to the import of what any particular lesbian has to say. [The voice of the therapist is saying, I think we've dwelled on this long enough. I'm sorry, our time is up.]

A good facilitator would rescind a lesbian's right to speak in direct response to even an accuser out of turn. Personal dialogues are deemed best left until after the meeting. [The voice of the therapist is saying, It seems you have some unresolved feelings with this person.]

Fourth, vocabulary has changed. Slowly, the concepts and jargon of therapy have replaced political language. Assertiveness (itself a middle-class concept) dissolved into their more comfortable middle-class stance of apparent chronic uncertainty and self-effacement. Assertiveness had taught middle-class feminists to leave behind ladylike manners. (And who else, I ask you, ever had them?) If your roommate borrowed your clothes and left them in a heap, you should tell her to knock it off. Middle-class lesbians never really got comfortable with this approach. Therapy worked much better for them. Therapy teaches that if your roommate repeatedly borrows your clothes and leaves them in a heap, you should tell her that this feels like a violation of trust to you, that you are flattered that she enjoys your taste in clothes enough to want to be seen in them, you are more than happy to allow her to share in the use of them, but she really must show more respect, so that your feelings for her can remain clean and uncluttered by your resentment.

I recall the lesbian who was the first in my experience to forbid direct confrontation, as facilitator, between any two lesbians at a meeting. At first, I thought it was only more of the fear often evinced by middle-class dykes at any sign of anger. (They sometimes act as though we're all about to pull knives.) When I saw that she also stopped all humor, I realized that emotion of all kinds made her feel uncomfortable, out of control of the meeting. She wished to conduct a calm, objective meeting.

Therapy, of course, is *the* training ground for the separation of intellect and emotion. I will not belabor the differences in kinds of therapy. The basic premise, stated or unstated, is that emotions need to be examined with the intellect. Instead of accepting our emotions as expressive of our thoughts, therapy teaches that they actually obscure our thoughts and our thought processes. Therapy is the definitive manifestation of middle-class alienation. Therapy has institutionalized one of the essential dichotomies of the patriarchy: that between intellect and emotion. In *Gyn/Ecology*[3], Mary Daly notes the dangers of therapy to revolutionary lesbianism in a very few, very pertinent pages, noting, among other things, that therapy "... fixes women's attention in the wrong direction, fragmenting and privatizing perception of problems. ..."[4]

Lesbians who find open emotion distasteful declare it off-limits for working-class dykes to express themselves with feeling, and still give vent to their own more circumspect sentiments by saying they are just putting out their personal needs, to which, of course, no one dares object. The personal has superseded the political.

What is the distinction between intellect and emotion? *Webster's New Collegiate Dictionary* gives us some clues:

> *Intellect:* The power of knowing, as distinguished from the power to feel and to will.
>
> *Emotion:* A psychic or physical reaction (as anger or fear) subjectively experienced as strong feeling and physiologically involving changes that prepare the body for immediate vigorous action.

Hadn't we better question a preference for thought divorced from the "power to feel and to will?" A working-class friend of mine once described this as "the difference between feeling and talking about feeling." The political result is the difference between change and talking about change. A movement aimed at subverting a system (of government, society, religion and personal relationships) many tens of centuries old should welcome "strong feelings" leading to preparation for "immediate, vigorous action."

But some of our sisters—notably those from middle-class and/or WASP backgrounds—were raised to believe that expressions of emotion signify lack of control. There are thousands of lesbians who will say, in all earnestness, "I am very angry with you" in a perfectly serene tone of voice. As the years go by, they grow more and more distant in their phrasing, as "I feel some anger around this," or even "I have some anger here." The distance grows: I am, I feel, I have. Meanwhile, charges of hostility, divisiveness, and male-identification are leveled at lesbians who don't need to announce that they are angry, because their feelings are clear, from their every word and gesture.

Therapists thrive on the belief that feelings are a threatening fog veiling the world, to which, with a counselor's help, the lens of the intellect must be applied.

Emotions are not uncontrollable, primitive forces forming a screen between lesbians and our world; it is not necessary or advisable to think of them as such, for to do so leaves us open to those who wish to be our interpreters to ourselves.

And so we have the basic set-up of feminist process. Therapists teach their clients/patients that they have a right to "put out their needs" while routinely exorcising the demon of open emotion. [The voice of the therapist is saying, "Now, let's calm down and see if we can't work to get to the true source of this pain.] Open emotion has at least a better chance at being honest, and is much easier to challenge.

Middle-class womyn have had to go through very few changes to adapt to feminist process, to "sharing" feelings, to sublimating and laying a coating of sophistication over their feelings. They operate on the tacit assumption that everyone in a feminist political gathering will understand the importance of using the (male-identified) concepts of therapy.

Feminist process, we are often told, has been developed so that the business of certain vocal persons dominating the group can be avoided. Through process, we can prevent the yelling bouts, the interruptions, the shouting over each others, the emotional expression of ideas, *the mixture of intellect and emotion* that have characterized other political movements. Many working-class dykes are actually shamed into a silent compliance with what is really middle-class manners newly defined as feminist process. And why not? By the equation the privileged have developed, feminist equals middle-class and working-class equals patriarchal. The either/or proposition is: feminist process or patriarchal power games. I maintain that the one is the other. The way we of the lower classes have related all of our lives is now labeled "male-identified," "politically incorrect."

Middle-class folks have often been threatened by my readiness to express my anger (or even my sarcasm). They never implied I would strike them or attach bombs to the ignition switches of their cars, but they said repeatedly that my anger frightened them. In the course of their various therapies, they would mention this problem to their counselors.

What happens next may be clarified by an incident of mine from the late 1970s. After a concert of a lesbian band at a local bar, a rather esoteric evaluation ensued. Though repeatedly asked to participate, I said I had nothing to add. I am scarcely a non-critical person, but it felt like a test: say something educated, give a (preferably negative) critique. Finally, annoyed, I said, truthfully, that the band had been fun and their discussion had an elitist and campus-y tone and I declined to play. My companions were both offended; the middle-class one began weeping and was consoled by my working-class friend.

A few days later, I ran into the middle-class woman, who had, by now, seen her therapist, and they had discussed how my "attack" had hurt her. She resented my having accused her of classist behavior. She told me that I had had no right to make any "judgments" about her musical opinions because everyone (including some mutual friends whom she had no better grace than to name) knew how rigid I am about music. (Her elaboration of this had to do with the fact that though she knew me to be extremely shy about it, I play the piano.)

In short, I said she did something classist. She was angry about this. Unable to say so, she "took back her own power" by trying to make me self-conscious about ever playing in public again. I was, in fact, momentarily humiliated, but I had time to see the look of triumph on her face. She felt she had cut me down to size and no longer had to deal at all with the truth or falsity of what I had said in the bar. I had been honest. She had been cruel. This is power-over. She still hadn't "expressed her anger," if you will; but she felt better and could duly report in her next therapy session that she had "dealt with" the situation.

I have eaten it more times than I can count, thanks to lesbian therapists. Since the middle-class friends of mine who went to them were never explicit that what made them uncomfortable with me was not what I said but that I *could* say it, what I got in return was abuse.

When we prohibit the right to honest anger, we inhibit justice among ourselves, for the balance should be one of truth for truth: honesty and an apology. Therapy gives us a balance of hurt for hurt: honesty and cruelty.

Because middle-class lesbians feel bad when I am forthright or yell, and I feel bad when they are cruel, they delude themselves that we are doing the same thing. But, of course, they remain therapeutically calm and objective, which gives them enormous power; in a classist culture, emotional outbursts in response to such cool would be so tacky. Both parties are judged by the standards of white, Protestant, middle-class America.

As meetings progress, and decisions must be made, the only mode now acceptable to feminists is consensus, a concept classist in practice. (Groups such as Abalone Alliance have published statements detailing the consensus process. A pamphlet called "Blocking Progress" is a statement by an Abalone member who finds consensus rife with abuse, especially classism.)

Consensus is said to give everyone an opportunity to speak and to object to group decisions, even if the majority approves them. I have never seen anyone but the most privileged members of any group successfully block a consensus decision.[*] Being consistently outvoted is decidedly frustrating. Consensus requires that every person be satisfied (the American Dream); no one is declared the loser of the vote (a horror to privileged folks); formidable pressure is brought to bear on the dissenter. Now, any objection to losing a consensus vote is deemed childish, because everyone theoretically had the chance to stop any vote from going through. The fact that dissenters must carry the onus of having selfishly stopped the entire group's progress is not officially acknowledged.

To close meetings, we are offered criticism/self-criticism, perhaps the most jarring item of feminist process for those of us from lower class backgrounds. This allotment of time at the end of meetings for the expression of feeling means implicitly that feelings are taboo during the meeting. Explicitly, it means only that emotionally expressed thoughts are forbidden. Intellectually (read: therapeutically) expressed emotions, the domain of the middle-class are very much indulged. Crit/self-crit is the first element of process to which working-class lesbians objected. When first introduced, it was no secret that it was a therapeutic concept. When we began objecting, they came up with the argument that since it *really* originated in China, with the Communist party, it was both racist and anti-revolutionary to resist.

Crit/self-crit serves to allow abusive or manipulative lesbians to say anything they wish in the course of meetings, knowing that the facilitators will not tolerate direct confrontation. A working-class dyke friend has recounted to me that her audacity in offering real criticism of middle-class lesbians' *exercise of privilege* was consistently punished by

---

[*] The important exception is the instance in which lesbians attend meetings solely to block decisions. Consensus is dangerous in this way, too. A small group of womyn attended the opening sessions of an anti-nuke group I was in some years ago only to make sure that neither the word "lesbian" nor the word "womon" appeared in the title of the group. They blocked consensus, the group was named as they wanted, and we never saw any of them again.

responding criticisms of her *style*. She was castigated in vague therapy terminology about her offensive, unconstructive attacks. This was intended to silence her protests against oppression. Yet, what middle-class dykes said about her never had to do with realities like privilege and oppression (the content of her criticism); only that some delicate spirit experienced her honesty as being hurtful. If she couldn't learn to do it right, she simply had no credibility.

Lesbians whose low-income backgrounds have placed us in the position of struggling against scorn all our lives sometimes just fail to grasp the benefit of chastising oneself in the presence of others whose respect one might like to have. We tend to take the brunt of the criticism (which should tell, once again, what and who is being silenced by feminist process) because we do not use the jargon of feminist process. It is not taught in lower-class homes to preface everything we say with the phrases: *I think, I feel that, In my opinion, I could be wrong but.* We speak with the bluntness for which we are stereotyped. During crit/self-crit, we are often attacked for opinions we expressed, because we neglected to provide ourselves and our listeners, in the fashion of feminist process, with those verbal escape clauses. The emphasis in middle-class *language* is not on the "I," but on the words "think," "feel," "opinion."

Alternatively, when such phrases are not used by middle-class lesbians, then the opinions are delivered with no "agent" at all. Mary Daly has referred in lectures to the diluted emotions of what she calls "therapized" lesbians as "plastic passions." Saying, "There seems to be some energy around this," removes the fire from the feeling. You don't, in fact, feel anything at all: you have some remote blob of ersatz emotion to be dealt with.

Therapy teaches self-doubt by its basic premise that womyn (who are the patients of all forms of therapy) need interpreters to understand their own spirits. The willingness of working-class lesbians to simply say what we want to say and take the consequences is an affront to the devotees of therapy. With such responses as "Speak for ourself!", when no one had claimed to be doing otherwise, middle-class lesbians make clear their discomfort with, and need to discredit, the fact that working-class dykes do not negate our own statements. They claim that we are less open to criticism when in fact, we are more open. We take the risk of making statements that can't be easily withdrawn like those beginning with *I'm not sure, but it seems to me that....*

Humanism
> ... there has been resurrected an individualism which, flowing directly from the human potential movement, emphasizes taking one's own space, defining one's own reality, taking care of one's own needs. For many, concern over the quality of life is personal, individual, and focused on one's well-being.
>
> Kathleen Barry[5]

Middle-class lesbians depend on self-centeredness and freedom from challenge. Although feminism as a movement probably no longer exists, feminists certainly do; and the majority have succumbed to the "therapeutically polluted environment,"[6] needing above all else to feel good about themselves.

This is a handy focus to have for oneself in a time when lesbians are trying to challenge each other about privilege and oppression. For example, I tried once to approach a lesbian about her class-oppressive notions and attitudes. Utterly unmoved by the pain she had inflicted on me, she said that she would like to promise to do better. However, she had never felt really good about herself and was trying—with the help, of course, of a feminist therapist—to acquire a better self-image. Therefore, much as she was sorry for my feelings, she would be unable to do anything about her classism. To acknowledge her privileged oppression of me would make her feel like a bad person. And her prime motivation at this time of her life was to feel good about herself.

The pursuit of a contentment with oneself *as one is*, without wishing to grow and change—wishing in fact to avoid growth and change—is the symptom of a self-centeredness which is overtly threatening to a revolutionary lesbianism. What kind of revolution waits until its warriors are happy and fulfilled before confronting the enemy? The answer is: one which has abandoned revolution for "therapy as a way of life."[7]

Feminism is no longer respected, even by most feminists, as a valid movement to which a lesbian could dedicate her life's energies. It is seen now as a step on the way to humanism: patriarchy in drag. All the values and attitudes radical feminists started out battling are contained within the humanist approach, disguised by "psychobabble," which the author who coined that term says, "must be seen as the expression not of a victory over dehumanization but as its latest and very subtle victory over us."[8]

Lesbian Relationships

Process is also required now in lesbian relationships. Dykes no longer seek partners with whom they can relax, with whom they have much in common, with whom they feel deep happiness or even love. Lesbians have been seeking "fixes" of various kinds. Alcohol and drugs, to be sure, but more and more frequently, "psychological 'fixes'" in the form of therapy sessions and the drama-filled relationships which provide the symptoms for which are sought therapeutic "cures."[9]

Class oppression distorts personal relationships between middle-class and working-class lesbians via the therapeutic concept of "getting one's needs met." Lover-relationships have been redefined as a place of struggle, not a refuge from the outside struggles of our lives. Therapy has been instrumental in closing off lesbians' awareness of these outside struggles: sexism, racism, and classism, etc., are too painful to deal with, and the circle is complete.

A lesbian *needs* food, clothing, shelter; secondarily, she

may need, in order to have a full life, satisfying work, productivity and usefulness, to love and to be loved, the achievement of inner peace and spiritual growth. What each of us *wants*, however, is a matter of individual taste and the choices we have made in our lives. Needs are now, in feminist/lesbian circles, anything a dyke wants or to which she feels entitled.

Seeking to get their needs met, lesbians with enormous differences and with vastly varying visions of a good relationship can remain together indefinitely. Manipulative behavior by one or both of them and the adjustment skills of a good lesbian therapist can keep the lovers struggling to process their differences, instead of separating because of them. Therapy greatly aids in this circumstance because it doesn't deal in facts, e.g., that the relationship is no good for you, but in personal feelings about facts, e.g., that you are unhappy about elements of the relationship, but therapy can help you change it and get your needs met.

If a therapist's patient was expected—or even *allowed*—to say, "I am in a relationship which limits my freedom of movement, inhibits my expression of ideas, threatens my peace of mind, and invades my privacy," chances are an intelligent and caring friend, or even counselor, would say, "Get out of it!" But the report is—as it is expected to be—phrased as, "I feel she doesn't trust me, or respect my opinions. I have a lot of anxiety and because of her insecurity, I have less free time than I need." Now there is something a therapist can work with: fears, anxieties, insecurities. The relationship could go on for years with the therapist encouraging better communication, more efforts to deal with these differences, perhaps even mediation. Moreover, being in a successful relationship (by therapeutic standards, ones where you struggle and make it last) is the hallmark of health to therapists, who are in the business of recommending and facilitating adjustment to existing circumstances.

It has been easy, therefore, for privileged lesbians to take advantage of working-class dykes in relationships. Middle-class people hire therapists and any number of others to provide service for them. We do not expect others to do for us.

Working-class etiquette says you don't expect everything in life. Outright demands would likely be met with scorn and a parental reminder that the world, after all, did not owe you a living! To "take power" in a situation you can't change means "taking power" *over* those whose obligation you think it is to provide for you. Power-over is not desirable. The natural empathy of working-class culture brings a willingness to help when *and if* possible. What one wanted or needed was never named, opening no one to public disappointment; the responsibility of fulfilling needs was given (by putting them out to others) to no one, opening no one to feelings of guilt and failure. It is a matter of pride, mutual respect, and consideration.

Contact with mixed-class society is a culture shock for working-class dykes on many levels. We are accustomed to keeping our private desires to ourselves, unless we have certain knowledge that someone with whom we are intimate can help. Then it is asked, respectfully, as a favor, to be reciprocated when possible. A refusal to help meant an inability to help, which also was treated with respect. This is how things would function between people of my background. Pointing up the absence of something material (even to the point of asking for sugar for coffee in someone's home) might be exposing temporary or permanent poverty. We all knew that we gave whatever we had; if you didn't see it, you didn't ask for it. Trust was built in widening circles, within which things could be taken for granted.

For working-class lesbians, there is more at heart than the absence of a personal therapy experience. There is the basic contempt in which therapy is held in working-class environments. For instance, I not only never experienced therapy myself, I was acquainted with no one who had until I was about 21. People at survival level have a justifiable disdain for the privileged, whose leisure time and money can be squandered on having a total stranger solve their problems for them.

Middle-class lesbians go through their lives with the expectation to varying degrees that their desires can and will and *should* be satisfied. There is a selfishness, a shortsightedness, in this attitude that is shocking to me, for everything they want or like or prefer in life is labeled a need.

Trained in proper etiquette involving the suppression of emotion, middle-class lesbians seek therapists to teach them about emotion. They spend their childhoods being repressed when trying to express emotion; being told that their feelings are invalid and in need of re-examination with the help of professionals. In other words, they are taught to doubt their ability to perceive the world through their own judgment. Therapists then lead them into a web of exploring feelings, denying feelings, examining feelings, analyzing feelings, trying to experience feelings, dealing with feelings, dealing with how others deal with their feelings, and how that affects their own ability to deal with these others. In short, they enter on an absorption with self, acquiring an ability to talk about feelings, but not to trust simply feeling.

A key factor in community life is missing because, not trusting her feelings—never in fact *feeling* them—the middle-class lesbian is unable to comprehend those of us who do, and empathy is beyond her. If it were not, the practices of the privileged over the oppressed would have to become obsolete; standing in another's shoes makes one more considerate.

Meanwhile, a working-class dyke relating intimately to middle-class dykes is unprepared for the outright demands, the assertion that needs be met; she is shocked by the accusation of failure if she doesn't meet them. What we consider true needs are those things the lack of which mark one as inferior in the U.S. I repeat, we express ourselves with emotion, and pride is an emotion. Our druthers we do not refer to as needs. And, since working-class lesbians expect empathy in other womyn (I have found this to be true even in those from the coldest, most non-nurturing homes imaginable), and because of the class dynamics I laid out above, nonprivileged dykes are sometimes unable, and usually unwilling, to state their emotional needs. We are therefore (conveniently, I can't resist noting) assumed to have none. So, those accustomed to asking for things, do so; those who are unaccustomed to asking for things, don't. And the class system marches on.

I categorically refuse the assertion of the middle class that we all learn to put our needs out. When it becomes valid to say, *I need not to have meetings scheduled on Thursdays, I need you not to use that expression because it reminds me of an ex-lover, I need you not to raise your voice because my mother used to yell and then hit me*, it occurs to me that silence may truly be golden. I grew up around too many alcoholics, constantly putting out their needs, with family members indulging them and fulfilling the needs, not to comprehend the danger in this. I, for one, have no desire to live in, let alone help create, a world of self-centered therapy addicts. The current "model" for lesbian relationships is based on one seeking the fulfillment of her needs by another and one feeling worthwhile because she succeeds in meeting those needs. This is a dependency model, much like alcoholic families. Similarly, "falling in love" brings together two lesbians, each feeling incomplete, hoping the relationship and the person in it will bring wholeness. A mature love/friendship would be the meeting of two lesbians, each complete in herself, or at least seeking to be, coming together for further happiness.

The Path Back To Radical Feminism

The Therapists

Therapists are, very simply, lesbians who believe the tenets they learned as students or patients themselves and who choose to think they are helping by offering these services to others. There is, really though, no earthly reason why lesbians should have turned over such authority and power to any specific group. If it is true that none of us has escaped indoctrination in the distortions of the patriarchy (and it is true), it is especially true that lesbians who have taken specialized training in one of the power structures of the mainstream society should not be given such absolute trust.

Therapists are not the objective listeners or wise counselors they are widely accepted to be. They bring all of their own biases and personal experiences to each session with them. Some have admitted to encouraging or discouraging some behavior, such as ending a relationship, depending on how well that aspect of their own lives is going at the moment. Lesbians approaching a therapist for help in escaping an abusive or destructive relationship should not be subjected to the prejudice of a therapist who suggests preserving the relationship because the therapist is content with her lover right now.

Moreover, we must question what they, as lesbians who so deeply believe in getting needs met, are getting out of these sessions themselves, besides their often outrageous fees.

Therapy is a part of the mental health establishment. How do we dare ignore the pitfalls of embracing, as central to our community life, even this lesser form of an institution which tortures and imprisons lesbians?

By the equation the feminist movement has accepted, all too eagerly, middle-class = feminist, while working-class = patriarchal. Yet, there are many qualities from poor and working-class lives which others would be wise to emulate: honesty, straightforwardness, a natural blending of intellect and emotion, a notion of female competency, empathy, self-reliance, a sense of the interwoven nature of life, and not least of all, survival.

It is important to understand that therapy is one of many abuses which have combined to destroy lesbianism as a movement. But while racism, classism, reformism, and other oppressive elements serve each a single purpose of the patriarchy, therapy has the double effect of *being* oppressive in and of itself, *and* of reinforcing, making possible, all of the others by the use of language and concepts which shield oppression. Therapy and the middle class are the two places where anger is presumed to mask some other emotion. Middle-class manners and values reign in the lesbian community, disguised by therapy and masquerading as feminism.

What We Have Lost

The physical space for which we fought so very hard, in which we had hoped to discover ourselves and each other, our commonality as lesbians, our shared oppression in the patriarchy and our shared strengths as those who had, so far, survived that patriarchy, no longer exists. Exclusion (of, for instance, men) would violate the tenets of humanism, which was peddled to lesbians by therapy as the step beyond feminism. Instead of the invaluable womyn-only or lesbian-only space where we reveled in our freedom to learn and grow together, we now have the ubiquitous "safe, supportive environments," formerly known as womyn's or lesbian centers. Now they exist for personal growth where lesbians learn not from each other as peers, but in therapist-led or -facilitated groups. They offer not revolution, not even assertiveness, but adjustment.* Self-sufficiency, in the form of hands-on workshops and concrete lessons in survival, are gone; in their stead we have not even self-defense, but self-improvement.

And what sort of improvement is being taught? Defeating racism or classism? not really: just "unlearning" them. The former is political and involves group movement; the latter is a realignment of ideas, having nothing to do even with community.

The feminist maxim, "the personal is political," was distorted like so many other things. It has been made to mean that anything a lesbian does, whether or not she involves herself in the furtherance of lesbian liberation, *is* political activism. It is not, although every aspect of our lives does have political implications. That, and the fact that the

---

*Twelve Step groups, patterned on Alcoholics Anonymous, are blossoming everywhere as the means of coping with every imaginable aspect of life. Despite the successes of AA—in lives saved—we should be more than a little alarmed at the popularity of a program whose First Step is for each person to admit her complete powerlessness over some area of her life.

oppression we suffer in our lives is not a personal issue but a political one was the original meaning. The present-day lesbian has acquired the right to live an utterly personal, self-centered life because, after all, the personal *is* political. She may seek completely private solutions, through therapy or its related themes, to what we had once defined as universal female problems. With a personal/therapeutic slant and humanist influence, even lesbian spirituality is making its contribution to the individualization of lesbian politics.

The truism that each of us must start the revolution with herself was not intended, by its originators, to mean that everyone could retreat into prosperity workshops, parental-paid educations, professions and the professionalizing of every aspect of lesbian liberation (licensed psychics, certified relationship mediators, professional organizers, Ph.D. witches) and the religion of once-a-week therapy. Start with yourself, yes; start and end with yourself, no.

Therapy is the religion of middle-class-oriented political lesbians, and those who oppose it are indeed heretics. There is an element of coercion here that we are not facing.

What We Could Have

Understanding the classism made possible by lesbian therapy does not mean that from now on our groups can have no structure or form. It means that any group's structure must be arrived at as at least a synthesis of working-class and middle-class experience and values. Whoever is facilitating a meeting must question whether she makes decisions and suggestions for the true benefit of the whole group and all of its members, or for the comfort of the group's middle-class members (who don't like raised voices and sudden interruptions) and her own continued power.

It doesn't mean that anyone should be allowed to pitch a fit in the middle of meetings or indulge in any sort of temper tantrum. It means recognizing, when a middle-class lesbian uses subtle manipulations of a group's rules or structure, invoking the principles of therapy which give her the right to demand that others deal with her feelings, that she is on a power trip. It means that when middle-class lesbians, skilled at speaking interminably while sounding humble and altruistic, calmly demand attention to their opinions, taking far more than their share of time, they are interrupting at least as much as a working-class lesbian who yells about the oppressiveness of the rules. We have come to view the middle-class mode as objectively right because we live in a classist society that has taught us all to respect and aspire to middle-class values, even if we don't understand any way in which they are workable in our own lives; even if they mean denying our traditional class and race and ethnic backgrounds.

It does not mean that there can be no politeness, no respectful treatment of one another in meetings. It means realizing that feminist process, while it *may* prevent yelling bouts (not always evil, you know), also prevents simply the excited expressions of ideas, the interruptions of each other, *the mixture of intellect and emotion* that have characterized other groups. Feminist process is not automatically egalitarian. The lesbian community ignores the facts that assuming the necessity of "sharing feelings" in a specified time slot means that those feelings must be hidden (essentially forbidden) until the appropriate time; that many people talking at once does *not* mean that no one gets heard (only that it might be a challenge for someone to hold the floor solely to herself for very long, a fact which I am sure upsets those accustomed to undivided attention); that silence while one lesbian speaks does not necessarily imply attention in the listeners; that calm, objective political discussions sometimes indicate (and often create) boredom in many working-class lesbians.

It does not mean that any one should be permitted to dominate group dynamics. It means realizing that feminist process *may* have put an end to one kind of hierarchical domination of group interactions but has instituted another kind. Both forms of control exclude working-class lesbians. In both formats, the middle class rules. Under feminist process, only objectified feelings, which one has analyzed and dealt with, are acceptable. Our liberation movement was not created to provide a solitary stage for each lesbian who felt entitled to one. The system we know as feminist process has become static, a fixed and rigid presence in our community, which we can ill afford if we are ever to become a movement again.

It does not mean that middle-class lesbians have no rights. It means acknowledging that working-class lesbians have had to learn to relate in the forms acceptable to middle-class lesbians for years—and I do mean *had* to. The complete denial of our way of life has been a means of coercing us into conformity with a way foreign to us. A middle-class lesbian relating with a working-class lesbian should no longer feel completely free to find the solutions to her own problems within the relationship without considering the methods and results of her solutions. Is she making demands which are acceptable according to middle-class standards, but which are painful for a working-class lesbian? Has she ever considered the vast differences in those standards and whence they arise?

It is incumbent upon middle-class lesbians to stand aside from the privilege they have assumed for themselves and really listen to their sisters who perceive things differently. This means an ongoing assessment of choices.

Solid friendships are a better place than therapy to talk about problems. Politics is a better weapon than therapy against our oppression, within and without the movement. That many oppressed lesbians (subject to classism, racism, anti-Semitism, etc.) end up in this "helping" profession is not a surprise. We all too often serve the upper classes, and act as a buffer for them.

The anger of working-class lesbians is an expression of raw pain, the unsophisticated anger to which middle-class lesbians once felt attached and to which they are now hostile. Acknowledgment of that pain would be many-faceted. It would involve a recognition of the psychic suffering of the affluent housewife (your mother, perhaps); the loneliness of the inner-city widow; the terror of the institutionalized woman, abandoned by everyone (including most of us); the hopelessness of the enslaved prostitute; the entrapment of the incest victim; the struggle of the unemployed pregnant teenager; the bureaucratic nightmare of lesbians and poor and Third World mothers whose children are "adopted" right out of their homes by social welfare agencies; the isolation of the incarcerated womon: the sadly endless list of nonprivileged lesbians whose lives our rhetoric has never touched.

Relief from oppression must come to all of us or none. We cannot settle for academic and employment gains for those who had at least limited access to such privilege—albeit, sometimes, through men—even before feminism. A revolution of lesbians cannot make privilege more comfortably accessible to the already privileged. *"Feminism demands more than private solutions or even private solutions stated in political terms."*[10]

Life, after all—especially lesbian life—is a progression of relationships in the truest sense: from the momentary to the life-long, the vital touching of one spirit with another. We *should* draw laughter and tears from one another, and we must learn to find them in ourselves. Separation of intellect and emotion, the *raison d'etre* of therapy and its primary function, is one of the most deadly dichotomies of the patriarchy: one to which we, always stereotyped as controlled by our emotions, are especially susceptible. Above all things, this dichotomy must be struggled against. Certainly, we must not perpetuate it ourselves.. Otherwise, defeat is imminent. A successful battle, however, could give us back ourselves: whole, integrated, prepared to seek the joy of freedom, individually experienced, but collectively achieved.

Notes

This article appeared originally in *Lesbian Ethics* 1:3, 1985, published by Jeanette Silveira, who also edited my first draft. It has been shortened considerably for this publication with some line editing to compensate for the deleted segments. Additionally, I have taken the opportunity of this reprint to be conscientious in the use of the word lesbian in *all* cases where I knew this identity to be so or when I was referring to the lesbian community exclusively. It was an oversight on my part not to have done that in the first edition.

[1]Kathleen Barry, *Female Sexual Slavery* (Englewood Cliffs, NJ: Prentice-Hall, 1979), p. 237. (Emphasis mine.)

[2]*Ibid*, p. 223.

[3]Mary Daly, *Gyn/Ecology* (Boston: Beacon Press, 1978), pp. 275-283.

[4] Ibid., p. 276.

[5]Kathleen Barry, *Female Sexual Slavery*, p. 223.

[6]Mary Daly, *Gyn/Ecology* (Boston: Beacon Press, 1978) p. 276.

[7]*Ibid.*, p. 280.

[8]R.D. Rosen, *Psychobabble* (New York: Atheneum, 1978), p. 13.

[9]Mary Daly, *Gyn/Ecology*, p. 280.

[10]Kathleen Barry, *Female Sexual Slavery*, pg. 237, (emphasis mine).

The View from Over the Hill

Notes on Ageism between Lesbians

Baba Copper

Youth sees itself as immune to the threat of ageing. I can remember the day when I would use the phrase "over the hill" to describe an old woman. The implications of the phrase, and my complicity in those implications, never crossed my mind. Now, from experience, I understand that someone "over the hill" is metaphorically out of sight. In my youthful complacency, I was banishing old age from my awareness by that phrase. Now that I am old, I have become increasingly curious about why I needed to reassure myself in this way.

Every one of us gets older from the day she is born, but there are great variations in the impact of this fact upon different lives, and upon different times in those lives. There are endless unexamined contradictions in the prejudice which women feel toward the old woman they themselves are or are becoming. Lesbian ageism is probably the ultimate extension of these self-defeating contradictions. It is this that I need to examine, since the greater part of my experience of ageism has been with lesbians. As the years beyond fifty-eight have accumulated, I have found it increasingly difficult to participate in the social and political life of the lesbian community. This difficulty has reflected a change in my status as ascribed by other women, not in my capacity for effective or enjoyable involvement. A subtle transition has taken place in which I have slipped from the category of "tolerated" (passing for middle-aged) to a new and shunned identity which has no name but "old."

The old woman finds herself captive to stereotypes which drain her initiative and shatter her self-respect. The mythic prototypes of the Wicked Old Witch, with unnatural powers; the Old Bad Mother, with neurotic power needs; and the Little Old Lady, of absolute powerlessness, cloud the individuality of every woman past sixty. Since childhood, all of us have been bombarded with systematic distortions of female ageing in fairy tales, legends, books, movies, plays and TV. Age prejudice encourages substitution of these manufactured realities for the real human being, with real personal powers, whom we encounter. Ageism rationalizes the discarding of old women—as workers, friends, lovers, relatives.

Feminism has taught me to closely scrutinize male reversals of women's truths. The blatant reversal of old women's reality, not only in our culture, but cross-culturally and down through patriarchal history, tells me something about the psychological and political needs which stereotypes such as the Wicked Old Witch fulfill. *One of the primary definitions of patriarchy is the absence of old women of power.* Shimmering in the psyche of the Father are his ancient fears of the old matriarch and her potential use of power—preferential treatment of the Daughters over the Sons, matrilineal inheritance, or incitement to marriage resistance. The accumulated experience of old women has always been a part of what Adrienne Rich named "the enormous potential counterforce (that) is having to be restrained."[1]

I believe that there is an important reservoir of lesbian energy locked away by this false consciousness, the "othering" of the old lesbian. The doors to that reservoir are being guarded by women acting upon unexamined traditions of expectation and behavior. They are rewarded by increased power within our limited world. But in carrying the double-edged sword of ageism, they wound themselves. Ultimately, they serve the interests of male dominance.

One of the pledges I made when I found myself going "over the hill" was that I would learn to articulate the great complexity of the experience of ageism as it takes place between women. Detailing the particulars, especially the startling erosion of the relative safety of middle-age, will not satisfy me. Rather, I need to explore the root sources of my dilemma, speculating about the conscious and unconscious motivations of the women who seek to diminish me. I recognize that my present and future pain is identical with that which I have caused others. It is time that we stop this intergenerational warfare. I would like to believe that I am not the only one dissatisfied with the low priority which lesbian feminism has assigned to these divisions between us.

Inventing Lesbian Identity—Who We Are, or Could Be

If lesbianism ever becomes a mass phenomenon, it will be because it offers women the opportunity to explore a fundamentally new social identity. No longer subject to male sexual choice, we learn not only to choose, but to decide for ourselves on what ethical and erotic basis we will make choices of all kinds. Without being particularly conscious of what we are doing, lesbians are collectively forging an unprecedented female identity out of our living.

Choices are often made on the basis of assumptions. The assumptions which we make automatically and unconsciously, in default of rational decision, are the vast ground of all human relations. They are as necessary to action as being able to breathe without awareness. But default assumptions are also intimately tied to nuances of hierarchy, which in turn falsely inform our identity or sense of self. It is here that lesbian choices need politically guided attention. Patriarchal standards of taste—rules of esthetic and erotic choices—perpetuate male structures of power. If we allow male-defined standards of choice to be our default standards, then we maintain female powerlessness. We waste the opportunity which our lesbianism provides: to choose how to choose.

This is particularly true in relation to age prejudice, since so many of the default assumptions which diminish a woman as she ages are derived from sexism. Male contempt for the older woman as unfit for the reproducer/sex object roles filled by younger women (still the primary source of female power in the patriarchy) is the foundation of the old woman's powerless position. Being largely barred from the working world further diminishes our power image, where worth is measured by earning and workplace status. If we are not sex-objects or breeders or caretakers or wage workers, then we are loathsome, since it is these *roles* which legitimate females in male judgement. As Susan Sontag, in her deeply ageist and heterosexist article "The Double Standard of Aging," pointed out: "That old women are repulsive is one of the most profound esthetic and erotic feelings in our culture."[2]

Lesbians, as the group within women's culture most self-conscious about patriarchal values, cultivate the illusion that we waltz to our own tunes. Yet lesbians, like everyone else, are all getting older. Our community is so ill-prepared for this that old lesbians find ourselves disappearing right off the edge of reality. The ageism we encounter teaches us that we are obsolete; that we should not be able to imagine ourselves powerful, either physically or socially. It is a standard default assumption of the lesbian political community that old lesbians are conservative (or at least politically incorrect) and inflexible. Above all else we are expected to be submissive to women younger than ourselves who are the "right" age to exert power within the lesbian world. We are asked to be walking contradictions to the clichés of lesbian identity which all of us are in the process of inventing. Unless old lesbians are re/membered as sexual, attractive, useful, integral parts of the woman-loving world, then current lesbian identity is a temporary mirage, not a new social statement of female empowerment.

Why Haven't We Heard More About Ageism Before?

In trying to understand ageism, I can find few guides beyond my own feelings and experience. With the notable exception of Barbara Macdonald and Cynthia Rich's book *Look Me in the Eye*,[3] there has been no analysis of ageism from the lesbian feminist community. Susan Sontag did not question the cultural rejection of old women. Instead, she pleaded for a time extension of the acceptance which passing provides for the middle years. Her primary contribution in this work was to distinguish between the male experience of ageing and that of the female.

Even the more subtle discrimination suffered by mid-life lesbians has rarely been examined. Attention has focused instead on the "real" problems, as named by women in their twenties and thirties. It is as if ageism were a minor difficulty, something which can be cured easily by a little "right" thinking. Since no one differentiates between the adultism which young people suffer as they grow up, the ageism men experience, and the primal loathing and stereotyping which hits women when they grow old, everyone assumes they know what ageism is and how it feels. Sometimes it is included in the litany of "isms" with which we exhort each other, sometimes not. When it is, the visiting male septuagenarian Chairman of the Board, the local teen-aged breakdance champion, the mid-life lesbian politico, and I are all expected to feel equally included.

As I write this, breaking the silence which surrounds ageism feels very unsafe to me. By demanding that younger women share with old lesbians the respect and power generated among women, I am questioning their use of that power. (The hill I am descending is a hill of power.) More than this, I would like to destroy their smug closet of "age-refuge"—those safe, dishonest inner denials of the process of ageing. All women practice age passing as a method of coping with whatever aging "crisis" we currently imagine threatens our self-esteem. Age passing, like any other kind of passing, involves lying, first to others and ultimately, to one's self. By raising the issues of passing and power and identity, I am engaging in activities which are forbidden to my kind. Old women who find fault are seen as Bad Mothers. They are not forgiven, and are ostracized.

Why, you may ask, have old women themselves not raised these issues in the past fifteen years of women's negotiations with each other? I think the answer to this lies in the peculiarities of the experience itself. Unlike other oppressions by class or ethnicity or race, oppression by age steals upon us gradually, invading the defenses carefully constructed against it. Passing begins long before the ritually endowed age of thirty. It begins when women (lesbians included) start equating youth and well-being. Age passing becomes a state of mind, a measure of self-worth, a guide to choice. When we reflect "young" tastes in our clothing, cosmetics, activities, friends and lovers, we are passing. As Sontag pointed out back in 1977, growing older for women is mainly an ordeal of the imagination—the biological eventuality dims in comparison with the social judgement. As ageist negative experience begins to impinge seriously on our self-image, we deny. At the same time, we deepen our reliance upon whatever advantages our "relative youth" may provide us. The age-acceptance which we need from others, we refuse ourselves. Women in their forties and fifties, themselves victims of ageism, are often the most vicious in their dealings with women older than themselves. Many old women are increasingly ageist and self-hating, decade to decade, from sixty to ninety.

It isn't just ageism that sneaks up on one. The process of growing old—biological ageing—involves constant adjustments of one's responses and goals. Old age acts as a thief in the comfortable storeroom of the expected, forcing one to adapt to changes which arrive as strangers to the usual patterns of be-ing developed over the years. It seems important that these adaptations, or losses—if that is what they prove to be—are met as courageously as possible. Old women need positive reinforcement from others to meet these strangers.

What we do not need is silencing. Yet the single strongest social message an old woman receives is to "grow old graciously"—to *not burden others* with complaints. By complaining, an elder will only increase her own isolation—or so the saying goes. This veiled threat obscures for old women the importance of naming our experience honestly.

Not all of the pain "on the other side of the hill" is inevitable. Much of it is simply serving the interests, and increasing the power, of others. As long as lesbians see ourselves as empowered by diminishing other lesbians, then old women become real targets for these interactions. Above all else, all ages must acknowledge that the deafening political quiet surrounding ageism is simply more female compliance in masculinist values.

Is This What Young Lesbians Really Want?

Conforming to the Little Old Lady stereotype of absolute powerlessness should not be a goal for any lesbian, yet the pressure I feel going "over the hill" is to behave less assertively—to be "appropriately" submissive. This is the subliminal message from women, as well as men. It says: "Smile, or you will be seen as critical or grouchy! If you manage to camouflage your greyness or your wrinkles or your limp, then you will be more likely to deserve attention. You will be more acceptable." If I can't pass, then I must act powerless.

I feel as if I am involved in some subtle competition not of my own making. Although feminist lesbians attempt to resist participation in power/over scenarios, we still listen carefully for the subtle indicators of respect from other women. Competitiveness seems connected to the attention we pay to power differences. Sources of power such as looks, skills, sexual confidence, resources, political correctness—all play their part in the complex process of figuring out whether one is "ahead" (and feeling confident and easy because of it) or "behind" (and feeling uncomfortable). Although old lesbians often receive deference, I seldom experience a feeling of real respect from others. Almost never do I sense that I am being approached by a younger woman in the spirit of acceptance, learning or wonder.

My situation feels confined within my category—an old woman, potential scapegoat. I do not mean to say that all my experience is negative all the time. But the fear, contempt and rage which many women unconsciously carry for my category is latent, hovering over me. I have learned that the discharge of these irrational feelings is postponed only to the moment when I do not please. *I feel like a walking lightning rod.*

Over and over, I have had the same experience, both with lesbians near to my age and with those younger. When I exert my powers on "their side," in agreement or in service to them, all is well. The mirror they hold up to me reflects: "Capable, intuitive, likable, creative, interesting." But when I exert myself in my own interests, as opposed to theirs, or in my own defense, I find that I am not allowed to act authentically. What they want—no, demand—from me is unconditional love and service. Their efforts to control my behavior take many forms, but are often distinguished by explosive intensity or irrational anger. Suddenly I get lots of negativity and trashing, not the "I feel" kind but the accusatory "You are" kind. I have become the Bad Mother or the Wicked Witch. Then their mirror says "self-centered, overpowering, coercive, withholding."

I, in turn, must process this feed-back through the filter of my years. Have I suddenly gone through some startling personality change which makes me radically different from the woman of ten, twenty, thirty years before? What about the lesbian identity I am struggling to perfect— assertive, un-self-sacrificing, honest? How can I gauge whether or not these women are being ageist? Maybe this is the way they always act. But why, then, am I having so many of these experiences in the last few years? Why do others refuse to negotiate differences with me? What about our feminist determination to work things through, to not treat each other as men have treated us? The self-doubt built into these questions is bottomless. Always I ask myself, "Aren't you being too sensitive? Isn't this awkwardness perhaps *your* fault?"

I do not have answers. All I can do is list some of the ways in which old lesbians may find ourselves used within the lesbian community. Some are from personal experience, some from watching the experience of other old lesbians.

(Obviously not all women participate in these offenses, nor do all older women experience them.)

The old woman is one whose labor/energy can be assimilated by everyone. We are someone to listen to others' troubles without telling ours, the Wailing Wall, the dump where others are free to unload. Our emotional or physical nurturance is a part of others' support system, without anyone monitoring the return. It is not politically incorrect to extract money or favors from us without a fair exchange of goods, labor or services. We are subject to a different code of honor than other women. For instance, an old woman who owns her own home, who is near to retirement from a good paying job, or who has a little capital from a divorce settlement, can be branded as a "Rich Woman." The age barriers to further wage income for us—barriers which radically change old women's relationship to capital—are ignored with youthful chauvinism. We are a Class Enemy. We can be envied with impunity; ripped off, with righteous indignation. Any resistance we muster in our own defense is punished severely. *Self-defense is absolutely unallowable in a mother figure.*

There is a look of wary readiness in the eyes of many old women. Our bodies often unconsciously reflect our humiliation. We have demonstrated a remarkable ability to internalize our own coercion. The body language of many old women speaks of our position at the age/sex nadir—the ones who no one wants to be. We are seen as the cause of many frustrations, disappointments and failures. We are pushed away by emphasis upon our differences, our faults, our style, our mistakes, our lacks, our general *difficultness.* Although our experience—even our expertise—is needed, everyone avoids ceding us either leadership or credit. In typical patterns of rationalization, almost everyone agrees that we *ourselves* are the ones who caused the offenses committed against us.

Among those who cannot imagine identifying with us, judgement is passed from mouth to mouth, without crossing our ears. Often we are unsure of exactly what we are accused. We are usually short on allies, social power, and self-love. Thus women carry out the horizontal violence among ourselves, doing the essential work of preserving "woman's place."

Knowing the threat of all these possibilities, I try to be the kind of person everyone likes. I listen well, I nurture, I create goodies and give. I comfort and touch others, even though I am seldom touched. I don't complain a lot. I suppress my needs, ignore the contempt or sexual invisibility I experience. (I bite my tongue and walk around as if on eggs!) I find myself metamorphosed into the stereotypical granny, even as I judge the role intolerably demeaning. This violation of Self is unhealthy, as feminists have been quick to testify in relation to male definitions of appropriate heterosexual female behavior. The personality I feel I am being asked to assume as an old woman is even more docile/submissive than that asked of me as a woman throughout my life with men. It is the polar opposite of the independent assertive dyke that I smashed my traditional world into bits to become.

Whose Mother Are We Defeating and Why?

There is no way to talk about ageism between women without focusing on mother/daughter relations. Sometimes I feel as if ageism is misnamed; that the problem should be called Daughterism. One of the ways that a young woman can get a taste of her future fate is to be turned into a moth-er-figure by a peer, who may or may not be older. At the lesbian summer camp of Califia, where all are invited to generate workshops, I spontaneously wrote *Daughterism* on the schedule, interested to see how other women would respond. Forty young women showed up, eager to describe their confusion over being used as a mother by friends, fellow workers, or lovers. Thematic to their testimony was self-blaming speculation as to why their *looks* evoked this manipulative behavior in others. ("I just know that it is because I have these big breasts!") None had any theoretical framework through which to view their misery. From *my* vantage point, at that time nearly over the hill, all of these women were potential daughters, capable of using me as they had been used.

I have often wondered if it wouldn't be possible to make a fortune by manufacturing a T-shirt which, in large letters across the breasts, said: I AM NOT YOUR MOTHER. Most older women find ourselves stereotyped as mothers by younger women. This erasure of our individuality is unfair, but the psychological underside is downright ugly. If the older woman triggers childhood angst in the younger, the older may find herself bearing a burden of projected hostility without the slightest clue as to what is going on. (Psychologists seem to agree that many people need to recreate unresolved childhood experience.) All women have been taught to see mothers as fair prey, to be used as the giver-who-does-not-get, the non-reciprocal nurturer.

The other side of the mother/daughter coin is the legitimate rage of the daughter at being raised by her mother to fulfill goals that are largely in violation of her own self-realization, especially when seen through lesbian eyes. With few exceptions, lesbians have in common the experience of growing up mothered by a woman who abided by traditional patriarchal motherhood. It is the mother's *job* to prepare the daughter for the use of men. She must teach her, by example, how to assume the terrible responsibility for "maintaining the center"—the stabilizing core of family and the "private" world. She must instruct her in the self-defeating standards of taste which will govern the daughter's attitudes toward her own body and face, her personality, and her choices of life adventures. Successful mothering is still measured in terms of the daughter's attractiveness to men, her success in male-controlled work worlds, and her reproductive capacity. These successes depend to a large degree upon the daughter's ability to assimilate and use the aesthetic rules which deify female youth and teach allegiance to a hierarchy which will forever divide her from other women. I do not believe that true reconciliation between women is possible until daughter-rearing goals are radically modified. The betrayal of the Daughter by her loving Mother poisons the relationships between all women, but most clearly those between young women and old women.

In light of these fundamental tensions, one of the remedial steps lesbians can take is to make a clear distinction in our minds between old lesbians and our own mothers. Another is to sort out, and question, the *roles* which our default assumptions tend to assign to women older, or more "motherly," than ourselves. Barbara Macdonald points out the servant status of the older woman, deriving from that of the mother.

> Today, the evidence is all around us that youth is bonded with the patriarchy in the enslavement of the older woman. There would, in fact, be no youth culture without the powerless older woman. There can be no leisure elite consuming class unless it is off the back of someone. The older woman is who the younger women are better than—who they are more powerful than and who is compelled to serve them.[5]

I look back at my personal experience as a good patriarchal mother with the painful wisdom of hindsight and recognize my deep collusion in the generational divisions which now afflict me. Even though my own mother was a professional woman throughout her life (reflecting the influence of the earlier wave of feminism, as well as the fact that my father was a poor provider), I fell into wifely dependency, and filled the servant role for my children and husband. Like so many other women of my generation, I left a war-time job as a shipfitter to marry and become "Supermom" to a large family. Not only did I betray my daughters by teaching them the standards of taste learned from my mother, but I also complied with their expectations of maternal servitude, generated through an alliance with their father.

The children learned an assumption of privilege from their father, and he in turn became one of the children—legitimately passive, irresponsible. For him, the equal partnership in parenting I had expected meant giving me some help around the house when the children were young. Even this was considered very progressive by our contemporaries. The onus of parenting was truly mine, so that the children were psychologically single-parented. Not only did these circumstances infantilize an already emotionally stunted man, but my older daughters never witnessed any *exchange* of nurturance. In their view of how the world worked, mothers gave, and men/daughters received. Ours was such an isolated nuclear family that they literally never had any opportunity to witness me being nourished, sustained, taken care of, or emotionally supported. The *absence* of experience is just as effective a conditioner as repetitive experience. My older daughters, now in their thirties, are dutiful wives but still do not know how to extend nurturance to me, or to negotiate when we have a difference of interest. As Macdonald points out:

> It becomes more clear that the present attitude of women in their twenties and thirties has been shaped since childhood by patriarchy to view the older woman as powerless, less important than the fathers and the children, and there to serve them both; and like all who serve, the older woman soon becomes invisible.[6]

Only the youngest, who at twelve came with me when I escaped into the relative sanity of the lesbian world, saw me in loving and reciprocal interactions with a range of other people, including women lovers. Now only she, of my three daughters, is able to exchange nurturance with me; only she is relatively free of ageist interactions with me.

It is Macdonald's insight that the alliance of father with children in the exploitation of the mother helps to create ageist response to all older women. As the Victorian authoritarian husband/father was vanquished by an earlier wave of female emancipation, men have had to regroup within the family to maintain the slave status of the woman. Demands made by children on the mother are seen to be as fully legitimate as those of the husband. As the children grow up, they continue to relate to older women with the clear expectations of service. By then they have laid claim to a place of privilege in the power hierarchy.

Do Lesbians Really Need Old Victims?

By now, it should be clear that in many ways the landscape over the crest of the hill is different in degree rather than substance from the up-grade. Political struggles between women have focused on ethnic, racial and class divisions. Movement women have made some small progress in diminishing these tensions, but at the same time, all of us are well socialized in the ways of the Fathers. At an unthinking, irrational level our world is still divided into those who give and those who get; those who are decided for and those who decide; those who are victims and those who victimize. This we have learned from our family of origin and all the other power hierarchies we observed as we grew up. In the either/or victim/victimizer choice our internal need to escape the victim position transcends our raised consciousness. The choices we make whereby we become victimizers are made on the basis of default assumptions, unconscious stereotypes, adherences to standards of taste which are alien to our avowed politics. These choices are the primary inhibitors of significant political cohesion between lesbians.

Fear of contempt is the tool of social control lesbians exert upon each other. Avoidance—the averted gaze—is the whip of our system. Scapegoating, and the pack behavior which we learned within our family of origin, are used by us to establish and maintain power differentials. Much of woman-to-woman interactions consists of automatic scanning for, and assertion of, the dominant position (normally occupied by the male in mixed-sex situations). First we act out of terror of being the victim. Once we establish our non-victimhood, we then need to escape guilt. The Other-who-is-in-fact-one-of-us, such as the old woman or the fat woman or the disabled woman, becomes the victim—the one who is shunned, the contemptible one.

For the mid-life woman, and especially the mid-life lesbian, sexual erasure is the most urgent and emotionally devastating aspect of ageism. Mid-life can be a time of desperate passing. Confidence diminishes and doubts multiply. These feelings often coincide with pressures at work which are also age-related. The mid-life woman drinks of the milder poisons of age prejudice every day. It is not the distilled tincture which the old woman must survive, but it is the same poison. The mid-life lesbian is also very good at serving it up to those whose years threaten her pretense of passing.

I am describing the polarized dance lesbians have learned as women, surviving in the "real" world (of compulsory heterosexuality), where many of our chances in life are determined by our race, looks, class able-bodiedness and age. In the larger culture, lesbians often reap rewards in jobs according to how we compare with other women. In our own world of power, influence and sexuality, we maintain this comparative and judgemental hierarchy ourselves. Age is the underlying agent of change in circulating power within the class of women, robbing Garbo to pay Twiggy.

Youth provides women with a temporary illusion of opportunity in the work world. As youth is the primary requirement for the role of phallus stiffener, there are a great number of jobs for which only young women qualify. There is a chasm of identity which comfortably separates young women from women they perceive as not passing. Old women are segregated into a shunned category and desexualized by both men and younger women. This attitude tends to legitimate the presumption that all women not in that category are sexually accessible to men. "The woman who too decisively resists sexual overtures in the work place is accused of being 'dried-up' and sexless or lesbian."[7] A young woman's fear or horror of those identifications can reduce her will to resist. Fear of being seen as too old to harass may lead young women to participate in the displacement of older women workers. In the competition between women for work, younger women have played scab to the struggle of older women workers for recognized seniority and paid-for-experience. The position of the "new, prettier receptionist" or the "young, sexy replacement" is dubious ethical ground.

There is a limited period of time in a woman's life when she is allowed to exert the power which masculinist values bestow upon accessible sexual energy. My personal experience of street hassling illustrates this. As an adolescent, my need for recognition accepted any offering, even though I wondered constantly whether the whistle was for me—for my specialness. By seventeen, this question had found its answer. I began a long period of developing techniques of rebuff. As my body thickened and my hair greyed, there was a time when I simply forgot about harassment. Then suddenly I became aware that not only was unwanted attention absent, but my personal space—the ground ceded to me by those who passed me on the street—had shrunk. No one met my eye. This remarkable change in my corporeality was acknowledged by both women and men. Through the absence of harassment, I discovered the invisibility of age.

Invisibility needs to be described in all its subjective horror. It takes many forms, the most searing being its sexual form. One has scarcely recovered from the ambivalence which sexual objectification evokes when one is plunged into the emotional vacuum which its withdrawal triggers. Lesbian youth worship differs little from heterosexual youth worship. But the deprivation of sexual recognition between women which takes place after middle-age (or the point when a woman no longer passes for young) includes withdrawal of the emotional work which women do to keep the flow of social interactions going: compliments, questions, teasing, touching, bantering, remembering details, checking back, supporting.

These are ethical issues which younger lesbians need to consider in their relations with older women. What do lesbians want to do about those human connections which do not directly enhance the primary goals of career or personal gratification? Are we so captive to the cultural fear of female obsolescence that we let time and indifference gradually strip women of power, work, visibility, and finally human contacts? We need to negotiate a feminist code of honor between young and old, designed for our ultimate and mutual benefit. The call for this must come from young lesbians, as well as old.

What Do Old Lesbians Really Want?

It makes a lot of difference who names our circumstances. There are a few angry old lesbians who are speaking out against circumstances that others have never thought to question. As with naming sexism in the early 1960s, the first problem is establishing one's legitimacy, despite the voices which contradict. Whenever old women complain of ageism in a gathering of women, there are inevitably those in their late forties for whom it is important to deny the observation. "I have grown children," they testify, "so I certainly qualify as an older woman and I haven't experienced any discrimination!" It would help if women in their forties and fifties assumed, not that they were experts on ageism, but rather that they might be suffering from a kind of perverse crisis of fear which increases their alienation from old women.

However, all ages of women have a deep investment in denying age-hatred. To those lesbians who point out that they have friends whose lovers are twenty years different in age, I say: "But how often does that twenty years include a woman in her sixties? How many women in their seventies are your intimates? Who do you know who has a close friend in her eighties?"

Ageism appears to pollute women's experience at different ages, or at different stages of physical change or disability. For some, the dramatic changes in our experience do not happen until ten to twenty years later than they happened to the next old woman. Some older women are able to delay ageing—"outwitting Nature," it is called. Old women who are physically small, "cute," or who emanate the vibes of Daughter rather than Mother may succeed in passing far longer than their more bulky peers. They often deny other women's experience of pain.

The way to respond to *all* accusations of ageism is identical to how we must respond to accusations of racist, classist, physicalist or sexist behavior. Do a lot of listening, both inwardly and outwardly. Resistance, excuses or rationalizations only compound our problems. There are basic questions which fifteen years of feminism have taught us to ask: Who profits? What are the hidden assumptions? Why have we ignored it? How many of the culturally mandated attitudes have we internalized? This is not necessarily to say that the action or absence of action has been correctly named. But when an older woman raises the issue of ageism, do not explain to her what you *really* meant. Listen.

Since there are so few from my side of the hill making demands, or even expressing dissatisfaction, there are many who challenge me by demanding concrete examples of ageism. If I am not being pressed for a story about my past, I am being asked for an example which will illustrate the charges I have made. Both demands annoy me. Like most people, I am focused in my present, not my past. This "tell me a story about the way things were" syndrome feels like another affliction of age. I am not some walking museum of memorabilia, either camp or quaint, to be mined by others' curiosity. As for ageism, I find that I can say how it feels, or describe who it serves, or speculate about its roots. But there is no way for me to tell stories which will fully illustrate my losses because of it.

It is possible to illustrate stereotyping, but this is only a part of the pain. Let me give an example: I had come to a meeting at the home base of a country collective which published a magazine. As I greeted those I knew and found a seat, one offered me a drag from the reefer she was smoking. Without much consideration, I took a puff. This ordinary social action on my part evoked a long discharge of heavy-handed approval from another woman, whom I hardly knew. She was delighted to know that I smoked. She thought it was absolutely wonderful. It had never occurred to her that I would indulge. On and on. The only woman in the group who found her condescension disturbing was the woman who had shared her reefer. "But Baba's a *head!*" she murmured, knowing I needed *some* kind of defense.

Now, it is true that this is an example of ageism. By verbalizing a default assumption about white-haired women (one that may have been in the minds of others in the room), this woman was able to set me up as Other. She happened to be a woman of color. I remember various cutting rebuttals, including some with racist overtones, which flashed through my mind, none of which I used. She was exercising her age dominance, and I, in my discomfort, mentally reached for white dominance as a defense. It is not enough that we learn not to say these things. *We have to unlearn needing to think them.* To do this, we have to build for ourselves a Self-image that will not be served by these easy power gains. Such a story can forewarn women of "things not to say." But don't ask me for catchy stories, which cannot begin to describe the righteous rejections, trashings and betrayals which have made ageism my "primary state of emergency."

When there is no regular channel for redress, then I don't know what else to do but call on others to hear my testimony, to share my pain, and to help clarify for me the universality of my experience. I believe that ageism does not result from fear or envy of the accumulated experience of an elder, nor is it the reflection of some primal response to the inevitable march of time toward death, despite the repeated use of these clichés in the apologies of the young. These rationalizations of prejudice, like so many raised in defense of sexism, use their kernel of truth as a diversion. Ageism exists because it rearranges power between women. It robs old lesbians of their rightful place of respect and social equality. With all the strength of self-fulfilling prophecy, it shapes the lives of all lesbians, even the most self-defined and self-confident. It can diminish and warp us into faint parodies of our essential Selves.

As for how old lesbians want to be treated within the lesbian world, that is difficult to describe. There is a kind of care which we take with women we wish to know. We give them our attention. We make allowances for their peculiarities. We monitor our own behavior for impositions or assumptions which we cannot justify to ourselves, or to them. Caring treatment involves effort—emotional work well invested in the interests of friendship between women.

Let me speak for myself. First and foremost, I need lesbians with whom I can test possibilities, with whom I can exchange disagreement and anger, with whom I can be comfortably intimate—women to trust. I need, in order to be fully sane, a circle who can reflect me back to myself without having to judge or chastise or control me. Lesbians who can give me both resistance and validation. There is a lot of political work I can do with women who are aware of their responses, who know disagreement between us does not mean that I am bad. Also, I expect women younger than myself to acquaint themselves with issues that are important to my age bracket, and include them in *their* political life. If I nurture them, they must recognize that I want nurturance in return. I don't think that I am asking for anything different now than what I hoped for fifteen years ago, when I first came out.

The potential of energy which is dissipated through woman-to-woman ageism may not be obvious until one gets "over the hill." But it should be clear to all lesbians that ageism distracts us from the pursuit of our essential Self, the very identity which lesbianism makes possible. Active confrontation of our conditioned loathing of the old woman is only the first step. The second is to become consciously anti-ageist—a step toward self-love, away from the contempt and terror with which we evade our eventual future.

Notes

This essay first appeared in *TRIVIA: A Journal of Ideas*, vol. 7 (Summer 1985).

I want to thank the women who encouraged me to find the words for these ideas, and helped me with editing: Pia Chamberlain, Becky Meeley and Harriet Ellenberger.

[1]See Adrienne Rich, "Compulsory Heterosexuality and Lesbian Existence," *Signs*, Volume 5, No. 4, p. 642.

[2]See Susan Sontag, "The Double Standard of Aging," *Saturday Review of the*

Society, September 23, 1977.

[3] Barbara Macdonald and Cynthia Rich, *Look Me in the Eye* (San Francisco: Spinsters Ink, 1983).

[4] Sontag, p. 37.

[5] Macdonald and Rich, p. 39.

[6] Ibid., p. 40.

[7] "Compulsory Heterosexuality," p. 640.

How Inclusive Is
Feminist Political Theory?

Questions for Lesbians
Bette S. Tallen

I come to this work both excited and a bit sad. Excited because I feel like I am once again on the cutting edge of a new
kind of feminist theory, a theory that may yet bring feminist
theory back to its more radical nineteenth century roots, the
ideas that challenged the basic patriarchal institutions of
church and family. I am sad though, because I realize that
much of what is called feminist theory today is not an inclusive enterprise, that it is meant to exclude my life and my
experience. Most 'feminist theory' today is exclusionary of
many groups. As a Jewish lesbian I feel this omission keenly.
I begin this paper, then, with a call that it is time to recognize
that what we are doing in lesbian theory may be, in fact, far
more inclusive than is most feminist theory today.

I also begin this work remembering what happened to
me when I entered graduate school in political theory in
1971. I was taking a seminar on modern political theory and
one night I was going on and on about my favorite theorist
at the time, Jean-Jacques Rousseau and his ideas on man and
his environment. My teacher, who was also my dissertation
advisor (she became my advisor because she was the only
woman on the faculty and I was one of only four female
graduate students in my year), finally couldn't take it anymore and asked me, "Tell me, what is the fate of poor
woman?" My mouth dropped open—I had never heard such
a question. I stammered on and on how man was really a
generic term and that clearly Rousseau had meant to include

women in his discussion. She asked me if I had ever read Rousseau's *Emile*. I said I hadn't, so she sent me home with her copy that evening. I went home and eagerly opened the book and started to read. Well, *Emile* was all about the education of the ideal citizen, Emile, who of course was male. No problem, I thought, I'm used to identifying with males. After all, Holden Caulfield, the anti-hero hero of J.D. Salinger's novel of adolescent adjustment, *Catcher in the Rye*, had been the hero of my youth. Then I got to Book V of *Emile*, Rousseau's chapter on marriage. Here I met for the first time Sophie, who is there to help complete Emile's education. Imagine how I felt when I read,

> In the mating of the sexes each contributes in equal measure to the common end but not in the same way. From this diversity comes the first difference which has to be noted in their personal relations. It is the part of the one to be active and strong, and of the other to be passive and weak. Accept this principle and it follows in the second place that woman is intended to please man.[1]

Imagine my surprise! I then was forced to re-examine radically all that I thought I knew about any political theorist. Was I to be included in any of their visions and analyses, was I to be liberated along with all the others? Clearly the term man was meant to be exclusionary by Rousseau, what about the others? I began to think of John Locke, the seventeenth century English liberal theorist whose ideas on natural rights and democracy were so critical in the founding of America. I realized that he never really explicitly confronts whether women are truly to be included fully in his theory on natural rights. He does grant that even married women retain their right to life, but how about liberty and property (his other natural rights)? His silence and the silence of the other political theorists I read spoke volumes.

My second starting place for this work occurred in 1982 when Billie Potts published *Witches Heal: Lesbian Herbal Self-*

---

[1] Jean-Jacques Rousseau, *The Emile of Jean-Jacques Rousseau.* Translated by William Boyd. New York: Teachers College, Columbia University, 1962, p. 131.

Sufficiency,[2] the best all-round women's herbal I've seen. One of the reasons Billie had titled the book that was because all the women's herbals she had ever seen addressed only women's reproductive issues. She subtitled it a lesbian herbal not only because of her extensive work and commitment to lesbian health, but because she meant it to be a complete herbal for a woman's entire body. I have used this book as a text in several courses on women and health. Students loved the book but were, in the main, shocked and uncomfortable with the title. One student went on for pages in her journal yelling about the title and why she, a non-lesbian, should be forced to read this, and then went on to say that the section on arthritis saved her knee. Further, anytime I went into a women's bookstore that stocked the book it was inevitably on the lesbian shelf. Not once did I see a copy on the health shelf, although it clearly belonged on both. That was my first major indication that non-lesbians absolutely refused not only to identify with lesbians, but that many even refuse to utter the word. Recently this perception was reinforced when I was a judge for the Chicago Women in Publishing annual awards. One of the awards that I and another judge recommended was for the Iowa based periodical, *Common Lives, Lesbian Lives*. She and I were amazed at the lengths the other judges, all non-lesbians and all very high-powered women in the world of publishing, went to avoid uttering the L word (and here L stands for lesbian not liberal). It became kind of a game as we tried to get them to say the word and they continued to refuse. As feminists we reject the generic man and refuse to identify with exclusionary language. What does it mean when non-lesbian feminists refuse to identify with the term lesbian?

Do non-lesbians include or exclude us when they use the term woman or the word feminist? We all understand that terms like lady doctor or lady lawyer imply that doctors and lawyers are male. Why is it hard to see that the way non-les-

---

[2] Billie Potts, *Witches Heal: Lesbian Herbal Self-Sufficiency*. Ann Arbor, MI., Du Reve, 1988.

bians use the word feminist may be just as exclusionary? Women of color, such as Alice Walker, have pointed out that white feminists, who never put white in front of feminist, continue to do so for Black women. As a result, many women of color will not identify with the term feminist because they believe that white women are trying to exclude them. Some argue for the term womanist as more inclusive than feminist and in terms of usage they are clearly correct. I think of the times I have heard non-lesbians use terms like lesbian families, lesbian mothers, or the supreme redundancy, lesbian women. When I have pointed out to them that lesbian women as a term implies the existence of the ultimate oxymoron, lesbian men, they look at me as if I was no longer in the realm of the rational. Finally it has dawned on me that perhaps they do not use terms like family, mother, or even woman as inclusive ideas: they do mean to exclude lesbians. A dramatic example of this occurs in an interview with Linda Gordon, a prominent socialist feminist historian, who says, "The word *family* does have an ideological meaning that cannot be defined away simply by the decision of leftists to make it mean something else. The family does *not* mean two lesbians and a child."[3] Let me not be accused of quoting Gordon out of context. She makes it very clear that she does not embrace the pro-family politics of some feminist and left theorists. Still her omission of a lesbian defined family from the concept of family is significant. Does it mean that her work on violence within families cannot include a discussion of lesbian battering? I feel like I did when I first realized that Rousseau had not meant to include me in his political theory. Clearly the generic man did not include me, but now I find myself being excluded from the concept of woman. I believe that woman should be an inclusive term. The very basis of feminist theory and existence is that it applies to all women. The fact that non-lesbians exclude me so clearly is troubling. Perhaps the reason that non-lesbians look at me as if I am

---

[3] "Interview with Linda Gordon." In *Visions of History*. Edited by Abelove, Blackmar, Dimock, Schneer. New York: Pantheon, 1983, p. 84.

speaking nonsense when I challenge terms like lesbian woman is that they think that woman only applies to non-lesbians. How could woman be an inclusive term if they have to add lesbian to it?

Theory and Inclusiveness

Since graduate school I use as my litmus test to evaluate any political theory the issue of inclusiveness and accessibility. Specifically I examine to whom the theory is addressed and how inclusive is the analysis? Does it speak to women? All kinds of women? Does it pretend to be a general theory but only apply to a few? I see my work in feminist theory as part of the task to make political theory inclusive. I have always thought that the best feminist theory attempts to look at the situation of all women. When I began to realize that much of feminist theory, especially kinds of feminist theory that calls itself radical, were not inclusive, I had to radically rethink what is the basis of feminist theory. Is feminist theory only the property of white, middle-class, non-lesbians? Is it an enterprise I can work with or must I abandon it?

When I consider how inclusive or exclusionary the practice of feminist theory is I need to think about what I know about political theory and the emergence of feminist theory. Is the process of feminist theory doomed from the start because its roots, especially in liberal theory, are too entrenched in a patriarchal, heterosexualist context? Or can feminist theory speak to the lives and situations of all women? My immediate answer is that I believe that feminist theory can be inclusive, but only if all of us insist that it be and only if we confront and understand the implications of some of the roots of feminist theory. These roots, in English liberal theory, spell out some of the limitations of feminist theory. I would argue that these limitations can be dealt with, but must not be ignored.

Most political theory that calls itself feminist emerged as a reaction to liberal theory. Liberal theory opened up citizenship in the state and full participation in social institutions, in theory, to all men, regardless of class background. Once citizenship in the state was opened up to all men (excluding men who were slaves in the U.S.), women also began to agitate for inclusion. I, among others, have written at length on how the connection between liberal theory and feminist theory has both fueled and limited the emergence of feminism as a political movement.[4] Briefly stated here, according to liberal theory, the exclusion of women from the political state was done not on the basis of divine law, but on practical grounds or grounds of expediency (at least in the eyes of the male theorists). Women were guaranteed some rights (such as life), but were seen as not capable of exercising other rights (such as the right to vote). Women fought back on primarily two grounds: one, that justice demanded their inclusion (that their exclusion from the world of natural rights was arbitrary, an excellent illustration of this argument is seen in the Seneca Falls declaration), and two, that women, if given equal rights, could act as the great reformers of civilization (the earliest comprehensive statement of this is in Mary Wollstonecraft's, *A Vindication of the Rights of Women*, where she argues that giving women their rights will make them better wives and mothers). I am sure that to no one's surprise lesbians were invisible in this debate. It further should be noted that early liberal feminist theory focused primarily on woman's relationship to the state, a focus that presumed automatically that the state was a given, that the state was and is vitally necessary for the preservation of human peace. Liberal feminist theorists argued that the church and the family need to be preserved, albeit reformed. Even Elizabeth Cady Stanton, one of the most radical theorists of the nineteenth century, relied on the state as the major vehicle through which

---

[4]For further discussion of this see Bette Tallen, *Liberal Equality and Feminism: The Implications of the Thought of John Stuart Mill*. Ann Arbor: University Microfilms, 1980. Also see Juliet Mitchell, "Women and Equality." In *The Rights and Wrongs of Women*. Edited by Juliet Mitchell and Ann Oakley. New York: Penguin Books, 1976, pp. 379-399. Also see Zillah Eisenstein, *The Radical Future of Liberal Feminism*. New York and London: Longmans, 1981.

women needed to gain and exercise rights. Today, some feminist theorists do challenge the hegemony of the state, church, and family of the nineteenth century tradition, but how many non-lesbians challenge the heterosexualism of liberal theory? Socialist feminists, in particular, although often leading the fight against the assumptions of the assumptions of the liberal state, have not seriously questioned compulsory heterosexuality and its institutions. Their failure to do so is striking.

When one looks at modern feminist theory, one is struck by two things. Liberal feminists, such as Betty Friedan, still see the state as natural and vital for human interests. Socialist feminists, such as Linda Gordon or those I discuss below, focus exclusively on women's relations to men, to children, to the family, and to male-defined institutions such as the economy. None seem to see any possibilities for life for women outside of a male-defined context. The institutions they focus on not only are male-defined and male-dominated, these are also institutions that exclude lesbians and lesbian meaning. It is clear that one of the few things that unites liberal feminists and socialist feminists is their intention to maintain relations with men. Sheila Rowbotham, a prominent socialist feminist, takes this point even further when she says,

> I felt that the concept of patriarchy was one that I really couldn't handle as a historian. ...It seemed to me that the idea of patriarchy inevitably inclines toward separatist feminism...what I was really trying to say was that a feminist theory about the relationships between women and men needs to think in terms of mutual needs and relations, positive reasons for relating as well as conflict. You need the two together. ...you need to see why it is not a relation of total conflict, not a Hobbesian situation, otherwise it would deny the experiences of those who have either sexual, work or political relationships with men. I think this is an unreal aspect of separatism. ...The term 'patriarchy' implies that the forms of male domination are unchanging.[5]

---

[5]"Interview with Sheila Rowbotham." In Abelove, et. al., *op.cit.*, p. 60.

Here women and men become the yin/yang[6] of feminist analysis, the two opposites that unite to form the whole. So much for the dialectic (and this from a socialist feminist), a form of interaction that holds for the dynamic interaction of negation. In Rowbotham's view the dialectic becomes all synthesis and no conflict.

Several other points of interest can be derived from Rowbotham's statement. The first is her view that feminism is meant to facilitate women's relations with men. She equates all women's relations with men, even if they are limited to work relations, and then says that separatism denies all of these women's experiences. Clearly all those relations are not the same. Rowbotham's ignorance of separatism is startling, if not surprising. By denying the existence of women who choose, in whatever ways they can, to define themselves independently of the male context, she reaffirms a yin/yang view of male/female relations. Lesbian meaning and existence have no place in her analysis. What further interests me is Rowbotham's insight that the use of the term patriarchy inevitably inclines toward separatism. She seems to say that once you accept that men seek to dominate, control, and define the lives of women because they are male and because historically men have exercised that right then the only way to free oneself is to separate from men. Her own refusal to separate further underscores the nature of the non-lesbian feminist's dilemma. Rowbotham's last assertion, that the concept of patriarchy implies that forms of male domination are unchanging, is truly absurd. Would she say that the term capitalist implies an unchanging form of economic domination and exploitation and therefore is not a useful term? Perhaps the answer lies in her desertion of the Marxist dialectic for a yin-yang view of male-female relations. This yin/yang view of masculinity/femininity holds that these are universal unchanging principles. Marx's concept of the

---

[6] When I use yin/yang here, I am talking about how Rowbotham and many other feminists use male/female as immutable realities meant to be harmonious. This is connected to the new age version of yin/yang which I believe takes the concept out of context and represents another New Age rip-off of native people's spirituality. While one might think that socialist feminism and new age spirituality have little in common their confluence here is significant.

dialectic is not about the unity of opposites but rather about the nature of the conflict of opposed forces. As a socialist, Rowbotham's embracing of immutable opposites is significant. Why is the sex/gender system immutable in a way capitalism is not? The answer appears to lie in the reality of women who refuse to separate from men and to deny the existence of those women who do.

A survey of major women's studies texts and major non-lesbian theoretical works reveals the same tendency to ignore lesbians altogether or treat them as a special case. Linda Gordon, in the same interview cited above, states that the highpoint for her at one of the Berkshire Women's History Conferences was a paper on the history of the Buffalo lesbian community. She says we need to do more of this kind of scholarship, but then goes on to say, "since Carroll Smith-Rosenberg's wonderful article, much that has been written about women's culture, particularly in the more popular feminist press, is abstract, rhetorical, polemical or without critical analysis."[7] Earlier, Gordon draws a distinction between lesbian history and women's history when she states, "there is real energy now in lesbian and gay history, as there was in women's history ten years ago and that brings both strength and weakness."[8] Does women's history not include lesbian history? On the one hand, Gordon collapses lesbian history into women's culture and says that since one article on lesbians (written by a non-lesbian), nothing very good has been written. Has she not read Mary Daly, Marilyn Frye, Sarah Hoagland, among many others? Has she not looked at *Sinister Wisdom, Lesbian Ethics, Common Lives, Lesbian Lives, Trivia*, the old *Insighter*? Why does Linda Gordon only seem to link lesbian history with the history of gay men, is our history more similar to their history than to the experience of all women?

Perhaps Monique Wittig was right all those years ago when she wrote that lesbians are not women: that to be a

---

[7] "Interview with Linda Gordon." *Ibid.*, p. 92.
[8] *Ibid.*, p. 88.

woman means that one's existence and context are defined by one's relationship to men. Perhaps all lesbians should abandon the struggle to make feminist theory and the construct of woman inclusive of us. I am not yet ready to give up that struggle, but as each day passes I understand more why many lesbians no longer consider themselves feminists or women. Most non-lesbians who consider themselves feminist are not willing to be seen outside those relations with men, e.g., "I speak to you today as a wife and mother as well as a _____." Their absolute refusal to identify with the word lesbian shows their complicity in male domination.

Non-lesbian feminists, to the degree that they refuse to separate from men and masculine values and identify with lesbian existence, participate in the maintenance of patriarchal values. If the major focus of the feminist revolution is to facilitate women's better relationships with men ("dancing with chains" was my High School principal's description), then one really needs to question the revolutionary nature of feminism.

Feminist theory and process are exclusionary of others in addition to lesbians. As a Jew, I have long been disturbed by what I see as the exclusion of Jewish values and life from feminist politics and process. Evie Beck, in her introduction to *Nice Jewish Girls*, summed up many of my feelings on feminist process. I have long experienced feminist process as subtly Anti-Semitic. The focus on not interrupting, not being emotional or loud, are not only feminist priorities, but embody the values of WASP middle and upper class life. Jewish conversational style and cultural values are distinct. In my home to interrupt someone was an indication of interest, not of dismissal. Feminist process also is based on the concept of the 'good girl', the one who speaks when spoken to, who is not rowdy and obnoxious, who doesn't talk too fast, who is, well, nice. Within WASP culture Jews are not nice. Within patriarchal culture how many lesbians are nice?

Feminist Theory and Inclusiveness

As a Jew and a lesbian, I have long rejected the premises of liberal feminism; primarily its belief that adjustments can be made within the current context and that "revolution" can occur without upsetting the applecart. Too many systems of oppression, such as racism, classism, ablism, etc., will still exist unless we confront the entire range of privileges available within the patriarchal construct. Liberal feminism today is based on many of the same premises as the seventeenth century liberalism of John Locke (that people are endowed with natural rights, that the state is necessary for the preservation of human peace). The illusion that one can, by putting pressure on the state, achieve meaningful equality for all women, is a frightening one for me. First, the liberal state was set up to ensure the protection of unequal distribution of property. To imagine that the state, which was set up to protect the interests of wealthy and powerful white men, will protect women, let alone a Jewish lesbian, is absurd. Second, as a Jew, I am all too well aware of what reliance on the state can bring. As Hannah Arendt so convincingly argues in her work, *Anti-Semitism*, one of the primary reasons Jews stayed in Germany, even after Hitler came to power and before the massive deportations to the camps began, is that over the centuries Jews had looked to the secular state to protect them from Christian religious authorities and from the mobs inspired by the Church. To hear liberal feminists embrace the state as the guarantee of my freedom and life is not only foolish but chilling. It is ironic, though, that lesbians at least exist for liberal feminists, even if it is only in the civil rights context of liberal feminism's support for gay rights. On the whole, however, I do not find liberal feminist theory an inclusive theory.

If one then turns to socialist feminism to find an inclusive feminist theory, the disappointment is far more bitter. One would expect socialist feminists who do attack the premises of liberal theory and do certainly question systems of economic oppression, to attack other systems of oppression, such as race and heterosexualism, that impact on the lives of women. Their failure to do so underscores the limitations of their own theoretical underpinnings. Much of their writing seems to be either exclusionary or foolish.

This can especially be seen in one of the first, and still most comprehensive anthologies of socialist feminist writings, Zillah Eisenstein's volume, *Capitalist Patriarchy and the Case for Socialist Feminism*. In this long work of over twenty articles there are only two more than superficial references to lesbians. The first is an article by Linda Gordon on reproductive freedom, in which she argues that lesbians and gays will benefit also from reproductive self-determination. Gordon writes,

> In this respect again the lesbian liberation movement has made possibly the most important contribution to a future sexual liberation. It is not that feminism produced more lesbians. There have always been many lesbians, despite high levels of repression; and most lesbians experience their sexual preference as innate and involuntary. What the women's liberation movement did create was a homosexual liberation movement that politically challenged male supremacy in one of its more deeply institutionalized aspects—the tyranny of heterosexuality. The political power of lesbianism is a power that can be shared by all women who choose to recognize and use it: the power of an alternative, a possibility that makes male sexual tyranny escapable, rejectable—possibly even doomed.[9]

Lest I be accused of trashing Linda Gordon, whose work on the whole I admire, it must be noted to her credit that she is the only non-lesbian in the group of women included in the anthology who seriously considers lesbianism as a political issue. Her analysis, though, still links lesbians with gay men, as part of a distinct "homosexual" liberation movement. She states, with no footnote, that most lesbians experience their sexual preference as innate and involuntary. Although the Kinsey research does indicate that is true for most gay men, I have yet to see any serious research that says this is true for

---

[9] Linda Gordon, "The Struggle for Reproductive Freedom: Three Stages of Feminism." In *Capitalist Patriarchy and the Case for Socialist Feminism*. Edited by Zillah Eisenstein. New York and London: Monthly Review Press, p. 123.

most lesbians. My lesbianism was a personal and political choice, a choice to reject heterosexual privilege. So what is positive about Gordon's analysis gets lost as she treats lesbians as a group apart from women, as a group whose closer political ties are with gay men.

The other article in Eisenstein's book that deals with lesbianism is the "Combahee River Collective Statement". Their statement is strongly opposed to any separate lesbian analysis and action, "we are feminists and lesbians, we feel solidarity with progressive black men and do not advocate the fractionalization that white women who are separatists demand."[10] This is the extent of their statement on lesbianism.

The other articles in the anthology systematically ignore lesbianism as they focus on the more 'important' subjects of women's work in the family, mothering, and women's role in the work force. Lesbians are clearly not part of the analysis.

The Eisenstein anthology and the work of Linda Gordon are by no means the only socialist feminist writings which are not inclusive of lesbian meaning and existence. It is perhaps the ultimate irony that socialist feminists appear to be the worst offenders when it comes to the issue of dealing with lesbians and lesbianism. At least liberal feminists deal substantively with the issue of civil rights for gay people and do support lesbian custody fights, etc.

But some non-lesbians are seeing the double bind they are facing. As Erica Jong writes,

> Unless men give up their denial that the society they have created is deeply diseased, most women have no choice but to be either semi-slaves colluding in their own oppression, or militant separatists à la Dworkin. How to get past male denial when most men have so much to gain by denying the existence of female pain?
>
> Privileged groups seldom give up their privilege without bloody revolution, and it is unthinkable that women will take up arms against their own sons, brothers, husbands. However violent our

---

[10] "The Combahee River Collective: A Black Feminist Statement." *Ibid.*, p. 365.

dreams, we are tied by ties of love and loyalty. Men have always
know this and abused it.[11]

Jong is correct when she identifies that unless men give
up privileges women face two choices—to collude in their
own oppression, to get men to be more human and behave
themselves, or to separate from men. What a dilemma!

I am not writing this paper to take all lesbian-feminist
and lesbian theorists off the hook. Historically, much of our
own writing and language has been equally exclusionary.
Our theory has seemed at times to assume that all lesbians
are white, Christian, middle class, not disabled, but it must
be noted that most lesbian theorists and writers have taken
seriously the issues of exclusionary theory, privilege, and
accessibility. One only has to follow lesbian or predominantly lesbian publications for a short time to realize how diverse
are our perspectives and backgrounds. We struggle to take
each other's cultures and systems of oppression seriously
and attempt to understand the privileges from our own
backgrounds and situations. I often think of Alix Dobkin's
line when she sings, "We ain't got it easy but we got it."[12]
This is far from saying that our work is finished or even
mostly successful, for the struggle for inclusiveness in lesbian theory continues. I do think it is accurate to say that lesbians have been at the forefront of every fight in the feminist
movement to make it more accessible and inclusive. Further
lesbian theory has been far more responsive to charges of
omission than have either liberal or socialist theory. The fact
that we do so while many of our non-lesbian sisters systematically exclude us from their writing is of great significance.

Toward A Lesbian Theory

Usually when lesbians write theory they mean to be
inclusive of any women who is willing to identify with a les-

---

[11] Erica Jong, "Changing My Mind About Andrea Dworkin." In *Ms.*, Vol. 16, No. 12,
p. 64.
[12] Alix Dobkin, "Talking Lesbian." From *Lavender Jane Loves Women*. Preston Hollow,
N.Y.: Women's Wax Works, 1975.

bian context. Perhaps it is time that non-lesbians cease to see lesbian as an exclusionary term that does not include them. Lesbian may well be far more inclusive than either feminist or woman, as non-lesbians use those terms.

What would a theory that is explicitly lesbian, and both inclusive and revolutionary, look like? Clearly it cannot start from the assumptions that seem to underlie both liberal and socialist feminist theory. It is not a theory that takes as a given an accommodationist politic with men and male-dominated institutions and it cannot take as its end product the 'reconciliation' of men and women. A lesbian theory cannot deny that men do oppress other men, that racism, Anti-Semitism, classism, among others, are real for men as well as for women. But it must be a theory that challenges the yin/yang assumption that the end product of theory is the unity of opposites. Such a yin/yang view posits the necessity of both categories, and that either category needs the other in order to achieve meaningful existence. A separate lesbian meaning and existence is invalidated and rendered invisible.

In my opinion, a theory that is explicitly lesbian and revolutionary is a profoundly separatist theory. Such a theory must separate from women's traditional roles in the family and it must challenge the use of 'motherhood' as a dominant political metaphor. We need to remember that some feminists of both the nineteenth and twentieth century use that metaphor as their primary argument to extend equal rights to women. If we want to define ourselves independently of that context we must seek to create new meaning. Only then can we start with woman as a central focus: woman as a separate and autonomous being, separate from a male-defined reality. We must examine our relations with each other, by analyzing not only the nature of lesbian oppression, but also the issues of bonding, responsibility, ethics, and how other systems of oppression work in our lives.

The necessity for lesbians doing this work can be seen if we examine what happened at the 1988 Sisterfire Music Festival (when two lesbian separatists asked two Black men to leave their crafts area because it was womyn-only space, an altercation ensued and at least one of the womyn was hit by one of the men). When some lesbians defended the actions of these two Black men because of the reality of racism in the U.S.A., they ended up justifying woman-hating. Lesbians (and feminists) must stop excusing men's violent and oppressive behavior because of some men's lack of privilege. We must continue to deal with differences between us, but we can no longer allow our understanding of the oppressions that some men face as an excuse or rationale for their actions.

Events like the Sisterfire incident only teach me how much more theory and understanding we need to do. We also need to continue to confront non-lesbian feminists on their failure to create an inclusive theory. Non-lesbians must begin to identify with the L word. I am not saying they must become lesbians, but that they understand that a lesbian context and meaning can apply to their own lives, the part of their lives they define separate from men. Their continued failure to identify with a lesbian meaning represents the true divisiveness in feminism.

If being a feminist means 'working it out' with men, count me out. As long as the practice of feminist theory continues to be exclusionary we must both struggle with non-lesbian feminists and create our own more inclusive lesbian theory. If being a lesbian and being involved with lesbian theory means working together with other women-identified-women to build a community, a movement, and ultimately a safe planet, count me in. The more non-lesbian feminists continue to deny their complicity with male supremacy because of their fear of being labelled a 'man-hating' lesbian, the more we all lose.

Let us continue to create our lesbian theory and give voice and meaning to lesbian existence. In so doing let us end the divisiveness and the exclusionary aspects of feminism. Let the non-lesbians among us do more of their own homework and examine their own woman-hating and lesbophobia. Ultimately it is the non-lesbians' fear of us that is the true divisiveness of the feminist revolution.

Note

An earlier version of this paper was presented at the 1988 NWSA conference in Minneapolis as one of the papers on the Lesbian Theory panel. A revised version appeared in *Sinister Wisdom*, No. 37, March, 1989.

The World as Will and Representation

MICHÈLE CAUSSE
TRANSLATED BY ELÉANOR H. KUYKENDALL

The science of woman that we ourselves develop as subjects can and must become cause and effect of the only epistemological revolution that matters to us.

In occidental and, more particularly, European civilization, the speaker *par excellence* is the philosopher. Now philosophy as we know it has not been able to pass beyond the sufficiency of the Same, its identification as oneness with itself, its egoism. The scandal of alterity or otherness (which emerges in the notion of the dialectic developed by the nineteenth century philosopher, Georg Wilhelm Friedrich Hegel) assumes the tranquil identity of the Same, a freedom sure of itself, unscrupulously exercised, to which the outsider brings only constraint and limitation. This philosophy which does not call the Same into question is the philosophy of Injustice. Some people today take it upon themselves to denounce this obsessional narcissistic discourse but, for millennia, at least half of the phylum, the feminine half, has paid the price for it.

"Everything is displayed before our eyes," said Ludwig Wittgenstein. "Nothing is concealed, except what is too evident." Indeed, only the evidence is invisible. But to track it down, it would suffice, nevertheless, that the ear hear. That the ear lend itself to the evidence, give itself over to it. Unto the loss of the eardrum. It would suffice that the eye read. If only that it might become blinded and, struck by lightning, recover sight.

Péres-versions: Paternal Versions/Perversions

Those who have not been duped are mistaken. Their unconscious admits it. The most famous of the non-duped. The most famous of the fathers. *Père-versions par excellence.* In language, they hear only what is spoken in the masculine. We must listen to them. For the sake of *memory.* In order that there may be proof. So that the proof may not be lacking, allowing denial to settle in. At the risk of repeating ourselves *ad nauseam*, let us see what remains, even now, of their favorite image-referent, of she who they banished from signs and to whom they gave names: "I named 'woman.'"

What shall we think, for example, of Emmanuel Levinas (one of the most influential contemporary French thinkers), always so concerned with the Other in his writings, that I, deceived, believed he included woman in this concern. Listen to him in *Totality and Infinity*: "This weight of non-significance, heavier than the weight of informed reality, we shall call femininity."

And, still more recently, there is nothing more devious than those who write that the Subject must know itself unmasked, dislodged, dismissed. Jacques Derrida in *Spurs*: "Woman needs the results of castration, without which she would know neither how to seduce nor to incite desire; but evidently she does not believe in it. She who does not believe in it and who benefits from it is woman."

No longer having to support the patriarchal regime, playing it like masters, they can even titillate the Neuter, the multiple, that is, the "coming minority", and soft-spokenly, exhort us.

Felix Guattari and Gilles Deleuze in *A Thousand Plateaus*:

> It is indispensable that women carry out a molar politics with respect to a conquest that they are bringing about of their own organism, their own history, their own subjectivity. 'We as women' would then appear as the subject of a statement. But it is dangerous to repeat oneself on such a subject, which does not function without drying up a spring or stopping a flow. The song of life is often intoned by the dryest women, moved by the spirit of revenge, by the will to power and by cold mothering.

To the good woman who listens, silence. Today, that is what has become of the dissemination of sense. Of semen, let us say frankly. Or of philosophy (and its derivatives) like semiology. "Textual marking replaces sexual marking," Madeleine Ouellette-Michalska says rightly.

What is this writing but a phallocentrism that admires itself, plays with itself, and congratulates itself? Everyone is supposed to think that "Everything which works well is a penis for the unconscious." And for each One to congratulate himself for thinking, for thinking us thinkable, as objects of thought and therefore as nothing but objects.

And that is why your daughter is mute.* Why she takes the place of the dead in the game of life. "Let woman keep silence on the subject of woman," Friedrich Nietzsche had already said over and over, in a phrase taken up recently by Michel Pontalis: "Nothing insures that the feminine discourse on femininity should be, by its position, truer than the masculine discourse."

This assertion would make us laugh until we cried if it didn't sound so familiar. Now in order to have access to our interior certitudes, to the evident truths of our bodies, we must suppress the familiarity imprinted into the flesh with a red-hot iron, set aside the speech and the stare of the one who never risked speaking of himself without immediately idealizing himself and setting himself up as the norm.

A difficult and arduous task, even though we practice, as did Virginia Woolf, the vow of derision or, more simply, even though we regain a clear surprise, amazement, before this fact which is so startling, used by some to discredit the *Mouvement de libération des femmes*, although only that movement has denounced it: *the dichotomy of the species.*

We have just heard it: the dichotomy of the species has been posited and reiterated by one gender, the masculine, which has decided, by himself alone, to represent and to

---

* I generally say that women are mute (not organically) because they have been reduced to silence, to *"mutisme."* You could say instead of "mute," "mutified" (a word I invented).

qualify what is human. Because of him, the two poles, masculine and feminine, are not symmetrical. Man subsumes woman. Through a semantical game of catch. Half of humanity has stolen humanity from the other half. A will to power has opened onto an annihilation, so that, truly and paradoxically, there remains no more than one gender, the feminine: the masculine being the general, the normal, and therefore, the norm. Denied, this domination bears the name of "the difference between the sexes."

Not letting ourselves be deceived, we shall call gynophagic, woman-devouring, the half of the social body that has swallowed up the other half, making that half *its* own thing, exploitable and exhaustible without mercy. We shall call gynophobic the half of the social body that has made of the other half non-beings, an imaginary construction, a rhetorical, analogical, metaphorical category, a particularization of which the writing, feminine in fact, would be only the last avatar, or phase, the last biological production.

Besides, who among us would still call ourselves *humans*, the equals of men, little men, nor-males? The denial of our identity assured at the interior of a caste system which we have diagnosed as the source of our privation and oppression.[1] Who among us would still call ourselves *women*: creatures who are half-surgicalized, structuralized, functionalized, stamped, mutilated, hardly recognizable, identified with the imagination of their enemy and thereby defined as "true" women (which at the very least supposes that one is not born a true woman—a fish rather?) such that the gigantic work of phallic simulation is necessary: "Each woman becomes for the other woman the image of her abjection."[2]

Don't forget: "This thing, what it is, how it is, isn't it that in the name of its name?" Martin Heidegger is right. The words 'women' and 'humans' are murderous nominations, lethal representations which do not represent us. To escape these representations, as multiple as they are monotonous, is of utmost urgency.

"Nothing is there where the word is lacking." Friedrich Hölderlin, poetically, puts his finger on the wound. We always listen to poets. Engaged as we women are from now on in a process of dismantling, decoding which allows us to have access, finally, to feminine being,[3] we rebel against all ontological-carnal hierarchy.

How do we gain access to feminine being? Informed of her oppression, a woman is immediately transformed into a political woman, changing the very nature of her oppression by the consciousness which she has of it. By her *will* to bring it to an end. In effect: "Singular consciousness which conceives itself as will no longer accepts its limitation or its alienation."[4]

"Consciousness" and "consciousness raising" are key words for whoever was never anything but an object (of cancellation, appropriation, oppression, discourse). If we can believe Clair Lejeune: "When an object reflects upon itself to the limits of its condition, it necessarily engenders itself as subject."[5]

With one blow the ex-object, called 'woman', has done with constituting herself in terms of haunting, repeating dramas (evoking the masochist triad: castration-rape-childbirth). And the process is irreversible. Through a strange turnabout of History which, truly, strikes the masochist triad into immobility if not nullity, the only known subject, the dominant subject, becomes object of the thought of she who has been dominated. That hardly says that he won't start again. For him it is the end of the world, the end of *his* history.

For us this optical reversal is the first, revolutionary, chapter of an ethic. If indeed optics can be an ethic.[6] The only ethic possible, under the circumstances, is that—freeing ourselves from a misshaped and distorting thought—we bring about a total *refounding of the given*. And man, revealed as not at all a protagonist with whom a woman could enter into a dialectical relation, compels us to recognize in him a given, the most cruel given. And to deny its negativity.

Three Moments of Revolutionary Consciousness

During the past ten years, this enterprise has developed (at least among French-speaking theorists, it seems to me) in three phases. I have undertaken to study these phases in the restricted field of writing, and of French-language writers primarily. My choice of texts is highly subjective and proceeds from obvious affinities. Three practices of awareness are at work in these texts, marking different steps in the conquest of an *I*. An *I* which we will see progressively modify itself.

During the first phase, writing consists in a statement of the damages. It is a statement of facts, testimony. Consciousness exists only in the form of thinghood. She who writes becomes a thing whose very existence has consisted in the fact of being used. As Jeanne Hyvrard says, "The having 'agreed' to be their thing. Their object. Their cast-off."[7]

Primacy of the object which woman is for the other. To be for the other. Yet the mere fact of writing history from the point of view of the victim is a revolutionary act. She who writes is already self-poetic. Even when her thematic is a semiotics, the breaking up, translation of a body de-centered, dis-inhabited, colonized, hystericized, forbidden to remain. Lucid in regard to her position in the writing itself:

> I am to writing what prostitutes are to love. The expression of collective disaster. The witness of common misery. The scum of society. The bottom of the glass that couldn't be emptied. I am the scum of literature. The residue of decantation. The mother of evaporated deposits. The bitterness of our common memory.[8]

If one thing is really common to us, we will see, it is the memory of our erasure and of our survival. The act of remembering presents itself as a murderous ascetism in which each must confront the hemorrhage of repetition.

> The crushing of all these women dead before me. The crushing of this line of women made crazy. From mothers to daughters. From grandmothers to granddaughters. . . until the memory of it is lost. Up to she who agrees to die rather than to kill.[9]

The autobiography of she who takes account of the disaster makes apparent the attunement between a devasted biology and a devastating history. It is the expulsion of that which, in daily life, mutifies, a legitimation of the intimate through its exteriorization. Autobiography displaces these perspectives: the infinitely great of the One that is feminine being nothing but the infinitely small of the One that is masculine, the only one who believes that he *risks* his life. So writing is an infraction of the interdiction to the symbolic, even though the act of writing makes obvious, for a woman as subject, the impossibility of being in relation with he who is other than herself. The only history that women will agree to is a history of intransitive love: "Write to heal. To succeed in giving birth to myself. To agree to die in order finally to live."[10]

To die to mortifying representations. Certainly. But she who writes herself discard-cast-off-object is not yet she who makes civil disobedience her business, her busyness. She is bled dry, powerless. Exempt however from setting up the seduction, that distance between self and body, she deserves more than the seduction that belongs to the languages of latency, deprived of institutional power. And she writes, at least, in the name of her martyred gender. Exceeding her category in the movement which makes her designate it. And if she replays her being put to death, it is so that the sense may be freed from it: "The rediscovered body. Ever-present fervor. Transformed into ardor. Joy. Splendor. Harmony. Life to live."[11]

She is no longer that castrated being who is a woman without consciousness of the perpetrated damages. Denouncing the body as nature, as reserve of the erogenous, she transforms it into a social body, a body politic. From her tormented senses, she draws the sense.

Actually, each intuition involving her pain and sorrow is transformed into a needle and each needle nourishes a science of oppression, a knowledge which pursues you and allows you no respite: because the real leaps at your throat, because it insists on raising an opposing complaint. All restraint, all cowardice in a woman writer is for she who writes a mistake against her entire gender. Writing no longer appears only as *ergon*, or deed, but also as *energia*, power: its true function can be no other than genetic, parthenogenetic. What we must seek in the text, more than its formal achievement (which is often extreme), is its power of connection, that is, its capacity to transmit its energy to other fields, to other bodies, even to other texts. She who writes is conscious that, self-generating, she engenders her gender which, escaping the imposed boundaries of particularization (sex/nature/immanence), recovers the generality that has been denied, a confiscated, forbidden, dimension of entry into the game, a metaphysical dimension in the most general sense ("all speculation about the world, about her place in the world").

This question is addressed by a writer of the second epistemological revolution, a woman from the United States who is almost unknown, Laura Riding Jackson, author of *The Telling*: "Most mute, as rememberers of First Things and perceivers of Last Things, and knowers of ourselves as that in which First and Last are bound together, are women."

Once again, notice the word *memory*, attribute of the feminine. The research Laura Riding Jackson presents is most appropriate for bringing to light a subject. A transcendental subject given over to a cognitive practice which permits the question of sense to enter in and to assert itself. To make sense. There, where our urgency alights.

> The minds of women are not, as seems, either partners or competitors to men in the reading of the mirror of the self. It is through mere love that they live according to men's self-reflecting half-world. Their love, fed upon the praise and favor of men, is of that world, but not their honor. And men will be preserved neither by their own self-love nor the love of women, but by the ultimate honor of women, the prior motive of their souls, and the principle of their minds—put by fate ever and ever out of harm's daily way into Reason's last keeping.

We will keep the word honor. The implacability of the diagnosis. Which nevertheless is not exempt from the nostalgic concern to convince even a man who is deaf, a man who will not listen. An ecumenical concern shared by a number of women authors of this phrase who, at great effort, mourn the loss of complementarity, this ever-familiar and little-questioned "evidence." Laura Riding Jackson cannot believe that there exists only one relationship of address, one single face-to-face encounter. And her awareness is in deep mourning.

It is not the same for the dismantlers/discoverers of a third phase. Presaging what future when their present, already, is read in the future? I mention Monique Wittig and Nicole Brossard. I could have mentioned others. But the latter hold me body and soul. In that they demonstrate that utopian vision (a-topian or poly-topian, as Françoise Collin would say) is the only political vision. All political vision being only a vision of what is after the event.

Monique Wittig and Nicole Brossard achieve the founding murder. They kill their speaker.[12] Without striking a blow. But not without brandishing a word. Euphoric or tranquil, they admit the for-itself. They elevate the certainty of being for Self to truth, in the Other and in themselves.[13] Thus they make themselves an identity. On their very body—for there is no science but of bodies—they have learned a lesson: "Because it is not in itself, the thing (understand woman as defined above) can be exchanged and consequently compared, quantified, and in consequence, lose its identity.[14]

The discoverers, they in the feminine [*elles*], not only are no longer threatened with the loss of their identity, but they avert the threat of those who, when reading them, understand that to be it suffices to desert the places where something has been taken away, to assert, generate, define, recognize one's self without ever allowing the male subject, whose identity is constituted by the negation of their own, any power of misrecognition or recognition. It is *ego* who says *ego*.[15] Ceasing to be a product, woman ceases to circulate in Bluebeard's digestive tract.[16]

Lesbians who write in a utopia of the present to come which is already here have only one addressable relationship: those like them, as much like them as possible, those who, upon reading them, become feminine beings whom one can no longer despoil. In brief, "They recognize themselves as recognizing themselves reciprocally."[17] Now we are not unaware that "each consciousness of self is for itself, actually, by means of the Other who recognizes her."[18] Since the beginning of the 1970s the *Mouvement de la libération des femmes* will have given women that pleasure. With the effects of desire which flow from it.

Nevertheless, notice that to read Wittig's *Les Guérillères* or Brossard's *These Our Mothers or: The Disintegrating Chapter*, it is necessary from the start to sketch, on a *background of absence*, what is said. It is necessary to exorcise labels, codes, centuries of memory and to arrive at a more ancient memory, an Amazonian cellular memory, and to forget a body which was forcibly phallicized. One must have recourse to an eminently atrophied function, an imaginative function (see Louky Bersianik, *Agenesis of the Old World*), for what is new is the perception that a woman writer communicates, a perception that most often is not incidental to the experience of a woman reader. And for a good reason. In summary, the words of a text are not the expression of a thing but of its *absence*, for she who reads. Herbert Marcuse has defined this phenomenon very well: "What is, pushes back what is not. The absent must be rendered present because the greatest part of truth is in this absence" How can we have precisely the imagination of Absence? For a woman discoverer, it is already presence. In a life which is aleady other. Giving itself to be read as a proposition and making us gauge, exactly, in what state of lack (to imagine) we lived, and still live. Therefore, the initial unreadability of these women discoverers is not always the fact of the writing (which can be a great formal shock, as in the case of Nicole Brossard, or a changing of textual reality in the two cases: the language inseparable from a certain praxis, breaking cliches, attitudes and habits), but rather the incapacity of a woman reader to represent to herself the unrepresentable: that which was not—and for good reason—ever represented.

A lesbian who writes herself is not duped. Thus Nicole Brossard writes:

> I said in beginning with the word 'woman' that utopia would not assure our insertion into reality, but that a utopian testimony on our part could stimulate in us a quality of emotion that is appropriate to our insertion into history.[19]

In other words, things will be born from words. Bodies will arise from words. The linguistic element showing itself to be as material as the body which produces it. To the point that History, in my opinion, is not pertinent to women. Issue-oriented, political, told by men, it forecloses the actual experience and the creation of women, rebels or victims, all of whom have clarified, illuminated, inspired, and nurtured a scene designed for their eviction. From then on, women's honor is transmitted through this resistance to the History that is our memory, the only memory capable of judging what makes history for us and was never recorded.

Monique Wittig is explicit: "Don't say, there have been periods of chaos. As if we had known other times. Dark age after dark age, such has been our historical account."[20] Echoing Ernst Bornemann: "All the history of humanity is the history of masculine aggression. One might even say that history is explained only as that." From now on, then: "Only a theatre of memory can be erected as a final court of appeals."[21] The role and the function of memory are always emphasized by utopian women writers.

Thus Nicole Brossard writes: "To revive *memory*, for women, is to be confronted with the fiction of self, with non-existence. The real body of a writer originating in her fictional body."[22] Or again, "I confuse times because there subsists in me a vital abstraction which makes me tend to multiple *memory*."[23] And Monique Wittig: "You say that you have lost *memory*. Remember. Try to remember. Or, failing that, invent."[24]

Wittig and Brossard appeal to an archeological memory and to its contrary or corollary, a prospective memory, both powerful forces of *de-* and of *re*-territorialization. In fact, these two discoverers are extraordinarily receptive to a collective memory. Collective memories are at once the expression of knowledge accumulated by our gender (which implies, very obviously, that of the other gender erected as human: cf. 'Nothing human is alien to me,' alas) and the transcendence of that knowledge. A transcendence that leads to a discovery of some of the real needs of their group, of our group. Indeed the discoverer's collection of information is such, her capacity of synthesis so overwhelming, that she immediately presses on to create new structures "cut off from the myths, names, ideologies, social structures that break the original and creative movement of the self."[25] From the outset women discoverers get down to basics. Never confusing desires with needs.

Nicole Brossard writes: "It is necessary to think the body with precision, beyond History,without delusion, without its text."[26] And Monique Wittig states: "They [*elles*] say that they know their bodies in their totality."[27] This knowledge is not a paltry miracle but a stopping of masculine fantasy, fetishism and synecdoche—that figure of speech which consists in taking the part for the whole. Thus woman's sexual organs became woman, so that to say "le sexe" in French is to say "woman." This coming to know our bodies is what men will call, obviously, separatism, because it concerns a practice of reappropriation, of self-legitimation. Freedom finally presents itself as what it is: an ontological category which brings it about that we are, indeed, the subjects of our own existence.

In this regard, Wittig's and Brossard's propositions of existence are remarkable. They place us before an important fact, namely, that the general form of the answer is such that at a given moment the question no longer exists. (In order not to leave unechoed Gertrude Stein's words on her deathbed.) Freed, indeed, from the obsession of constraining images and bringing to an end the collective fiction that has become incarnate in each of us, Brossard and Wittig create for us propositions in the sense of Wittgenstein: "It belongs to the essence of a proposition to be able to communicate a new sense."

And Nicole Brossard, in fact, does not hesitate: "We dare the imagination of our knowledge. Our thoughts manifest. Our thoughts make a thinking which is on the lookout." Or again: "All vision is in itself a mathematics of imaginary space, it bears in itself the evidence."[28]

Wittig and Brossard have broken with man's tautological system: "the world is what it is". For them, there is no doubt that everything that is imaginable, when imagined, is called upon to become real.

Brossard says, "I know that everything that I imagine has a sense. . . one day I tried to conquer reality. On that subject I fabricated a knowledge of what I had learned."[29] And Wittig: "They [*elles*] say that they invent a new dynamic. They say: you are invincible, be invincible".[30]

And their propositions, which just a few years ago seemed deviant, have taken on a new appearance, because suddenly the context has changed. Changed, precisely, in and because of their "blasphemous" hypotheses, exhortations, anticipations. From fragment to Integral that is the long march of their *I*.

Active, they create new dimensions of reality, new perspectives; activists, they subvert language and the social. They make fluid, indeed, melt solidified thoughts.

Thus, when Brossard writes, in *These Our Mothers or: The Disintegrating Chapter*: "I have killed the womb and I write that," she states a fact that is real, rather than symbolic. The tradition of a will put into action. Namely, in order that the kinship system of filiation [*filiation*] might no longer be a system of tradition passed from son to son [*une filature, fils*=son], the father never being a biological father but the erection of a Capital Letter.[31]

A woman reader not previously warned—and how can she be?—can only shudder at the nature of the murder. Each one strikes, not from fear of light when facing the light of the statement, but from an incapacity to conceive the inconceivable: the refusal of conception. But, paradoxically, a lesbian who kills the womb is alone at the origin of an ontogenesis capable of influencing the species, that half of the phylum that has been thrown off track, led astray, hidden from view for millennia. Finally bringing that half into view, saying it (while telling it to herself) a woman discoverer, in fact, changes it. Nicole Brossard is clear: "I want to see the form of women organized in the trajectory of the species." And for that to happen: "Making visible all sorts of forms and all colors, asserting themselves before the gaze of the Other before he imposes himself."[32]

Utopia? No, for a lesbian who generates herself by freeing herself does not weaken the Other, making him infirm, but only forbids him to do harm by refusing to serve any longer as a *receptacle* for his semantics. She uses her new knowledge of herself as an outside authority, which, of course, meets resistance, that of the authority of the Same; the representative masculine thought embedded in a contingent content which it takes care not to revise. The fact remains that a woman writer knows for herself—and for she who wants to hear it—that *feminine existence* would possess veritable being if its possibilities were fulfilled, in other words, if there were an identity between its existence and its concept. She, a conscious and reflective subject, shows herself able to realize, by herself, her concept which has sprung precisely from her existence. "She is in her own being her own concept."[33] For the concept is at the same time the self-movement of the thing and the act of understanding it. Thus Nicole Brossard writes: "I cannot live deferred, delayed from transformation."[34] And Monique Wittig states: "We must bring about a political transformation of key concepts, that is, concepts which are strategic for us."[35]

This implies a rejection of all of the sciences which use as their foundation not only the categories of sex but also their most blatant and therefore most hidden consequence, the oppression of one sex by another, in other words, a rejection of all human sciences which, reproducing this masculinity of which they are one of the effects, are afflicted with invalidity as much in the assumptions as in their conclusions.

Women's access to being requires no less than an epistemological revolution.

Our consciousness creates the world.

*Our world is a veritable accomplishment of the consciousness
of Self.*

Our work, the reality which consciousness gives to itself. The
work is. That is, it is for other individualities.[36] Thus we can
say:

The I that we are.

The we that I am.

We know very well that truth rises up where a being separated from the Other does not become submerged in the
Other, but speaks to the Other. Speech-emotion. Writing-
emotion. Transformation of the world.

A gynesthesia is substituted for an anesthesia. The world
becomes our will. And in consequence our representation.
There is no longer a gap between the movement of the heart
and decision.

"The law of the heart, through its actualization, ceases to
be law of the heart. It receives by its actualization the form of
being and it is now universal power."[37] Our genesis is an epi-
genesis. Slow. We know it to acquire in our utopians the cuttings and grafts that will become our flesh. In tune with the
injunction-intuition of Nicole Brossard.

"Invent the essential in yourself." Certainly, each of us
may not always objectify the will through poetic expression.
But each of us can objectify the character of her self. To
become for the other a center of reference. However our will
my sustain us. For "everywhere that there is will, there is life,
and finally a world."[38]

Each of us remembers Monique Wittig's warning: "They
say, if I appropriate the world for myself, may that be to
immediately dispossess myself of it, may that be to create
new relationships between myself and the world."[39]

Thus fiction produces the irreducible and as yet incalcu-
lable effects of gynility. Of this we can only rejoice.

Notes

This essay first appeared as "Le monde comme volonté et comme représentation" in VLASTA, vol. 1.

The incompleteness of the following notes is intentional.
1. Cf. Adrienne Rich.
2. Sartre.
3. Cf. Mary Daly.
4. Hegel. (All citations are from *The Phenomenology of Mind*.)
5. Cf. *The Studio*.
6. Levinas.
7. *Murderousness*.
8. *Ibid*.
9. *The Plums of Cythère*.
10. *Ibid*.
11. *Ibid*.
12. Cf. Serge Sartreau, *Outside*.
13. Hegel.
14. *Ibid*.
15. Benveniste.
16. Therèse Plantier.
17. Hegel.
18. *Ibid*.
19. *Picture Theory*.
20. *Les Guérillères*.
21. Cf. Françoise Delcarte.
22. *Le Sens apparent*.
23. *Picture Theory*.
24. *Les Guérillères*.
25. Mary Daly.
26. *Le Sens apparent*.
27. *Les Guérillères*.
28. *Le Sens apparent*.
29. *Picture Theory*.
30. *Les Guérillères*.
31. Françoise Delcarte.
32. *Picture Theory*.
33. Hegel.
34. *Picture Theory*.
35. "The Straight Mind."·
36. *Ibid*.
37. Hegel.
38. Schopenhauer.
39. *Les Guérillères*.

Lesbian Ethics and Female Agency

SARAH LUCIA HOAGLAND

Introduction

It is possible for us to engage in moral revolution and change the value we affirm by the choices we make. It is possible for lesbians to spin a revolution, for us to weave a transformation of consciousness.[1]

My focus is lesbian for several reasons. A central element of lesbian oppression has been and remains our erasure by the dominant society. If lesbians were truly perceptible, then the idea that women can survive without men might work its way into social reality. This suggests that lesbian existence is connected logically or formally in certain ways with female agency: the conceptual possibility of female agency not defined in terms of an other.

Besides a logical possibility, I find a more concrete possibility. By affirming our lesbianism, lesbians have questioned social knowledge at some level. In spite of our varied assimilation (including absorption of dominant, oppressive values), through lesbian existence comes a certain ability to resist and refocus, an ability which is crucial to the sort of moral change I think can occur. And because of this my focus is lesbian.

In naming my work 'lesbian' I invoke a lesbian context, and for this reason I choose not to define the term. To define 'lesbian' is to succumb to a context of heterosexualism, to invoke a context in which lesbian is not the norm.

By 'heterosexualism', I do not simply mean the matter of men having procreative sex with women. Heterosexualism is men dominating and de-skilling women in any of a number of forms, from outright attack to paternalistic care, and women devaluing (of necessity) female connection and engagement. Heterosexualism is a way of living (which actual practitioners exhibit to a greater or lesser degree) that normalizes the dominance of one person in a relationship and the subordination of another. As a result it undermines female agency.

I focus on 'lesbian' because I am interested in exploring lesbianism as a challenge to heterosexualism, as a challenge to the matter of men (or the masculine) dominating women (or the feminine), whether that be as protectors or predators, whether that domination be benevolent or malevolent. And I am interested in exploring ways to work the dominance and subordination out of lesbian choices.

I think of lesbian community as a ground of lesbian being, a ground of possibility. Once we thought it enough to just come out as a lesbian, now we know better; we know that at most it creates the possibility of a certain kind of female agency. And that involves the area of ethics.

My overall thesis is that the foundation of traditional anglo-european ethics (and I use "foundation" in the Wittgensteinian sense of an axis held in place by what surrounds it) is dominance and subordination, that its function is social control, and that as a result it serves to interrupt rather than promote lesbian connection and interaction. My focus is not a new standard of behavior, but rather concerns what it means to be a moral agent under oppression. In what follows I discuss the appeal to the feminine and the concept of self-sacrifice as a feminine virtue because I want to challenge these concepts and realize a different concept of female agency from within a lesbian context.

The Feminine Principle

We appeal to altruism, to self-sacrifice, and in general, to feminine virtuousness in a desperate attempt to find grace and goodness within a system marked by greed and fear. However, while these virtues may herald for us the possibility of ethics—the possibility of some goodness in an otherwise nasty world—nevertheless, as Mary Daly has pointed out, they are the virtues of subservience.[2]

Under modern phallocratic ethics, virtue is obedience and subservience,[3] and the virtuous are those who remain subordinate (accessible). The function of phallocratic ethics—the master/slave virtues—has been to insulate those on top and facilitate their access to the resources of those under them.

Despite this, and because of the effects of men's behavior, we can be tempted to regard the feminine as more valuable than the masculine. Many suffragists defended votes for women by appealing to women's "moral superiority."

Currently, some women are developing an ethics based on the feminine, noting values that pass between women and developing theories about these values, including an ethics of dependence. Without going this far, Carol Gilligan has argued that, in ethical matters, women tend to focus on interpersonal relations while men's ethical considerations involve principles.[4] In the process, she has attempted a vindication of what she perceives as women's morality.

Claudia Card has written a significant critique. Among other things, she argues that Carol Gilligan does not take into account women's oppression and, consequently, the damage to women of that oppression. And, she argues, the fact that women have developed necessary survival skills under oppression does not mean these skills contribute ultimately to women's good.

For example, while Carol Gilligan revalues women's concern for approval as actually a concern for maintaining relationships, Claudia Card reminds us that the approval women seek is usually male approval, which is granted for "obedience to conventions requiring affiliation with men, respect for their views, empathy for them, etc." Or again, while Carol Gilligan revalues the so-called weak ego boundaries of women as a capacity for affiliation, Claudia Card reminds us that only certain affiliations are pursued. Lesbian relations, for example, are more often than not a source of terror for women.[5]

In addition, it may be that women have a greater capacity for empathy. However, women tend to direct that empathy to men of their own race and class, not to women of other races and classes, or even women of their own race and class. (Early radical feminists called this male-identification.)

Further, Claudia Card points out that intimacy has not cured the violence in women's lives; instead, it "has given the violent greater access to their victims." She goes on: "Without validation of success in separating, we may learn to see our only decent option as trying to improve the quality of bad relationships." She adds:

> More likely to be mistaken for a caring virtue is a misplaced gratitude women have felt toward men for taking less than full advantage of their power to abuse or for singling them out for the privilege of service in return for "protection."[6]

Claudia Card argues that misplaced gratitude is a form of moral damage women have suffered; and she suggests there are others such as women's skills at lying, being cunning, deceit, and manipulation.[7]

Actually, I go a step further and argue that, while men have designed 'the feminine' for their own purposes, women have refined these virtues in defense and resistance, developing them as a means of obtaining some control (individual and limited) in situations which *presume* female self-sacrifice. Women have developed the "giving" expected of them into survival skills, strategies for gaining some control in situations where their energy and attention are focused on others.

That is, the power of control can be exercised from the subordinate position, and under heterosexualism women have refined and developed the feminine virtues for just that purpose. Under heterosexualism, female agency involves manipulation and cunning—for example, a woman getting what she needs for herself and her children by manipulating a man in such a way that he thinks it was all his idea. And this power is the essence of female agency under heterosexualism.

I will add here that manipulation, cunning, and deceit are not peculiar to women. Men are also extremely manipulative and deceitful, and can exhibit considerable cunning, for example, in keeping their dominance over their peers or subordinates from appearing overt, or in enlisting women to support them. The difference, finally, between men and women under heterosexualism may lie in who maintains dominance — though not, in every instance, in who maintains control.

Dominance is maintained by violence or the threat of violence—which, in the long run, means by destruction or the threat of destruction.[8] If nothing else works, men will disrupt or destroy what is going on. Thus, to be different from men, women stress nonviolence. Under heterosexualism, manipulation and control are not challenged; what is challenged is only the threat of disruption or destruction. Women want men to "play fair" in the game of manipulation and control by not resorting to the oneupmanship of destruction.

While many claim that there is a feminine principle which must exert itself to counterbalance masculinism pervading world cultures, what they seem to ignore is that the feminine has its origin in masculinist ideology and does not represent a break from it.* Further, the counterbalancing

---

*This dualism is related to the manichean good/evil dualism and the taoist yin/yang dualism. The manichean approach holds the two opposites in constant conflict, each attempting to dominate and vanquish the other. The taoist approach embraces the conflict but strives for harmony and balance of the two opposites. And while the taoist ideal involves harmony and balance, the nature of the opposites is significant: yin/yang, female/male, dark/light, black/white, cold/heat, weakness/strength. The one is the opposite of the other because it is the absence of it. Thus, strength is the absence of weakness as weakness is the absence of strength. Further, one of the pair is the absence of the other because it is a void. While there are two opposites, in the long run, there is only one essence. The dualism is actually a monism.[9]

In discussing the new spiritualism, Susan Leigh Star argues that the new mystics have managed to mask male identity beneath the guise of androgyny. Further, she points out, "Amidst the escalation, it is vital for us to understand that the new mysticism has to do with the control of women; that it may be seen as a sexual as well as a spiritual phenomenon; that it represents a subtler form of oppression, not a form of liberation."[10]

works both ways. Because of the non-discriminatory nature of feminine receptivity, that is, a lack of evaluating or judging what the feminine responds to, the feminine requires the masculine to protect it from foreign invasion.

Within lesbian community, many lesbians embrace a feminine principle and suggest that self-sacrifice and a romantic ideal of mothering and all-embracing nurturing, are desirable ethical norms in our relationships. I want to challenge this.

'Selfishness', 'Self-Sacrifice', and Choice

Consider, first, the use of the label 'selfish'. Those who are judged to be selfish are often those who do not respond to demands from others: the question of selfishness is a question of whether a person thinks only of herself. This consideration often develops into a complaint that the person deemed selfish does not act in ways that contribute to a social structure such as the nation, the family, the synagogue or church, the corporation, the sewing circle, or the collective. Significantly, when a person goes along with the group, even if she is only thinking of herself—being "selfish"—she may well be considered ethical for doing the "right" thing. Further, someone who is perceived as selflessly opposing the group nevertheless often is judged immoral and unethical. Thus someone can be "selfish" and yet "good"—as well as "unselfish" and yet "bad."

Apparently, the relevant factor in judging a person to be selfish is, not whether she considers herself first, but whether or not she goes along with the group (or conforms to a higher order) in one of a number of prescribed ways. It seems that selfishness is not of prime concern; rather, the label is used as an excuse to manipulate our participation toward someone else's end.

Secondly, masculinist ideology suggests that true female nature affirms itself through self-sacrifice. Mary Daly defines 'self-sacrifice' as the handing over of our identity and energy to individuals or institutions.[11] This ethical value encourages a woman to give up pursuit of her needs and interests in order to dedicate her efforts to pursuing others' needs and interests, usually those of her husband and children.

Self-sacrifice appears to be a sacrifice of self-interest. Yet women face limited options: men limit women's options through conceptual, physical, and economic coercion. As a result, when a woman engages in self-denial, acquiesces to male authority, and apparently sacrifices her own interests to those of a man in conformity with the dictates of the feminine stereotype, she may actually be acting from self-interest, doing what she deems necessary to her own survival.[12]

One consequence is that, except perhaps in extreme cases of female sexual slavery, when a woman is in a situation in which she is expected to shift her identity to that of a man or a child, the stage is set for her to work to control the arena wherein her identity is located. She has not sacrificed her self: by altruistically adopting another's interests, she has transferred that self, or rather it has been arrogated by the man.[13] And while she may have given up pursuit of her own unique interests and needs in favor of those of her husband (and to a lesser extent those of her children), she will pursue their interests and needs as her own.

This, in turn, gives rise to a double bind of heterosexualism: While she is expected to attend to everyone else's projects, she has no final say in how they are realized. She thus becomes the nagging wife or the fairy-tale stepmother. For example, mothers may "live vicariously" through their children and some wives may be "domineering." And those mothers who pursue their children's needs and interests too enthusiastically are criticized for not being passive enough.

Thirdly, the concepts of 'self-sacrifice', 'altruism', 'selfishness', and 'self-interest' may appear to be factual descriptions, but the implications we can draw from sentences containing these words depend significantly on how we use them. Someone may "self-sacrifice" because it makes her feel good and so she is actually acting from "self-interest." "Self-sacrifice" may even be "selfish" if someone refuses to take her own risks or becomes a burden if she doesn't take care of herself as a result. We can play around with these concepts and come up with all sorts of interesting results; and through all this, acting in consideration of our own needs and limits does not exist as a moral consideration.

Fourthly, the selfish/selfless (or egoism/altruism) dichotomy does not accurately categorize our interactions. Often we do not consider our interests and the interests of others as being in conflict.[14] Concern for ourselves does not imply disregarding the needs of others.[15] In addition, doing good for others need not involve disregarding ourselves.

Now, fifthly, in challenging the concept of 'self-sacrifice', I do not mean to suggest that the sort of "selfish" behavior which self-sacrifice is supposed to counter does not exist among lesbians. For example, a lesbian may consistently act as if her feelings are the only ones, that she is warranted in interrupting anything else going on to demand attention (the strategies for this are many and varied). However, while the problem is real, the solution does not lie in advocating self-sacrifice. When a lesbian is acting this way, often it is because she hasn't a firm sense of herself in relation to others and is threatened; advocating self-sacrifice will only compound the problem.

Egocentrism is the perception that the world revolves around oneself. Now, it is important to have a healthy sense of oneself, centered and in relation to others. But egocentrism is our judgment that those around us have no other relationships, needs, commitments, or identity than that which they have with us. Egocentrism is perceiving and judging others only in relation to ourselves. Hence it is a confusion of our needs, reactions, and choices with those of others. Egocentrism is a form of "selfishness," for it entails a lack of consideration for others—it involves a lack of awareness that others are different and separate from us, and have needs distinct from our own.

In the community we tend to promote self-sacrifice as a virtue and a proper antidote for behavior resulting from egocentrism. However, self-sacrifice cannot solve the problem because egocentrism involves a confusion of needs similar in form to the confusion that occurs with self-sacrifice: my perception of my needs and concerns becomes so entwined with my perception of others that anything relating to the other must relate to me and vice versa.

The difference is that in the case of self-sacrifice we cease to have a distinct sense of ourselves. In the case of egocentrism we cease to have a distinct sense of the other. Thus, advocating self-sacrifice as a corrective measure to selfishness really feeds an underlying problem of ego boundary: the solution actually nurtures the problem.

And this brings me to my main point. We tend to regard choosing to do something as a sacrifice. I want to suggest, instead, that we regard choosing to do something as a creation. From heterosexualism we tend to believe that any time we help another, we are sacrificing something. Thus, we might regard helping a friend fix a carburetor, spending an evening listening to her when she's upset rather than going to a party, or helping her move, as a matter of self-sacrifice. But these acts do not necessarily involve self-sacrifice. Rather, they involve a choice between two or more things to do, and we will have reasons for any choice we make. Often we have choices to make. But that we have to make choices is not itself a matter of sacrifice.

There is another way of approaching this: we can regard our choosing to interact as part of how we engage in this living. Such choices are a matter of focus, not sacrifice. That I attend certain things and not others, that I focus here and not there, is part of how I create value. Far from sacrificing myself, or part of myself, I am creating; I am weaving lesbian value.

As I engage in lesbian living, I make choices—to start this relationship, to work on this project, to withdraw now, to dream now. I make daily choices; and at one time I may choose to help another, at another time not. But in choosing to help another, I am not thereby sacrificing myself. Instead, this is part of what I involve myself in. When we regard interacting with others as a sacrifice and not as an engagement, it is time to reassess the relationship.

Nor, when we make a choice to engage here rather than there, do we need to regard ourselves as sacrificing or compromising parts of our selves. When we interact, we pursue certain interests. We may have other interests, and we can choose which we want to develop, involving ourselves elsewhere for some. In any given engagement, what is possible exists only as a result of how those involved connect—as a result of what each brings to the engagement and of how it all works out. So when we decide to interact, we do not need to regard ourselves as compromising or losing anything, but rather as embarking on an adventure.

For example, a lesbian develops a friendship with another lesbian. They may have a common interest in the martial arts and work out together. In the process, they create possibilities that were not there, maybe eventually deciding over time to open a lesbian martial arts school. They may develop strategies specific to women and lesbians. And in the process they have created a connection between them, one that changes over the years. During this time, they are not opening a bookstore, writing a book, building a house—actually, they may take on another project, but there will be things they do not do. And they may create other possibilities with other lesbians, their lovers, for example. My point is that in making their choices, they have not sacrificed themselves or other projects. They have created something that did not exist.

There is an idea floating about to the effect that if we cannot do everything, if we have to choose some and let other things go, then we are sacrificing something. Given traditional anglo-european philosophy and u.s. imperialist ideology, u.s. lesbians, in particular, tend to think the whole world exists for us, that everything is potentially ours (or should be), so that when we have to choose between two or more options, we feel we are sacrificing something or that we have lost something. But everything is not ours; everything is not even potentially ours. In fact, nothing out there that exists is ours. Thus in acting, engaging, making choices—in choosing one thing rather than another—we are not losing anything.

In acting, engaging, making choices, we are creating some-thing. We create a relationship, we create value; as we focus on lesbian community and bring our backgrounds, interests, abilities, and desires to it, we create lesbian meaning.

What exists here as lesbian community is not some pre-determined phenomenon which we opted for, but rather a result of what we've created. And the same is true of all our relationships. Thus, the choice to engage here rather than there is not a sacrifice of what's "out there"; to engage is to create something which did not exist before. I want to sug-gest that revaluing choice is central to Lesbian Ethics.

Now, if we decide to regard choice as a creation, not a sacrifice, situations requiring difficult decisions will still arise between us. However, we can regard our ability to make choices as a source of power, an enabling power, rather than a source of sacrifice or compromise. Thus by revaluing choice we begin to revalue female agency: female agency begins to be, not essentially a matter of sacrifice and manipu-lation, but rather a process of engagement and creation.

Mothering and Amazoning

Understanding choice as creation, not sacrifice, helps us better understand choices we make typically considered "altruistic." We often are drawn to helping others. That is one reason so many are drawn to healing, to teaching, to vol-unteering to work at shelters, to practicing therapy, to work-ing at community centers or in political campaigns, to going to nicaragua—to all kinds of political work. In doing such work, we feel we are creating something, that we are partici-pating in something; we engage and we make a difference.

However, there remains the danger that we treat choice and engagement as "handing our identity over to individu-als or institutions," or even as "acting in, as though in, my own behalf, but in behalf of the other." In heteropatriarchy, engagement and creation for women amount to mothering. Mothering, perhaps, most clearly embodies the feminine virtues, is itself a feminine virtue. And appealing once again to the 'feminine', we tend to romanticize 'mothering' as women's function and regard it as unconditional loving, as a matter of selflessly protecting and nurturing all life.

In the first place, mothering is women's *function* only given the values of heterosexualism. What appears to be a factual statement about women's function is actually a disguised value statement in that men have picked one of the many things women do and decided to call *that* women's function.

If I were to pick one thing and claim it is women's function these days, I would suggest it is amazoning. Some women do it, and many women are capable of it. And, in my opinion, it is far more necessary than mothering. While some might focus on mothering, the vast majority might answer the call to amazon. Further, they would accomplish through amazoning what they keep trying to accomplish through mothering—appropriate atmosphere for children, self-esteem for girls, caring, room to grow and flourish.

The idea that mothering is women's function appears in women's spirituality, which is rushing to claim the 'feminine'. Women's spirituality embraces mothering as nurturing and as an ideal for all women.[16] Mothering, for many, is the paradigm of women's creativity and power, whether mothering takes the form of nurturing children (boys or girls or men) or saving the world and being the buttress of civilization.[17] The idea that all women are or should be mothers in one way or another is not only not challenged, it is pursued.

Mothering is one way of embracing and developing one ability to make a difference in this living; it is creating a quality of life through choice. As such, it does not always involve protecting living things, nor is the energy involved only nurturing energy. More significantly, we must challenge the concept of mothering as it is institutionalized in heteropatriarchy.[18]

As Jeffner Allen notes, mothering reproduces patriarchy and serves men.[19] And as Monique Wittig and Sande Zeig note, mothers are separate and distinct from the amazons:

> Then came a time when some daughters and some mothers did not like wandering anymore in the terrestrial garden. They began

to stay in the cities and most often they watched their abdomens grow. . . . Things went so far in this direction that they refused to have any other interests.[20]

Thus some lesbians who have given up on the movement have turned to mothering as an alternative, presumably to work on the next generation. Further, as Baba Copper suggests, "heteromothering cannot break away from the heterosexualism of female socialization into subjugation." She argues that only "lesbian group-mothering can begin to rear daughters who will be capable of female bonding."[21] Perhaps then those who are called mothers will again ride with the amazons.

Baba Copper suggests that lesbians can develop a cosmology which can explain to a female child how she can learn to differentiate from and identify with others without dominance and subordination. She adds, "we will have to do all this without motherly domination of those same daughters in their infantile dependence, and without self-sacrifice on the part of the lesbian mothers and shareholders."[22] It may be that we come to deconstruct 'mother' as we do 'woman' and 'feminine'. In this respect, amazoning is more appropriate for girls and others to experience than mothering.

Secondly, the ideal of 'mothering' appeals to 'unconditional love'. So we must ask whether we want an ideal of unconditional opening or giving. Perhaps the paradigm of unconditional loving lies in the stereotype of the mammy. Bell Hooks writes:

> Her greatest virtue was of course her love for white folk whom she willingly and passively served. The mammy image was portrayed with affection by whites because it epitomized the ultimate sexist-racist vision of ideal black womanhood—complete submission to the will of whites. In a sense whites created in the mammy figure a black woman who embodied solely those characteristics they as colonizers wished to exploit. They saw her as the embodiment of woman as passive nurturer, a mother figure who gave without expectation of return, who not only acknowledged her inferiority to whites but who loved them. The mammy as portrayed by whites poses no threat to the existing white patri-

archal social order for she totally submits to the white racist regime. Contemporary television shows continue to present black mammy figures as prototypes of acceptable black womanhood.[23]

As Baba Copper argues, the unidirectional ideal of mothering undermines reciprocal interaction between mothers and daughters and so encourages incompetency and ageism among us.[24] In discussing Barbara Macdonald's thesis that children and husbands combine in exploiting mothers, helping to create ageist responses to older women,[25] Baba Copper describes her own experience:

> The children learned an assumption of privilege from their father, and he in turn became one of the children—legitimately passive, irresponsible. ...[M]y older daughters never witnessed an exchange of nurturance. In their view of how the world worked, mothers gave, and men/daughters received. Ours was such an isolated nuclear family that they literally never had any opportunity to witness me being nourished, sustained, taken care of, or emotionally supported. ...My own daughters, now in their thirties, are dutiful wives but still do not know how to extend nurturance to me, or to negotiate when we have a difference of interest. ...As the children grow up, they continue to relate to older women with the clear expectations of service. By then they have laid claim to a place of privilege in the power hierarchy.[26]

In other words, the ideal of 'unconditional loving' as embodied by the stereotype of the mammy is not a distortion of unconditional loving but rather an accurate realization of it. To pursue the ideal of mothering as unconditional loving or total nurturing, to pursue this sense of female agency, is to pursue oppression. The masculine and the feminine are not significantly different in what they engender. Again, amazoning at this time is more appropriate and will provide a better atmosphere in which children can develop.

Thirdly, mothering as unconditional love is self-sacrifice. And in general I want to suggest that when we equate self-sacrifice with virtue—something we must exhibit to be considered ethical—and we act accordingly, control begins to enter our interactions as a logical and acceptable consequence. For if we do not perceive ourselves as both separate and related, we will be off-center and forced to control or try to control the arena and those in it in order to retain any sense of agency, of ability to act.

If my identity rests with another and her actions, then I am going to have to try to affect her choices and actions because, at the very least, they reflect back on me. For example, I may choose to help someone who is ill. Now, if I regard my choice as self-sacrifice, then who I am will be caught up in whether, how, and how soon she gets well. As a result I may well go beyond helping, to attempting to control her choices in certain key ways. And in exercising such control, I may not be allowing her time to heal in her own way, on her own terms, by her own means.

My goal in exploring the feminine virtues lies in uncovering the kind of interacting we enable—the sense of female agency we promote—when we believe that self-sacrifice, altruism, and unconditional loving are part of ethical behavior. The feminine virtues, virtues which accrue to the less powerful, are developed as strategies for manipulating and gaining control in a relationship of dominance and subordination. When self-sacrifice and altruism — rather than self-understanding — are regarded as prerequisites for ethical behavior, control — rather than integrity — permeates our interactions.

Conclusion

I am not simply saying that at times we don't behave as well as we might. I am saying, instead, that the *structure* of the feminine virtues will thwart even our best efforts because these virtues don't function to promote a female agency which stems from self-understanding and which is both related and separate. And far from facilitating our ethical interaction, the feminine virtues actually interrupt attempts among lesbians to connect and interact ethically by promoting control and distance and by erecting barriers. If we are to achieve a moral revolution, rather than possible moral reform or perhaps remain stuck in the status quo, it is important to understand the feminine as born of the masculine.

Finally, if we regard choice as creation, not sacrifice, we can regard our ability to make choices as a source of enabling power, rather than as a source of sacrifice or compromise. As a result, we can revalue female agency, developing it independently of the manipulation and control of the position of subordination of heterosexualism. Female agency becomes, not essentially a matter of sacrifice, but rather a process of engagement and creation.

Notes

[1] This paper is excerpted from a chapter of my book, *Lesbian Ethics: Toward New Value*, published by the Institute of Lesbian Studies, P.O. Box 60242, Palo Alto, CA 94306. A note on style: in the text I capitalize the phrase 'Lesbian Ethics', the word "i", names of books and journals, names of people, and first words of sentences only. I follow Marilyn Frye in using single quotation marks when referring to words or concepts. And I use double quotation marks around words or phrases I wish to stress as remarkable in one way or another, which remarkableness should be clear from the context.

[2] Note *Beyond God the Father: Toward a Philosophy of Women's Liberation* (Boston: Beacon Press, 1973) and *Gyn/Ecology: The Metaethics of Radical Feminism* (Boston: Beacon Press, 1978).

[3] Claudia Card, conversation.

[4] Note, for example, Carol Gilligan, *In a Different Voice:Psychological Theory and Women's Development* (Cambridge, Mass.: Harvard University Press, 1982).

[5] Claudia Card, *Virtues and Moral Luck*, Series 1, Institute for Legal Studies, Working Papers, University of Wisconsin-Madison, Law School, November 1985, pp. 14-15.

[6] Claudia Card, *Virtues and Moral Luck*, pp. 16, 17.

[7] Ibid., p. 23.

[8] Conversations, Deidre D. McCalla, Anne Throop Leighton.

[9] Conversation, Marilyn Frye.

[10] [Susan] Leigh Star, "The Politics of Wholeness: Feminism and the New Spirituality," *Sinister Wisdom* 3 (Spring 1977): 39.

[11] Mary Daly, *Gyn/Ecology*, pp. 374-75.

[12] Marilyn Frye, "In and Out of Harm's Way: Arrogance and Love, in *The Politics of Reality: Essays in Feminist Theory* (Trumansburg, N.Y.: The Crossing Press, 1983, now in Freedom, Calif.), p. 73.

[13] Ibid. pp. 66-72.

[14] For further discussion, note Judith Tourmey,"Exploitation, Oppression, and Self-Sacrifice," in *Women and Philosophy*, , ed. Carol C. Gould and Marx W. Wartofsky (New York: G.P. Putnam's Sons, 1976), pp. 206-21; and Larry Blum, Marcia Homiak, Judy Housman, and Naomi Schemen, "Altruism and Women's Oppression," in

Women and Philosophy, pp. 222-47.

[15] For further discussion, note James Rachels, "Morality and Self-Interest," in *Philosophical Issues: A Contemporary Introduction*, ed. James Rachels and Frank A. Tillman (New York: Harper & Row,1972), pp. 120-1.

[16] Note, for example, Z. Budapest, *The Feminist Book of Lights and Shadows*; and Billie Potts and River Lightwomoon, *Amazon Tarot* and *New Amazon Tarot* (Bearsville, N.Y.: Hecuba's Daughters, n.d.); for information, write Billie Potts, 18 Elm Street, Albany, NY 12202. Jean and Ruth Mountaingrove edited *Womanspirit* from 1974 to 1984.

[17] Marilyn Frye, "A Note on Anger," in *The Politics of Reality*, p. 92.

[18] Note for example, Adrienne Rich, *Of Woman Born: Motherhood as Experience and Institution* (New York: W.W. Norton & Co., Inc., 1976).

[19] Jeffner Allen, "Motherhood: The Annihilation of Women," in *Mothering: Essays in Feminist Theory*, ed. Joyce Trebilcot (New Jersey: Rowman & Allanheld: 1984), pp. 315-330; republished in *Lesbian Philosophy: Explorations*, Jeffner Allen (Palo Alto, Calif.: Institute of Lesbian Studies, 1986), pp. 61-86.

[20] Monique Wittig and Sande Zeig, *Lesbian Peoples: Material for a Dictionary* (New York: Avon, 1979), pp. 108-9.

[21] Baba Copper, correspondence.

[22] Ibid.

[23] Bell Hooks, *Ain't I a Woman: Black Women and Feminism* (Boston: South End Press, 1981), pp. 84-85.

[24] Baba Copper, "The View from Over the Hill: Notes on Ageism Between Lesbians," *Trivia: A Journal of Ideas* 7 (Summer 1985): 57, revised and reprinted in *Over the Hill: Reflections on Ageism Between Women* (Freedom, Calif., The Crossing Press, 1988).

[25] Barbara Macdonald with Cynthia Rich, *Look Me in the Eye: On Women, Aging and Ageism* (San Francisco: Spinsters Ink, 1983, now Spinsters/Aunt Lute).

[26] Baba Copper "View from Over the Hill," p. 57.

WRITING DESIRE

Lesbian Desire As Social Action

Nett Hart

To be lesbian, to act and name oneself as a lover of women, presents an unmitigated challenge to the belief system that structures reality. While arguably there are different *experiences* of reality depending on age, race, class, physicality, education, origin, and most especially, sex/sexuality, the *structuring* of reality is generally held uniform by the belief system of those who control the resources, the dominant/dominating. The experience of reality by the non-dominant often has its reference in the reality of the dominators, even when as feminists do, those experiences are used to analyze and challenge. This relationship maintains the hegemony of the dominators' reality. If, instead, we challenge the belief systems that sustain that reality, that is, if we take the underlying beliefs to be arbitrary, we begin to understand reality itself as changeable. It is then that we contribute a new structure to reality, rather than argue for the inclusion of our experience in the dominated reality.

For a social change movement to honor the various *experiences* of reality, it necessarily comes from a perspective outside the dominator reality, outside what is perceived as the only possible reality. When a people disenfranchised within that existing system validates their own identity as a starting point for their world view, elemental change can happen because the structure through which reality is apprehended becomes fluid. For me, to be Lesbian is elemental social action, not a metaphor, not an example, but social change itself. For this reason, my approach is specifically Lesbian. My text is Lesbian experience. A Lesbian separatist perspective is implicit because this approach stands on its own as a movement created of itself, not derived, not reactive, but self-created, self-authorized. This approach validates the intellectual/emotional/psychic shift of Lesbian reality toward authentic new being.

Duty and Desire

Twinned in each of us, Duty and Desire stand often at odds, pulling us this way and that inconclusively. Duty asks that we fulfill our commitments: those we make and those we perform out of obligation. Duty speaks from the world view of the society, to evaluate, analyze, direct the action.

Desire wants what she wants, burns with her own passion, acts outside reason in faith that things will right themselves in her wake. Where Duty is "mature", cool, able, Desire is willful, unpredictable, brilliant and dangerous. She runs by her heart, often to excess. There is no reining her energies, no channeling her force. She flows in the most erratic of manners toward the least likely of goals. When she succeeds, she creates new worlds. This possibility alone directs her movement.

Duty can never be faulted except by failure to succeed according to her own standards. Her performances are mundane, socially constructed, proven. Her risks are minimal. The values she embodies replicate themselves in the being of every responsible person. She is fervently loyal to the status quo, to the expectations others have of her. There is no necessity to explain motivation, no redaction of means. Her acts are self-evident in the reality to which she is wedded. Duty reflects the concerns of her society.

Desire promises no such stability, no confirmation of the rightness of her action. Her movements spring from the permutations of her heart without pattern. Yet, of the two, it is Desire I trust implicitly.

Wanting Woman

What separates us as Lesbians from our socialization is our self definition. While we may be called willful, indulgent, selfish, headstrong, we have always existed, flourished within a world of our own making, whose culture was rarely transmitted. We move contrary to the judgement and concern of friends, intimates and family, inversely to socialized expectations and longings. That is to say, we move by desire.

To move by desire we must name it, own it, claim it. We have been socialized against desire and in particular *this* desire, *this* longing, this pleasure in women. Yet, as Lesbians, we experience a reverence, a bond, unheard in this misogynist society. We love women. In loving women we love ourselves. We love women as a class and we love specific women. We embrace the concept that women can be loved, that women are inherently worthy of love. When we claim desire we disenfranchise the notion that we are worthy of love only when we are selfless, that is, to the extent that we do not love ourselves. Full of our desire we appear selfish, self-loving and loving women.

To move by desire is to understand choice, to undertake the risk of making choices. We choose to act in accord with our feelings, to connect the power of these feelings to action. We choose to listen to our hearts and accord priority to that knowing. We choose to be our own authority, trusting ourselves more than we trust the beliefs of society.

The desire of which I speak is for the community formed by the self/mutual love of women, the love of women for women. This desire is for the wholeness, the remembering of our selves, the giving of our attention to women as a whole, as a class. We accept the worthiness of that attention; we accept that we in turn are worthy of the attention and devotion of other women. We are a separate self, a whole self. We are loveable apart form what we do, how well we actualize what is expected of us. We can focus our attention on what we want. Knowing what we want makes us trustworthy.

In focusing on our wants, we discover we have them, that we can name preferences. We have never been asked before. We exercise this new skill. So accustomed have we been to not getting what we want, not having attention focused on our needs, that we as women become passive about our very lives. In naming our wants we choose to validate our power. Our wants are not petty or vain. Our wants are not for fashion or control. Our desires are for life, life loving actions, life responsive institutions. When we connect with our desire at this level, we pierce socialized difference to find our common bond as women. What we want is nothing less than a just world where the quality of all lives is honored, where there is enough resources and choice, enough community and spirit. We do not move to this vision step by step, dismantling the rationale we've been taught. When asked what we want, we know, have always known.

In loving women as a class, we accept as our own the lot of woman as a class worldwide. Where our socialization would contradictorily have us see women as both powerless *and* responsible for our condition, by loving ourselves as women we see all women as potentially potent, aware of which values promote life and which are used to oppress. We are not separated from each other by our political, economic, religious boundaries, because all of these boundaries are delineated by misogyny. We break through our socialized self hatred and inherit as sisters all women in the world. We take on not only the material conditions of all women as our own, but in this formation we are the strength of the majority. We are not only capable of envisioning change, witness our love of women, we are powerful to enact it.

How we come to know our desire, our power to envision and enact a new reality, is by *experiencing* our desire, allowing it to lead us out of confinement to duty. Just this once, we tell ourselves, we will risk damnation and disapprobation. The fire inside breaks through. What we discover is that no risk from following our desire is as deadly as not doing so.

In naming ourselves Lesbian, we choose the epithet "Lesbian," that has been hurled at us to keep us in line. We become the gorgon by choice. In stepping out of line, we see the relationship between things on the line. We see how much wider a perspective is possible. We see things we could not see in our dutiful position. From this perspective we can rename and set free. In becoming the Lesbian threat, we have nothing more to fear.

The Shape of Desire

We come to our Lesbian self in the revelation that we (can) love a woman. We disprove, call to question, everything else we have been taught. If what was impossible, to love women, is now possible, so might anything else be possible. Duty turns a dour face on our revelation. She knows where this could lead. Without our fearful obedience, who will maintain patriarchy?

Lesbian desire is the most powerful force we can know, increasing as we come to know the self intimately, not through social screens and standards, but as a self. We cultivate who we each are individually: our pleasures, our tolerances, our passions. We explore/indulge the self in pleasures of the body, mind and heart because we know we can be pleasured, satisfied. We do not grope for unnamed vague satisfactions. We are satiable, not a bottomless void of want. We learn our pleasures are specific, possible and constituent of our being.

Our desire is replenishable. It is not exhausted by indulgence. We are full of life, pulsing with energy. We experience want as an expression of ourselves, growing as we grow. Our desire is not self-absorbed, voraciously drawing all experience into a vacuum. There is an integral self that experiences, a self that experiences other selves. This self is in the world, conscious of the world, a self to whom, and from whom, energy flows. We are interactive, yet distinct from our environment. We are affected and affecting, able to make choices. We can be open because we have a nucleus of self that can engage and disengage, expand and retract. We are a vortex of energy, a gravitational field that makes possible/necessary relationship among peers who are neither ourself, nor a part/reflection/extension of ourself, but their own vortex of energy. We are neither egocentric nor self sacrificing. We exist in the community we make.

Our desire is relational. We may have a generalized level of sexual excitement or become awakened to our feelings by someone we do not intimately know, but our desire for a specific Lesbian or Lesbians takes in her whole being, her Self. We want to engage her, not possess her. We want the power of her self to interact with our own. In fact, what we find attractive about her is her self, her self awareness, self confidence, self possession. We may dream, scheme, seduce and court her, but she comes willingly, willfully, or not at all.

Our desire is from our self. We choose to focus it on specific Lesbians with whom we feel a meeting of energy: emotional, psychic, physical. But desire is always *our* desire, enflamed by our emotional power. If we are drawn in by desire for another Lesbian, it is our motion toward her vortex. We swim; we are not swallowed.

Lesbian desire is propellant. We meet our desire on the frontiers of the self, the most intimate, least socially constructed edge. We spill over the nouns and adjectives we fashion as self image. We flood the new territory with emotion unleashed. We are overwhelmed, tumbled in the undertow of passion. Our desire sweeps into itself tightly held beliefs, and gathers them as sediment upon which to build new ground. We know what we could not come to know without the surf. The wind and water and sky and earth are all one piece, are all in the surf. All the elements are intact yet commingled. They will generate new relationship after the passion. The chemical constituents of our bodies remain, but in new molecular form. Our desire is life altering. It creates a new landscape/seascape. It creates its own home.

When we create a place for our desire, a context for its fulfillment, we inhabit the world, are fully present to the life around us. Our desire brings us to the world. It does not bring the world to us. We dissolve our separateness, our alienation from the consciousness of all life. We are animated by that which animates everything. We dissolve boundaries, open our selves. We flow into the expanse our desire has created. We are our self, our own, a constituent of the whole, a hologram of life. We exist in the whole. Our desire brings us home, into relationship, safe from fears that would keep us outside. We belong to the natural world and it is only by the most stubborn, the most self negating beliefs and behavior that we can keep ourselves outside, beyond reach of this consciousness.

Our desire is specifically Lesbian. We arrive at our place in the whole through our most precise identity. We arrive with clarity through focus. Our identity is a truth about ourselves we have chosen to honor and in this choice we create our own being. We stand true, in our element. We fulfill our nature.

When we claim our Lesbian identity, we bond with Lesbians of all possible definitions. We bond in our choice to love women. We are an international/intergalactic movement. We embrace all races and geographies. We have no need to be the same, as if sameness confirmed our choices. We are the power of change in the world. Our diversity is essential to our strength. We are together to be open, to challenge without malice, to love without fear. We defy anything that could separate us from one another, prodding one another out of habits and fears that keep us from community. We will not be separated, pitted against one another in a scarcity economy. We create our own abundance from our desire for one another. We each receive/can receive all that we need. We are enough in return.

To be members of this Lesbian body, this Lesbian community, we must be authentic. We cannot afford to disappoint the capacity of our desire. We cannot withhold our self, our presence. We cannot hold ourselves to control, to performance by duty. We trust ourselves to flow true to nature, ceasing to act from fear. We do not alibi our complicity in patriarchy; we separate our power from its purposes. Desire authors a more inclusive good than duty. It stands responsive to the whole picture.

Desire Creates Freedom

To accept our desire is to accept ourselves, to trust ourselves. Only a self who can be trusted can create a new world. From this self trust we exercise our authority, act authentically. We live free and make possible that reality for others as well.

In our choice to act authentically, live as a free being, as a Lesbian, we strengthen our ability to do so. What we do from this posture has tremendous implications for the universe. We, like everything else, create ourselves in freedom. If we are free, we are not only free of oppression, free of another's control, we are free to act/interact in freedom; that is, we engage animate others including the earth and creatures, as free beings themselves. We are incapable of oppressing/abusing/destroying the other we perceive as free.

The truly authentic act is that in which the self takes the risk of freedom, of acting in her own freedom to authenticate the freedom of another. We do not liberate, but in exercising our freedom we allow, in the broadest sense, another to exercise her freedom. In taking the risk of authenticity there is room for error. There is room for self judgement. We do not act from the certainty oppression provides. The authentic self learns to act in circumstances that are ambiguous, in situations where we may fail to achieve our desire. Self love permits tolerance for action within ambiguity, for feeling one's way through uncharted acts.

Lesbian World Lovers

The power of social change lies in the heart. The motivation for creating a world of justice and joy is our desire. This is not to privatize social action, naming personal fulfillment the epitome of social acts. Instead it confirms first of all that those who would will into being a world of justice and joy are those whose sense of self-love, of self, tells them that nothing less will do, that we must create the reality of this vision because it accords with the power and purpose of the universe, outside of which there is only alienation, that is to say, no social action/interaction. For social action to be true, it must embrace the highest good, the authentic being of all lives. We need an abundance of love, of hope, of vision to right this global circumstance. We need radical lovers, Lesbian lovers, to take the risk of new being, to begin in new premise, to move in the world with assurance/boldness, to settle for nothing less than what we want.

By flowing to our desire we have created an island of new being, a place from which to view the rest of society and being, a perspective of reality from which genuine social change is possible. This requires new method in effecting change. We have had vision before, but we petitioned those perceived to be in power to effect the changes. We now understand ourselves capable not only of vision but of the action; inseparably we call upon our desire to be both the dream and its manifestation. We nourish our selves, our power to dream, and in so doing nourish the dream. We create a new world from within it, fully engaged in its form, embraced by its destiny, our own. We risk everything to become authentic, to create ourselves in our own image, to find our place within the universe. With this same boldness, we engage the world, creating it as we do so.

Lesbian "Sex" *

MARILYN FRYE

The reasons the word "sex" is in quotation marks in my title
are two: one is that the term "sex" is an inappropriate term for
what lesbians do, and the other is that whatever it is that lesbians do that (for a lack of a better word) might be called "sex"
we apparently do damned little of it. For a great many lesbians, the gap between the high hopes we had some time ago
for lesbian sex and the way things have worked out has
turned the phrase "lesbian sex" into something of a bitter joke.
I don't want to exaggerate this: things aren't so bad for all lesbians, or all of the time. But in our communities as a whole,
there is much grumbling on the subject. It seems worthwhile
to explore some of the meanings of the relative dearth of what
(for lack of a better word) we call lesbian "sex."

Recent discussions of lesbian "sex" frequently cite the
finding of a study on couples by Blumstein and Schwartz,[1]
which is perceived by most of those who discuss it as having
been done well, with a good sample of couples — lesbian,
male homosexual, heterosexual non-married and heterosexual married couples. These people apparently found that lesbian couples "have sex" far less frequently than any other

---

* When I speak of "we" and "our communities," I actually don't know exactly who
that is. I know only that I and my lover are not the only ones whose concerns I
address, and that similar issues are being discussed in friendship circles and
communities other than ours (as witness, e.g., discussion in the pages of the *Lesbian Connection*). If what I say here resonates for you, so be it. If not, at least you
can know it resonates for some range of lesbians and some of them probably are
your friends or acquaintances.

type of couple, that lesbian couples are less "sexual" as couples and as individuals than anyone else. In their sample, only about one-third of lesbians in relationships of two years or longer "had sex" once a week or more; 47% of lesbians in long-term relationships "had sex" once a month or less, while among heterosexual married couples only 15% had sex once a month or less. And they report that lesbians seem to be more limited in the range of their "sexual" techniques than are other couples.

When this sort of information first came into my circle of lesbian friends, we tended to see it as conforming to what we know from our own experience. But on reflection, looking again at what has been going on with us in our long-term relationship, the nice fit between this report and our experience seemed not so perfect after all.

It was brought to our attention during our ruminations on this that what 85% of long-term heterosexual married couples do more than once a month takes on the average 8 minutes to do.[2]

Although in my experience lesbians discuss their "sex" lives with each other relatively little (a point to which I will return), I know from my own experience and from the reports of a few other lesbians in long-term relationships, that what we do that, on average, we do considerably less frequently, takes, on average, considerably more than 8 minutes to do. It takes about 30 minutes, at the least. Sometimes maybe an hour. And it is not uncommon that among these relatively uncommon occurrences, an entire afternoon or evening is given over to activities organized around doing it. The suspicion arises that what 85% of heterosexual married couples are doing more than once a month and what 47% of lesbian couples are doing less than once a month is not the same thing.

I remember that one of my first delicious tastes of old gay lesbian culture occurred in a bar where I was getting acquainted with some new friends. One was talking about being busted out of the Marines for being gay. She had been put under suspicion somehow, and was sent off to the base psychiatrist to be questioned, her perverted tendencies to be assessed. He wanted to convince her she had only been engaged in a little youthful experimentation and wasn't really gay. To this end, he questioned her about the extent of her experience. What he asked was, "How many times have you had sex with a woman?" At this, we all laughed and giggled: what an ignorant fool. What does he think he means, "times?" What will we count? What's to *count*?

Another of my friends, years later, discussing the same conundrum, said that she thought maybe every time you got up to go to the bathroom, that marked a "time." The joke about "how many times" is still good for a chuckle from time to time in my life with my lover. I have no memory of any such topic providing any such merriment in my years of sexual encounters and relationships with men. It would have been very rare indeed that we would not have known how to answer the question "How many times did you do it?"

If what heterosexual married couples do that the individuals report under the rubric "sex" or "have sex" or "have sexual relations" is something that in most instances can easily be individuated into countable instances, this is more evidence that it is not what long-term lesbian couples do...or, for that matter, what short-term lesbian couples do.*

What violence did the lesbians do their experience by answering the same question the heterosexuals answered, as though it had the same meaning for them? How did the lesbians figure out how to answer the questions "How frequently?" or "How many times?" My guess is that different individuals figured it out differently. Some might have counted a two- or three-cycle evening as one "time" they "had sex"; some might have counted it as two or three "times." Some may have counted as "times" only the times both partners had orgasms; some may have counted as "times" occasions on which at least one had an orgasm; those

---

* This is the term used in the Blumstein and Schwartz questionnaire. In the text of their book, they use "have sex."

who do not have orgasms or have them far more rarely than they "have sex" may not have figured orgasms into the calculations; perhaps some counted as a "time" every episode in which both touched the other's vulva more than fleetingly and not for something like a health examination. For some, to count every reciprocal touch of the vulva would have made them count as "having sex" more than most people with a job or a work would dream of having time for; how do we suppose those individuals counted "times?" Is there any good reason why they should *not* count all those as "times?" Does it depend on how fulfilling it was? Was anybody else counting by occasions of fulfillment?

We have no idea how the individual lesbians surveyed were counting their "sexual acts." But this also raises the questions of how heterosexuals counted *their* sexual acts. By orgasms? By *whose* orgasms? If the havings of sex by heterosexual married couples did take on the average 8 minutes, my guess is that in a very large number of those cases the women did not experience orgasms. My guess is that neither the women's pleasure nor the women's orgasms were pertinent in most of the individuals' counting and reporting the frequency with which they "had sex."

So, do lesbian couples really "have sex" any less frequently than heterosexual couples? I'd say that lesbian couples "have sex" a great deal less frequently than heterosexual couples: by the criteria that I'm betting most of the heterosexual people used to count "times," lesbians don't have sex at all. No male orgasms, no "times." (I'm willing to draw the conclusion that heterosexual women don't have sex either; that what they report is the frequency with which their partners had sex.)

It has been said before by feminists that the concept of "having sex" is a phallic concept; that it pertains to heterosexual intercourse, in fact, primarily to heterosex*ist* intercourse, i.e., male-dominant-female-subordinate-copulation-whose-completion-and-purpose-is-the-male's-ejaculation. I have thought this was true since the first time the idea was put to me, some 12 years ago.[3] But I have been finding lately that I have to go back over some of the ground I covered a decade ago because some of what I knew then I knew too superficially. For some of us, myself included, the move from heterosexual relating to lesbian relating was occasioned or speeded up or brought to closure by our knowledge that what we had done under the heading "having sex" was indeed male-dominant-female-subordination-copulation-whose-completion...etc. and it was not worthy of doing. Yet now, years later, we are willing to answer questionnaires that ask us how frequently we "have sex," and are dissatisfied with ourselves and with our relationships because we don't "have sex" enough. We are so dissatisfied that we keep a small army of therapists in business trying to help us "have sex" more.

We quit having sex years ago, and for excellent and compelling reasons. What exactly is our complaint now?

In all these years I've been doing and writing feminist theory, I have not until very recently written, much less published, a word about sex. I did not write, though it was suggested to me that I do so, anything in the SM debates; I left entirely unanswered an invitation to be the keynote speaker at a feminist conference about women's sexuality (which by all reports turned out to be an excellent conference). I was quite unable to think of anything but vague truisms to say, and very few of those. Feminist theory is grounded in experience; I have always written feminist political and philosophical analysis from the bottom up, starting with my own encounters and adventures, frustrations, pain, anger, delight, etc. Sometimes this has no doubt made it a little provincial; but it has at least had the virtue of firm connection with *someone's* real, live experience (which is more than you can say for a lot of theory). When I put to myself the task of theorizing about sex and sexuality, it was as though I *had* no experience, as though there was no ground on which and from which to generate theory. But (if I understand the terminology rightly), I have in fact been what they call "sexually active" for close to a quarter of a century, about half my life, almost all of what they call one's "adult life," heterosexually, lesbianly and auto-erotically. Surely I have experience. But I seem not to have *experiential knowledge* of the sort I need.

Reflecting on all that history, I realize that in many of its passages this experience has been a muddle. Acting, being acted on, choosing, desiring, pleasure and displeasure all akimbo: not coherently determining and connecting with each other. Even in its greatest intensity it has for the most part been somehow rather opaque to me, not fully in my grasp. My "experience" has in general the character more of a buzzing blooming confusion than of *experience*. And it has occurred in the midst of almost total silence on the part of others about their experience. The experience of others has for the most part also been opaque to me; they do not discuss or describe it *in detail* at all.

I recall an hours-long and heated argument among some eight or ten lesbians at a party a couple of years ago about SM, whether it is okay, or not. When Carolyn and I left, we realized that in the whole time not one woman had said one concrete, explicit, physiologically specific thing about what she actually *did*. The one arguing in favor of bondage: did she have her hands tied gently with ribbons or scarves, or harshly with handcuffs or chains? What other parts of her body were or weren't restrained, and by what means? And what parts of her body were touched, and how, while she was bound? And what liberty did she still have to touch in return? And if she had no such liberty, was it part of her experience to want that liberty and tension or frustration, or was it her experience that she felt pleased or satisfied not to have that liberty...? Who knows? She never said a single word at this level of specificity. Nor did anyone else, pro or con.

I once perused a large and extensively illustrated book on sexual activity by and for homosexual men. It was astounding to me for one thing in particular, namely, that its pages constituted a huge lexicon of *words*: words for acts and activities, their sub-acts, preludes and denouements, their stylistic variation, their sequences. Gay male sex, I realized then, is *articulate*. It is articulate to a degree that, in my world, lesbian "sex" does not remotely approach. Lesbian "sex" as I have known it, most of the time I have known it, is utterly *in*articulate. Most of my lifetime, most of my experience in the realms commonly designated as "sexual" has been pre-linguistic, non-cognitive. I have, in effect, no linguistic community, no language, and therefore in one important sense, no knowledge.

In situations of male dominance, women are for the most part excluded from the formulation and validation of meaning and thereby denied the means to express themselves. Men's meanings, and no women's meanings, are encoded in what is presumed to be the whole population's language. (In many cases, both the men and the women assume it is everyone's language.) The meanings one's life and experience might generate cannot come fully into operation if they are not woven into language: they are fleeting, or they hover, vague, not fully coalesced, not connected, and hence not *useful* for explaining or grounding interpretations, desires, complaints, theories. In response to our understanding that there is something going on in patriarchy that is more or less well described by saying women's meanings are not encoded in the dominant languages and that this keeps our experience from being fully formed and articulate, we have undertaken quite deliberately to discover, complete and encode our meanings. Such simple things as naming chivalrous gestures "insulting," naming Virginia Woolf a great writer, naming ourselves women instead of girls or ladies. Coining terms like "sexism" "sexual harassment" and "incestor." Mary Daly's new book is a whose project of "encoding" meanings, and we can all find examples of our own more local encodings.*

---

* I picked up the word "encoding" as it is used here from the novel *Native Tongue*, by Suzette Haden Elgin (NY: Daw Books, Inc., 1984). She envisages women identifying concepts, feelings, types of situations, etc., for which there are no words in English, and giving them intuitively appropriate names in a women-made language called Laadan.

Meanings should arise from our bodily self-knowledge, bodily play, tactile communication, the ebb and flow of intense excitement, arousal, tension, release, comfort, discomfort, pain and pleasure (and I make no distinctions here among bodily, emotional, intellectual, aesthetic). But such potential meanings are more amorphous, less coalesced into discrete elements of a coherent pattern of meanings, of an *experience*, than any other dimensions of our lives. In fact, there are for many of us *virtually no meanings* in this realm because nothing of it is crystallized in a linguistic matrix.*

What we have for generic words to cover this terrain are the words "sex," "sexual" and "sexuality." In our efforts to liberate ourselves from the stifling women-hating Victorian denial that women even *have* bodily awareness, arousal, excitement, orgasms and so on, many of us actively took these words for ourselves, and claimed that we *do* "do sex" and we *are* sexual and we *have* sexuality. This has been particularly important to lesbians because the very fact of "sex" being a phallocentric term has made it especially difficult to get across the idea that lesbians are not, for lack of a penis between us, making do with feeble and partial and pathetic half-satisfactions.** But it seems to me that the attempt to encode our lustiness and lustfulness, our passion and our vigorous carnality in the words "sex," "sexual" and "sexuality" has backfired. Instead of losing their phallocentricity, these words have imported the phallocentric meanings into and onto experience which is not in any way phallocentric. A web of meanings which maps emotional intensity, excitement, arousal, bodily play, orgasm, passion and relational adventure back onto a semantic center in male-dominant-

---

* Carolyn Shafer has theorized that one significant reason why lesbian SM occasioned so much excitement, both positive and negative, is that lesbians have been starved for language—for specific, detailed, literal, particular, bodily talk with clear non-metaphorical references to parts of our bodies and the ways they can be stimulated, to acts, postures, types of touch. Books like *Coming to Power* feed that need, and call forth more words in response.

** Asserting the robustness and unladylikeness of our passions and actions, some of us have called some of what we do "fucking."

female-subordinate-copulation-whose-completion-and-pur-pose-is-the-male's-ejaculation has been so utterly inadequate as to leave us speechless, meaningless, and ironically, accord-ing to the Blumstein and Schwartz report, "not as sexual" as couples or as individuals of any other group.

Our lives, the character of our embodiment, *cannot* be mapped back onto that semantic center. When we try to syn-thesize and articulate it by the rules of that mapping, we end up trying to mold our loving and our passionate carnal inter-course into explosive 8-minute events. That is not the timing and ontology of the lesbian body. When the only things that count as "doing it" are those passages of our interactions which most closely approximate a paradigm that arose from the meanings of the rising and falling penis, no wonder we discover ourselves to "do it" rather less often than do pairs with one or more penises present.

There are many cultural and social-psychological reasons why women (in white Euro-American groups, but also in many other configurations of patriarchy) would generally be somewhat less clear and less assertive about their desires and about getting their satisfactions than men would gener-ally be. And when we pair up two women in a couple, it stands to reason that those reasons would double up and tend to make relationships in which there is a lowish fre-quency of clearly delineated desires and direct initiations of satisfactions. But for all the help it might be to lesbian bodies to work past the psychological and behavioral habits of femi-ninity that inhibit our passions and pleasures, my suggestion is that what we have never taken seriously enough is the *lan-guage* which forecloses our meanings.

My positive recommendation is this: Instead of starting with a point (a point in the life of a body unlike our own) and trying to make meanings along vectors from that point, we would do better to start with a wide field of our passions and bodily pleasures and make meanings that weave a web across it. To begin creating a vocabulary that elaborates and expands our meanings, we should adopt a very wide and general concept of "doing it." Let it be an open, generous, commodious concept encompassing all the acts and activities by which we generate with each other pleasures and thrills, tenderness and ecstasy, passages of passionate carnality of whatever duration or profundity. Everything from vanilla to licorice, from puce to chartreuse, from velvet to ice, from cuddles to cunts, from chortles to tears. Starting from there, we can let our experiences generate a finer-tuned descriptive vocabulary that maps and expresses the differences and distinctions among the things we do, the kinds of pleasures we get, the stages and styles of our acts and activities, the parts of our bodies centrally engaged in the different kinds of "doing it," and so on. I would not, at the outset, assume that all of "doing it" is good or wholesome, nor that everyone would like or even tolerate everything this concept includes; I would not assume that "doing it" either has or should have a particular connection with love, or that it hasn't or shouldn't have such a connection. As we explain and explore and define our pleasures and our preferences across this expansive and heterogeneous field, teaching each other what the possibilities are and how to navigate them, a vocabulary will arise among us and by our collective creativity.

The vocabulary will arise among us, of course, only if we talk with each other about what we're doing and why, and what it feels like. Language is social. So is "doing it."

I'm hoping it will be a lot easier to talk about what we do, and how and when and why, and in carnal sensual detail, once we've learned to laugh at foolish studies that show that lesbians don't have sex as often as, aren't as sexual as, and use fewer sexual techniques than other folks.

Notes

This essay first appeared in *Sinister Wisdom*, vol. 35 (Summer/Fall 1988). In its first version, this essay was written for the meeting of the Society for Women in Philosophy, Midwestern Division, November, 1987, at Bloomington, Indiana. It was occasioned by Claudia Card's paper, "Intimacy and Responsibility: What Lesbians

Do," (Published in the Institute for Legal Studies Working Papers, Series, 2, University of Wisconsin-Madison, Law School, Madison, WI 53706). Carolyn Shafer has contributed a lot to my thinking here, and I am indebted also to conversations with Sue Emmert and Terry Grant.

[1] Philip Blumstein and Pepper Schwartz, *American Couples*, (NY: William and Morrow Company, 1983).

[2] Dotty Calabrese gave this information in her workshop on long-term lesbian relationships at the Michigan Womyn's Music Festival, 1987. (Thanks to Terry for this reference).

[3] By Carolyn Shafer. See pp. 156-7 of my book *The Politics of Reality* (The Crossing Press, 1983).

Learning To Touch Honestly

A White Lesbian's Struggle With Racism

Kim Hall

In the early morning we sleep peacefully entwined in the warmth of rays streaming through the window. Opening my eyes, stretching, I feel the soft heat of your skin against my stomach and breasts. As I watch you sleeping, I think of our love-making during the night. Your fingers trickling along the length of my back, my tongue caressing your firm brown nipples. Kissing the back of your neck, I snuggle closer, my skin ghost-like next to your brown skin . . .

I have been struggling for quite some time wondering how I could possibly write about my experiences as a lesbian who is trying to come to terms with my whiteness, trying to be specific about my experiences, wondering how I can love womyn better. As I begin to write, the pain and difficulty of this process nearly overwhelm me. Seized by a sudden lack of vocabulary and faced with an immense writer's block, I feel afraid.

Afraid of what? I am afraid of what I have been denying, afraid of seeing what I have not wanted to see. I am afraid that when I look at racism, I will discover my own white face. I am afraid that I will do it all wrong and that, instead of creating a connection, I will create an even greater distance. How can I write without straying to another focus that feels safe to me? How can I prevent white guilt from thwarting my efforts before I even begin? What does it mean that I am writing as a white lesbian? How can I climb this wall?

I have become increasingly aware of an awkward silence surrounding the experience of racism and white skin privilege among white lesbians.[1] I have read books written by womyn of color. Particular turning points in my awareness have resulted from my readings of *Ain't I A Woman* by Bell Hooks, *Sister Outsider* by Audre Lorde, and *This Bridge Called My Back: Writings By Radical Women of Color* edited by Cherríe Moraga and Gloria Anzaldúa. I have attended conferences on feminist theory at which Chicana, Latina, and Black womyn have read their papers. I have also read books, poems, articles by white womyn on the subject of racism and explorations of how to come closer to a lesbian world. Works by Minnie Bruce Pratt, Adrienne Rich, and Elly Bulkin come to mind here. Certainly the subject has been discussed and written about — I am not the first to do so by any means. So why am I complaining about a silence surrounding racism and white skin privilege among white lesbians?

I do not mean to devalue or neglect the previous work by white lesbians. These works have inspired me and provided glimpses of the possibilities for change. However, the inspirations have been too few and too far between.

More often, I have noticed a white lesbian's brief acknowledgment of the fact that she is writing from her position as a white lesbian, only to continue with the development of her theory in the pages that follow. It's not enough to say, "As a white lesbian . . ." Don't get me wrong. I am certainly not suggesting that white lesbians have to begin to

---

[1] One obstacle that I have encountered in writing this paper is the dilemma of the "we" and the "I". I use "we" to refer to white lesbians, not in order to abstract from my own involvement; I am very much included in the "we". Rather, I use "we" out of a felt need to connect with other white womyn in order to work collectively on our racism. I in no way assume that the "we" refers to a homogeneous group of white lesbians. On the contrary, I imagine the "we" to refer to a group of lesbians who differ enormously in our experiences but who are on the oppressor-side of racism due to our whiteness.

Also, in this paper I am writing from my experiences as a white lesbian who happens to be in academia; therefore, I often refer to writing, conferences, and so on. I do not mean to suggest that writing is the only place where change can occur. Certainly I want to work on other aspects of my life in addition to writing.

write from within experiences other than our own. My concern stems from my belief that these acknowledgments have all too often been empty acknowledgments. Frequently, white lesbians acknowledge the existence of racism within lesbian relations only to abstract our personal experiences from the all-too-brief conversation that follows, as if racism exists "somewhere over there" and our lesbian lives exist here.

"We're called 'Flips'," you say matter-of-factly, your voice cracking like thunder in my ears. Why did you say that? Doesn't it make you angry? I shudder wishing that I had not hear it. I look down at my hand holding yours, my whiteness a neon sign that hurts my eyes. Even as we sit side by side, your hips brushing mine, I feel the earth open between us, trees are uprooted. I want to hold you close, you slip and spin away . . .

Have our acknowledgments changed the *way* we speak, the *way* we write? What does it mean that I can pick up a book written by a white lesbian in 1987, only to discover that she continues to erase the experiences of womyn of color, continues to talk about *all* womyn. By ignoring the significance of the differences between womyn, she creates an exclusively white context even if this is not her intention. Addressing her own racism (or, for that matter, addressing racism at all in her writing) would put the very foundation of her work into question.[2] What does it mean that womyn of color write from within their experiences and that white womyn can only analyze whiteness from a distance, as if whiteness was an object located only in the heteropatriarchy and as if white lesbians can separate ourselves from white

---

[2]In her latest book, *Websters' First New Intergalactic Wickedary of the English Language* (Boston: Beacon Press, 1987), Mary Daly writes about "the Race of Women," inferring that all womyn experience the same oppressions as womyn and thus ignoring the many different sources of oppression experienced by womyn who have racial and ethnic backgrounds other than her own. This is especially disturbing when I remember May Daly's lack of response to Audre Lorde's "An Open Letter to Mary Daly," *This Bridge Called My Back: Writings by Radical Women of Color*, eds. Cherríe Moraga and Gloria Anzaldúa (New York: Kitchen Table, 1983), pp. 94-97.

skin privilege in the same way that we have separated ourselves from men? Have we acknowledged our whiteness only to be politically correct?

I am made painfully aware of the abyss between the efforts of womyn of color and the efforts of white lesbians. I must ask, "Have we really listened to womyn of color at all?" The point is not to simply acknowledge what we as white lesbians have done (although that's a big part of it); the point is to *change* what we are doing.

I live my life in the world as a white lesbian; therefore, my focus is on lesbian relations. Because all of my loyalties and attention remain with womyn, my approach and dealing with racism and white skin privilege will differ sharply from those of a white heterosexual or bisexual woMAN. In other words, I have no desire or interest in working for equality with white men. White woMEN's desire for equality with white men is also a desire to participate with white men in racial dominance.[3]

I am trying to meet womyn of color out of love. Because I am white, I have benefited and continue to benefit from white skin privilege, even though being a lesbian has denied other privileges. Being a lesbian does not change the fact that my physical being in the world is safer than that of a lesbian of color. My white skin remains.

Spinning, you take with you all of my hopes that, as lesbians, we are the same in some way. I wanted to believe that racism is a problem only in the heteropatriarchal world. I wanted to believe that here, in our lesbian world, we were two lesbians loving each other. That's all. I didn't want to realize that we were both carrying pieces of the heteropatriarchy that would appear and disappear at various tim . . .

---

[3] Marilyn Frye, "On Being White: Thinking Toward A Feminist Understanding of Race and Race Supremacy," *Politics of Reality: Essays in Feminist Theory* (Trumansburg, New York: The Crossing Press, 1983), p. 125.

More and more, I am astonished at the spaces between white lesbians when it comes to working on racism. Too much of the process occurs in isolation, too much of the process remains buried in silence.

Recently, I listened as María Lugones read her paper about the ways in which white womyn have not seen her. During the reading, I am in agreement with her and move my body in ways to make my agreement clear to her and to other womyn of color in the room. I did not want the womyn of color at the reading to place me in a slot labelled "White Womon", even though that's what I am. Simultaneously, I avoided making any kind of contact with the other white womyn in the room. I tried to create as much distance as possible between myself and the other white womyn present, as if I want to say to the womyn of color, "Yes. I know that I am a white womon, but I am aware. I have worked on/am working on my racism. It's them — those white womyn. They are the problem!"

Needless to say, this is not what I consider to be one of my proud moments. Looking back at it and writing about it are very difficult. Instead of pointing my finger at myself, I was too quick to point my finger at the other white womyn in the room. Why did I act this way?

Surely there have been other white womyn who have felt similarly in similar situations. The problem is that we rarely talk about it. We put vast distances between ourselves as if the distance somehow dissolves our white skin. However, even though our experiences may vary, whiteness *is* a collective experience, and working against racism is our collective responsibility. We cannot expect womyn of color to do it for us. White womyn need to take action, to make working against racism an integral part of our feminist work. We need to touch the depths of our love, our passionate love for other womyn.

In my lack of realization, I failed to love you. I failed to see the lesbian of color that you are, I failed to see the white lesbian that I am. I failed to see the places where we drift apart as well as the places where we touch in warm embrace. I wanted to believe that our les-bian world was colorless. I did not realize that in the process of wanting this I was whitewashing you and that we were drifting further apart. You tried to share your piece of the truth, and I did not want to listen . . .

What remains absent from white lesbians' struggle against racism is the incorporation of caring and touch which characterize a world of lesbian relating. Abstractness dissolves when we explore our past and present relationships with womyn of color and each other in ways that touch both the pain and the joy of our experiences, in ways that make white womyn accountable for our racism and white skin privilege. New exciting possibilities of relating unfold.

Touching in a caring way is something done out of love. It is a touch that seeks not to conquer or to possess or to silence, but to meet, to let exist, to caress. It is a touch that welcomes differences, a touch that does not seek to know all. It is a touch that delights in both the places of connection and the places of separation.

In our work on racism, white womyn have yet to realize the "power of touching another woman's difference."[4] Touching the difference of another womon generates sparks spinning into the wilderness, creating something new.

Part of touching another womon's difference is not coming empty-handed; it means touching each other honestly. Touching honestly is extremely difficult because it makes hiding behind my racism and white skin privilege and lying about my experiences impossible. Lying is a refusal to look at racism in the face; it is a refusal to touch my memory, a refusal to change. For a white lesbian, lying makes working on racism and white skin privilege much easier than it is or ought to be.[5]

---

[4] Audre Lorde, "The Uses of Anger: Women Responding to Racism," *Sister Outsider* (Trumansburg, New York: The Crossing Press, 1984), p. 133.
[5] Adrienne Rich, "Women and Honor: Some Notes on Lying," *On Lies, Secrets, and Silence* (New York: W.W. Norton and Company, 1979), pp. 187-188.

White womyn need to be honest, to face the difficulty of the task, to meet womyn of color out of love. In their work womyn of color have shared pieces of their worlds. Womyn of color have been honest. But what have white womyn done? What have we done to meet womyn of color half-way?

You look at me not understanding my reaction. What did I want you to do — not say it? Did I want you to never mention the word, racism? Did I want you to remain silent forever? No. I know that you had to say it and that I had to hear it. I am angered that I have the luxury of choosing whether or not I hear it, of selecting among your words. I lean forward and try to listen to you more closely . . .

By remaining silent, by creating spaces between ourselves and other white lesbians, by not being specific about our experiences, by acting as if racism does not exist in lesbian relating, by pretending that white lesbians have somehow "transcended" whiteness, we have not touched the difference of womyn of color or each other honestly. We have not even ventured to put one toe on the bridge. For example, if you come to me willing to share a piece of your world, and I come to you not willing to share anything (or worse, hiding the parts that I am afraid for you to see), I am not meeting you honestly. I am expecting you to do all of the work while I do nothing, risk nothing. Instead of spinning in new directions creating new meaning, we remain at a stand-still.

I go to the library and check out a ton of books. You know so much about my world — you had no choice. I know so little about your world, almost nothing. Between us, I do not want to be in the position of not having to know, of being able to ignore. I love you. I want to read about your world, to come to you with some knowledge. Then, maybe, if you want, I can talk with you . . .

Touching another woman's difference with honesty is a process of re-membering. Until I am willing to explore the caverns of my memory, until I am willing to be honest about my life experiences, I will remain empty-handed. Without remembering the places where I have absorbed heteropatriarchal values, as well as the places where I move beyond them, I remain dis-membered from myself and other lesbians. The absence of this exploration renders impossible the creation of new meaning and places a lesbian world[6] beyond my fingertips. Only in confronting the demons of my memory will I be able to wipe out their existence. Of course, this does not mean that the color of my skin will miraculously change and that I will no longer be white. It does, however, mean that I will be able to meet womyn of color honestly, enabling our relationships to spring into new dimensions.

Remembering is not only a movement backward; it is also a movement forward. Remembering forward is an exploration of the unknown, a movement in which the possibilities of relating unfold and begin anew.[7] Remembering involves not placing myself only in a negative relation to womyn of color. If, in my remembering, I stop and say, that I have oppressed you, that I have silenced you, and nothing else, I not only do not see you, I also do nothing to change myself. Remembering means realizing that the process of remembering is undertaken with the positive goal of change in mind. It involves the realization that you are not only a survivor of racism and that I am not only an oppressor.

There are many things that I cannot see, many things that I am trying to learn how to see, many things that I will never see. However, the existence of the worlds of womyn of color is not contingent on what I do or do not see.

---

[6] Even though I refer to lesbian world in the singular, I do not mean to suggest that lesbians are a homogeneous group. I am talking about a community where diversity is celebrated, not feared or ignored. I am also not talking about a world that I create alone. Such a world can be created only by the efforts of many different lesbians. There are many threads that connect and shape a lesbian world; however, not all of these threads connect with each other. I cannot see all of the connections. Many of the connections are quite independent of me, a white lesbian.

[7] Jeffner Allen, *Lesbian Philosophy: Explorations* (Palo Alto, California: Institute of Lesbian Studies, 1986), p. 25.

You tell me about your problems with your family — they have traditional values and you are a womon. Laughing, you tell me how you tried to explain to your mother how you know a white womon, a white womon who is older than you, a white womon who lives in another state. None of your other friends are white. You tell me about your visits with relatives and about how none of the womyn are allowed to go out. I relish the twinkle in your eye as you tell great tales of resistence — how you go out anyway. I watch you dancing with your friends. Looking at you, I do not see only a survivor of racism, a womon who has no existence apart from my whiteness . . .

A Childhood Memory: I remember walking into the drug store in my small southern hometown with my mother. Everyone says hello to me, and while my mother gets her prescription filled, I busy myself in the aisle where all of the toys are located. No one follows me. A few minutes later, a black girl, who is about my age, walks in with her mother. While her mother walks to the prescription counter, she joins me in picking up various toys and examining them. She is followed by a white man who works there, and he does not take his eyes off her. A little later, her mother finds her, scolds her for touching things on the shelf, and says that it's time for them to leave. When they have gone, I hear the white man say, "You can't take your eyes off them for one minute." But he does not watch me, and I realize that he trusts me not to steal because I am white.

I invite you to come with me to my mother's house. You are nervous and ask many questions. You ask whether or not my mother knows that you are not white. I reply that it had not occurred to me to mention it to her and try to assure you that everything will be OK. You are skeptical and say that you would rather not go . . .

Years later, I go to a conference to hear a U.S. Latina womon whose work I have admired for quite some time. There are many womyn of color there, and I listen to them speak. I try to remove the wax from my ears, I lean forward, trying to listen. I listen to María Lugones read about how white womyn have not seen her, how white womyn are afraid of the selves that we see when we look in her eyes. I am breathless, unable to move during the reading. I look down at my white hands in my lap. I look into her eyes as she reads her paper.

Afterwards, I want to tell her how beautiful I thought her paper was, how much it touched me and moved me deeply. I hesitate — it is more than my usual shyness. How many more times do I have to read the writings of womyn of color before I do something? Haven't they told me enough already?[8]

I look into her eyes and see a white woman who has read and done little. I look down at my white hands and realize that I cannot go to any more of these conferences until I know that I am doing something. I look into her eyes and see the white/Anglo lesbian that I am, the U.S. Latina lesbian that she is. I tell her how beautiful I thought her paper was.

You and I are sitting side by side on a step. You gently rest your hand on my thigh generating sparks of electricity racing through my body. I feel warmth surge between my legs as I reach over and run my fingers through your straight, short, black hair. You turn to me and smile . . .

María Lugones   Jeffner Allen   Gloria Anzaldúa   Naomi Littlebear Wendy Rose   Joyce Trebilcot   Ntozake Shange Bell Hooks   Audre Lorde   Mary Daly   Anne Mamary Jordana Brown   Barbara Cameron   Chrystos Cherríe Moraga Paula Gunn Allen   Adrienne Rich   Donna Kate Rushin Caryatis Cardea   Anna Lee   Combahee River Collective Elly Bulkin   Minnie Bruce Pratt   Marilyn Frye   Barbara Smith Sara Lucia Hoagland Nicole Brossard Nellie Wong Ruth Frankenburg   Marie . . .

---

[8] Nellie Wong, "When I Was Growing Up," *This Bridge Called My Back: Writings By Radical Women of Color*, eds. Cherríe Moraga and Gloria Anzaldúa (New York: Kitchen Table, 1983), p. 8

Lesbian Body Journeys

Desire Making Difference
JACQUELYN N. ZITA

The notion of "body journeys" occurred to me after reading Adrienne Rich's "Notes toward a Politics of Location" (1986), a writing in which Rich eliminates some of the essentialist[1] commitment of her earlier work. Unlike the romanticized female body in *Of Woman Born*, where the body represents "the unity and resonance of our physicality, our bond with the natural order, the corporeal ground of our intelligence," (1973, p. 21), one finds in this later essay a very concrete and historically-located body: "To write 'my body' plunges me into lived experience, particularity." (1986, p. 215) This body, "born in the white section of a hospital which separated Black and white women in labor and Black and white babies in the nursery, just as it separated Black and white bodies in its morgue," (1986, p. 215) had more than one identity *from the outset*. Whereas in Rich's earlier writing "the diffuse, intense sensuality radiating out of the clitoris, breast, uterus, vagina; the lunar cycles of menstruation; the gestation and fruition of life which can take place in the female body" (Rich, 1977, p. 21) furnished a resource for female-centered intelligence and power, her new writing contextualizes this body by revealing its locational meanings. "To locate myself in my body means more than understanding what it has meant to me to have a vulva and clitoris and uterus and breasts. It means recognizing this white skin, the places it has taken me, the places it has not let me go. The body I was born into was not only female and white, but Jewish —

enough for geographic location to have played, in those years, a determining role. (1986, pp. 216-217)

A lived body is always deeply contextualized in its location and meanings, whether these be historical and culturally-specific meanings imposed on the form and function of the body or the inscription of social difference, dependent on the meanings of race, sex, class, age and physical type, marking bodies into social kinds. From the outset and throughout life, the psyche embraces the memory and experience of multiple differentiations and markings, meanings which are continuously re-constituted and challenged through the body's serial displacements in location and relationship. Thus, the body is a situated and irreducible site where social difference and meaning are inscribed and contested. "Body journeys" consist in this residual process — the continuous constitution of body meanings and social difference — transversing the private and public locations of one's lifetime.

In this essay I will explore the concept of body journeys through three autobiographical accounts, Audre Lorde's *Zami: a new spelling of my name* (1982), Minnie Bruce Pratt's "Identity: Skin Blood Heart" (1984), and Joan Nestle's *A Restricted Country* (1987).[2] In these personal journeys, the complexity of the authors' multiple-identities is not readily assimilated into a reductive lesbian essentialism, which subordinates race, class, ethnic and even erotic differences to the primacy of "Lesbian" as a central and normative defining category of "self".[3] These journeys also bring into focus points of contestation and disjuncture — where difference is *felt* as a boundary, a barrier, a grieved loss of connection, a reason for leaving or fighting back, heroically if necessary. Such points of disjuncture do not represent steps in linear growth, but periods of expansion or constriction, where the meaning of difference in the context of lesbian experience is explored. From the collected testimony of these three autobiographical writings, collective unity carved into a lesbian essence,[4] committed to an analytics of sameness and denial of difference, seems oddly disrespectful and dishonest.

Identity Points

Audre Lorde. Black. Lesbian. Ky-Ky. West-Indian-American. Afrekete. . . . *Minnie Bruce Pratt.* White. Southern-usa. Anglo. Christian-raised. Lesbian. . . . *Joan Nestle.* White. Jewish. Working Class. Lesbian. Sexradical. Femme. Freak. . . . Where nouns and adjectives name and depict important aspects of our lives, we traverse "identity points,"[5] each marking a difference, making claim on a receding center. There is no one difference, no one stabilizing identity, only partial coherencies disrupted by shifting locations. The ordering can be rearranged or stabilized, however unstable. Claiming any one identity is not a precondition for the unity of self, but at times a precondition for self-preservation. Claiming a lesbian identity often diffuses into difference, once its locations are made physical, real, and lived.

Points of Disjuncture

For a white Anglo[6] woman the journey into difference is the growing recognition of one's multiple-identities, instead of none or one, instead of the "boundaries of protection" which created the meanings of her "whiteness" through omission, denial, distance, and control. (Martin and Mohanty, 1986) For such a woman, "home" is a tenuous structure, with its insurgencies found in difference, what cannot be included, including female "promiscuity and wantoness," lesbian or otherwise.

"Home" "Unity" "Sameness" "Community" all insufficient. Disjunctures when experienced become impetus to continue one's journey: a reason for leaving, a desire to fill in the gaps, to stay and fight, to disrupt, become obnoxious or resist. These disjunctures create a "free space", where individuality and uniqueness is constituted in a discourse of negations.

Being women together was not enough.   We were different.
Being gay-girls together was not enough.   We were different.
Being Black together was not enough.   We were different.
Being Black women together was not enough.   We were dif-
ferent. Being Black dykes together was not enough.   We
were different. (Audre Lorde, p. 226)

And finally, in my own recent life I have entered the domain
of public sex. I write sex stories for Lesbian magazines, I
pose for explicit photographs for Lesbian photographers, I
do readings of sexually graphic materials dressed in sexually
revealing clothes, and I have taken money from women for
sexual acts. I am, depending on who is the accuser, a pornog-
rapher, a queer, and whore. (Joan Nestle, p. 159)

By the amount of effort it takes me to walk these few blocks
being conscious as I can of myself in relations to history, to
race, to culture, to gender, I reckon the rigid boundaries set
around my experience, how I have been "protected." In this
city where I am no longer of the majority by color or culture,
I tell myself everyday: In this *world* you aren't the superior
race, and never were, whatever you were raised to think. . . .
(Minnie Bruce Pratt, p. 13)

SKINNED ZONES

"The skin is a line of demarcation, a periphery, the
fence, the form, the shape, the first clue to identity in a
society. . . and, in purely physical terms, the formal precondition for being human. It is the thin veil of matter
separating the outside from the inside." (Dworkin, 1987,
p. 22) The body's surface, its morphology and ancestry
of genetic flesh, is a primary site for the inscription of
social difference. We are, however, differently stationed
with respect to this cutaneous sign. For some, it signi-
fies no right of passage into restricted zones. For others,
traversing new zones calls for a careful shedding of its
semantic transparency, its whiteness. In living the body,

we can take in these meanings as deep infractions or strange twists of shyness.

As a very little girl, I remember shrinking from a particular sound, a hoarsely sharp, gutteral rasp, because it often meant a nasty glob of grey spittle upon my coat or shoe an instant later. My mother wiped it off with the little pieces of newspaper she always carried in her purse. Sometimes she fussed about low-class people who had no better sense nor manners than to spit into the wind no matter where they went, impressing upon me that this humiliation was totally random. It never occurred to me to doubt her. It was not until years later once in conversation I said to her: "Have you noticed people don't spit into the wind so much the way they used to?" And the look on my mother's face told me that I had blundered into one of those secret places of pain that must never be spoken of again. (Audre Lorde, pp. 17-18)

Huddled in the privacy of our room, my mother and brother told me what the manager had said. Since it was off-season, he was willing to compromise. If we told no one that we were Jewish, if we left and entered through the back door, and if we ate our meals by ourselves, we could stay. We looked at each other. Here was an offer to the Nestles to pass as Gentiles. To eat and walk in shame. . . . In a strange twist of feeling, my anger had turned to shyness. I thought of the priest I had noticed sitting on the table the night before, and I could not bear the thought of making him see we were human. (Joan Nestle, p. 31)

"I said I kin give you a take out, but you can't eat here. Sorry. . . . Straight-backed and indignant, one by one, my family and I got down from the counter stools and turned around and marched out of the store, quiet and outraged, as if we had never been Black before (Audre Lorde, p. 70)

When I am trying to understand myself in relation to folks different from myself, when there are discussions, conflicts about anti-Semitism and racism among women, criticisms, criticism of me, and I get afraid: . . . when I feel my racing heart, breath, the tightening of my skin around me, literally defenses to protect my narrow circle, I try to say to myself: Yes, that fear is there, but I will try to be at the edge between my fear and outside, on the edge of my skin, listening, asking what new things will I hear, will I see, will I let myself feel, beyond the fear. (Minnie Bruce Pratt, p. 18)

BODY, LOCATION, DISCIPLINE

Body. Discipline. Rules proscribing body acts. Rules despising body functions. Rules denying body secretions. Language as rules determining the limits of the body's semantic and sexual space, its pleasure and capacities. Through the imposition of social order on the body, a "second nature" is created, but it must be constantly watched or kept under guard. Transgressions are subject to punishment.

Pat Califia: "Knowing I was a lesbian transformed the way I saw, heard, perceived the whole world. I became aware of a network of sensations and reactions that I had ignored my entire life." (Califia, 1980, p. 165) Is she also dangerous? Should I watch her? Guard against her?

For myself, knowing that I was a woman transformed what I say into a way of being seen. Knowing that I was a lesbian (and knowing that I would be watched for this) transformed how I saw the straight world. I also started watching and wanting women. Knowing women, redefining "woman".

What I was feeling was that I would spend the rest of my life going round and round in a pattern that I knew by heart: being a wife, a mother of two boys, a teacher of the writings of white men, dead men. I drove around the market house four times a day, travelling on the suface of my own life, circular, repetitive, like one of the games at the country fair, the one with yellow plastic ducks clacking one after the other on a track, until they fall abruptly off the edge, into inevitable meaningless disappearance: unless, with a smack, one or two or three vanish from the middle, shot down by a smiling man with a gun. For the first time in my life, I was living in a place where I was afraid because I was a *woman*. (Minnie Bruce Pratt, pp. 21-22)

But the most searing reminder of our colonized world was the bathroom line. Now I know it stands for all the pain and glory of my time, and I carry that line and the women who endured it deep within me. Because we were labeled deviants, our bathroom habits had to be watched. Only one woman at a time was allowed into the toilet because we could not be trusted. . . . Guarding the entrance to the toilet was a short, square, handsome butch woman, the same every night, whose job it was to twist around her hand our allotted amount of toilet paper. She was us, an obsenity, doing the man's trick so we could breathe. (Joan Nestle, p. 38)]

Besides, among us there were always rumors of plainsclothes women circulating among us, looking for gay-girls with fewer than three pieces of female attire. That was enough to get you arrested for transvestism, which was illegal. Or so the rumors went. (Audre Lorde, p. 187)

The states also drew up litanies of control defining the multitude of ways prostitutes could lose their social freedoms. In fifteenth-century France, a prostitute faced up to three months imprisonment if she was:
  1. to appear in forbidden places
  2. to appear at forbidden hours
  3. to walk through the streets in daylight in such a way as to attract the notice of people passing. (Joan

Nestle, p. 162)

Dykes and whores, it appears, have an historical heritage of redefining the concept of woman. (Joan Nestle, p. 161)

SEX: IN THE ALTOGETHERNESS

The erotic. Sex. Touch. Lesbian collisions of sensuousity. Desire uncoded by adjustments to a male body. "Sometimes, the skin comes off in sex. The people merge, skinless. The body loses its boundaries. . . . The skin collapses as a boundary — it has no meaning; time is gone — it too has no meaning; there is no outside." (Dworkin, 1987, p. 22) Yet the differences return once the skin returns. For a heterosexual woman this return brings into view another body unlike her own: it is sometimes said that this difference is worth dying for. For lesbians, the return can be surprising, in the discovery of difference where the sameness in morphologies promised sameness everywhere. The erotic for lesbians, as a colonized people, is a fragile identity point, bridging completely, though momentarily, differences which can stop our touching, our desire . . . simultaneously feed them . . . : "the erotic for us, as a colonized people, is part of our social struggle to survive and change the world." (Joan Nestle, p. 104) There is no simple unity here.

Our bodies found the movements we needed to fit each other. Ginger's flesh was sweet and moist and firm as a winter pear. I felt her and tasted her deeply, my hands and my mouth and my whole body moved against her. . . . The sweetness of her body meeting and filling my mouth, my hands, wherever I touched, felt right and completing, as if I had been born to make love to this woman, and was remembering her body rather than learning it deeply for the first time. . . . So this was what I had been so afraid of not doing properly. How ridiculous and far away those fears seemed now, as if loving were some task outside of myself rather than simply reaching out and letting my own desire guide me. It was all so simple. I felt so good I smiled into the darkness. Ginger cuddled closer. (Audre Lorde, pp. 139-140)

You came in dazzling waves of freedom, you came on shores never to be visited again, and I knew even before your body slid back into its full weight that I had lost you again. When the revelation has passed, you lay beside me. Carrying my history on my lips, I bent my head between your legs to taste, to soothe, to speak to you in the language of my love, but it was too much. You pushed my head away. The secret glory had burst and the curtains again descended, long heavy drapes of custom and of fear. There could be no acknowledged touch outside the frenzy of deliverance. The next morning, a kiss was not allowed. We stood before the mirror, Mara braiding her long hair, opening her face to the morning light. I stood behind her, a shadow, touching the crack in my lip with my tongue. The earth for one brief instant had split open, letting loose the storm of years, but now in the light, only a thin red line on a woman's lip marked the place where the center had burst. (Joan Nestle, p. 73)

In the bars of the late fifties and early sixties where I learned my Lesbian ways, whores were part of our world. We sat on barstools next to each other, we partied together, and we made love together. . . . This shared territory broke apart, at least for me, when I entered the world of lesbian-feminism. Whores and women who looked like whores became the enemy or at best, misguided oppressed women who needed our help. (Joan Nestle, pp. 158-159)

Between Muriel and me, then, there was one way in which I would always be separate, and it was going to be my own secret knowledge, if it was going to be my own secret pain. I was Black and she was not, and that was a difference between us that had nothing to do with better or worse, or the outside world's craziness. Over time I came to realize that it colored our perceptions and made a difference in the

ways I saw pieces of the worlds we shared, and I was going
to have to deal with that difference outside our relationship.
This was the first separation, the piece outside of love.
(Audre Lorde, p. 204)

This was the first separation, the piece outside of love.
There were others, as the sisterhood re-collected into pieces.

COMMUNITIES OF DISLOCATION

There had to be some place, however factious, sectarian, and
fissionable, and local.

The important message seemed to be that you had to have a
place. Whether or not it did justice to whatever you felt you
were about, there had to be some place to refuel and check
your flaps. (Audre Lorde, p. 225)

Most of the women I knew in the Sea Colony were working
women who either had never married or who had left their
husbands and were thus responsible for their own economic
survival. Family connections had been severed, or the families were poorer than the women themselves. These were
women who knew they were going to work for the rest of
their Lesbian days to support themselves and the homes they
chose to create. They were hairdressers, taxi drivers, telephone operators, who were also butch-femme women. Their
feminism was not an articulated theory; it was a lived set of
options based on erotic choices. (Joan Nestle, p. 105)

During the time that I was first feeling all this information,
again I lived in a kind of vertigo: a sensation of my body
having no fixed place to be: the earth having opened I was
falling through space. I had had my home and children taken
away from me. I had set out to make a new home with other
women, only to find that the very ground I was building on
was the grave of the people my kin had killed, and that my

foundation, my birth culture, was mortared with blood. (Minnie Bruce Pratt, p. 35)

. . . a sensation of my body having no fixed place to be . . .

A Desire Which Left Her Homeless

Pariah's desire. If anything lesbians know our desires and sex acts can throw us by the wayside of family circles, some of us never to return again. Desires leaving us homeless often cause longing for another home in community or relationships. "The assumption of, or desire for, another safe place like "home" is challenged by the realization that "unity" — interpersonal as well as political — is itself necessarily fragmentary, itself that which is struggled for, chosen, and hence unstable by definition: it is not based on "sameness," and there is not perfect fit. But there is agency as opposed to passivity." (Martin and Mohanty, 1986, pp. 208-209) There has to be some place to go, "to refuel and check your flaps," to just be.

But I *had* expected to have that protected circle marked off for me by the men of my kin as my "home": I had expected to have that place with my children. I expected it as my *right*. I did not understand I had been exchanging the use of my body for that place. I learned, finally: I stepped outside the circle of protection. I said, "My body, my womb, and the children of my womb are not yours to use." . . . The inner surface of my arms, my breasts, and muscles of my stomach were raw with my need to touch my children. (Minnie Bruce Pratt, p. 27)

We need to know that we are not accidental. . . . I need to remember what it was like to walk the streets as a young femme with my butch lover. I need to remember what it was like to fight for sexual territory in the time of Joseph McCarthy. I need to remember the humiliation and the courage of standing on the bathroom line. I need to remember the flashing red light that signaled police visits and the closed faces of the vice squad, the paddy wagons carrying off my friends. I need to keep alive the memory of passing women and their wives, the memory of Lesbians who because they "looked like men" were ridiculed, beaten, locked up, hidden away. These women presented gender challenges at a time when only the deviants questioned gender destiny. I need to keep alive the memory that in the 1940s doctors measured the clitorises and nipples of Lesbians to prove our biological strangeness. When transvestites and transsexuals are beaten by the police, as they were at Blues, this history calls me to action. I cannot turn away from it. My roots lie in the history of a people who were called freaks. (Joan Nestle, pp. 111-112)

I was gay and Black. The later fact was irrevocable: armor, mantle, and wall. Often, when I had the bad taste to bring that fact up in a conversation with other gay-girls who were not Black I would get the feeling that I had in some way breached some sacred bond of gayness, a bond which I always knew was not sufficient for me. This was not to deny the closeness of our group, nor the mutual aid of those insane, glorious, and contradictory years. . . . The question of acceptance had a different weight for me. (Audre Lorde, pp. 180-181)

It was a while before we came to realize that our place was the very house of difference rather than the security of any one particular difference. (And often, we were cowards in our learning.) It was years before we learned to use the strength that daily surviving can bring, years before we learned fear does not have to incapacitate, and that we could appreciate each other on terms not necessarily our own. (Audre Lorde, p. 226)

• • • • • • • •

My excerpts from these lesbian autobiographies are arranged in a purposefully fragmented order, providing the reader with a glimpse of how these texts intersect in new ways of writing one's "self". This "self" is not grounded by a notion of an essence, but is constructed in and through partial coherencies within the immediacy of daily transactions. It is a self which finds "the very house of difference" as shelter. The unity of "home", while nostalgically sentimentalized, is foiled by fidelity to the political meanings of difference and to the imbeddedness of difference in relations of power, domination and historical reality. These differences cannot be wiped away by new ethical practices, by the spiritual unity of "sisterhood", by play-acting with historical relations of power in bedroom scenarios, by the bonds of lesbian sanctity or by the appeal to the structures of normalization, having babies, getting married, buying property together. They are differences originally cut and cut deeply by the violence of history, implicating us in each others' lives through the recognition of disunity, distrust and unsteady coalitions.

Within these body journeys of lesbians consciously exploring the meanings of multiple oppressions and resistances, the foregrounding of one particular difference shifts into the background, as another identity point is foregrounded against it. The "self" moves through these journeys, always informed by and informing of a body marked by many differences and partial "homes". As Audre Lorde writes "there was a piece of the real me bound in each place, and growing", irreconcilable with the coherent and unified "security of any one particular difference."

For these lesbians, loving across differences brings into focus the power of an eroticism which dissolves boundaries while simultaneously colliding upon them as sources of power, pleasure, separation and loss. "This was the first separation, the piece outside of love." Such experiences belie the notion of lesbian eroticism as an eroticism of sameness, in which sanctum from the male body allegedly eliminates the presence and disturbance of social difference. Likewise, Joan

Nestle's erotic writing further problematizes the notion of a unified and normative lesbian sexuality. Her writing brings into focus a fierce permutation of desire and pleasure, unheeding the requirements of any ideological purification or disremberance. All three autobiographical writings honor a faithfulness to the details of everyday life and history, to the survival of women struggling through multiple marginalizations and partial assimilations. What is affirmed is the diversity of lesbian experience, disrailing any simple abstraction of sameness.

Is it then at all possible to say that these three autobiographies share at least something in common, as *lesbian* autobiographies? Here the claim to some lesbian commonality, a "lesbianess" which is not essentializing, is marked within the text itself, in the primacy of sexual desire and pleasure which pulls these women through the journey of a maverick life. Surprisingly and pleasurefully, these autobiographical narratives return to the body, over and over again, as a point of desire, pleasure, and connection while traversing constant recontextualization across the differences of class, race, gender, sexualities and history.

Entry into such journeys begins with the recognition of a desire disruptive to the erotic ontologies of a hetero-sexed culture. Released from heterosexual imperative, lesbian journey is re-located *on the other side*, where desire begins to move in a different direction: "we dared for connection in the name of woman, and saw it as our power, rather than our problem." (Audre Lorde, p. 225) To live this is to break with the erotic ontologies of socially-constructed hetero-sex (quite simply, *her body is no longer over there*) and to assume a full repertoire of sexual pleasure, power, positions, permutations, and postures, whether coded by gender or not, with *one who is also no longer over there*.[7] This cannot be summarized by any positive unity, nor should it be. The error made in lesbian essentialism, in forging unity, sameness and coherency, where there exists difference, discontinuity, and contradictory heterogeneity, is in taking the dominant cultural view too seriously, as if the social/clinical category of "lesbian" designated a homogeneous kind.

To build a politic and theory on the reification of this homogeneous kind is wrong-ended. To build a politic and a theory anchored in the reclamation of "forbidden sexual acts and desires" opens a new view of body politic and female sexual agency. This body is not separable from its history, culture, and other social contexts, since it is within these contexts that the body's lived meanings are created. This is also a body relocating zones of pleasure and sexual meaning on behalf of women's erotic complexity:

> Shame and guilt, censorship and oversimplified sexual judgments, the refusal to listen and the inability to respect sexual difference is not the world I have fought to create. The real challenge to all of us, Lesbians and feminists, is whether we can eliminate violence against women without sacrificing women's erotic complexities. I do not want to become a dictator of desire. . . . (Joan Nestle, p. 117)

To allow for this erotic venture, sexual moralism which focuses exclusively on acts and rules must be replaced by new analyses of sexual contexts, meaning, and relationships — of sexual pluralisms negotiated across bodies and pleasures. Likewise, questions about limits call for a different approach, one uninhibited by homophobia, somato- and erotophobia, yet attentive to the dynamics of oppression, abuse, and harm, the risks encountered.[8]

Lesbian theorizing must begin with sexual desire and erotic relationship as a line of demarcation. It need not sanitize this or essentialize a sublimated content or unify its permissible acts. The ontological load of lesbian essentialism is unnecessary in the marking of this difference. All too often, normative lesbian essentialism marshals together collectivities and ontologies which invite us to rewrite our "selves" or our pasts and futures in allegiance to political orthodoxies, substituting these fictions for reality. I would like to move away from this, towards a different materiality — towards a politic of body journeys, where lesbian authorship of "self" recognizes that sexual desire makes significant difference, whatever else we make of it.

A lesbian identity point is thus a site of negation,[9] articulating the possibility of a sexual desire outlawed by the dominant culture. Lesbian existence begins here, with the body, *no longer over there*. What meanings lesbians bring to this location rests upon agency, desire, the vicissitudes of experience, politics and pleasure. Commonality exists in so far as the lesbian subject is one of a sexual people, constructed and defined *in sexuality* across the multiple locations of class, race, language, and social relations. This is not an essence, but a point of departure, a mark of difference, allowing for the expression of other differences among and within lesbians.[10]

To those among us who wish to screen out this diversity or raid the bars and the past of its deviant underworld, I recommend that we reconsider the historical and social construction of marginalized sexualities, that we wander the margins more openly, sit thigh-to-thigh with our differences, live there, taking seriously the existence and meaning of our diversity. In the thick of such dissonance and within these locations, our talk of essential unity will no longer serve us. What then do lesbians have in common? Sex, if only, and not a lot more. And such a difference does not make all the difference.

Notes

This short article belongs to a much larger writing project, which will appear in a forthcoming book (*Body, Desire, and Violence: Textualities of Soma*) and an essay on lesbian epistemology (manuscript presented at the National Women's Studies Conference, Minneapolis, Minnesota, 1988).

[1] I define essentialism as a belief system committed to the existence of intrinsic natures underlying phenomena. "Lesbian essentialism" would be committed to the belief in some intrinsic nature which separates lesbians from others or real lesbians from other lesbians. This essence can be defined descriptively or normatively. In either case, I will suggest that such an "essence" is not fixed by any ontic base, but should be construed as a discursive inscription which derives identity from sexual practice. More traditional essentialist writing can be found in the work of Mary Daly (1978), Susan Brownmiller (1975), Susan Griffin (1978), and the earlier works of Adrienne Rich (1977, 1980).

[2] Hereafter page references to these texts will be parenthetically indicated by author and page number.

[3] I use this word "self" cautiously, since I do not want to imply that there is a hidden self to be discovered in "the search for identity". Rather I believe that we construct "partial coherencies" in and through our daily interactions which have the semblance of a "self", as a locatable and embodied reference for first-person pronouns. This embodied "self" is relationally and interactively constructed, continuously constituted through memory, principles of coherency, rules of meaning and value, and materialities which set limits and opportunities for individuation and experience.

[4] Strategies to recoup an essentialist meaning for lesbianism include a quest for the inner Self (Daly, 1978), a normative gender thematic of woman-identification (Radicalesbians, 1971), a "continuum of women caring for women" (Rich, 1980), an oppositional ethical practice couched in terms of psychological qualities, values and meanings (Hoagland, 1988), a semantic realignment of meaning with the female body (Wittig, 1986), etc.

[5] The notion of "identity points" was first coined by Teresa de Lauretis. (1986, p. 9) I use it here to replace the baggage of essentialism and to indicate a common point of departure and reference in lesbian existence, the meaning of which is negotiable and local. The demarcation of this difference is located in the body and in the intersections of experience where meanings are constituted.

[6] My own experience as a white Anglo lesbian includes the growing and at times quite painful awareness of my own multiple identities, stationed as I am as the oppressor to some and the oppressed by others. Claiming these various identity points and deciding what to do about them represent a significant change from my earlier less fractured identity, when as a radical feminist my politics, life and theory-making were organized primarily around and through the concept of "woman." Here I direct the reader to Minnie Bruce Pratt's (1984) essay.

[7] My contention here may set off the alarms registered in Janice Raymond's "Putting the Politics Back into Lesbianism" (1989), which characterizes the new "lesbian libertarian lifestyle" as "increasingly preoccupied with fucking as the apogée of lesbian existence" (p 149) and as a backwards move into the hetero-conservative view "that for women sex is salvation." (149) Raymond's analysis reproduces the standard and by now strained polarization of the feminist sex debates between sex radicals and radical feminists. (Ferguson et. al., 1984) Her critique of the sex radicals, selectively focused on the Samois, is a critique of a specialized and highly stylized sexuality, which makes essentialist claims in its call to liberate repressed female sexuality. Raymond's response reconstitutes the question of lesbian sexuality as a debate over sexual essentialisms, rather than abandoning a commitment to essentialism altogether. In the autobiographies used in my analysis, sexuality is centralized as a moving force in the creation of a life; it is always historically-located, not isolated within the "reality-free zones" of Samois practice and not anchored by any essentialist claims which arrest its content.

[8] In the area of sexuality, I am not advocating that '"anything goes", but I do believe that the boundaries and limits set by the rhetorical moralism and extreme polarization in the feminist sex debates have robbed feminist discourse of a more sophisticated analysis. See Ferguson (1983) and Cohen (1986) for some exploratory analyses on how new boundaries can be determined and negotiated in a contextualized approach to sexual pluralism.

[9] I realize that some readers may be concerned about nonsexual or asexual lesbians in this characterization of an identity point. Here the category of negation includes all women who have no primary sexual desire for men, which would include a woman who claims to be a nonsexual or asexual lesbian. However, I feel

uncomfortable with this inclusion, since a woman committed to asexual or nonsexual body journeys, where sexual desire is totally absent, could claim a different way of naming herself. I also feel a need to include and honor lesbians who live out the risks and dangers of lesbian desire. Here meaning is constructed from a desire which moves beyond the negative moment of a life erotically focused on men in a primary way.

[10] I have paraphrased here from Teresa de Lauretis (1987, p. 159) who makes a similar point with respect to the category "woman": "the female subject is en-gendered, constructed and defined in gender across multiple representations of class, race, language, and social relations: . . . differences among women are differences *within* women, which is why feminism can exist despite those differences and, as we are just beginning to understand, cannot continue to exist without them." (de Lauretis, 1987, p. 139) In substituting "lesbians" for "women", this construction allows for the recognition of lesbian pluralism, defined by its location in sexual desire and inclusive of social diversity and sexual pluralism.

References

Brownmiller, Susan. 1975. *Against our Will: Men, Women, and Rape* (New York: Simon and Schuster).

Califia, Pat. 1980 *Sapphistry. The Book of Lesbian Sexuality* (New York: The Naiad Press) 165.

Cohen, Cheryl H. 1986. "The Feminist Sexuality Debate: Ethics and Politics" *Hypatia* vol. 1., no. 2, pp. 71-86.

Daly, Mary. 1978. *Gyn/Ecology: The Metaethics of Radical Feminism* (Boston: Beacon Press) 381.

Dworkin, Andrea. 1987. *Intercourse* (New York: The Free Press).

Ferguson, Ann, Illene Philipson, Irene Diamond and Lee Quinby, and Carole S. Vance and Ann Barr Snitow. 1984. "Forum: The Feminist Sexuality Debates" *Signs* vol. 10, no. 1, pp. 106-135.

Ferguson, Ann. 1983. "The Sex Debate within the Women's Movement: A Socialist Feminist View" *Against the Current* (September/October), pp. 10-16.

Griffin, Susan. 1978. *Woman and Nature: The Roaring Inside Her* (New York: Harper and Row).

Hoagland, Sarah Lucia. 1988. *Lesbian Ethics: Toward New Value* (Palo Alto, California: Institute for Lesbian Studies).

de Lauretis, Teresa. 1986. "Feminist Studies/Critical Studies: Issues, Terms, and Contexts: *Feminist Studies/Critical Studies* ed. Teresa de Lauretis (Bloomington: Indiana University Press), pp. 1-19.

de Lauretis, Teresa. 1987. *Technologies of Gender: Essays on Theory, Film, and Fiction* (Bloomington: Indiana University Press).

Lorde, Audre. 1982. *Zami: a new spelling of my name* (Watertown, Mass.: Persephone Press, Inc.).

Martin, Biddy and Chandra Talpade Mohanty. 1986. "Feminist Politics: What's Home Got to Do with It?" *Feminist Studies/Critical Studies* ed. Teresa de Lauretis (Bloomington, Ind.: Indiana University Press), pp. 191-212.

Nestle, Joan. 1987. *A Restricted Country* (New York: Firebrand Press).

Pratt, Minnie Bruce. 1984. "Identity: Skin Blood Heart" *Yours in Struggle: Three Feminist Perspectives on Anti-Semitism and Racism* (New York: Long Haul Press) pp. 11-63.

Radicalesbians. 1971. "The Woman Identified Woman" *Notes From the Third Year,* reprinted in *Radical Feminism* ed. Ann Koedt.

Raymond, Janice. 1989. "Putting the Politics Back into Lesbianism" *Women's Studies Int. Forum,* vol. 12, no. 2, pp. 149-156.

Rich, Adrienne. 1977. *Of Woman Born* (New York: Bantam).

Rich, Adrienne. 1980. "Compulsory Heterosexuality and Lesbian Existence" *Signs* 5, no. 4 (Summer 1980).

Rich, Adrienne. 1986. "Notes toward a Politic of Location" (1984) *Blood, Bread, and Poetry: Selected Prose 1979-1985* (New York: W.W. Norton and Company), pp. 210-231.

Wittig, Monique. 1986. *The Lesbian Body* trans. David Le Vey (Boston: Beacon). French edition published in Paris by Editions de Minuit, 1973.

The Trojan Horse

Monique Wittig

At first it looks strange to the Trojans, the wooden horse, off color, outsized, barbaric. Like a mountain, it reaches up to the sky. Then little by little, they discover the familiar forms which coincide with those of a horse. Already for them, the Trojans, there have been many forms, various ones, sometimes contradictory, that were put together and worked into creating a horse, for they have an old culture. The horse built by the Greeks is doubtlessly also one for the Trojans, while they still consider it with uneasiness. It is barbaric for its size but also for its form, too raw for them, the effeminate ones, as Virgil calls them. But later on they become fond of the apparent simplicity, within which they see sophistication. They see, by now, all the elaboration that was hidden at first under a brutal coarseness. They come to see as strong, powerful, the work they had considered formless. They want to make it theirs, to adopt it as a monument and shelter it within their walls, a gratuitous object whose only purpose is to be found in itself. But what if it were a war machine?

Any important literary work is like the Trojan Horse at the time it is produced. Any work with a new form operates as a war machine, because its design and its goal is to pulverize the old forms and formal conventions. It is always produced in hostile territory. And the stranger it appears, nonconforming, unassimilable, the longer it will take for the Trojan Horse to be accepted. Eventually it is adopted, and even if slowly, it will eventually work like a mine. It will sap and blast out the ground where it was planted. The old literary forms, which everybody was used to, will eventually appear to be outdated, inefficient, incapable of transformation.

When I say that it is quite possible for a work of literature to operate as a war machine upon the context of its epoch, it is not about committed literature that I am talking. Committed literature and *écriture féminine* have in common that they are mythic formations and function like myths, in the sense Barthes gave to this word. As such they throw dust in the eyes of people by amalgamating in the same process two occurrences that do not have the same kind of relationship to the real and to language. I am not speaking thus in the name of ethical reasons. For example, literature should not be subservient to commitment, for what would happen to the writer if the group which one represents or speaks for stops being oppressed? Would then the writer have nothing more to say? Or what would happen if the writer's work is banned by the group? For the question is not an ethical one but a practical one. As one talks about literature, it is necessary to consider all the elements at play. Literary work cannot be influenced directly by history, politics, and ideology because these two fields belong to parallel systems of signs which function differently in the social corpus and use language in a different way. What I see, as soon as language is concerned, is a series of phenomena whose main characteristic is to be totally heterogeneous. The first irreducible heterogeneity concerns language and its relation to reality. My topic here is the heterogeneity of the social phenomena involving language, such as history, art, ideology, politics. We often try to force them to fit together until they more or less adjust to our conception of what they should be. If I address them separately, I can see that in the expression *committed literature* phenomena whose very nature is different are thrown together. Standing thus, they tend to annul each other. In history, in politics, one is dependent on social history, while in one's work a writer is dependent on literary history, that is, on the history of forms. What is at the center of history and politics is the social body, constituted by the people. What is at the center of literature is forms, constituted by works. Of course people and forms are not at all interchangeable. History is related to people, literature is related to forms.

The first element at hand then for a writer is the huge body of works, past and present—and there are many, very many of them, one keeps forgetting. Modern critics and linguists have by now covered a lot of ground and clarified the subject of literary forms. I think of people like the Russian Formalists, the writers of the *Nouveau Roman*, Barthes, Genette, texts by the *Tel Quel* group. I have a poor knowledge of the state of things in American criticism, but Edgar Allen Poe, Henry James, and Gertrude Stein wrote on the subject. But the fact is that in one's work, one has only two choices—either reproducing existing forms or creating new ones. There is no other. No writers have been more explicit on this subject than Sarraute for France and Stein for the United States.

The second element at hand for a writer is the raw material, that is, language, in itself a phenomenon heterogeneous both to reality and to its own productions. If one imagines the Trojan Horse as a statue, a form with dimensions, it would be both a material object and a form. But it is exactly what the Trojan Horse is in writing, only in a way a little more intricate, because the material used is language, already a form, but also matter. With writing, words are everything. A good many writers have said it and repeated it, a lot of them are saying it at this very moment, and I say it—words are everything in writing. When one cannot write, it is not, as we often say, that one cannot express one's ideas. It is that one cannot find one's words, a banal situation for writers. Words lie there to be used as raw material by a writer, just as clay is at the disposal of any sculptor. Words are, each one of them, like the Trojan Horse. They are things, material things, and at the same time they mean something. And it is because they mean something that they are abstract. They are a condensate of abstraction and concreteness, and in this they are totally different from all other mediums used to create art. Colors, stone, clay have no meaning, sound has no meaning in music, and very often, most often, no one cares about the meaning they will have when created into a form. One does not expect the meaning to be interesting. One does not expect it to have any meaning at all. While as soon as something is written down, it must have a meaning. Even in poems a meaning is expected. All the same a writer needs raw material with which to start one's work, like a painter, a sculptor, or a musician.

This question of language as raw material is not a futile one, since it may help to clarify how in history and in politics the handling of language is different. In history and politics words are taken in their conventional meaning. They are taken only for their meaning, that is in their more abstract form. In literature words are given to be read in their materiality. But one must understand that to attain this result a writer must first reduce language to be as meaningless as possible in order to turn it into a neutral material—that is, a raw material. Only then is one able to work the words into a form. (This does not signify that the finished work has no meaning, but that the meaning comes from the form, the worked words.) A writer must take every word and despoil it of its everyday meaning in order to be able to work with words, on words. Chklovsky, a Russian Formalist, used to say that people stop seeing the different objects that surround them, the trees, the clouds, the houses. They just recognize them without really seeing them. And he said that the task of a writer is to re-create the first powerful vision of things—as opposed to their daily recognition. But he was wrong in that what a writer re-creates is indeed a vision, but the first powerful vision of *words*, not of things. As a writer, I would be totally satisfied if every one of my words had on the reader the same effect, the same shock as if they were being read for the first time. It is what I call dealing a blow with words. As a reader, I find that some writers give me this shock, and it is how I keep on understanding what is happening with words.

What I am saying is that the shock of words in literature does not come out of the ideas they are supposed to promote, since what a writer deals with first is a solid body that must be manipulated in one way or another. And to come back to our horse, if one wants to build a perfect war machine, one must spare oneself the delusion that facts, actions, ideas can dictate directly to words their form. There is a detour, and the shock of words is produced by their association, their disposition, their arrangement, and also by each one of them as used separately. The detour is work, working words as anyone works a material to turn it into something else, a product. There is no way to save this detour in literature, and the detour is what literature is all about.

I said history is related to people while literature is related to forms. As a discipline, however, history like all disciplines uses language in communicating, writing, reading, understanding, and learning. History, ideology, and politics do not question the medium they use. Their domain is the domain of ideas, which is currently considered to be apart from language, issuing directly from the mind. These disciplines still rest on the classical division of body and soul. Even in the Marxist and post-Marxist traditions, there are, on the one hand, the economic order, the material one, and, on the other hand, ideology and politics, considered as the "superstructure." They do not examine language as a direct exercise of power. In this conception, language, along with art, is part of what they call the superstructure. Both are included in ideology, and as such express nothing but the "ideas" of the ruling class. Without a reexamination of the way language operates both in the domain of ideology and in art, we still remain in what the Marxists precisely call "idealism." Form and content correspond to the body/soul division, and it is applied to the words of language and also to ensembles, that is, to literary works. Linguists speak of signifier and signified, which comes to the same distinction.

Through literature, though, words come back to us whole again. Through literature then we can learn something that should be useful in any other field: in words form and content cannot be dissociated, because they partake of the same form, the form of a word, a material form.

One of the best examples of a war machine with a delayed effect is Proust's work. At first everybody thought it was only a *roman à clef* and a minute description of Parisian high society. The sophisticates feverishly tried to put a name to the characters. Then in a second stage they had to change around the women's and men's names, since most of the women in the book were in reality men. They therefore had to take in the fact that a good many of the characters were homosexuals. Since the names were codes for real people, they had to glance back to their apparently normal world, wondering which of them was one, how many of them were, or if they all were. By the end of *La rechereche du temps perdu*, it's done. Proust has succeeded in turning the "real" world into a homosexual-only world. It begins with the cohort of the young men populating the embassies, swarming around their leaders like the maids around Queen Esther in Racine. Then come the dukes, the princes, the married men, the servants, the chauffeurs, and all the tradesmen. Everybody ends up being homosexual. There are even a few lesbians, and Colette reproached Proust with having magnified Gomorrah. Saint-Loup, the elegant epitome of a ladies' man, also turns out to be gay. In the last book Proust, describing the design of the whole work, demonstrates that for him the making of writing is also the making of a particular subject, the constitution of the subject. So that characters and descriptions of given moments are prepared, like so many layers, in order to build, little by little, the subject as being homosexual for the first time in literary history. The song of triumph of *La recherche* redeems Charlus as well.

For in literature, history, I believe, intervenes at the individual and subjective level and manifests itself in the particular point of view of the writer. It is then one of the most vital and strategic parts of the writer's task to universalize this point of view. But to carry out a literary work one must be modest and know that being gay or anything else is not enough. For reality cannot be directly transferred from the consciousness to the book. The universalization of each point of view demands a particular attention to the formal elements that can be open to history, such as themes, subjects of narratives, as well as the global form of the work. It is the attempted universalization of the point of view that turns or does not turn a literary work into a war machine.

Note

This essay is excerpted from *The Straight Mind and other Essays*, by Monique Wittig (Beacon Press, 1990, forthcoming). Reprinted by permission of Beacon Press.

Coincidence

NICOLE BROSSARD
TRANSLATED BY MARLENE WILDEMAN

In male conditioning, male heterosexuality is linked to the male prerogative of a human identity; in female conditioning, female heterosexuality is linked to the denial of that same identity.

The purple september staff

MELTING: I need to find a way to make you understand that I am with you and that my desires are not separate from yours. This thought inspired my body to find the means; later we gave it a name. We called it 'melting.'

Isabel Miller,
quoted by Monique Wittig
and Sande Zeig in
*Brouillon pour un dictionnaire
des amantes*

This body was like extremely reticent to use the usual or, at least, the official body language. It's not homosexuality I have in mind here, though it too seems to have balked at conventional scenes.

Viviane Forrester

It is not by accident that we manage to coincide *women among women*; rather it is the pleasant effect of slowly passing through the initiation leading the body to where rapture is imminent: mobility at the heart of the species, primed in space like an instinctive strategy toward consciousness. Meanwhile, my luminous body has a vivid consciousness of chaos, history, and knowledge, all of them at once, doubly dense.

You can't write *women among themselves* without having to consider the magnitude of this little expression: "do without a man," without hurtling against the writing on the patriarchal wall where all laws that keep us separate from ourselves, that isolate us from other women, are inscribed.

i look at myself and voilà there is present to conquer; I've been daydreaming it all along a tenuous string of words. Circling around the subject, seeking out my spaces. The body, wanting to live, looks for a way to stretch. I don't have to go back to *once upon a time*; I simply look in our saliva for movement, desire's axis, which would have me speak of me, us, now.

this salty air which marks the beginning of transitory palpitations. Little by little, the text begun will begin, tangible. An embrace in the widest part of the liquid flow. I hear, not far away, breathing. It's the times which get confused with time: would I have a past?

i cannot imagine myself confined to vegetation for soon, very quickly, metal, stones, the city, surround me, confine me. This is how spaces have come to be then: from an acute sense of survival. Imperative that we step lively on each front, our muscles agile as a thousand allusions make the circuit of our bellies.

we are the night lights, watchful, highly visible, in the city.

spent the night together. Once in bed we're on our guard, because men are on the prowl all over the neighbourhood and we are—we know this—the *very pulse of their prey*. Space, for us, is a sign of resistance: to keep our distance. Not only to protect each one's vital space, but to make sure daily that the enemy (the one that can seize you at any moment) doesn't come by night as well as day to divert your attention, catch hold of your body, capture thus your proud bearing.

we have never had enough space. And on finding it it's like convergence; you know full well, in the happy posture of hands on hips, a sexual tenderness that covers all urban distance.

where there is space, there are tracks. The still warm tracks of those who have gone before us. Hardly visible these traces, buried, hidden, as we often are, from one another. But traces take up more and more space in our lives. They re-appear as us, come up from out of our childhood, where we were forced to learn the female roles in a vulgar humiliating show before parents and friends.

patience and ardour we must constantly renew in order to make it across the opaque city of the fathers, always on a tightrope, having to keep our balance, and on all sides, the abyss. For we work without nets.

and everywhere, what meets the eye is only the usual: sex, one's sex, life, childbirth, the 'petites morts'[1] and other circumstances of fictive reality. And one forgets that sex is not this ambiguous representation of the other, that it has sense only in reality, and that this reality in turn has sense only *in the moment,* that is, when reality gets us into *such a state.*

as for desire, it resides only in that space where the cue for the other woman's desire is found. Otherwise, it's something else: 'proxy.'

---

[1]A French commonplace for male orgasm.

then there is this obsession held by the overwhelming reality
(patriarchy at full gallop in our lives, running after us as if on
the last hunt, a final assault on our bodies as women-loving
women, lesbians, suddenly forced to react, face to face with
reality. The confrontation must take place.

combat:

)

then, this other reality, from where we begin to exist, and in
which girls again find themselves full of intensity, in the process
of project, like an essential force circulating among the spaces.

distances: space which in perspective gives the impression of drawing further away. Space which is not a void when I cross it on my fingertips, to be able finally to set down my hand, when your hand with its same identity, offset by the light, comes closer slowly to touch just ahead of me the hand which is transformed cell by cell for the temperature rises and the palm, an echo of late nights, suddenly comes alive for a dance of numbers. Then we can breathe, just at this moment. Distance abolished, we enter into the dense centre of fiction, with which I am obsessed, quite as much as by fictive reality.

whence this other persistent thought, that while cognizant of reality (this does happen to me), I am nonetheless taken with all metaphors enhancing the body. The body perceived like a familiar analogy. All scenarios given sway there: what's never been and—no doubt—what's already very well known, these and other scenarios where one recounts oneself and encounters others civilly in the political figure.

which assures the permanence of desire. And for oneself, fecund necessity as one proceeds. The space between us: allowing our eyes to open slowly in an exercise of precision.

women in search of: seeking perspective in the usage of words come from everywhere to capture our attention, this time, in order to write.

another loving technique: commit an indiscretion with respect to memory, in the water, after remembering a fluent voice close to the ear.

this is how I imagine that one can intercept space so that, above oneself, the body of the other woman is not for one second kept in suspense. Shaken up by all the shams of patriarchy, omnipresent as an automatic slap . . . at the moment I write these lines, at the moment where the text is possibly about to begin with a series of expressions such as: the lesbian citizen; watchful women, the night-light lovers; the enchanted lesbian.

and words will then be committed to speaking modalities of anger, humiliation, fear; then the mouth (I know, I am familiar with which foods give the appetite for) will open itself on the enthusiasm for figures which, in the rainstorm, have already changed and change again, day after day, the images of reality.

hole: Languorous holes are made by digging in the sand. Languorous holes are inhabited by one or several women lovers. These are good spots to practice languor, when the sun is hot and you can hear the ocean.

Monique Wittig, Sande Zeig,
Brouillon pour un dictionnaire
des amantes,
Grasset, Paris, 1976

HOLE: Symbol of the aperture on the unknown; what opens onto the other side (beyond, in concrete terms) or what opens onto what is hidden (beyond, in terms of what seems apparent)...

On the imaginary plane, the hole is richer in meaning than the simple void.

Jean Chevalier, Alain Gheerbrandt,
Dictionnaire des symboles,
Robert Laffont/Jupiter, Paris, 1969

void/hole: she says "I am a hole," believing by this, as she's often been informed, that she is of mere nothingness or only this horrible wound that men cannot bear to look at. We know the carnage which ensues.

I say that the text begins here. At the hole, this place that fulfills, overfills me, because it is my *in*tention, a happy tension which makes me let go like matter in expansion (and here there is no centre, no axis, and this is in no way chaos). This is the opening (thought, the boundless activity of the body, often comes of it). I say that she who has swallowed, who swallows what comes out of a man's hole, closes herself again with that man's anguish inside her and this is *closure* to all others. Her belly, her arms, her hands, are restless, eager to find the opening once again. In vain, she exhausts herself "in love." And each attempt at fabulated love buries her ever more deeply under her hole, puts her in the hole, causing her, in this way, to lose her opening. But the male lens always sees a hole there, sees first and foremost only a *rap*acious hole there (cf. rape: "this hole begged me for it," says he, before his accomplices on the jury).

I say that by my own energy I know the hole, its texture, its landscape, its rhythm. I am no longer turning in circles in my woman's hole. I acknowledge myself: I am thus capable of knowing. And intervening in the city (the lesbian citizen), with all the other women who acknowledged one another from the moment there was opening.

I am, having gone out through my opening, *of the other side.* Male fantasies and the code they dictate are thus reduced, in my psychological space, to their just proportion, as are those who take their nourishment there. It's crossing the mirror and not the static seduction of it, and I understand this now having another woman before me, that the gaze flickering into life has nothing to do with *setting one's sights.* I do not catch sight of myself in another woman; I cross into a new dimension. And this can't help but affect the number, the wavelengths, the music inside.

Note

"La coïncidence," written April 1978, was first published in *La Lettre aérienne* (Les Editions du remue-ménage: Montreal, 1985). This English translation appears in *The Aerial Letter,* translated by Marlene Wildeman (The Women's Press: Toronto, 1988).

Certain Words

NICOLE BROSSARD
TRANSLATED BY MARLENE WILDEMAN

Amid the worst possible misfortunes, the most daring nights of adoration, tragic death, and the softest skin, by the shores of all seas, and clothed in a utopian body and ecstasies, we proceed along the relief of words, agile among the sharp coral of la Isla de las Mujeres. Dressed in a woman's body, patiently we mark time at the edge of the page; we are await-ing a feminine presence. With wet fingers, we turn the pages. We are waiting for truth to break through.

From one reading to another, words relay back and forth as though to test our endurance around an idée fixe, around the few self-images we have, images which apply to us only in the fictive space of our particular version of reality. From one reading to another, we fabulate stories from our desire, which is to identify what inspires us and what plunges us into such a state of "indescribable" fervour.

When this fervour comes over us, we say we are captivat-ed by our reading and we advance slowly / rapidly toward our destiny. Our destiny is like a project, a life woven into us by innumerable lines; some are called the lines of the hand holding the volume. These lines innervate our entire body, like the logic of thought derived from the senses. Engrossed in our reading, we become aware of (being) the cause and the origin of the faces and landscapes surrounding us for we make allusion to them as one does to childhood, a desire, an inclination. Engrossed in our reading, we hear murmurs, entreaties, cries; we hear our voice looking for its horizon.

In our reading, there are mauves, some indigo, terrible looks, women adorned in jewels and silence. Bodies, sorely tried. Stirring visions. We open and close our eyes on them in the hope of a sonorous sequence, or a vital discussion perhaps. Our fervour sweeps into the text in order that from the discussion, truth might break through.

Amid the rhetoric, the logic of the senses, the paradoxes, and the sensation of becoming, we advance through our intention of forms. Sometimes, in the middle of the night, we might wake to re-read a passage, to see again the women we desire. And as we read it over, in our breast is an "indescribable" sensation which keeps us awake until dawn. At dawn, our spirit is extravagant; it wanders freely in forbidden zones and we have no choice but to explore them. I've heard that some women write at dawn, when they are in this state. I've heard that sometimes they burst into tears.

"I know the rhythms of the voice; I know how it jumps about. I know the experience and the adventure of the gaze." Toward this we soar with each reading, incredulous before truth, which, like a memory of shadow and of fervour, bursts in on us.

The words we notice speak to us and they fill us with unrest and pleasure. These words are revelations, enigmas, address. We transform them by an unconscious method, yet our consciousness finds itself enlightened by the process. Women reading, we become the allusion and the tone of a text.

What animates us in a sentence or an expression is a decision to be it. Inclined to become one with the text in order to seize in the fire of the action the brilliant exploit of our desire, we are astonished before the unanimity forming within us. Each intense reading is a beam of action.

Amid the equations, the pivotal axes, the intoxicating audacity, and the light which criss-crosses over us, we advance in our reading the way in theory we become what we desire. We advance toward a subtle and complex woman who reflects the process of our thinking and its forms of development. Words are one way to devour the desire which devours us with comparisons, taking us to the place where we become the appetite of knowledge and the knowledge of consciousness.

When we turn the pages with our wet fingers, going from terror to ecstasy, we confront eternity; we are believers and disbelieving before the sum total of bodies, craniums, orgasms; we confront the beyond of the whole and become desire's precision in the unrecountable space of the brain.

Truly, the sensational effect of reading is a feeling we cannot express, unless we underline. _With each reading, the intimacy of eternity is an intrigue we invent_. All reading, every reading, is a desire for image, an intention to re / present which gives us hope.

Note

"Certain mots" appeared in the journal *Tessera*, No. 2, *La Nouvelle Barre du Jour*, No. 157 (September 1985). This English translation appears in *The Aerial Letter*, translated by Marlene Wildeman (The Woman's Press: Toronto, 1988).

She Ate Horses

Gloria E. Anzaldúa

Prieta turned to face the ocean. Behind her she could sense
Llosí watching her. She shouldn't have let Llosí talk her into
coming back to Padre. Her toes gripped the wet sand. Get a
grip on, get a grip on. She buried her feet deeper into *la arena*
and felt the small tug of the sea, the gentle suck. The waves
coming in, going out. The shore was swaying, not the sea,
and she was swaying with the shore but she didn't fall. Her
feet were buried in the sand and they had roots.

She bent from her waist, her long black *cabello* almost
touching the waters. She plunged her fingers into the sand,
anchoring both hands and feet. Something sharp cut into her
palm. With a smooth movement she rose from her waist and
pulled it up. A sawtooth sea pin shell, half of a bivalve shell,
nestled in her hand. Somewhere on the beach with the hun-
dreds of other shells was the other half, or in someone's
pocket or dresser top. *La concha* was pretty on the inside, she
thought, but neither the beauty nor the shell last long. The
ligament holding the two valves together breaks, the halves
fall apart. A stallion roared and neighed. Prieta's head
snapped up, the image had been so real.

She remembered when she became afraid of horses. She
was a little girl. They had three horses, one of them a skittery,
skinny horse who shivered when humans approached, even
child humans. She'd gotten on it by climbing up on the fence

and vaulting over onto its bare back. A tremor had passed through its body, the rippling of its flesh against her soft inner thighs always surprised her. The horse snorted, then took off in a mad gallop. She clung close to its sleek neck. She was beginning to revel in the muscles rubbing against her legs, the smell of horse flesh, the harsh breathing, the spray of spittle. The vegetation so green and alive, everything in sharp detail, and then she was sailing

over the horse's head, felt a shuddering jar, then stillness. She found herself on the ground where she'd slammed her face, the thought that she'd broken something brought a sickening weakness to her chest and arms. She lay stunned watching the back end of the horse disappear, tail raised in the air.

Her father had found her on the ground. "*Es un caballo mañoso*," he had explained. "It takes revenge on humans for previous floggings, goes down on its forelegs as if to kneel *y zas* while the rider flies over its *cabeza*.

"*Mi hijita*, you have to show it who's boss. *Nunca, nunca sueltes* the reins. Never, never let it have its head. Always keep a tight rein, always stay in control. *Dale un palazo*, use the stick when it balks." The beating of wings as the gulls rose and hovered low over the water brought Prieta back to herself.

She looked up at the gulls, watched the amber feet folded back together against their tails, amber beaks looking down below in search of food riding the waves along with the pieces of mica mirroring the sun. Their white bodies and grey wings looked lost in the sky. The sounds of the Gulf of Mexico and a sea that seemed to go on forever soothed Prieta. She threw the shell that had once had a counterpart into the water, turned around to see that Llosí was still watching. She turned around again and walked away from the lip of the sea.

She remembered her first time with Llosí. Something inside her had taken form—animal shape—and was sending out tingling sensations of heat and cold from the middle of her body. Something inside her was pulling, sucking in her stomach, tightening, loosening, tightening, loosening her stomach muscles. As the excitement rose she felt that she was dying. She tried to squash that reflex inside her that was making her breathe hard, that was sending *la sangre* pumping faster and faster through her veins, that was making her *corazón* beat faster, faster. The reflex was taking over. She would not let it. She tried to flatten it, to numb it, deaden it; to hold the animal, reflex, back. She had willed her lungs to breathe slower, deeper. When her vagina stopped gulping air and no feeling went below her waist she let herself relax. *Oh, Papá*, I can't stay in control. She had burst into tears and Llosí had held her in her arms all night.

Her feet sank into the hot sand as she climbed the dune. It was hot. Her upper lip beaded with sweat, beads of *sudor* ran down between her breasts, sweat trickled down her scalp. The fur on her nape was wet, her pubic hair, *esos pelos de elote*, was saturated. She scratched and her fingers came away wet. She lifted her hair from the nape of her neck, felt the breeze cool it. She dampened a white handkerchief and spread it on her breasts to cool them. She knew why Mexicans eat a lot of chile. In arid climates it makes you sweat, leaving the skin dry and cool. She could only wear cloth that breathes, cotton, rayon, nothing else. She liked white, mint blue, and icy pastels. She couldn't stand colored sheets, especially the sheets with flowers. Llosí can have the sheets with flowers, she thought, we'll divide the cats, one and a half for each. The plants. Who takes the *molcajete*?

She glanced back and stared at the tracks she had made, they looked crooked and a little sad. And further down below stood Llosí watching her. She was too far away for Prieta to see the look in her eyes. She watched Llosí walk slowly toward her. She looked away, felt more than saw the tawny strands of sea oats edging the sea dune. When she turned back Llosí was standing before her. Prieta saw anger in her eyes, and trying to hide behind it, the hurt. Side by side they began to walk up the beach.

Why is this happening to us? *¿Por qué nos esta pasando ésto, Llosí?* Had she spoken the words? They stopped and turned to look at each other. As Prieta turned her head to one side to let the wind blow her hair out of her eyes, she saw the two sets of tracks on the sand. Their *huellas*, side by side, were almost identical. There'd once been wildlife on the dunes of Padre Island. *Masteños*: she'd seen their unshod hoof prints crossing the trails of the smaller deer tracks.

"We love each other, Llosí, but that doesn't seem to help." She kneaded, fingers and nails raking the sand, obliterating the tracks. *Con dedos y uñas rastrillando la arena borrando las dos huellas.* "What are you doing?" said Llosí. "You'd like to erase me out of your life as easily as you do those *huellas*, wouldn't you."

"*Huango, Llosí, todo esta huango.* Something got loose and flat, lost the tension holding us together. Snap and we went flying off the edges. Llosí, we lost the feeling of belonging, of being part of the other, the ligament that kept us together." She opened her hand and showed Llosí the shell. She saw something subtle shift in Llosí's eyes. Then Llosí was walking fast, away from her, kicking the *botellas de cerveza* on her path. Padre was beginning to resemble Coney Island. Crossing Laguna Madre to South Padre on the Queen Isabella Causeway, they had seen huge chain hotels and condominiums; cabin cruisers, luxury beach hotels, golfcourses. The surfing crowd was riding the high waves, the clear waters. The travel agents call Padre Island a "vacation frontier." Once these shores were empty. Now Padre was a town full of Mexicans, Germans, Austrians, Anglos. But no horses. She remembered when she and Llosí used to come here as kids. Before MacDonald's, before the car-covered beaches and the rich people's private saunas and cinemas, before South padre incorporated into a city. Had that idyllic paradise really existed, or was it too a fantasy?

She heard the rustling sound of the tawny strands of sea oats edging the sand dune. The sight of them bent almost double by the strong sea breeze riveted Prieta's attention. Time had stopped, making nature more alive, animated. Streamers of sand whipped up by the winds dusted the fine sheen of sweat on her body with their pollen.The same wind blew a spittle of sea water on her face and pulled tears from her eyes. Through blurred vision she looked at the ripples of the sand dune. The sand was liquid and of the same substance as the sea. Molten sand—how air would seem if it was a solid.

She dropped down to rest by a bunch of big yellow primroses, buttercups they were called, watched them quiver in the wind. Sea oats and grass fell out of the dune pockets. She felt like she was falling. She was under the horse's hooves, clumps of sand fell on her arms and face. Abruptly she realized that Llosí had come back, that Llosí was squatting before her, that Llosí was shaking her, that Llosí was peering intently into her face, that Llosí wanted her too much. Too much, too close. Prieta sucked in her breath but no air reached her lungs. She was suffocating.

"¿Qué tienes?" Llosí was saying. "Are you alright honey? Come on." When Llosí tried to pull her up out of the sand dune she involuntarily drew back. Llosí dropped her arms and stiffened, the hurt look back in her eyes.

She did not know what she had wanted most to change by allowing Llosí to talk her into coming back here, only that she wanted everything to change, everything. She could not tolerate the way things were between her and Llosí one more day. There was a force inside her that was angry and raging and hopeful and loving, yes loving, a force that could no longer be shut up in a drawer.

She rose up and hurried to catch up with Llosí. "Chin," she said as she stepped on a wiener half buried in the sand, jumping away—aborting the gesture to grab Llosí's arm, a half dance step that scared the seagulls, their shrill cries irritating her as they scrambled away and lifted off into the blue. She returned to Llosí's side. They had to weave in and out of running kids and beach balls, blankets; male eyes leering at their boobs from behind sunglasses. Heads swiveled toward them, checked out Llosí's butch haircut, the dark hair on Prieta's legs and underarms, pegged and labelled them *de las otras*, lezzies, *marimachas*.

The rays of the setting sun beat the surface of the water into shifting sheets of hammered gold. The wind whipped Prieta's hair across her face and she saw the horse again, its blood-colored name rising and falling, heard again the thunder it made on the wet sand. White, everything was white, white sand, white shells. For one hundred and thirteen miles. That was how long the island was, and two miles wide. Prieta stared out at the shallow strip of water separating Padre from the mainland. It was called Laguna Madre. Her father had said the water was never more than six feet deep. Waves lapped her feet; she felt a sand crab nibble her toe. She dug her feet deeper into the wet sand.

"*Madre Dios* I'm tired of you flinching whenever I touch you," Llosí said, raking back her short hair.

"Sometimes I want to be left alone, I need to be left alone." Prieta replied.

"Why?"

"Because I need to think things out. I can't think while you're standing over me trying to ferret out every little secret."

"Eh, like what?"

"Things. We each protect the secret hidden parts. We've not only closed *las pinchas puertas*, but barred them. It's a fucking stand-off."

"Yeah, I haven't shut no doors, I don't have any secrets. You know what I think? I think you've changed. *Tú no eres la de más antes*—you're not like you used to be. *La otra es la que yo quiero*—I want the old you, I want you back."

"Oh, so that's it. Don't dare change on you, 'cause your identity's based on me maintaining mine. Is that it?" said Prieta.

"You want me to change and I *don't* want you to change, Prieta. Why can't things be like before, *como más antes*?" said Llosí, her voice entreating. When Prieta didn't say anything she continued, "Let's eat." She reached into her backpack and pulled out a bag of fruit. She held out a big ripe mango to Prieta.

"Neither one can tolerate changes in each other," Llosí said. Silence.

Prieta bit into the lush mango. The mango peel gave her mouth a rash. Prieta brought her hand up slowly, her hand and arm felt heavy, and tried to rub off the tingling around her mouth.

"It's something in the oil," said Llosí. "You have to be exposed to the oil at least once before your immune system will recognize it as an allergen and react to it."

"Allergen?"

"Yeah, the oil, like the oil in poison ivy, oak or sumac," said Llosí. "*Mira*, Prieta, we both know you've fucked up plenty. But I gave you the space to go into *veredas* full of thorns and rattlesnakes curled up under the *nopales*. I had faith that you'd get yourself out of whatever fuckups you got yourself in."

"Space?" said Prieta, "You gave me space? Ha! You followed me into those *veredas* stuck to me like a prickly pear thorn. You know what you're doing now? You're always leaning on me. I want you to get the hell out of my head. Even when you're clear across the other end of the apartment out of sight, I feel you watching me, thinking about me, making plans about us."

Slap.

"You hit me! *Cabrona. Pos 'ora sí, Llosí, 'tas bien zafada.*"

"You used to like it, Prieta, my getting close to you, remember? You never wanted us to get out of bed."

"I couldn't tell you, Llosí, but after a while it didn't feel as good anymore."

"Why didn't you say anything?" said Llosí.

"What was I supposed to say—that I wanted you to make love to me differently? You would have felt like I was rejecting you sexually. The few times I asked that you...you know, it put you off," said Prieta.

"Well, you never told me what you did with your other lovers, nor even who they were," said Llosí.

"You were crowding me, Llosí, trying to get inside my head, wanting to know everything. You never could understand that at times I need to be alone. At times I need a little distance from people."

"I'm not people, I'm your *novia*!" shouted Llosí. Then in a softer voice she said, "I hope you're satisfied, Prieta. We finally did it, put up a wall between us.

Prieta shook her head and turned away. "Llosí, I couldn't even masturbate. You were jealous even of my fantasies."

"Why would you want to get it off by yourself—you had me. But no, you had to have that fucking gadget," said Llosí, voice thick with tears.

"You always want to control everything in bed, including me," said Prieta.

"That's not me you're talking about, it's yourself, Miss Control," said Llosí, stepping into the water and thrashing about.

She knows it's over. It can't be over. How can I tell her? Llosí can't take it, she thought, realizing that she wanted Llosí to be the one to end the relationship, absolving her of guilt. A lie had slipped into bed with them, slept between them. Love was slinking through a slit under the door trying to get out, but Llosí seemed oblivious to the quiet racket it was making. But no, Llosí had to know. Why else was she trying to do the right thing, trying to work things out when she'd never cared to before? Why else insist on coming back to the island to the waters where they had made their vows?

She watched Llosí walk toward a patch of grass burned brown by the sun, saw her run from a clump of grass to a clump of grass, her burning feet sinking into the shadows. Walking barefoot in the sand in south Texas in the summer was like thrusting your feet into embers. Like plunging headlong into love, so hot, Llosí was dancing in agony. Prieta knew that Llosí was waiting for Prieta to say, *This is the end, it's over, estaba esperando que le diera la calabaza.* Prieta wanted to remain "friends." But she knew Llosí well enough to know that Llosí would refuse and that that would be her revenge. If they were going to break up Llosí would want another chance, not a complete severance. Prieta opened her hand and stared at the sawtooth sea pin. No, she couldn't leave Llosí. She couldn't. It would kill Llosí.

Sensing her nearby, Prieta looked around and saw Llosí walking back to her, saw the anxiety in her eyes. Something bitter backed up into her throat. She clamped down on the nausea, swallowed hard. Don't lose it now, don't lose control.

"Will you calm down," she said to Llosí. "*Madre Dios, Llosí,* we're members of the same tribe. We know each other so well. Maybe that's the problem. We no longer have surprises for each other. Everything is so predictable—ugh." Her bare foot had stepped on a dead fish lying on the sand on her path. I have to watch where I'm going, she thought.

"You got suspicion in your eye, girl," Llosí was gesticulating wildly now, her bare foot kicking hard at an empty Coca Cola can, sending it scuttling across the sand. "Every time you look at me I feel like I got lice or something and that you don't want to come near me. Don't I take enough baths? The gringos shoved your face in dirt and you're still obsessed with it. We should never have moved from the Valley. Why don't you answer me?"

Prieta tried not to stop listening to Llosí. She saw Llosí's mouth move, saw annoyance, anger, impatience flicker in and out of her face, felt the tension in Llosí's body. She even heard the words. The words she'd heard a hundred times before. Llosí's interpretation of the "argument" was different from hers. She was tired, bone tired of it all. Along with the smell of salt and fish the sea breeze brought the smell of mayonnaise and bologna and coconut tanning lotion. The mixture of smells made her want to throw up.

"*Mira, Prieta, tú no entiendes.* Shit, things are really getting bad. *Tú ya no vives conmigo, mija.* You no longer live with me. *Tu ya te fuiste pa' otra región adonde yo no peudo seguirte.* You've wandered into that other place and I can't follow you. *Chingao, Prieta, yo soy la que no puedo aguntar.* You kept yourself out of it, Prieta, didn't you? What were you saving it for, Prieta? You never laughed enough, nor wept, nor raged. You didn't care enough. Oh, you have plenty of love, Baby. Plenty of rage, plenty of everything—only you sat on it. You rationed it. You hoarded it."

"Don't put it all on me," Prieta said. "I was right there with you in the beginning. But then you had to go into The Clutch and hang onto me as though your life depended on it."

"*¿Y qué?* What's wrong with wanting to be with my lover? We married each other right here, maybe told our vows to the sea on this very spot. *Te acuerdas*, Prieta? We swore that no matter what we would always be there for each other."

"*Sí*, I remember," said Prieta softly. "How could I forget? *No me dejas olvidar nada.* When you think I'm behaving differently from you, you panic, *la pierdes, Llosí.* You think a little autonomy on my part *o de la tuya* would kill it, *verdá*?" She could hear the shrillness growing in her voice and she clamped down on it.

"*Y tú, mi Prieta*, are afraid I will take too much, afraid I will stomp into your soft exposed places with hiking boots. A brown woman afraid of the animal inside, of losing control."

"You do take too much, you have stomped into me. You have tried to tame me with soft words. *Llosí, me quieres amansar como un potrillo.* You've been trying to tame me for as long as I've known you."

When had she reached the point when she'd said, No, I don't want to look too closely at our different needs anymore; I don't want to listen to the hunger in her voice—it was too rapacious; I don't want to think about how it is my fault that I can't make her understand. *At that point,* she knew she'd reached *una orilla,* an edge of some sort. For the relationship to work, they had to stay near the edge—her edges, Llosí's edges. But finally it had been that edge that had split them. By stopping they had created the edge.

They stopped and stood at the edge of the sea and watched the emerald waves drive spume over their feet. There were fewer people here. *"Que fea me siento ahorita, horrible," dijo Llosí.*

"¿No tan fea como me siento yo? Look at me, *tengo la boca llena de ceniza,* my mouth's full of ashes, Llosí. They've outlawed fire on the beach, did you know that?"

"Yeah, and horses," said Llosí. And Prieta *vio otra vez el caballo bayo salir galopeando del mar*—and Prieta saw again the coyote dun gallop out of the sea. The tall majestic beast shot down the side of one of the sand dunes, showering sand in all directions, making a drum of the wet earth, then plunging straight into the sea. She heard the hollow thud as the horse hit the water and saw spray sluicing up from its body. Then it surged out again, its hooves making the earth quake. The *caballo* galloped toward her. She stood very still, but inside of her something was twitching, flinging itself against the walls of its cage. *El caballo bayo* loomed over her, wide eyes pulled back, black pupils, no white showing. As it cast its shadow over her the horse swallowed the red sun. She saw the sun's rays through its tail, combing its mane, outlining its dark arched neck in gold and red. The sleek powerful thighs rippled and brushed slightly against her as the horse sped past. She stood there trembling, the heat of her...

. . . . body seeping into the sand, legs folding. Until now she hadn't known it lived inside of her. She'd been seven or eight when she'd first encountered the *mesteño* on the beach. Since then she encountered it only in her dreams. Sometimes it was a black horse, sometimes yellow; always wild. *Mesteños,* half-Spanish, half-wild were harder to tame, her father had told her. The first thing she had ever drawn as a child had been a horse. The first thing she had painted when she started experimenting with oils had been a horse. She had photographed horses, sweat running down their slick flanks. She dreamed of horses, their hooves striking the earth, making gouges in the earth, water welling up where their hooves had struck. When she was twelve, someone had given her a clay mare for her birthday, knowing how much she loved horses—having read *Black Beauty*, *The Mustang* and every horse book she could get her hands on. She had taken that clay mare, wrapped it in soft white muslin and placed it gently in the bottom drawer of her dresser. Then she had locked it and dropped the key between the floorboards.

Prieta and Llosí stood watching a man straddling a shiny black inflated inner tube. He turned, saw them looking, and began jumping up and plopping down on the inner tube, waving his arms like a bird. Kids with orange surfboards, holding cokes and sprites and slices of *sandía* looked over occasionally, yelling out encouragements in Spanish.

She saw the mare shake her head. *Vio a la yegua sacudir la cabeza.* She crouched down and turned to face the mare. *Ella, agazapada, voltió.* She wasn't going to pit her life against that wild mare. *No iba a estrellar su vida contra esa yegua ladina. El sordo palpitar la acompañaba.* Prieta turned away, the mare's breathing accompanying her. The sea was a woman, wallowing. A giant woman breathing, her breath a tart tanginess, the slough of the sea. She breathed into the wind, pulled the smell of salt and tart into her body. Abruptly the wind changed and the smell of dead fish was a slap in her face. Death rode the velvet tanginess of the sea.

"I'm going back to the car, get us some cold drinks," Llosí said. "Are you ready for a lunch?"

"I'm not hungry but you go ahead," Prieta told her,

getting that exasperated look again. "You can't synchronize our appetites, our hungers, Llosí."

Prieta listened to the crunch of feet on sand as Llosí, the woman she loved, walked away. The wind shifted and she smelled salt. *'Taba bien salada,* luck had passed her by. In their relationship nothing had flowed. Nothing except details. Love had stood still, stagnated. *Sintió el momento decisivo* come washing up with the waves, slapping her legs. *¿Qué iba hacer?* The time had come for her to decide. What was she going to do? People were leaving the beach and she was beginning to feel cold. *La gente se retiraba de la playa y le estaba dando frío.* She looked at her watch. She was going to lose her *novia,* her *mejor amiga,* her *hermana,* her *mamá,* her lover if they didn't do something quick.

She squirmed her lower body into the sand where the wind had made a hollow, peered over the rim of the hole into the gulf trying to discern the invisible boundary between grey sea and grey sky. It had all started out so well. *Todo había comenzado tan bien, y se estaba acabando tan mal. Ni pleitos, ni celos.* No fights, no jealousies. Each had to learn to listen to what lay behind the words, had learned to speech the pauses. What had gone wrong? No movement. Love, that instinct to unite, had forgotten its counter-movement, the loosening, the letting-go, the acceptance of the contradictions. They couldn't live with that. It had to be one way or the other. Somehow they hadn't learned to hold on and let go simultaneously. And here she was in the middle of the blow out area, the hollow. Like sand in a storm the wind had shifted love to a distant lot.

They were two *mexicanas* afraid in different ways of the dark blood in their veins, dealing in different ways with the wild horse making thunder One woman had tried to tame the animal, to break the spirit of the horse that had eaten the sun; the other had protected that horse, had sheltered and hidden it and had ended up fettering it.

The chilled feathers of the wind hitting her face numbed

her nose and cheeks. People had packed and driven away in their pickups and cars and now she was the only one on the beach. Maybe they'd heard storm warnings on the radio, telling them to evacuate the island. She felt utterly alone. Llosí had not returned with the cold drinks and sandwiches. She'd probably gotten a ride back to the mainland. Or maybe she'd taken the car. Prieta again heard the words they'd said earlier to each other. "I stake everything on this relationship. *¿Tú crees que voy amar a otra mujer?* You think I'm going to love another woman?"

"*Ni modo.*"

"*Me quieres o no? Do you still love me?*"

"*¿Ya ni se si te amo o te odio?* I don't know if I love you or hate you, probably both?" The conversation played itself out in her mind. After each quarrel the same conversation. She knew it by heart.

The broad white beach encrusted with shells was bordered by dunes that were as high as two story buildings. Her feet sank into the soft sand as she scrambled up and down the sand dunes, pulling herself up by the sparse grass, *el zacatal quemado,* that grew in clumps on the dunes. She pictured the twenty Spanish galleons and pirate ships—an entire treasure fleet—driven by a hurricane in 1553, wrecking on Padre, Spanish doubloons spilling from split chests onto *las playas de* Padre. Even now people occasionally found gold coins buried in the sand. She knew that if she looked for treasure, she would only find cockle and moonsail shells.

Dunes and sand and sea turned into an orange haze as the sun sank into the ocean. Three sea gulls skimmed over the water, then rose and disappeared to the north. No shadows on the ground followed them. The long stiff brown grass was bent double by the wind. She too was pushed downwind. *Tenía que amellar,* she had to pee. She squatted down on the sand *y se mio en la arena.*

La noche se le atrepaba encima, night mounted her. *La hundía en la arena,* it pushed her body into the sand. *Contra su cuerpo vio la huella de la pezuña de algún animal, de un caballo.* Longside her body on the sand she saw the hoof mark of an animal, of a horse. *Y ahí entre yerbas la soledad le pegó como un leño.* Amidst the salt stiffened grass solitude knocked her down like a blow from a log. Waiting for the horse, *esperando,* she listened to the silence. *No más oyó el suspiro del mar* but only heard the breath of the sea. *El aire se había puesto escaso.* The air had become scarce. She lay on her back and let night find her.

She dug her hands into the wet sand, clenched her fists tighter and tighter until in their trembling they resembled two fish jerking in the sand. She always thought that if one of them left, it would be her. Maybe she could just walk into the dark water, there at that spot where the moon in its cradle, the sea, was rocking back and forth. The horse had slipped out of the sea from the moon in the water.

Why not? She'd have good company; Alfonsina, Sappho, Virginia. It was almost midnight, *la mala hora,* no one on the beach but her. No one to see her. She'd sink out of sight, disappear forever. She dismissed the notion almost as soon as she'd thought it. Too late. *No se atrevó a darse al mar,* she did not dare give herself to the sea, she for whom giving herself was nearly impossible. *Pa' ella era casi imposible entregarse.* The decisive moment had come *y se había ido,* and gone. *Aquí se le acabó su jornada,* here her journey had ended, her flight, *su huida,* and she had stayed at the edge of the sea. *Se había parado allí en la orilla del mar*—a woman who feared horses, who had betrayed the animal.

She dug a hole in the sand, curled up in it. It still retained a little of the heat of the sun. She did not intend to sleep. She woke, remembering the dream. She had stood by the horse looking into its face. A small stripe of white ran across its face at an angle that is called a "race". A red orange ribbon extended from its mane to its tail. *Un caballo bayo*, a coyote dun with feathered legs. She saw the long hairs growing on the cannon and backs of the fetlocks. She mounted its smooth and glossy back and rode it *a la jineta* like the Berber Arabs. Together they made thunder and their feet shook the earth. The woman who feared horses rode smoothly on its back. She knew that she'd start her period sometime the next day. Her dreams were always more vivid and real just before her menses. She looked up to find the moon.

The wind that touched her was icy when she uncurled from her hole. The stars were crystal lights in the sky as she walked toward the sea. The full moon was a silver coin. *Era una mujer hecha pedazos*, she was a woman in pieces, pieces lapped thin by the tongues of the sea. *Algo caliente y salado en su boca salía de una herida que apenas había comenzado a conocer.* Something hot and salty in her mouth bled from a wound that she was only now becoming aware of. Swallow me, swallow me. Too late.

She wiped the tears from her cheeks with the back of her hand. She had to give up the illusion that to quit now was to fail with this woman. Failing was a luxury out of her reach. Brown women from the *colonia* had to try harder. She had been called many names, but not one had ever called her quitter, *rajetas*.

She ran headlong back into the sand dunes, away from the sea. It was then that she saw the horse-headed woman, slick neck arched, nostrils flaring. It had human arms and human skin that looked both frail and strong. She stopped in her tracks, veered off and ran on. She looked back, the horse-faced woman was following her. She ran harder. It was like trying to escape the sound of the breath of the sea, that persistent and permanent heartbeat. The horse woman was *la llorona* and it was in her body, in her mind, and at war. Yes, she feared the animal inside her—she'd been taught to distrust her instincts and to trust outsiders. She had to lead the animal out, get it away from its tether. But once the horse was loose, what then? In the morning would the shore patrolman catch her sprawled among the sea oats behind the dune and drag her screaming into a closed van?

When she woke *con un despierto de golpe*, the moon was riding low on the water. She walked into the water then turned her back to the sea. The water receded, tugging the sand from around her feet. She felt as if she were in back of a bus looking backwards, under her, the land was travelling away.

She heard the beating of wings as the gulls rose and hovered low over the water. *Se hincó y metió su cara en el mantel de espuma. Hizo sus abluciones* then tugged her towel around her and followed the tracks. She wanted to be there when the horse-woman emerged from the sea.

She began digging with her bare hands. She'd dug a three foot hole when she touched moisture and water flowed up into her hands. She put her wet finger into her mouth. She instinctively knew it wasn't pure enough to drink. She thought of the jellyfish beached on the sand, the diamond-back rattlesnake in the dunes, the strong breezes combing back the salt grass and the coastal dropseed. In the grasslands she pictured the meadowlarks, blue herons and the great horned owls. Like the mare the sea was untamed, *el mar como yehua no era mancito*. She saw herself astride the *llorona*-faced mare, felt the wind on her face, felt the power vibrating from the mare into her body. Her legs become the hind legs of the horse, her arms its front legs, her hair its flaming mane. She had become the horse, *una yegua con alas*, a mare with wings. As they both plunged into the sea they became a single ray of light, *un rayo de luz*, they became lightning, *se hicieron relampago*.

Allí se quedó en la arena mirando el mar. She stayed on the sand and looked at the sea. The wind had stopped blowing. She knew Llosí had come back and was waiting for her in the car. There at the edge of the sea she gave up her taming powers. It would start here. She would eat horses, she would let horses eat her.

Note

"She Ate Horses is from Gloria Anzaldúa, *Entreguerras entre mundos/ Civil Wars Among the Worlds*, forthcoming Spinsters/Aunt Lute, Fall 1990.

On The Seashore,
A Writing of Abundance

JEFFNER ALLEN

The economy of scarcity that I live daily makes difficult and vital the conception of a writing of abundance. Writing, when reduced by the economy of scarcity to an instrument in the service of something other than itself—even when used as a means for 'revolution', or a tool for the acquisition of 'knowledge'—vanishes from thought.

Yet the wonder I find is that the powers of writing defy eclipse: are not the physical, emotional, and intellectual famines of life under patriarchy ended, at least in part, when writing, remembered, brings forth a writing of abundance?

There was a time before there was a war, before abundance was rendered scarce and the many were dominated by the Same.

I am drawn to this time, to the shores of a writing which *is* an abundance. Abundance, flowing with the waves and without bounds, is an inexhaustible plentitude.

In a field of wildflowers where never has there been any question but that each is herself, gentle Gaiety, Revelry, Radiance, and Muses with lovely hair offer a welcoming embrace. 'Woman', the word which has betokened the constriction of female existence as womb and wife of man, dissolves in myriad currents: womon, womyn, wimmin.

A time before there was a war, a time of abundance, is an invention. An invention is not plucked out of the air and imposed on reality as if that were a blank slate awaiting definition. Invention approaches that which is there. When I invent a time I come to a time which already comes to me.

I set down my pen, I close this book and writing does not stop. I open this book, I pick up my pen, and writing does not begin. The writing is not a gimmick I manipulate by whim, but an event with its own histories.

Writing is the greeting in which a writing births herself. Writing is the welcoming of that freedom.

Writing is not the mark that would impress itself on random points in empty space. Nor is writing the frame that would captivate language by its pre-formed focus, stasis. The institution of a center, the confinement to the Same, miss the freedom of writing.

Writing *is* in the open rapport of the many. Writings of the past, star writings of the future, traverse again and again the plants, earth, self, with which they are inscribed.

A writing is in company with, and not imposed on, parchment, clay tablet, consciousness. A writing is ancient and contemporary, she discovers herself with others.

The coming to be of a writing as she *is* is a conception by parthenogynesis.

Goddesses are born of writing; goddesses each of whom brings forth a writing. The ancient wisdom of H.D., "blue as the blue-poppy, / blue as the flax in flower," she who knows our fears, remembers, and who does not falter, the meditative knowledge of Elsa Gidlow, a "knowledge standing stark under the sky / feet naked to earth," is each a goddess of writing free from the disguise of authority, bold, and beautiful.

The shore is effervescent: shifting sands, rubble washed by the sea, layers under layers upon layers. There is a transformation of energies in these multiple, shifting, grounds.

Among the tens of thousands of languages, the language I speak is a language situated in writing. Where writing is, worlds in writing and the being of worlds are inseparable.

I emerge with writing: a nebular I.

The I of authority, disciplinary I that would judge writing from a distance, transparent I for whom writing must be to become legible for everyone even if indecipherable for oneself, loses hold before an I of shifting densities, darknesses, florescence.

Clitoral currents trace shimmering galaxies of visceral desire.

The effulgences of lesbian love and writing celebrate the intensities of mutual delight. It is a matter of significance that clitoral currents are lesbian: warm, billowing, radiant.

Sensual and scriptural configurations are at play when writing is cyprine.*

Alphabets of wimmin, the many alphabets of each womon, survive: the clay tablets and cuneiform of Nidaba of Sumer, the letters of the three Fates, parthenogynic daughters of the Great Goddess, and of Io, the violet flower, moon

---

*A secretion of lesbian lovers [from *Cyprus*, birthplace of Aphrodite].

that encircles the Mediterranean. How could I have thought the syllables of Sarasvati, signs of Kali, hieroglyphs of Isis, whom Serpot of Syria, Amazon queen, invoked as goddess of the land of womyn, woman's contribution to *the* alphabet?

Alphabets, delightful surfaces, magical signs, cosmic vibrations intertwine, making writing festive.

On the shore, amid rubble washed by the sea, I live. My memory is a beginning, not first, but as always, opening to times spaces Myceneas future and past.

My memory travels with a writing before which the dissolution of patriarchy is a matter of fact.

The dead live when the moist lotus open along Acheron.

Lost continents of writing, where I, not shade or shadow, flourish, are sites from which I see the horrors and undergo healing.

I forget the claim to reality that is made by the Same when, aware that that claim is being made, I move apart from its hold.

Lovers of writing turn the leaves of memories and books, tending, patching, mending.

The mysteries of writing are not a secret to be withheld, but an experience that in her freedom is brimming with life.

Yet where is the writing when our books are so few, and when so many are banned, lost?

Writing, too, travels with memory. By this power writing preserves herself when memory endures the flames in which a writing is burned. On byways such as these Sappho's lyric poetry survives the destructions of Alexandria by Christians and Moslems.

But at times, a writing is burned, and the more that is written the more quickly it is burned, or suppressed . . . out of date, incomplete, unreal, disquieting. If you are squeamish don't prod the beach rubble, which washes up when what will not assimilate is expelled.

No longer the captivity of writing!

On indigenous grounds a writing thrives. Her powers cannot be made to grow on alien terrain.

With a magic eye, tooth, and Gorgon face, the three Fates find at each season a writing: twigs scattered by the wind, drifting sands, the flight of birds.

But if this writing in her freedom were to meet the limit once, and once again, the eye of mastery that would seize her in its grasp, the sickle that would cut her off from perception, divination, rebirth, the craneskin bag that would contain her, the mask that would frighten away her friends, if she were to encounter Hermes, hermeneut who thinks stones are mute, he who would bring her from unintelligibility to intelligibility—according to whom?—she might forget life, were not she tenacious.

The lie: that Hermes has the alphabet. That by cunning theft Hermes stole writing from the three Fates. That he was given the gift of writing by the three Fates. That he is the origin of writing and language.

Writing is not one and writing cannot be possessed. The three Fates did not give writing to Hermes, nor did Agluaros give Hermes her daughter, Herse, moon goddess of the morning dew.

I remember the attempts made by force, over time, to break the power of memory; to instill the belief that writing must be captive.

I remember the teaching that writing is a writing of servitude, porno-graphy, a writing that affirms its submission to the Same, that writing must comply when the chain of command of a grammar where the subject governs verb and thereby possesses object comes to power. I remember the attempts to inculcate the lesson that I, if I am to write, must also be captive.

Hermes, communications technology satellite, circles the earth, while wild mares frolic on the shore.

The attempt to use writing counting cattle and counting wimmin, counting what cannot be counted, is at the origins of scarcity and civilization.

Civilization would turn writing against herself.

The history of writing in the West, as set forth in vase painting, 600 b.c.—300 a.d., in mainland Greece, the Black sea, Anatolia, and Europe, depicts a history in which men, but never wimmin, write. That history attests to the fact that wimmin who write, and all wimmin caring for pleasure and freedom, live in ways that escape representation by civilization.

A writing of six hundred ideographs circulates solely among womyn in Jiangyong County, Hunan province, 960 a.d. to the present. The womyn, barred from school and confined to the home, write. While weaving, the womyn read the writing to each other.

Young womyn form families of sworn sisters and write of these sisterhoods in womyn characters. They continue to communicate in the writing after marriage. They burn their writings so that in the next life they can enjoy them. The womyn believe that the script came to Hu Xiuying during her loneliness at the imperial palace.

Wimmin often have no option between non-literacy and literacy: sixty-two percent of the non-literate people in the world are wimmin, sixty percent of the non-literate wimmin live in countries whose average per capita income in 1980 was below $300, United States currency, the gap between the percentage of wimmin and men who are non-literate is increasing.

Wimmin who are literate often are obliged to a literacy that would confirm the legitimacy of civilization.

In memory

Two womyn teachers in Afghanistan, 1984, are raped, mutilated, and burned on a fire of school books. The womyn taught reading and writing and did not wear veils.

Over five thousand years ago, in Sumer, a region of southern Babylonia, Nidaba appears with clay tablets and cuneiform, prior to any of the male gods who attempt to replace her. Yet by 1880-1550 b.c., wimmin in Sippar, a city in northern Babylonia, write in the *gagûm*: a locked house inside the walled temple dedicated to the sun god, Sămas̄. The wimmin who write are *nadītu*, the barren ones: without children and without property.

Iltani, who composes her last text when she is more than seventy, Inaan-amamu, Amat-Mamu, a scribe for at least forty years, and Awāt-Aja, are among the *nadītu* who write the lives of the one hundred to two hundred wimmin who reside, at the same time, in the locked house.

The *nadītu* often live to be old, for they do not die in childbirth, which shortened the lives of many womyn. They offer each other mutual support. Within the confines of the locked house, they enjoy a degree of personal freedom exceptional for womyn at that time.

At birth the womyn are marked, given names to show they are destined for the locked house. They are sent to the *gagûm* so that, upon their death, their share of the paternal estate will be inherited by their brothers. Under an administrative staff comprised exclusively of men, the *nadītu* keep records of sales and profits from the land.

At the center of the city womyn write, provided that womyn and writing are walled in.

Cloaked, wimmin with writing walk in the heart of the city. Axiothea, in the fourth century b.c., leaves home and travels to Athens where, disguised as a man, she becomes a student. Hypatia, 375-415 a.d., casts a cloak around herself and appears in Alexandria, where she teaches and writes mathematics, astronomy, philosophy, and mechanics. Hypatia is killed when men tear off her cloak and mutilate her body because she is a womon, because she will not convert to Christianity, because she will not leave the city with her teaching and writing.

Wimmin with writing walk in the city by assuming the appearance of men, and at the will of men.

Why do I write?

I leave the blue springs and blazing sun, the tropics, pink azaleas and palms, to live in the city with a lesbian writing. At my job, I circulate among languages, none of them my own, and when I write I am told, "not philosophy," "poetry," "....using language as it was not intended."

I partake in migrations not sought, but taken on, to be to myself a writing companion and for economic sustenance, to make real a world that enlivens my senses, to be with friends. I live with the excitement of beauty in the open, a writing of cultures of womyn on the lost coast, llamas, red hummingbirds, wild berries, sea gulls, when I am told, "not the ideal woman we had in our minds."

And now, on the frontier, a bare winter after years of sea and sun, why is this winter so cold?

Is it possible to write without moon, sun, stars, the warmth of wimmin?

The mysteries

The war is over what is not. Writing is not possessed by Hermes, womyn are not in civilization, counting counts only its own numbers, marks only its bills of ownership and sales, the limit limits itself.

I write over, under, across the limit, apart from the limit, without the limit.

In psychic gathering I find a writing that lives with the cosmic. I meet with a time that flows.

Through magic greater than the force of Hermes, a time before there was a war becomes also a time that is now.

Silver streaks from waves to shore, a writing, buoyant, arrives with a gasp. She brings with her gentle breezes, a cosmic shedding. A writing that may exceed language, she brings feeling, touch, free movement.

On the seashore boats at sunset and sunrise bring local crops, quilts, seashells, scrolls. Lavender ribbons, currency from a time when wimmin recorded ownership and debt, pile up in disuse. Nets shine with new values.

Wimmin glean curiously shaped alphabets from events on boat and shore, telling the stories, pain, anger, and joys, which are and can be in the present of our lives.

A writing discovers herself with others

SAPPHO H.D. ELSA GIDLOW SAPPHO H.D. ELSA
GIDLOW SAPPHO H.D. H.D. NICOLE BROSSARD
MONIQUE WITTIG H.D. MICHELLE CAUSSE SAPPHO

Susan Guettel Cole, "Could Greek Women Read and Write?" *Reflections of Women in Antiquity*, edited by Helen P. Foley, 1981

"Secret Women's Writing," Audrey Mindlin, *SpareRib* 1986

"500 Million Illiterate Women Worldwide: Female/Male Gap Increases," *WIN News* 13.1:36

The Status of Women in Afghanistan," *WIN News* 12.4:48

Margaret Alic, *Hypatia's Heritage*, 1986

Rivkah Harris, "Biographical Notes on the *Naditu* Women of Sippar," *Journal of Cuneiform Studies* 16 (1962): 1-12

Ulla Jeyes, "The Nadītu Women of Sippar," *Images of Women in Antiquity*, edited by Averil Cameron and Amelie Kuhrt, 1983

SAPPHO H.D. BRYHER MICHELLE CAUSSE
ELSA GIDLOW NICOLE BROSSARD MONIQUE WITTIG
SAPPHO H.D. H.D. SAPPHO

Contributors

JEFFNER ALLEN is the author of *Lesbian Philosophy: Explorations*, and co-editor of *The Thinking Muse: Feminism and Modern French Philosophy*. I teach philosophy at SUNY Binghamton. My writing appears in *TRIVIA: A Journal of Ideas, Amazones d'hier lesbiennes aujourd'hui, HYPATIA: Journal of Feminist Philosophy*, and other publications in women's studies and philosophy. I like to walk with friends by the ocean. At present I am completing a new book of lesbian theory.

GLORIA E. ANZALDÚA is in graduate school at the University of California, Santa Cruz. She is editor of the anthology, *Haciendo Cara: Making Faces Making Souls: Constructing Colored Selves, A Reader of Creative and Critical Perspectives* (San Francisco: Spinsters/ Aunt Lute, 1990) and author of *Borderlands/La Frontera: The New Mestiza*. She is co-editor of *This Bridge Called My Back: Writings by Radical Women of Color*, winner of the Before Columbus Foundation American Book Award. Her work has appeared in *Third Woman, Cuentos: Stories by Latinas, IKON, Bilingual Review, Conditions*, and she has been a contributing editor for *Sinister Wisdom* since 1984.

NICOLE BROSSARD was born in Montreal in 1943. Poet, novelist and essayist, she has published more than twenty books since 1965. Seven of them have been translated into English. Among those: *A Book, French Kiss, These Our Mothers, Lovhers*, and *The Aerial Letter*. She is co-founder of the magazine *La Barre du Jour* (1965) and she co-directed the film *Some American Feminists* (1976). She is twice winner of the Governor General's Award for poetry. Her most recent novel is *Le Désert mauve*. Nicole Brossard lives in Montreal.

CLAUDIA CARD is a Fully Revolting Hag in the Department of Philosophy at the University of Wisconsin-Madison where she teaches ethics, feminist theory, and lesbian culture. She has articles in *Philosophical Review, American Philosophical Quarterly, Ethics, Canadian Journal of Philosophy, Journal of Social Philosophy, Hypatia*, and *Women's Studies International Forum*. She is at work on a book on character and moral luck.

CARYATIS CARDEA is a lesbian separatist. She studies history and writes lesbian theory in poetry and prose. Born in 1950 to working-class parents of Irish and French Canadian heritage, she now lives in the Bay Area of Northern California. Her writing has appeared previously in the journals *Common Lives/Lesbian Lives, Lesbian Ethics, Sinister Wisdom*, and the recently published anthology, *For Lesbians Only*.

MICHÈLE CAUSSE is a writer of poetry, fiction, biography, and essays as well as a prolific translator. Born in France, she has lived in Italy, Tunisia, the U.S., and Martinique, and now hopes to make Montreal her home. Her own books include *L'Encontre* (Des Femmes), *Berthe ou un demi-siecle auprès de l'Amazone* (Tierce), *Lesbiana, Seven Portraits* (Nouveau commerce), and most recently (   ), (Trois). I am obsessed by lesbianism and the condition of Lesbians in the WHOLE WORLD; this is why I am nomadic. I care for a lesbian land (or possibly a lesbian sea) with lesbian economics, ethics, etc. . . . At the moment (as always) I live the most separatist life I can live. Translating only Lesbian books, for Lesbian publishers. Writing only Lesbian texts. And the only women who inspire me are Lesbians. (Dead or Alive).

BABA COPPER was an old lesbian. She purposefully reclaimed and empowered those two words. An artist, writer, mother, and reluctant prophet, she strove to illuminate and undermine the forces that serve to oppress and isolate old women. Her book, *Over the Hill: Reflections on Ageism Between Women*, is published by Crossing Press, 1988. She lived by the sea in Fort Bragg, California, until her death in August, 1988.

ANN FERGUSON is a lesbian socialist feminist who teaches Philosophy and Women's Studies at University of Massachusetts/Amherst. She has published articles on androgyny, the feminist sex debate on pornography, Adrienne Rich's theory of the lesbian continuum and on motherhood and sexuality. Her book *Blood at the Root: Motherhood, Sexuality and Male Dominance* (Pandora/Unwin and Hyman, 1989) develops the theory that different forms of patriarchy are based in "modes of sex/affective production"—historical ways of constructing sexuality, parenting, nurturance and social bonding. She is presently working on a collection of old and new essays called *Sexual Democracy: Women, Oppression and Revolution* (Westview).

EDWINA FRANCHILD, a.k.a. Trish Kelly, has a B.A. in English from the University of Minnesota. Born during the Truman administration, she still seeks a sense of belonging. She considers herself an activist and a survivor, is on the board of directors of the Womyn's Braille Press, and hopes to write the Great Radical Blind Lesbian Novel or Play.

MARILYN FRYE'S primary occupations are philosophizing, teaching philosophy and feminist theory, building lesbian life and value with lover, friends and others. Not necessarily in that order. She authored *The Politics of Reality: Essays in Feminist Theory* (Crossing Press, 1983), and has been working for a long time now on how "theory" (whatever that is) can be pluralist without dissolving into politically useless mush. She thinks it can.

NETT HART is a country dyke with a passion for dykes, gardening, building, thinking, tinkering, canoeing, languages, and herbcraft. She is a graphic designer/illustrator and runs her own studio in Minneapolis. She is a partner in Word Weavers, a Lesbian publishing company, which produces Lesbian positive books and magazines. Her book, *Spirited Lesbians: Lesbian Desire As Social Action*, of which this article is an excerpt, will be released Fall, 1989. She is a naturalized Labian.

KIM HALL. At the present moment I am a graduate student of philosophy at SUNY Binghamton. I enjoy long walks, visiting with friends, pleasant dreams, fireplaces, laughter, hugs, kisses, sunrises, and sunsets.

SARAH LUCIA HOAGLAND is a chicago dyke and a philosopher. She came out in 1975, a year after being labeled p.d.o.f. (potential dyke on faculty) by her lesbian students, and she named herself 'separatist' in 1976. She has been teaching philosophy and women's studies at northeastern illinois university in chicago since 1977, and has given talks in lesbian communities around the u.s. for thirteen years. She is the author of *Lesbian Ethics: Toward New Value*, published by Institute of Lesbian Studies, and along with Julia Penelope she has co-edited *For Lesbians Only: A Separatist Anthology*, published by Onlywomen press of London.

ELÉANOR H. KUYKENDALL, Chair of the Philosophy Department and Coordinator of the Linguistics Program at SUNY New Paltz, has published on feminist linguistics and French feminist theory and is writing a book on French feminist linguistic theory.

ANNA LEE. I am a black lesbian separatist who has finally returned to the midwest.

VIVIENNE LOUISE. I am an African-American lesbian separatist, originally from Washington D.C. I now reside in Oakland, California and am working on a collection of personal writing. I presently derive a great deal of personal joy from the organizational/political growth of the African-American lesbian community in the San Francisco Bay Area.

MARÍA LUGONES was born in Buenos Aires, Argentina in 1944. She emigrated to the U.S. in 1967. She is associate professor of philosophy at Carleton College and a community organizer among Hispanos in the North of Nuevo Mejico. Her book, *Peregrinajes/Pilgrimages: Essays in Pluralist Feminism* is forthcoming with SUNY Press.

JULIA PENELOPE, author of the internationally acclaimed "Mystery of Lesbians," co-editor of *For Lesbians Only* (1988) with Sarah Lucia Hoagland, co-author of *Found Goddesses: From Asphalta to Viscera* (1988) with Morgan Grey and co-editor of *The Original Coming Out Stories* (1989) with Susan Wolfe, has completed an analysis of the patriarchal universe of discourse (PUD), which will appear in the Athene Series of Pergamon Press in the spring of 1990. She lives in Massachusetts with Sarah Valentine, Noot, and

Pagan; in her spare time she bags groceries to make ends meet. When they don't, she calls on Moola-Moola for help.

MARTHE ROSENFELD. Born in Antwerp in 1928, I grew up in Belgium and soon felt the effects of the rise of fascism and the resurgence of anti-Semitism in Europe. As a Jewish refugee in World War II, I was fortunate to be able to immigrate to the United States. In New York city, where I lived from 1941 to 1959, I pursued my studies in French. Since the 1970s I have been teaching French and Women's Studies at Indiana University-Purdue University at Fort Wayne. My fascination with Jewish lesbians in France stems from my own experience as a Jewish lesbian with a franco-phone background.

BETTE S. TALLEN is a thirty-nine year old Jewish lesbian separatist who chairs the Women's Studies department at Mankato State University (home of the only M.S. in Women's Studies in the u.s.a.). A New Yorker, she is thrilled by the Minnesota countryside but is trying hard to adjust to the land of the *Prairie Home Companion.*

JOYCE TREBILCOT is author of *In Process: Ideas for Wimmin,* forthcoming from SUNY Press.

KITTY TSUI was born in the year of the dragon in the City of Nine Dragons and immigrated to Gold Mountain in 1968. She has been active as a community organizer and cultural worker in the Third World and gay communities since the mid 1970s. She is the author of *Words of a Woman Who Breathes Fire* (San Francisco: Spinsters-Aunt Lute). Her work, both poetry and prose, has been widely anthologized, most recently in *Gay and Lesbian Poetry, In Our Time* (St. Martin's Press 1988). Tsui, an alcoholic, survived the slip, and is again in recovery.

MARLENE WILDEMAN is a writer, English teacher, and lesbian feminist activist who lives in Montreal. She translates truth, beauty, love, desire, and ecstasy . . . and she takes life very seriously.

MONIQUE WITTIG is the author of *The Opoponax, Les Guérillères, The Lesbian Body, and Across the Acheron* (which first appeared in French as *Virgile, non*). She has co-edited, with Sande Zeig, *Lesbian Peoples: Material for a Dictionary,* has translated several books, and is the author of a number of short stories, critical essays, and plays, including *The Constant Journey.* Monique Wittig has been a visiting professor at Vassar College, University of California, Davis, and University of California, Berkeley.

JACQUELYN N. ZITA is Associate Professor of Women's Studies at the University of Minnesota. Her interests include feminist theory, issues related to sexuality, gender, and women's health. She is currently completing a book of feminist theorizing on the body, desire, and violence, textualities of soma.